BEYOND VALUE
AT RISK

Beyond Value At Risk

The new science of risk management

KEVIN DOWD

JOHN WILEY & SONS

Chichester • New York • Weinheim • Brisbane • Singapore • Toronto

National   01243 779777
International (+44) 1243 779777
e-mail (for orders and customer service enquiries): cs-book@wiley.co.uk
Visit our Home Page on http://www.wiley.co.uk
or http://www.wiley.com

Reprinted September 1998, January and August 1999, April 2000

Other Wiley Editorial Offices

John Wiley & Sons, Inc., 605 Third Avenue,
New York, NY 10158-0012, USA

WILEY-VCH Verlag GmbH, Pappelallee 3,
D-69469 Weinheim, Germany

Jacaranda Wiley Ltd, 33 Park Road, Milton,
Queensland 4064, Australia

John Wiley & Sons (Asia) Pte Ltd, 2 Clementi Loop #02-01,
Jin Xing Distripark, Singapore 129809

John Wiley & Sons (Canada) Ltd, 22 Worcester Road,
Rexdale, Ontario M9W 1L1, Canada

Library of Congress Cataloging-in-Publication Data

Dowd, Kevin.
    Beyond value at risk : the new science of risk management / Kevin Dowd.
        p.   cm. — (Wiley series in Frontiers in Finance)
    Includes bibliographical references and index.
    ISBN 0-471-97621-0. — ISBN 0-471-97622-9 (pbk.)
    1. Financial futures.   2. Risk management.   I. Title.
    II. Series
    HG6024.3.D68   1998
    658. 15′5—dc21   97–31514
                                                                         CIP

British Library Cataloguing in Publication Data

A catalogue record for this book is available from the British Library

ISBN 0-471-97621-0 (hb)
ISBN 0-471-97622-9 (pb)

Typeset in 10/12pt Times by Vision Typesetting, Manchester
Printed and bound in Great Britain by Bookcraft, Bath Ltd, Avon
This book is printed on acid-free paper responsibly manufactured from sustainable forestation, for which at least two trees are planted for each one used for paper production.

Contents

Preface

YOU are responsible for managing your company's foreign exchange positions. Your boss, or your boss's boss, has been reading about derivatives losses suffered by other companies, and wants to know if the same thing could happen to his company. That is, he wants to know just how much market risk the company is taking. What do you say?

You could start by listing and describing the company's positions, but this isn't likely to be helpful unless there are only a handful. Even then, it helps only if your superiors understand all of the positions and instruments, and the risks inherent in each. Or you could talk about the portfolio's sensitivities, i.e., how much the value of the portfolio changes when various underlying market rates or prices change, or perhaps option deltas and gammas. Even if you are confident of your ability to explain these in English, you still have no natural way to net the risk of your short position in Deutsche marks against the long position in Dutch guilders. (It makes sense to do this because gains or losses on the short position in marks will be offset almost perfectly by gains or losses on the long position in guilders.) You could simply assure your superiors that you never speculate but rather use derivatives only to hedge, but they understand that this statement is vacuous. They know that the word 'hedge' is so ill-defined and flexible that virtually any transaction can be characterised as a hedge. So what do you say? (Linsmeier and Pearson, 1996, p. 1)

The obvious answer, 'The most we can lose is . . .' is clearly unsatisfactory, because the most one can possibly lose is everything. So either one lies or one tells the board that they can lose everything, an answer that ought not to impress them. Consequently, Linsmeier and Pearson continue, 'Perhaps the best answer starts: "The value at risk is . . .".'

But what is value at risk, and what is all the fuss over value at risk about? Put simply, value at risk (VaR) is the maximum amount we expect to lose over some target period – our maximum likely loss. The notion of value at risk is important because it leads to a whole new approach to risk management, and one that has taken off in the last three years or so and is already in the process of revolutionising both the theory and the practice of risk management. Moreover, while this VaR revolution is led by some of the major financial institutions, its implications go well beyond financial institutions and well beyond the handling of market risks on which VaR initially focused. Value at risk is not so much a particular technique or set of techniques – although it does have these – as a radically new approach to firm-wide risk management, and one that can be applied to credit risks, liquidity risks and other risks, as well as market risks. Yet despite this novelty, VaR has its philosophical roots in the portfolio theory first developed by Markowitz in the 1950s and can, indeed, be viewed as the natural development of that theory.

Outline of the Book

The book gives an overview of VaR, viewed in its broader risk management context. The book has three parts. Part One is an introduction, which discusses the origins (Chapter 1) and basics (Chapter 2) of VaR in the context of recent developments in the theory and practice of risk management. Part Two deals with the measurement of VaR, with different chapters each dealing with different approaches to VaR measurement: Chapter 3 deals with the variance-covariance approach, Chapter 4 with historical simulation, Chapter 5 with Monte Carlo simulation, and Chapter 6 with stress testing. Part Three then deals with risk management issues from a VaR perspective: Chapters 7 and 8 look at decision-making rules, such as investment and hedging rules, Chapter 9 deals with credit risks, Chapter 10 deals with liquidity, operational and legal risks, Chapter 11 deals with capital allocation, and Chapter 12 deals with firm-wide risk management.

Intended Audience

The book is aimed at three main audiences. The first consists of practitioners in risk management – those who are already using VaR and related risk systems, and those who are thinking of getting into them. The second audience consists of students in MBA, MA and MSc courses in finance, risk management and banking. The book can be used as a textbook for courses on VaR itself, risk management, or derivatives. The third audience, of course, consists of academics interested in risk management issues, most particularly accountants, economists and finance specialists.

To get the most out of the book requires a reasonable knowledge of statistics, some mathematics, and some prior knowledge of finance, most particularly of derivatives and (to a lesser extent) of fixed-income theory. I therefore suspect that most practitioners and academics would have relatively little difficulty with it, but for students it is perhaps best taught after students have already done quantitative methods, derivatives and other 'building block' courses.

Nonetheless, readers without this background should still be able to follow many of the arguments, at least outside Part Two, which deals with VaR measurement issues. I have tried to design the chapters so that they can be dipped into, and readers who are interested in some topics but not others should be able to dip into the bits they are interested in quite easily. In addition, non-specialists interested in risk management (e.g., senior managers, or students in related disciplines such as accountancy or economics) should also be able to get something from the book by reading selectively and taking the parts they are not sure of on trust.

Acknowledgements

It is a real pleasure to thank the many people who have contributed in one way or another to the book. I thank the many people who have written in this area who were kind enough to send various papers which I have, I hope, made good use of here. In this context, I would particularly like to thank Barry Schachter, whose website on VaR –

http://pw2.netcom.com/~bschacht/varbiblio.html – has been immensely valuable to me in tracking down literature and making contact with other writers in this area. I strongly recommend this website to anyone interested in this area. I also thank librarians at the University of Sheffield, Sheffield Hallam University, the Chartered Institute of Bankers, and the Bank of England, and I am particularly indebted to Kath Begley from the library of the Bank of England. Thanks also to Vicki Fitt and *Risk* magazine for permission to quote from her article 'Confessions of a regulator', which appeared in the July 1996 issue of *Risk*. I am also very much indebted to the team at Wiley, and most especially Richard Baggaley, Isabel Park, Nick Wallwork and David Wilson. I also thank many colleagues and friends for a whole variety of different contributions. I apologise in advance to anyone inadvertently missed out, but I would particularly like to thank Tony Berry, Mark Billings, Dave Campbell, Dave Chappell, Paul Cowdell, Brian Dowd, Paul Glasserman, Duncan Kitchin, Mark Reedman, James Watson, and two anonymous referees. I am also very grateful to David Cronin and Conor Meegan of the Central Bank of Ireland who were kind enough to go over some of the draft chapters for me and give me valuable feedback. I am particularly indebted to Conor on that account. Finally, my biggest debt, as always, is to my family – to my parents and brothers, and above all, to my wife, Mahjabeen, and my daughters, Raadhiyah and Safiah. They not only provided much needed moral support, but also had to put up with a book taking far more out of me, and taking up far more of my time, than I had bargained for, again. I would therefore like to dedicate the book to them.

Kevin Dowd
Sheffield
July 1997

PART ONE

Introduction to VaR

The Risk Management Revolution

1. INTRODUCTION

1.1. Risk and Risk Management

EVERYTHING changes, and changes can be good or bad for those affected by them. Change therefore leads to risk, the prospect of gain or loss, and risk (or, more precisely, the risk of loss) is something that we must all come to terms with. Coming to terms with risk does not mean eliminating risk from our lives, which is clearly impossible; nor does it mean that we should do nothing about risks and accept consequent losses fatalistically, as if we could have done nothing about them. It means that we must manage risk: we must decide what risks to avoid, and how we can avoid them; what risks to accept, and on what terms to accept them; what new risks to take on; and so on. We therefore buy insurance and watch out before we cross the road, we live with other risks, and we buy lottery tickets and speculate on the stock market.

1.1.1. The Nature of Corporate Risk Management

Firms face much the same problems, and their managers must decide how to deal with them. The risks firms face can be broadly divided into the following categories:

- *Business risks* are those risks specific to the industry and market in which the firm operates. If the firm produces steel, its business risks would be those specific to the steel industry and the market for steel, and so on.
- *Market risks* are the risks of losses arising from adverse movements in market prices (e.g. equity prices) or market rates (e.g. interest or exchange rates). Market risks, in turn, can be subdivided into interest rate risks, equity price risks, exchange rate risks and commodity price risks, depending on whether the risk factor is an interest rate, a stock price, or whatever. These risks are also very common, as evidenced by a recent (1995) survey by the US Treasury Management Association which showed that over 90% of organisations polled faced interest rate risk, three-quarters faced foreign exchange risk, and over a third faced commodity price risk.[1]
- *Credit risks* are the risks of loss arising from the failure of a counterparty to make a promised payment.
- *Liquidity risks* are the risks arising from the cost or inconvenience of unwinding a

position. We bear liquidity risk when we hold an asset that we may have to sell on disadvantageous terms because buyers may be hard to find.

● *Operational risks* are risks arising from the failure of internal systems or the people who operate in them. Operational risks can vary from the very minor (e.g. the risk of photocopiers breaking down) to the critical (e.g. the risk of bankruptcy because of breakdowns in management control, as happened with Barings Bank in 1995).

● *Legal risks* are risks arising from the prospect that contracts may not be enforced. We bear legal risk when we enter into an agreement with another party, not knowing whether we will be able to get the contract enforced if our counterparty defaults.

Managers must therefore manage their firms' exposures to these different risks. They must decide on the risks they want to bear, assess the risks they currently bear, and alter their exposures accordingly so that they bear the risks they want to.

1.1.2. The Risk Management Revolution

Both the theory and the practice of risk management have developed enormously in the last two and a half decades. The theory has developed to the point where risk management is now regarded as a distinct sub-field of the theory of finance, and risk management is increasingly taught as a separate subject in the more advanced master's and MBA courses in finance. The subject has attracted a huge amount of intellectual energy, not just from finance specialists but also from specialists in other disciplines who are attracted to it. This is illustrated by the large number of Ivy League theoretical physics PhDs who now go into finance research, attracted not just by high salaries but also by the challenging intellectual problems it poses. One prominent researcher, Tim Bollerslev, has aptly observed that finance research now generates an atmosphere of excitement that matches some of the great eras of science, such as the quantum physics research of the 1930s.[2]

The transformation of the practice of risk management is no less dramatic, and two factors in particular stand out as contributing to this transformation. One factor is the development of new theory and its rapid translation into practical applications. A good example of this process was the rapid adoption in the 1970s of the famous Black-Scholes option pricing model as a practical tool. The Black-Scholes option pricing equation and others like it are now routinely programmed into the hand-held computers that traders use to go about their business. They use them to price options, but also to guide them when constructing hedges against the various risks they face. A more recent example of this process was the rapid adoption of the Heath-Jarrow-Morton framework for the analysis of fixed-income securities (e.g. bonds) and their various derivatives. This research was published in the early 1990s and rapidly became industry-standard. The HJM model enables traders to price fixed-income securities and calculate hedges for them. It is far more complex than Black-Scholes, but all that a trader requires to use it in practice are a sufficiently powerful computer and the skill to plug in the relevant parameters and interpret the output.

The other factor, and one that is in the process of altering risk management almost beyond recognition, is the development of Value at Risk (VaR). The VaR approach began as a methodology for measuring market risks, but it was soon realised that it could do much more than merely provide VaR figures to report to shareholders or guide internal decision-making. It can also be used to guide investment decisions by adjusting expected returns for risk; it can provide information to evaluate investment decisions after the event, which is very useful when designing rules to remunerate investment managers and traders; it can provide for a more consistent and integrated treatment of risks (including derivatives risks) across the institution; and the logic it embodies leads to robust new control systems that make it much harder for fraud and human error to go undetected. It was also realised that the VaR methodology can be extended to measure and manage other risks as well, including liquidity risks, credit risks, cashflow risks and even some operational and legal risks. In short, VaR opens up a radically new approach to firm-wide risk management, the full implications of which have still to be worked out.

2. BACKGROUND FACTORS

2.1. A Volatile Environment

A number of background factors contributed to this transformation of risk management, and one obvious factor was the high level of instability in the environment within which firms operated.

2.1.1. Exchange Rate Instability

Exchange rates have been volatile ever since the breakdown of the Bretton Woods system of fixed exchange rates in the early 1970s. Occasional exchange rate crises have also led to sudden and significant exchange rate changes, a good example being the bust-up in the exchange-rate mechanism (ERM) in September 1992, which led to significant falls in the values of sterling and the Italian lira. There have also been major changes in exchange rates as the result of shifts in monetary policies, such as the large appreciation of sterling in the period 1979–81 in the wake of the tighter UK monetary policies of the new Thatcher administration. Firms have therefore had to come to terms with ever-present and sometimes very significant exchange rate risk.

2.1.2. Interest Rate Instability

There have also been major fluctuations in interest rates, with their attendant effects on funding costs, corporate cash flows and asset values. Interest rates rose to very high levels in the developed countries in the mid-1970s, largely as a consequence of previous inflationary monetary policies, and subsequently came down again in the later 1970s. Interest rates in the US and the UK then both shot up in 1979, peaked in 1981, and gradually came back down again. In the UK, interest rates rose yet again in the late 1980s and early 1990s, and then fell sharply after sterling's unceremonious ejection from the ERM in 1992. In the US, interest rates have risen and fallen three more times since 1983, and the last major rise – that of 1994 – is believed to have led to losses of $1.5 trillion on capital invested in bonds and other fixed-income securities.[3]

2.1.3. Stock Market Volatility

Stock markets have also been extremely volatile. Stock prices rose significantly in the inflationary booms of the early 1970s, then fell considerably a little later. Stock markets then recovered, fell again somewhat in the early 1980s, and rose to a peak in 1987. They then fell precipitously throughout the world on 19 October of that year. In the US, they fell 23% and in the process knocked off over $1 trillion in equity capital. In most countries, equity markets then recovered and proceeded to grow right through until 1997. In Japan, however, stock prices fell over 50% over the period from 1989 to 1991, and in the process wiped out $2.7 trillion in capital.[4]

2.1.4. Other Sources of Instability

The period since the early 1970s has also witnessed all manner of other sources of instability. There were the oil price hikes of 1973–74 and 1979, and subsequent falls in oil prices, and there was also very considerable volatility in other commodity markets. There were drastic shifts in legal and regulatory environments, the growth of offshore banking (i.e., banking systems largely beyond the reach of national regulators), and the massive transformation and, indeed, globalisation, of the financial services industry, as manifested by the erosion of barriers between different types of financial firms and the emergence of a new breed of financial multinationals operating on a worldwide scale. There were also increases in the level of world trade and profound changes in trade patterns, major changes in trade policy, and, for much of this period, the prospect of major trade wars. And, of course, there were also other changes of major historical importance: the collapse and subsequent opening up of the Soviet empire, the expansion of the EEC, the transformation of China and India into great economic powers, the emergence of the Asian tiger economies, and so on.

2.2. IT Developments

Another factor contributing to the development of risk management was the rapid advance in the state of information technology. Improvements in IT have made possible huge increases in both computational power and the speed with which calculations can be carried out. Improvements in computing power mean that new techniques can be used (such as computer-intensive simulation techniques) and so enable us to tackle more difficult calculation problems. Improvements in calculation speed then make these techniques useful in real time, where it is often essential to get answers quickly.

This technological progress has also led to IT costs falling by about 25–30% a year over the past thirty years or so. To quote Guldimann,

> Most people know that technology costs have dropped dramatically over the years but few realise how steep and how continuous the fall has been, particularly in hardware and data transmission. In 1965, for example, the cost of storing one megabyte of data (approximately the equivalent of the content of a typical edition of the *Wall Street Journal*) in random access memory was about $100 000. Today it is about $20. By 2005, it will probably be less than $1.
>
> The cost of transmitting electronic data has come down even more dramatically.

In 1975, it cost about $10 000 to send a megabyte of data from New York to Tokyo. Today, it is about $5. By 2005, it is expected to be about $0.01. And the cost of the processor needed to handle 1 million instructions a second has declined from about $1 million in 1965 to $1.50 today. By 2005, it is expected to drop to a few cents. (All figures have been adjusted for inflation.) (Guldimann, 1996, p. 17)

These falls in cost then make the new technology economically (and not just technically) feasible.

Improvements in computing power, increases in computing speed, and reductions in computing costs have thus come together to transform the technology available for risk management. Decision makers are no longer tied down to the simple 'back of the envelope' techniques that they had to use earlier when they lacked the means to carry out more involved calculations. They can now use sophisticated algorithms programmed into computers to carry out real-time calculations that were not possible before. The ability to carry out such calculations then creates a whole new range of risk measurement and (therefore) risk management possibilities.

2.3. Growth in Trading Activity

Another factor behind the transformation of risk management is the huge increase in trading activity since the late 1960s. In the New York Stock Exchange, to give one example, the average number of shares traded per day has grown from about 3.5 million in 1970 to around 40 million in 1990.[5] Foreign exchange activity has grown even more, and is said to have grown from a few billion dollars a day in 1965 to more than a trillion dollars a day by 1996.[6]

There have also been massive increases in the range of instruments being traded over the past two decades, and trading volumes in these new instruments have grown very rapidly as well. New instruments have been developed in the Euro (i.e., offshore) markets, in new corporate bond markets (such as the commercial paper market in the UK), in repo markets and, more recently, in the newly emerging financial markets of eastern Europe, China, Latin America, Russia, and elsewhere. New instruments have also arisen for assets that were previously illiquid, such as mortgages, consumer loans, commercial and industrial bank loans, and similar assets, and these markets have grown very considerably since the early 1980s.

2.4. Development of Derivatives

There is also the development of derivatives contracts and the associated growth of derivatives activity. (Derivatives are contracts whose values or pay-offs depend on those of other assets, and are explained more fully in the appendix to this chapter.) The growth of derivatives activity has been phenomenal. Until 1972 the only derivatives traded were certain commodity futures and various forwards and options that were traded over the counter (i.e., directly between provider and purchaser). Then, in May 1972, the Chicago Mercantile Exchange started trading foreign currency futures contracts, and in 1973 the Chicago Board Options Exchange started trading equity call options. T-bond futures were introduced in 1975, and a large number of other financial derivatives contracts were introduced in the following years. There are now a huge variety of different derivatives contracts traded at exchanges all over the world or over the counter. These include, among others, all sorts of swaps (e.g. various types of interest rate swap, foreign currency swap, equity swap, and others), many different futures (e.g. commodity futures, interest-rate futures, stock-index futures), many different options (e.g. American and European call and put options, Asian options, barrier options, binary options, credit options, currency options, cylinder options, index options, multicoloured rainbow options, quanto options) and countless forward contracts. There are also many hybrid derivatives which are combinations of simpler contracts: options on options, options on futures, futures on options, options on swaps, futures on swaps, collars, caps, floors, range forwards, index amortising rate swaps, and many different types of structured notes (e.g. inverse floaters, leveraged floaters).

Box 1.1:   Marking to market

The process of securitisation has developed hand-in-hand with the spread of marking-to-market accounting practices: valuing and periodically revaluing positions in marketable securities by means of their current market prices.

Marking to market provides a relatively objective and reliable means of valuing positions. It facilitates accountability by making it harder for managers to hide profits and losses, since managers can no longer resort to the smoke and mirrors of the accrual valuation methods that were used previously. By quickly revealing profits and losses, marking to market also gives managers feedback on their investment strategies. A failing strategy will make losses that highlight its failure, and this loss signal will enable managers to change strategy before their losses grow much further. With accrual methods, losses were often revealed only when securities matured, when it was too late to do anything about them.

Marking to market also makes reported profits and losses more volatile.[7] This greater volatility then makes managers more aware of risk – and more aware of the benefits of risk management.

There has also been a staggering growth in derivatives trading activity. From negligible amounts in the early 1970s, the notional amounts involved in derivatives contracts grew to about $50 000 billion – that is, $50 trillion – by 1995.[8] This figure is over 7 times total US GNP, and well over the total amount invested in stocks and bonds in the US. However, this figure is misleading, because notional values give relatively little indication of what derivatives contracts are really worth. The true size of derivatives trading is therefore better represented by the replacement cost of outstanding derivatives contracts, and these are estimated to be between 4% and 5% of the notional amounts involved. If we measure size by replacement cost rather than notional principals, the size of the derivatives market in 1995 was upwards of $2 trillion – a figure which, to put it into perspective, is still about six times the total equity of all US banks.

3. DEVELOPMENTS IN RISK MANAGEMENT

3.1. 'Traditional' Risk Management

We now turn to consider various approaches to risk management. It is convenient if we focus first on the more straightforward (i.e. more traditional) approaches and leave the others till later.

The first point to appreciate is that all sensible approaches have the same first step, i.e., we formulate a corporate risk management philosophy to impose some guidelines on risk management decision-making. This tells us what kinds of risks we wish to bear, what risks we want to avoid, what sort of options we will consider to manage our risks, and so forth. Usually, we will readily bear those risks that we have some particular expertise in handling (e.g. risks unique to our particular line of business), but there will also be other risks that we will usually wish to avoid (e.g. the risk of our factory burning down). This philosophy should also give us some indication of what attitude we should take towards the many other types of risks we might face – when we should bear them, when we should not bear them, and the like.

3.1.1. Quantifying Risk Exposures

We then quantify our risk exposures. There are a number of approaches we can choose from at this point: gap analysis, duration analysis, statistical analysis or scenario analysis.

Gap Analysis[9]   One approach developed by financial institutions to give a simple, albeit crude, idea of interest-rate risk exposure is gap analysis. Gap analysis starts with the choice of an appropriate horizon period – one year, or whatever. We then determine how much of our asset or liability portfolio will reprice within this period. These give us our rate-sensitive assets and rate-sensitive liabilities. The gap is the difference between these. Our interest-rate exposure is then taken to be the change in net interest income that occurs in response to a change in interest rates, and this in turn is assumed to be equal to the gap times the interest-rate change:

$$\Delta NII = (GAP).\Delta r \qquad (1.1)$$

where ΔNII is the change in net interest income and Δr is the change in interest rates.

Gap analysis is fairly simple to carry out, but has its limitations: it applies only to on-balance sheet interest-rate risk, and even then only crudely; it looks at the impact of interest rates on income, rather than on asset/liability values; and it can be sensitive to the choice of horizon period.

Duration Analysis[10]   Duration analysis is another method traditionally used by financial institutions for measuring interest-rate risks. In loose terms, the duration of a bond (or any other fixed-income security) can be regarded as the term to maturity of the security, adjusted for the maturities of interim coupon payments. More specifically, duration (D) is defined as the weighted average term to maturity of a bond's cash flows, where the weights are the present value of each cash flow relative to the present value of all cash flows:

$$D = \sum_{i=1}^{n} [i.PVCF_i] / \sum_{i=1}^{n} PVCF_i \tag{1.2}$$

where $PVCF_i$ is the present value of the period i cash flow, discounted at the appropriate spot period yield. The duration measure is useful because it gives an approximate indication of the sensitivity of a bond price to a change in yield:

$$\% \text{ change in bond price} \approx -D.\Delta y \tag{1.3}$$

where y is the yield and Δy the change in yield. The bigger the duration, the more the bond price changes in response to a change in yield. The duration approach is very convenient to use because duration measures are easy to calculate and the duration of a bond portfolio is a simple weighted average of the durations of the individual bonds in that portfolio. It is also better than gap analysis because it looks at changes in asset (or liability) values, rather than just changes in net income.

However, duration approaches have similar limitations to gap analysis: they ignore risks other than interest-rate risk; they are crude,[11] and they are not suited to non-financial firms. However, even with various refinements to improve accuracy,[12] duration-based approaches are still inaccurate relative to more recent approaches to fixed-income analysis (such as HJM models). Moreover, the main reason for using duration approaches in the past – their (comparative) ease of calculation – is no longer of much significance, since more sophisticated models can now be programmed into microcomputers and give their users more accurate answers very rapidly.

Statistical Analysis   We can also use statistical analysis to quantify our risk exposures. Statistical analysis can be applied to equity, foreign exchange (FX), commodity and other risks, as well as interest-rate risks, and is therefore of more use to non-financial firms.[13] The idea is simply that we postulate a measurable relationship between the exposure-variable we are interested in (e.g. the loss/gain on our bond or FX portfolio or whatever) and the factors that we think influence that loss or gain. We then need to estimate this relationship, which means that we need numerical estimates of its various parameters, and we usually estimate them by some econometric technique. These parameters then give us an idea of our different risk exposures, and these enable us to estimate the sizes of the hedges we would need to cover them.

This approach is limited by the availability of data (i.e., we need enough data to estimate the relevant parameters). It is also usually limited to market price risks, because we normally have data only on the prices of marketable securities. There are also worries of potential misspecification and instability in estimated statistical relationships.[14]

Scenario Analysis[15]   Finally, there is scenario analysis, in which we set out different scenarios and investigate what we stand to gain or lose under them. Scenario analysis can be applied to most kinds of risk, and is less limited by data availability than statistical approaches are.

There are four main steps in scenario analysis: (1) We select a scenario – a path describing how relevant variables (inflation, the exchange rate, or whatever) might evolve over a horizon period. (2) We postulate the cash flows and/or accounting values of assets and liabilities as they would develop under the scenario postulated. (3) We repeat these two stages for any other scenarios we are concerned about. (4) We use the results of these scenarios to come to some view about our exposure.

Scenario analysis is not easy to carry out. A lot hinges on our ability to identify the 'right' scenarios, and there are relatively few rules to guide us when selecting them. We need to ensure that the scenarios we examine are reasonable (e.g., do not involve contradictory or excessively implausible assumptions) and we need to think about the interrelationships between the variables involved.[16] We also want to make sure, as best we can, that we have all the main scenarios covered. Scenario analysis also tells us nothing about the likelihood of different scenarios actually occurring, so we need to use our judgement when assessing the practical significance of different scenarios. In the final analysis, the results of scenario analyses therefore depend entirely on the skill or other-wise of the analyst.

3.1.2. Responding to Exposures

Having determined the size of any given exposure, we then decide how to deal with it. In making this decision, we first need to refer back to our corporate risk management philosophy to determine how to manage our risk exposure and, in particular, whether to hedge it. Assuming we wish to hedge, we then have to decide how to do so. The basic choice here is between standardised exchange-traded instruments and tailor-made OTC instruments, and the trade-off is between instruments that are liquid (which would push us to exchange-traded instruments) and those that fit our needs closely (which would push us to OTC ones). In choosing among possible instruments, we also have to determine the size of the hedged position, assess its liquidity, and estimate the amount of residual or basis risk left over once the hedge is in place. We also have to decide how we would live with whatever liquidity risk or basis risk the hedge would involve.[17] Depending on the instruments involved, we might also have to deal with further issues such as those arising from having dynamic hedging strategies, from hedging contingent risks, or from other features of the hedging instruments such as the need to tail a futures hedge or price a swap.[18]

3.2. Portfolio Theory

A somewhat different approach to risk management is provided by portfolio theory,[19] which focuses on the interactions between different risks.[20] Portfolio theory starts from the premise that investors choose between portfolios on the basis of their expected return, on the one hand, and the standard deviation (or variance) of their return, on the other.[21] The standard deviation of the return can be regarded as a measure of the portfolio's risk. Other things being equal, an investor wants a portfolio whose return has a high expected value and a low standard deviation. These objectives imply that the investor should choose a portfolio that maximises expected return for any given portfolio standard deviation or, alternatively, minimises standard deviation for any given expected return. A portfolio that meets these conditions is efficient, and a rational investor will always choose an efficient portfolio. When faced with an investment decision, the investor must therefore determine the set of efficient portfolios and rule out the rest. Some efficient portfolios will have more risk than others, but the more risky ones will also have higher expected returns. Faced with the set of efficient portfolios, the investor then chooses one particular portfolio on the basis of his or her own preferred trade-off between risk and return. An investor who is very averse to risk will therefore choose a safe portfolio with a low standard deviation and a low expected return, and an investor who is less risk averse will choose a more risky portfolio with a higher expected return.

One of the key insights of portfolio theory is that the risk of any individual asset – as opposed to the risk of the portfolio of assets – is not the standard deviation of the return to that asset, but rather the extent to which that asset contributes to overall portfolio risk. An asset might be very risky (i.e., have a high standard deviation) when considered on its own, and yet have a return that correlates with the returns to other assets in our portfolio in such a way that acquiring the new asset adds nothing to the overall portfolio standard deviation. Acquiring the new asset would then be riskless, even though the asset held on its own would still be risky. The moral of the story is that the extent to which a new asset contributes to portfolio risk depends on the correlation (or, if one prefers, the covariance) of its return with the returns to the other assets in our portfolio. The lower the correlation, other things being equal, the less the asset contributes to overall risk. Indeed, if the correlation is sufficiently negative, it will offset existing risks and actually lower the overall portfolio standard deviation.

A prospective new asset will therefore be a worthwhile acquisition if its expected return is sufficiently high, relative to the risk it contributes to the portfolio. This principle then translates into an operational decision rule, i.e., we acquire a new asset i if its expected return, r_i, is equal to or exceeds a risk-free return, r_f, plus a risk premium, RP_i:

$$r_i \geqslant r_f + RP_i \tag{1.4}$$

The risk premium, in turn, is equal to the product of two factors: the excess of the expected portfolio return over the risk-free rate, and a risk factor, usually known as the beta (i.e., β_i), which is equal to the covariance between the return to asset i and the return to the portfolio, r_p, divided by the variance of the portfolio return:

$$RP_i = (r_p - r_f)\beta_i \tag{1.5}$$

where $\beta_i = \text{cov}(i, p)/\text{var}(p)$. To use this rule, we need to estimate the risk-free return r_f, the portfolio expected return, r_p, and the asset beta, β_i. We plug these into (1.5) to estimate the risk premium and use our estimates of the risk premium, the risk-free rate and the expected return to asset i (i.e., r_i) to see if (1.4) is satisfied. We acquire the asset if it is, and reject it if it is not.

Portfolio theory provides a useful framework for handling multiple risks and taking account of how those risks interact with each other. It is therefore of obvious use to, and is in fact widely used by, portfolio managers, mutual fund managers and other investors. However, in practice, it tends to run into problems over data. Remember that we can make use of it only if we have estimates of the risk-free return, the expected market return, and the relevant betas. The risk-free return and the expected market return are not too difficult to estimate, but estimating the betas is often more problematic. Each beta is specific not only to the individual asset to which it belongs, but also to our current portfolio. To estimate a beta coefficient properly, we therefore need data on the returns to the new asset and the returns to all our existing assets, and we need a sufficiently long data set to make our statistical estimation techniques reliable. The beta therefore depends on our existing portfolio and we should, in theory, re-estimate all our betas every time our portfolio changes. Using the portfolio approach can thus require a considerable amount of data and a substantial amount of ongoing work.

In practice users often wish to avoid this burden, and in any case they sometimes lack the data to estimate the betas properly in the first place. The temptation is therefore to seek a short cut, and the usual short cut is to work with betas estimated against some hypothetical portfolio, usually a market portfolio of some sort. This short cut then leads to practitioners talking about *the* beta for some given asset, as if the asset had only a single beta. However, this short cut gives us good answers only if the beta estimated against the hypothetical portfolio is close to the beta estimated against the portfolio we actually hold, and in practice we seldom, if ever, know whether it is. If the two portfolios are sufficiently different, the 'true' beta (i.e., the beta measured against our actual portfolio) might be very different from the hypothetical beta we are using, and we could end up making serious errors in our investment decisions.[22]

3.3. Risk Management with Derivatives Models

3.3.1. Uses of Models to Manage Derivatives Risks

When dealing with derivatives, we can also manage risks using derivatives models. These models can be used to manage derivatives risks by helping us to value positions, so we can infer the prices at which we should buy and sell them, and by helping us construct hedges by enabling us to estimate the sizes of hedge positions.[23] To illustrate, suppose we are dealing a simple derivatives contract such as a European call option. The Black-Scholes equation then tells us what the price of the option should be if it is to be consistent with a zero-arbitrage equilibrium (i.e., a state that rules out profitable, riskless trades). More particularly, it tells us that the current (i.e., period-t) price of such an option, $c(t)$, should be:

$$c(t) = N(d_1)S(t) - XN(d_2)e^{-r(T-t)} \tag{1.6}$$

where

$$d_i = [\ln(S(t)/X) + (r + \sigma^2/2)(T - t)]/(\sigma\sqrt{T - t})$$

$$d_2 = d_1 - \sigma\sqrt{T - t}$$

and where $N(.)$ is the standard cumulative normal distribution,[24] $S(t)$ is the current price of the underlying asset (e.g. a share), r is a risk-free interest rate, X is the option's strike price, T is the time when the option expires, and σ is the price volatility of the underlying asset. This equation effectively tells us that the price of the call option should be equal to that of a leveraged position in the underlying stock (i.e., a combination of $N(d_1)$ underlying shares financed by borrowing $XN(d_2)e^{-r(T-t)}$ dollars). If this condition does not hold, it is possible for someone to make risk-free profits by buying or selling options as appropriate, with the option position offset by a leveraged share position.[25] The equation also tells us that the call price depends on five variables: the risk-free interest rate, the underlying share price, the option's strike price, the option's term to expiry, and the share-price volatility. We can therefore determine the price of the call if we know (or can estimate) these variables, and we already know the first four. The only variable we don't know is the share-price volatility, and we can estimate that by using a suitable econometric procedure.[26] Once we estimate the volatility, we substitute its value and the known values of the other variables into (1.6) and determine the option's arbitrage-free price. This gives us the price to charge, give or take a mark-up.

The Black-Scholes model also gives us the hedging ratios for our call option. These include our delta and our gamma, but also some other sensitivities as well – the sensitivities of the call option price to the volatility, the interest rate, and the passing of time. These additional sensitivities are known as the option's vega, rho and theta, respectively. Like the delta and gamma, these are also useful for hedging purposes. For instance, the vega tells us how much we stand to lose from a change in volatility, and this information gives us the size of our hedge ratio if we wish to hedge ourselves against volatility risk. The actual sensitivities themselves can be obtained by differentiating (1.6) with respect to the relevant variable (e.g. the delta then turns out to be $N(d_1)$, and so forth). Once we have these formulas, we can program them into computers and easily work out the sizes of our hedge positions.

The same principles go for other derivatives: we use an arbitrage-free pricing model to tell us what their prices should be, and we use the sensitivity ratios derived from such models to tell us our hedge ratios. There are a wide range of models to choose from, each designed for a particular type of derivative: the Black (1976) model for options on futures, the Merton (1974), Roll-Geske-Whaley and other models for options on dividend-paying stocks, the Garman-Kohlhagen model for foreign currency options, and many others. There are also many models, often very sophisticated ones, designed specifically for fixed-income instruments and their derivatives.[27] These vary from simple models of duration (which give some, albeit limited, idea of interest-rate risk) through to highly sophisticated ones such as the Heath-Jarrow-Morton models and others like them that are now routinely used by industry professionals for pricing and hedging fixed-income positions.

We can also derive our instrument prices and hedge parameters by using numerical methods that crank out the answers we seek by brute computational force.[28] These methods are very useful when we are dealing with instruments for which we have no satisfactory analytical (i.e., mathematical, as opposed to computational) methods. We might use them, for example, when dealing with American-style options where the need to consider the exercise of the option at each point in time makes it impossible, or at least very difficult, to use analytical methods. We can then derive arbitrage-free prices by programming zero-arbitrage conditions into the computational package, and we can derive hedge ratios by carrying out calculations for two slightly different values of the relevant risk factor and comparing the two.[29] The drawback of these methods is that they require huge numbers of calculations,[30] and can therefore be slow. However, developments in computing power and improvements in the procedures themselves mean that they are becoming very much faster and therefore much more widely used.

When choosing among alternative procedures, we need to keep in mind that some are much better than others and that the state of the art is continually improving. Earlier approaches are being displaced by later, more accurate ones. A Wall Street specialist in fixed-income derivatives would never now use a duration approach, say, when he or she could use more accurate approaches that can be programmed into a computer. Similarly, improvements in numerical procedures mean that some of the less accurate early analytical approaches can now be abandoned. The need to use the better approaches should of course be obvious: a poor approach leads to inaccurate pricing and, hence, the danger of losing money to competitors with a better idea of pricing; and a poor approach also leads to less accurate hedging information and inferior hedging strategies.

3.3.2. Pitfalls of Using Models to Manage Derivatives Risks

These quantitative approaches need to be used *very* carefully. Clearly, users should try to use the best models available, but it is also very important that they understand how to use the models in a trading market context. There are two big traps to avoid here. The first is to avoid using these approaches mechanically, since traders who do so can leave themselves wide open to speculative attack. A standard example is the options trader who becomes a sitting duck because he or she does not appreciate that econometric estimates of volatility can sometimes be very biased. A trader might want to price options written on a particular exchange rate, say, and situations can arise where the exchange rate has low historical volatility (i.e., the exchange rate has not moved much recently) but is widely believed to be about to change (e.g., a devaluation might be imminent). If he or she is not careful, the trader might estimate volatility on the basis of historical data, get an unduly low volatility estimate, and underprice options as a result. Smarter traders would then take our trader to the cleaners by buying up his or her options for much less than they were really worth. The lesson to learn is that quantitative approaches should be used only by people who have some feel for the markets they operate in and who understand the limitations of quantitative approaches in trading contexts. Quantitative methods can be useful *complements* to more traditional trading approaches (i.e., the messy combination of rules of thumb, judgement, common sense and whatever else that traders use) but can be highly dangerous in the hands of those who unwittingly use them as *substitutes* for those approaches.[31]

We must also avoid getting caught out when using dynamic hedges. These hedges only work against small changes in risk factors, and only then if they are revised sufficiently frequently. The worry, alluded to earlier, is that these strategies fail to cover us against major market moves such as stock-market or bond-market crashes, or a major devaluation. We may have hedged against a small price change, but a large adverse price in the wrong direction could still be damaging: our underlying position might take a large loss that is not adequately compensated for by the gain on our hedge instrument.[32] Moreover, there is also the danger that we may be dealing with a market whose liquidity dries up just as we most need to sell. When the stock market crashed in October 1987, the wave of sell orders prompted by the stock-market fall meant that such orders could take hours to execute. Sellers then found themselves getting even lower prices than they had anticipated. The combination of large market moves and the sudden drying up of market liquidity can therefore mean that positions take large losses even though they are supposedly protected by dynamic hedging strategies. It was this sort of problem that undid portfolio insurance and other dynamic hedging strategies in the stock market crash, when many people suffered large losses on positions that they thought they had hedged. As one experienced observer later ruefully admitted:

> When O'Connor set up in London at Big Bang, I built an option risk control system incorporating all the Greek letters – deltas, gammas, vegas, thetas and even some higher order ones as well…And I'll tell you that during the crash it was about as useful as a US theme park on the outskirts of Paris. (Robert Gumerlock, 1994)[33]

The bottom line, again, is the need to use these models as an aide, rather than as a substitute for knowing the market.[34]

3.4. Value at Risk

3.4.1. Development of Risk Management Guidelines

The early 1990s saw an intensification of the ongoing debate about risk management practice, particularly as it concerned derivatives. Inevitably, the rapid proliferation of derivatives contracts and the growth in the number of contracts being traded led to worries about leverage, risk opacity and disclosure, the measurement of risks across different types of position, the handling of portfolios of derivatives risks, and various other issues. (The first two issues are discussed in more detail in the appendix to this chapter.) The growing demand for more accurate risk management tools also led to the increasing displacement of older but simpler approaches in favour of more complex ones, and there were also the various problems associated with managing risks in organisations of growing complexity. It was also clear that accounting and regulatory systems were out of date, especially as regards derivatives, but developments were so rapid that even the derivatives industry itself had great difficulty keeping up.

These problems led to a string of reports on good risk management practice. The most significant was a report on derivatives risk management published in July 1993 by the Group of Thirty, a New York-based consultative group of leading bankers, financiers and academics. This report was followed by a report by the US General Accounting Office in May 1994, a joint report issued by the Bank for International Settlements (BIS) and the International Organisation of Securities Commissions (IOSCO) in July 1994, and many other reports by the Derivatives Policy Group, the International Swaps and Derivatives Association (ISDA), Moody's, Standard and Poor's, and other interested parties. These reports made a number of sensible recommendations that have rapidly become benchmarks for modern financial risk management. They tended to focus particularly on derivatives risks, but their recommendations apply not just to derivatives providers and investment banks, but to other financial institutions and most corporates as well.

The main recommendations of these reports were much the same: the need for senior management to understand the risks of their business, and the importance of their overseeing the risks that more junior managers were taking; the separation of front (i.e., trading) and back (i.e., administrative) offices to help detect rogue trading and other forms of fraud; an independent risk management (or middle office) function that reports directly to senior management; the importance of thorough audit and control systems; the importance of good information systems; and the use of internal or value-at-risk models (about which more will be said shortly) for measuring and managing financial risks across the institution.

3.4.2. Recent Risk Management Disasters

The need for sound risk management was highlighted by a number of high-profile risk management disasters in the early 1990s. In each of these cases, a single individual or subsidiary company built up huge positions (apparently) without the knowledge of senior management or the parent company. The firms involved then suffered very large losses when the risks turned sour. Among the most noteworthy of these cases were:

- *Metallgesellschaft.* A US subsidiary of MG built up very large positions in oil futures in an attempt to hedge some long-term forward contracts it had sold. The fall in oil prices in 1993 then led to very large losses, and the German parent company intervened to liquidate the remaining futures positions. The ultimate loss was $1.3 billion.
- *Orange County.* The County Treasurer, Bob Citron, invested much of the County's Investment Pool in highly leveraged derivatives instruments that were, in effect, a very large bet on interest rates remaining low. The rise in interest rates in 1994 then inflicted huge losses on the Investment Pool – $1.7 billion in all – and led to the County's bankruptcy.
- *Barings Bank.* Nick Leeson, a trader working out of Barings' Singapore subsidiary, built up huge unauthorised positions in futures and options. The amounts involved vastly exceeded the bank's capital, and adverse movements in these markets forced the bank into bankruptcy in February 1995. The ultimate loss to the bank was about $1.3 billion.
- *Daiwa Bank.* A single trader, Toshihide Iguchi, managed to make and conceal losses from Treasury bond trades of over $1.1 billion over an 11-year period. The losses came to light only when Iguchi confessed them to his management in July 1995.
- *Sumitomo Corporation.* In June 1996, Sumitomo announced a loss of $1.8 billion. These losses had accumulated over a 10-year period from unauthorised trades by its chief copper trader, Yasuo Hamanaka, which he had managed to cover up.

In each of these cases, losses were well in excess of $1 billion. However, there were also many other cases where smaller losses were made in much the same way.[35] A recent example is the loss of £450 million announced by Deutsche Morgan Grenfell in September 1996, which was also ascribed to the unauthorised activities of a single individual. There are also many other cases that failed to hit the headlines, and it is quite possible that the combined losses of these more numerous, but smaller, financial disasters could exceed the amounts lost in the high-profile billion-dollar-plus cases. One can only speculate about how many other losses are made but covered up by embarrassed managers in efforts to protect themselves or prevent scandals becoming public. Nor, too, does anyone really know how often institutions have had near misses that could easily have led to disaster, but where disaster was averted by pure good luck.[36]

These disasters had some disturbing common features. Key individuals were able to make decisions that exposed their institutions to potentially huge losses, and to do so apparently without their superiors being aware of what they were doing. In many of these cases, the individuals involved were also able to subvert the institution's own risk-control systems by controlling the back office and feeding distorted information to head office. For their part, the head office people were often aware of weaknesses in their risk-control systems, but failed to act or even to ask fairly obvious questions about what their subordinates were doing. These institutions also tended to lack adequate systems to monitor compliance with position limits and other safety procedures. In addition, they also lacked good systems to audit their internal financial statements. Had they had them, these systems would have shown that the figures didn't add up and so told senior management that something was amiss. These disasters occurred not because of the activities of aberrant individuals, as such, but because the institutions concerned had very poor systems of risk management and management control that allowed these individuals to engage in the activities that led to these losses.[37]

∿3.4.3. The Origin and Development of VaR

In the late 1970s and 1980s, a number of major financial institutions started work on internal models to measure and aggregate risks across the institution as a whole. They started work on these models not just for their own internal risk management purposes, but also to support their management consultancy businesses and, ultimately, to sell to clients – other financial institutions and large corporates – who wanted such systems but were not in a position to develop them themselves.

The best known of these systems is the RiskMetrics system developed by JP Morgan. This particular system is said to have originated when the chairman of JP Morgan, Dennis Weatherstone, asked his staff to give him a daily one-page report indicating risk and potential losses over the next 24 hours, across the bank's entire trading portfolio. This report, the famous '4.15 report', was to be given to him at 4.15 each day, after the close of trading. In order to meet this demand, the Morgan staff had to develop a system to measure risks across different trading positions, across the whole institution, and also aggregate these risks into a single risk measure. The measure used was value at risk, or the maximum likely loss over the next trading day.[38] The measure was derived from a system based on standard portfolio theory, using estimates of the standard deviations of and various correlations between the returns to different traded instruments. While the theory was fairly straightforward, making the system operational involved a huge amount of work: measurement conventions had to be chosen, data sets constructed, statistical assumptions agreed, procedures determined to estimate volatilities and correlations, computing systems established to carry out estimations, and many other practical problems to be resolved. The devil was in the detail.

Other financial institutions were also working on their own internal models and there was considerable competition to establish a system that would become an industry standard. Some VaR software systems were also developed by specialist companies that concentrated on software issues, but were not in a position to provide data as well. The resulting systems differed quite considerably from each other. Even where they were based on broadly similar theoretical ideas, there were still considerable differences in terms of subsidiary assumptions, use of data, procedures to estimate volatility and correlation, and many other 'details'. Moreover, not all VaR systems were based on portfolio theory. VaR systems were also built using a historical simulation approach that estimated VaR from a histogram of past profit and loss data for the institution as a whole. These historical simulation systems were considerably easier to develop and use, but also had their own limitations. More sophisticated systems were also developed using Monte Carlo and other simulation techniques. These systems were extremely powerful and could in theory give better results than systems based on portfolio theory or historical simulation, but they were also more costly to develop and more difficult to operate.

JP Morgan then threw the gauntlet down to its rivals in October 1994 by making its RiskMetrics system public and making the necessary data freely available on the internet. This move encouraged many of the smaller software providers to adopt the RiskMetrics approach or make their own systems compatible with it. The resulting public debate about the merits of RiskMetrics was also useful in raising awareness of VaR and of the issues involved in establishing and operating VaR systems,[39] as well as in leading to improvements in the RiskMetrics approach itself. Making the RiskMetrics data available also gave a major boost to the spread of VaR systems by giving software providers and their clients access to data sets that they were often unable to construct themselves.[40]

Box 1.2: Portfolio theory and VaR

In some respects VaR is a natural progression from earlier portfolio theory (PT). However, there are also important differences between them:

- PT interprets risk in terms of the standard deviation of the return, while VaR approaches interpret it in terms of the maximum likely loss. The VaR notion of risk – the VAR itself – is much more useful.
- The variance-covariance approach to VaR has the same theoretical basis as PT – in fact, its theoretical basis *is* portfolio theory – but the other two approaches to VaR (i.e., the historical simulation and Monte Carlo simulation approaches) do not. It would therefore be a mistake to regard all VaR approaches as applications (or developments) of portfolio theory.
- VaR approaches can be applied to a much broader range of risk problems: PT is limited to market price risks, while VaR approaches can be applied to credit, liquidity and other risks, as well as to market price risks. VaR is also more flexible, in the sense that we can choose different VaR procedures to suit different circumstances.
- VaR approaches are better at accommodating statistical problems such as non-normal returns.
- VaR provides better rules than PT to guide investment, hedging and portfolio management decisions.
- VaR, unlike PT, also provides a more far-reaching methodology for firm-wide risk management. It has major implications for the structure of the firm, the organisation of risk management within the firm, the remuneration of traders and asset managers, and related issues. VaR provides a whole risk management philosophy, not just a procedure for estimating a given set of risks in a given organisational environment.

The adoption of VaR systems was very rapid, not only among securities houses and investment banks, but among commercial banks, pension funds and other financial institutions, and non-financial corporates. Already,

value at risk is used by most major derivatives dealers to measure and manage global market risk. In the 1994 follow-up to the survey in the Group of Thirty's 1993 global derivatives project, 43% of dealers reported that they were using some form of value at risk and 37% indicated that they planned to use value at risk by the end of 1995...The 1995 Wharton/CIBC Wood Gundy Survey of derivatives usage among US non-financial firms reports that 29% of respondents use value at risk for evaluating the risks of derivatives transactions. A 1995 *Institutional Investor* survey found that 32% of firms use value at risk as a measure of market risk, and 60% of pension funds responding to a survey by the New York University Stern School of Business reported using value at risk. (Linsmeier and Pearson, 1996, p. 2)

The use of VaR is continuing to spread, and it is now clearly only a matter of time before it becomes universal among financial institutions and all but universal among large non-financial corporates.

The state of the art is also continuing to improve and expand in coverage. VaR systems are getting better, and their coverage is being expanded to more instruments; those who develop and use them are becoming more experienced; the combination of plummeting IT costs and continuing software development means that systems are becoming more powerful and much faster, and able to perform tasks that were previously not feasible; and the VaR methodology itself is being extended to deal with other risks besides the market risks for which VaR systems were first developed. These other risks include credit risks, liquidity risks and cashflow risks, the latter being a particular (and self-evident) concern for non-financial corporates. Indeed, even as VaR systems continue to spread and improve, the emphasis is already shifting away from VaR systems to deal with market risks to the new challenges posed by credit at risk, cash flow at risk and other risks, and to the even more difficult problems of handling these risks in an efficient, integrated way. The goal for many firms is no longer a state-of-the-art VaR system to handle their market risks, but a state-of-the-art risk management system that can provide an integrated treatment of market risks, credit risks, cashflow risks and other risks all together.[41]

3.4.4. The VaR Approach to Risk Management: Attractions

So what is VaR, and why is it important? The basic concept was well described by Linsmeier and Pearson (1996):

> Value at risk is a single, summary statistical measure of possible portfolio losses. Specifically, value at risk is a measure of losses due to 'normal' market movements. Losses greater than the value at risk are suffered only with a specified small probability. Subject to the simplifying assumptions used in its calculation, value at risk aggregates all of the risks in a portfolio into a single number suitable for use in the boardroom, reporting to regulators, or disclosure in an annual report. Once one crosses the hurdle of using a statistical measure, the concept of value at risk is straightforward to understand. It is simply a way to describe the magnitude of the likely losses on the portfolio. (Linsmeier and Pearson, 1996, p. 3)

The VaR figure has two important characteristics. The first is that it provides a *common* consistent measure of risk across different positions and risk factors. It enables us to measure the risk associated with a fixed-income position, say, in a way that is comparable to and consistent with a measure of the risk associated with equity or other positions. VaR thus provides us with a common risk yardstick, and this yardstick makes it possible for institutions to manage their risks in a variety of new ways that were not possible before. The other characteristic of VaR is that it takes account of the correlations between different risk factors. If two risks offset each other, the VaR allows for this offset and tells us that the overall risk is fairly low. If the same two risks don't offset each other, the VaR takes this into account as well and gives us a higher risk estimate. Clearly, a risk measure that accounts for correlations is absolutely essential if we are to be able to handle portfolio risks in any meaningful sort of way.

The VaR figure can be used in various ways. (1) Senior management can use it to set their overall risk target, and from that determine risk targets and position limits down the line. If they want the firm to increase its risks, they would increase the overall VaR target, and vice versa. (2) Since VaR tells us the maximum amount we are likely to lose, we can also use it to determine internal capital allocation. We can use it to determine capital requirements at the level of the firm, but also right down the line, down to the level of the individual investment decision. The riskier the activity, the higher the VaR and the greater the capital requirement. (3) It can be used to assess the risks of different investment opportunities before decisions are made, as well as to evaluate the performance of business units after the event. (4) VaR can be very useful for reporting purposes, and many firms now make a point of reporting VaR information in their annual reports.[42]

Box 1.3: What exactly is VaR?

The term value at risk (VaR) can be used in one of four different ways, depending on the particular context:

(1) In its most literal sense, VaR refers to a particular *amount of money*, the maximum amount we are likely to lose over some period, at some specific confidence level.
(2) There is a VaR estimation *procedure*, a numerical, statistical or mathematical procedure to produce VaR figures. A VaR procedure is what produces VaR numbers.
(3) We can also talk of a VaR *methodology*, a procedure or set of procedures that can be used to produce VaR figures, but can also be used to estimate other risks as well. VaR methodologies can be used to estimate other amounts at risk – such as credit at risk and cash flow at risk – as well as values at risk.
(4) Looking beyond measurement issues, we can also talk of a distinctive *VaR approach to risk management*. This refers to how we use VaR figures, how we restructure the company to produce them, and how we deal with various associated risk management issues (how we adjust remuneration for risks taken, etc.).

However, VaR also has other, more far-reaching, uses. Once we start thinking about VaR, we begin to realise that we can go much further than merely producing VaR figures. Although it may not be apparent at first sight, VaR is a key that leads to a radically new approach to firm-wide risk management. This new approach goes well beyond mere risk management as conventionally understood and requires a major transformation in the way that firms structure and govern themselves. This new approach has many attractions:

- It gives senior management a much better handle on risks than they could otherwise have, thus leading to more informed and (hopefully) better risk management.
- It leads to robust new control systems that make it much harder for fraud and human error to go undetected. Such systems would go a long way towards preventing repeats of some of the major risk management disasters of recent years.

- It provides a consistent, integrated treatment of risks across the institution, leading to greater risk transparency and a more consistent treatment of risks across the firm.
- It provides new operational decision rules to guide investment, hedging and trading decisions. These rules take full account of the risk implications of alternative choices and substantially improve the quality of decision-making.
- It provides new remuneration rules for traders, managers and other employees that take account of the risks they take. It therefore helps to discourage the excessive risk-taking that occurs when employees are rewarded on the basis of profits alone, without any reference to the risks they took to get those profits.
- Systems based on VaR methodologies can be used to measure other risks, such as credit, liquidity and cashflow risks, as well as the market risks measured by VaR systems proper. This leads to a more integrated approach to the management of different kinds of risks, and to improved budget planning and better strategic management.
- This new approach enables firms to respond appropriately to regulations, particularly the capital adequacy regulations that financial institutions face. In particular, they tell institutions how to comply with such regulations whilst rearranging their portfolios to minimise the burden that such regulations impose on them.

3.4.5. The VaR Approach to Risk Management: Limitations

Of course, VaR systems have their own problems and limitations, and it is important that users understand these if their firms are to benefit from adopting a VaR approach. Three general limitations especially stand out. One problem is that all VaR systems are backward-looking. They attempt to forecast likely *future* losses using *past* data, based on the assumption, which may or may not be justified, that past relationships will continue to hold in the future. There is therefore always the danger of a major shift – an unexpected collapse of the stock market, say – that inflicts on us losses much bigger than anything a VaR model might have led us to expect. Someone once said that trying to use a VaR system was like trying to drive by looking through the rear-view mirror. The answer to this problem is not to give up on VaR, but to remain aware of this limitation and supplement VaR analyses with scenario analyses that tell us what we might lose under hypothetical circumstances such as a market crash. We need to remember that VaR systems cannot tell us what to expect in these circumstances because they are not designed to.

A second problem stems from the fact that all VaR systems are inevitably based on assumptions that may not be valid in any given circumstances, and our results might accordingly be compromised. The basic answer, again, is to get some feel for our models and our data, and be conscious of where and how our results might be affected. Where possible, we can also check out particular problems by comparing our results with those of other models, and we can sometimes avoid certain problems altogether by upgrading our model (e.g., if we are concerned about returns being non-normal, we can replace a model that assumes returns are normal with one that allows for non-normality). However, the main point is just to be aware of limitations and act accordingly.

Finally, there is the limitation that no VaR system is foolproof. However good the systems are, the fact remains that they are only tools, and they should be used only by people who know how, and how not, to use them. Even a relatively poor VaR system can therefore still be very useful in the hands of experienced operators who know how to use it properly; and even the best VaR system can lead to serious problems in the hands of those who don't know what they are doing. The solution, as always, is for management to hire good people, stay awake, and never forget that risk management continues to be as 'much a craft as it is a science' (Longerstaey *et al.*, 1996, *iii*).[43]

4. OUTLINE OF THE BOOK

Before proceeding further, it is perhaps useful at this point to give a brief outline of the rest of the book. This should, hopefully, give readers some idea of where the discussion is going. It is also important to enable readers to maintain some perspective on the subject and avoid getting bogged down in the detail: the detail is important, but it is more important to have some idea of how it all fits together.

Accordingly, we begin,[44] in Chapter 2, with a longer introduction to the notion of value at risk. This chapter explores the meaning of VaR and examines the significance of the parameters – the holding period and the confidence level – on which VaR figures are predicated. We also examine different ways, numerical and statistical, of estimating VaR. We then turn to the issue of estimation error in VaR, and develop the notion of incremental VaR (i.e., the VaR associated with individual decisions, as opposed to the VaR of a portfolio as a whole), which is of fundamental importance when examining the consequences of individual (e.g. investment) decisions. The appendix to Chapter 2 then addresses the problems involved in validating VaR numbers and assessing the reliability of the systems that generate them.

Part Two then considers different approaches to the estimation of VaR. We begin in Chapter 3 with the variance-covariance approach, whose distinctive feature is the use of a variance-covariance matrix to estimate VaR numbers. The most prominent and most straightforward version of this type of approach is based on the assumption that portfolio returns are normally distributed. This normal approach is very tractable and yields an easy formula for VaR as a multiple of the portfolio standard deviation. It is ideal for large 'straightforward' positions, but has difficulty when portfolio returns are non-linear functions of underlying risk factors (as will often be the case with options) or when the risk factors themselves are not normal. However, it is sometimes possible to modify this approach to approximate portfolio VaR even when the portfolio has non-linear or non-normal elements. Chapter 3 is followed by a brief appendix that reviews the estimation of the volatilities and correlations on which the variance-covariance approach depends.

Chapter 4 considers the historical simulation approach, which uses historical data to reproduce the distribution of our portfolio return, and then reads off the VaR from this reproduced distribution. This approach has the attraction of not relying on particular distributional assumptions such as normality, but has the drawback of being acutely dependent on the data set actually used. Nonetheless, evidence suggests that it often works reasonably well in practice.

Chapter 5 then considers the Monte Carlo simulation and related approaches to VaR. These approaches also estimate VaR from a simulated distribution, but in this case the distribution is derived by assuming particular theoretical return processes and simulating large numbers of random paths that returns could follow. The idea is that if we take a sufficiently large number of simulations, they will produce a simulated distribution that will converge to the unknown true distribution of portfolio returns. We can then infer the VaR from the simulated distribution. These techniques are very powerful and can handle almost any type of position, but they are also more difficult and more time-consuming than other approaches. We would therefore normally use them to estimate the VaRs of 'difficult' portfolios (e.g. those with large options positions) that are not readily amenable to simpler approaches.

The fourth approach is stress testing or scenario analysis, which we examine in Chapter 6. Strictly speaking, this approach does not estimate VaR at all. Instead, it offers a useful (and, in practice, essential) complement to other approaches by examining the effects on our portfolio of plausible scenarios that these other approaches do not consider. Scenario analyses are essential for looking at our vulnerability to unusual events that could plausibly happen but may not yet have happened, or else happen so rarely that VaR procedures cannot do them justice.

To round off Part Two, Chapter 6 is followed by two appendices. The first of these deals with a new approach to VaR, the extreme value approach, which estimates VaR using statistical extreme value theory. The second appendix provides a short comparison of the strengths and weaknesses of each approach and a brief summary of the empirical evidence on their relative performance.

Part Three deals with various risk management issues. We begin in Chapter 7 with the dual issue of how to make risky decisions and how to evaluate them after the event. The object is to derive an operational decision rule that will enable a manager or trader to make the correct choice when faced with alternative investment opportunities that have differing expected returns and differing risks. We also want to evaluate such decisions after they have been made so that we know what to pay our managers. The best decision/evaluation rule turns out to be a generalisation of the well-known Sharpe ratio. This generalised Sharpe rule is the key to risk adjustment. It is valid regardless of correlations with the rest of the portfolio return, and can be extended to deal with the financing as well as risk implications of investment decisions. Traditional decision rules, by contrast, are all seriously flawed (e.g., the standard Sharpe ratio is flawed because it ignores correlations between additional assets and our existing portfolio, the CAPM approach is flawed because it ignores our existing portfolio altogether, and so forth).

Chapter 8 then looks more closely at risk management decision-making, building on the decision rule developed in the previous chapter. It examines how the rule should be used, and looks particularly closely at its use in investment, hedging and portfolio management decisions. It also compares this VaR approach to decision-making with the more traditional approaches to decision-making found in pre-VaR literature.

Chapter 9 deals with the measurement and management of credit risk. The amount of credit risk depends on factors such as the amount of credit extended, the probability of counterparty default and the recovery value of counterparty assets in the event of default. Quantifying these factors leads to a number of different measures of credit risk, of which the most important are credit at risk (i.e., the maximum amount of credit at some confidence level) and default-related VaR (i.e., the maximum default loss at some confidence level). We then discuss various ways of handling credit risk: netting agreements to reduce credit exposure, periodic settlement of outstanding debts, the use of collateral, credit guarantees, position limits, and credit derivatives. The chapter ends with the difficult issue of integrating credit-related risks into the VaR analysis of earlier chapters which focused on market risks.

Chapter 10 then deals with other risks not covered in earlier chapters: liquidity risks, operational risks and legal risks. Liquidity risks relate to the costs of unwinding positions in illiquid markets, and can make a significant difference to VaR estimates. Operational risks relate to operational failures of one sort or another, and are extremely diverse and in some cases very dangerous: most institutions that fail do so because of a failure to control operational risks properly. While some operational risks can be measured and therefore managed, many operational risks, by their very nature, resist attempts to measure them. The key to handling operational risks is therefore to have good systems of control operated by competent people. Legal risks relate to legal uncertainties (e.g., the risk that default procedures will not be enforced), and generally need to be handled by getting access to good legal advice and keeping on top of legal risk exposures.

Chapter 11 considers the allocation of capital. At the level of the business unit, we need to ensure that position limits reflect performance (so we allocate towards the better performing units away from the poorly performing ones) and are set out in terms of VaR rather than nominal amounts alone (so that we can control the risks being taken). At the level of the firm, the key issue is the institution's capital requirement. This capital requirement will be determined either by its own internal risk policy, or by some regulatory capital requirement that forces the institution to maintain a higher level of capital than it would otherwise choose. In the former case, the institution has to decide its capital on the basis of its own risk policy; in the latter, the institution has to satisfy regulatory constraints, but it should also rearrange its portfolio to minimise the burden that those constraints involve.

An appendix to Chapter 11 briefly reviews and compares the main types of capital adequacy regulation faced by financial institutions, and also looks at some of the problems that capital adequacy regulation faces.

The final chapter examines risk management at the firm-wide level, and considers three main issues:

- The first strategic risk management. Management must set out a strategic risk management framework to determine the broad parameters within which individuals and business units will operate – the objectives of strategic risk management, the types of risk the firm will bear, the responsibilities of different business units, and the like. Senior management must then make strategic risk management decisions within this broader framework – they must anticipate new developments and plan ahead, decide on major investments and risk exposures, and determine policy on risk targets and risk limits for individual units.
- The second issue is enterprise-wide risk management which, in many ways, is what VaR is all about. To manage its risks most effectively, a firm needs a centralised system to collect and process data, carry out analysis and estimation, and feed the results to appropriate business units. Establishing such a system implies a major restructuring, but also produces very considerable benefits: most particularly, a better handle on risk management, greater efficiency in decision making, and increased checks against human error and fraud.
- Finally, we examine the usefulness of VaR to corporates, bearing in mind that their needs are generally different from and much more heterogeneous than those of the financial institutions on which the book has tended to concentrate so far. What do VaR approaches offer corporates, and why should corporate managers pay any attention to them? The short answer is that VaR can help corporates manage certain positions (e.g., FX or derivatives ones) and that the VaR methodology can also be very useful for

managing corporate credit risks and cashflow risks. This takes us into the important and growing area of cashflow-at-risk (CRaR) analysis.

The book then ends with some short risk management guidelines for senior managers.

ENDNOTES

1.   Field (1995, p. 2)
2.   Olsen and Associates (1996a, p. 5)
3.   Jorion (1996, p. 5)
4.   Jorion (1996, p. 5)
5.   Daigler (1994, p. 7)
6.   Guldimann (1996, p. 17)
7.   Reported profits and losses calculated under accrual methods showed less volatility, not so much because profits and losses actually were less volatile, but because accrual methods are essentially rules of thumb – extrapolation procedures and the like – that make little or no reference to current market events. Hence, they *could* not reflect genuine day-to-day developments in the markets for the securities they were trying to value.
8.   This estimate comes from Jorion (1996, p. 10), who bases it on figures from the Bank of International Settlements (BIS). Chorafas (1995, p. 273) gets much the same estimate by a different route. The other figures quoted in this paragraph also come from (or are based on those in) Jorion (1996, pp. 10–11).
9.   For more on gap analysis see, e.g., Smith, Smithson and Wilford (1992, p. 5) or Sinkey (1992, Chapter 12).
10.   For more on duration approaches see, e.g., Fabozzi (1993, Chapters 11 and 12) and Tuckman (1995, Chapters 11–13).
11.   They are crude in large part (a) because they take only a first-order approximation to the change in the bond price, and (b) because they implicitly assume that any changes in the yield curve are parallel ones (i.e., all yields across the maturity spectrum change by the same amount). Duration-based hedges are therefore inaccurate against yield changes that involve shifts in the slope of the yield curve. Moreover, as Chance (1996, p. 2) says, 'As if that is not enough, there is a little-known theorem in finance that shows that such parallel yield curve shifts, if they occur, admit arbitrage … And, as we know, such arbitrage profits cannot persist. We have to conclude that parallel shifts in the yield curve not only cannot be expected to happen by coincidence, they simply cannot happen in a well-functioning market.'
12.   There are two standard refinements. (1) We can take a second-order rather than first-order approximation to the bond price change. The second-order term, known as convexity, is related to the change in duration as yield changes, and this duration-convexity approach gives us a better approximation to the bond price change as the yield changes. (For more on this approach see, e.g., Fabozzi (1993, Chapter 12) or Tuckman (1995, Chapter 11).) However, the duration-convexity approach is open to the same problems outlined in the last footnote. Alternatively, if we are concerned about shifts in the yield curve, we can construct separate duration measures for specified yields (e.g. short-term and long-term yields), which would give us estimates of our exposure to changes in these specific yields and allow us to accommodate non-parallel shifts in the yield curve. (For more on this key rate duration approach see, e.g., Ho (1992) or Tuckman (1995, Chapter 13).)
13.   See Smith, Smithson and Wilford (1992, pp. 6–8).
14.   As is well known in applied economics and econometrics, estimated parameters can be very sensitive to the choice of proxies and the inclusion or exclusion of other variables. Relationships can also change over time, often quite dramatically, so there is always the danger of adopting a particular hedge, and still taking a loss because the relationship had changed and the hedge position was too large or too small to match our exposure to the relevant risk factor.
15.   For more on scenario analysis see, e.g., Holton (1996a) or Lawrence (1996, Chapter 9). Scenario analysis is also further discussed in Chapter 6.

16.   It is possible to examine scenarios that take correlations into account as well (e.g., correlations between interest-rate and exchange-rate risks), and it is often helpful to do so. However, we also need to bear in mind that correlations often change, and sometimes do so at the most awkward times (e.g. during a market crash). Hence, it is often good practice to base scenarios on relatively conservative assumptions that allow for correlations to move against us (see, e.g., Chew (1994)).

17.   We need to keep in mind that no hedge is ever perfect, and the instruments that involve lower basis risk (i.e., OTC instruments) also involve higher liquidity risk. The trade-off mentioned earlier thus boils down to one between basis risk and liquidity risk.

18.   See Campbell and Kracaw (1993, Chapters 8 and 10). These traditional approaches also have the limitation that they handle groups of risks by considering each risk separately. This ignores the extent to which risks offset each other or even just diversify, and therefore generally leads to overhedging. The only way to avoid this problem is to get to grips with portfolio theory, which then leads us into the VaR approach.

19.   Portfolio theory tends to be seen as a portfolio measurement tool rather than a risk management tool as such. Nonetheless, it *is* a risk management tool and, in fact, a very useful one.

20.   The origin of portfolio theory is usually traced to the work of Markowitz (1952, 1959). Later scholars – most notably, Sharpe (1964), Lintner (1965), Mossin (1966) and Fama (1968) – then developed the Capital Asset Pricing Model (CAPM) from the basic Markowitz framework. However, in discussing portfolio theory, I have sought to avoid the tangles associated with the CAPM. I believe the CAPM – which I interpret to be portfolio theory combined with the assumptions that everyone is identical and that the market is in equilibrium – was a pointless digression and that the current discredit into which it has fallen is entirely justified. (For the reasons behind this view, I strongly recommend Frankfurter's withering assessment of the rise and fall of the CAPM empire (Frankfurter, 1995).) However, in going over the wreckage of the CAPM, it is also important not to lose sight of the tremendous insights provided by portfolio theory (i.e., *à la* Markowitz). I therefore see the way forward as building on portfolio theory (and, indeed, I believe that much of the VaR literature does exactly that) whilst throwing out the CAPM and, hopefully, most of the CAPM terminology as well.

21.   This framework is often known as the mean-variance framework, because it implicitly presupposes that the mean and variance (or standard deviation) of the return are sufficient to guide investors' decisions. In other words, investors are assumed not to need information about higher-order moments of the return probability density function, such as the skewness or kurtosis coefficients. The mean-variance framework produces some elegant and appealing results, and I prefer to stick with it here because of its relative simplicity and, to be honest, because I am not up to the task of departing from it.

22.   There are also other problems. (1) If we wish to use this short cut, we have relatively little firm guidance on what the hypothetical portfolio should be. In practice, investors usually use some 'obvious' portfolio such as the basket of shares behind a stock index, but we never really know whether this is a good proxy for the CAPM market portfolio or not. It is probably not. (2) Even if we pick a good proxy for the CAPM market portfolio, it is still very doubtful that *any* such portfolio will give us good results (see, e.g., Markowitz (1992, p. 684)). If we wish to use proxy risk estimates, there is a good argument that we should abandon single-factor models in favour of multi-factor models that can mop up more systematic risks. This leads us to the Arbitrage Pricing Theory (APT) of Ross (1976). However, the APT has its own problems (e.g., we can't easily identify the risk factors, and even if we did identify them, we still don't know whether the APT will give us a good proxy for the systematic risk we are trying to proxy).

23.   The actual models themselves are standard fare and are explained in more detail in any good finance text. I particularly recommend Daigler (1994), Chance (1995b), Jarrow (1996) or Ritchken (1996).

24.   The standard cumulative normal distribution is the probability of a standard normal variable (i.e., a normally distributed variable with a mean of zero and a standard deviation of 1) being less than the particular figure in the brackets (i.e., d_1 or whatever).

25.   If the call price is above the value given by the Black-Scholes equation, we would sell options and go long on the leveraged share position. The risks should offset each other (i.e., any gain on the underlying position would be offset by an equal loss on the option position, and *vice versa*), so our combined position would be riskless. We can then pocket the difference between the option and

leveraged share positions as riskless profit. If the call price is below the Black-Scholes value, we buy the option and short the leveraged share position. Again, the risks offset each other and we pocket the difference as riskless profit. It is only when the Black-Scholes equation holds that riskless profits are eliminated, assuming, of course, that the assumptions (e.g. constant volatility, no jumps in the share price) of the model are appropriate to begin with.

26.   There is a large and still growing cottage industry producing different econometric procedures to estimate volatilities, and the issues involved are complex and highly technical. These procedures are discussed further in the appendix to Chapter 3.

27.   Fixed-income positions are especially difficult because certain common assumptions used elsewhere (e.g. when solving for the prices of equity derivatives) are highly inappropriate in a fixed-income context. One of these is the assumption of a constant volatility which is inappropriate in a fixed-income context because a bond's price is pulled towards par as the bond matures, and this pulling to par produces a declining volatility. Another common assumption that is even less appropriate when analysing fixed-income instruments is that of a constant interest rate. Strictly speaking, if interest rates are fixed, a bond price has no reason to move, unless there are changes in credit risks and such factors. It therefore makes little sense to try to model fixed-income instruments on the basis of an assumption that interest rates (of all things!) are fixed. These factors – a declining volatility and the interrelationship between bond prices and interest rates – are much of the reason why the analysis of fixed-income instruments is so difficult and why it has taken so long to develop fixed-income pricing models.

28.   The most common method is the binomial procedure, which simulates the movement of the underlying price by a discretised process that assumes that every so often (e.g. every few minutes) the price can go either up or down by particular amounts. We use this process to solve for the possible values of the underlying asset when the derivative expires, and then work back to infer what the current derivative price should be to eliminate any scope for arbitrage profits.

Other common methods are Monte Carlo simulation procedures. These simulate large numbers of possible paths for the underlying variable by taking random (or, more accurately, random-like) drawings of the random variables involved. Each path leads to a particular final value of the underlying variable and, hence, a particular final value for the derivative as well. We then take the average of these final derivative prices and discount appropriately to determine the current zero-arbitrage derivative price. These simulation methods are discussed further in Chapter 5.

29.   To illustrate: if we were interested in estimating an option delta, we might calculate the option price for one particular value of the underlying price and then calculate it again for another, slightly different value of the underlying price. The difference in the two option prices then gives us the sensitivity of the option price to a small change in the underlying price. The ratio of the change in option price to the change in underlying price then gives us the delta parameter we seek.

30.   Binomial procedures can be very computationally intensive, since each additional sub-period doubles the number of calculations. If there are n periods, the number of calculations is therefore 2^n, and the number of calculations rapidly becomes enormous. There is also a limit to how far we can cut down on the number of sub-periods we can use. The fewer the sub-periods into which we divide the total period between now and maturity, the coarser and less accurate the discretised approximation (remember that the binomial process takes a discrete approximation to a continuous price process) and the less accurate our results will be. Our results therefore need to have at least a minimum level of accuracy if there is to be any point using the binomial process in the first place. For their part, Monte Carlo and other types of simulation approach can easily require millions of 'random' drawings to produce results of sufficiently useful accuracy.

31.   Typical traders have a different mindset from the average quantitative sciences graduate, and this mindset gives them a natural edge in a trading environment. As Nassim Taleb nicely put it, traders 'are trained to look into reality's garbage can, not into the elegant world of models. Unlike professional researchers, traders are never tempted to relax assumptions to make their models more tractable' (Taleb, 1997b, p. 25). They make their living pursuing the statistical and other quirks that quantitative graduates actively dislike, and often try to ignore in an effort to make their world fit into their models. To quote Taleb again:

> Anytime I take a smart street kid with a strong Brooklyn accent and train him or her in quant methods, I develop a wonderful quant trader who knows how to squeeze the sitting ducks. When you take extremely quantitative trainees, particularly from the physical

sciences, and try to make them arbitrage traders, they freak out and become pure gamblers. They can't see the edge and become the sitting ducks. The world has too much texture, more than they can squeeze into the framework they're used to. (Taleb, 1997a, p. 40)

32.   This problem is associated with the gamma risk (i.e., the risk of a changing delta) and is a big worry in practice. As one risk manager noted:

On most option desks, gamma is a local measure designed for very small moves up and down [in the underlying price]. You can have zero gamma but have the firm blow up if you have a 10% move in the market. (Robert Bookstaber, quoted in Chew, 1994, p. 65)

The solution, in part, is to adopt a wider perspective. To quote Bookstaber again:

The key for looking at gamma risks on a global basis is to have a wide angle lens to look for the potential risks. One, two or three standard deviation stress tests are just not enough. The crash of 1987 was a 20 standard deviation event – if you had used a three standard deviation move [to assess vulnerability] you would have completely missed it. (Bookstaber, quoted in Chew, 1994, pp. 65–6)

33.   Quoted in Chew (1994, p. 66)

34.   Taleb (1997a, p. 37) argues that these models are positively harmful, because they encourage the mistaken belief that positions are hedged when they are not, which then leads to excessive risk-taking. However, the problem here is not with the tool, but with the way it is used. The possibility that misuse of the tool can harm a user is not an argument for getting rid of the tool, unless the tool is completely useless. Rather, it is an argument for the user treating the tool with respect.

35.   The overall losses from derivatives positions were very low (at least relative to the notional amounts involved) until 1993, but then rose dramatically. The estimates presented by Chorafas (1995, p. 269) suggest that the annual losses from such positions in the US were well below $1 billion until 1993, when they rose to just over $2 billion, and then jumped to $10.42 billion in 1994. Note, too, that this figure applies to the US only and excludes some of the spectacular losses made (although generally some years earlier) by Japanese corporations. The worldwide totals are therefore considerably higher.

36.   I know of two such cases, and there must be more. It is now a matter of public record that Nick Leeson accumulated large losses shortly after he went to Singapore, but managed to gamble his way out of them without his managers realising what had happened. The episode only came to light later, in the post-mortem over Barings' failure. For reasons best known to himself, Leeson then got himself into trouble again, and it was his efforts to gamble his way out of *that* mess that led to Barings' bankruptcy.

  I also know of another case in which a trader with an excellent previous record stayed late one night and bet his bank on the US Treasury market. The bank's position in US Treasuries was so large that it took days to unwind the position in an orderly way (and thus prevent the bank inadvertently pushing market prices down and destroying itself in the process). The bank was of course highly exposed over this period, and a significant adverse price movement would have killed it. Ironically, the market price rose, and by the time it had unwound its position the bank had made a small profit. The bank's management were keen to hush the whole episode up, and as far as I know, no one outside the bank was ever aware of what had happened. City and Wall Street insiders no doubt know of many other cases of near misses that have also been hushed up.

37.   Ironically, these losses sometimes occurred in institutions whose managements watched other institutions go down and thought that they had covered themselves against such disasters befalling them. After Barings failed, the management of Deutsche Morgan Grenfell, among other banks, apparently satisfied themselves that they were covered against the rogue trader syndrome. Yet they were clearly wrong, as the activities of Peter Young subsequently demonstrated. One suspects that the managements of many other vulnerable financial institutions also think they are covered.

  Managers who think they are covered against such risks should think seriously about the preliminary results of a survey of investment banks recently carried out by Cap Gemini. Apparently,

No fewer than three-quarters of risk managers questioned believe their organisation is immune to a Barings-style trading scandal. But almost the same number of traders believe the opposite: furthermore, 85% of traders believe they could hide trades from their risk managers. (Paul-Choudhury, 1997, p. 19)

If that doesn't wake up managers from their complacency, I don't know what will.

38.   Note that the literature put out by JP Morgan (such as the *RiskMetrics Technical Document*) uses the term 'value at risk' somewhat idiosyncratically to refer specifically to the maximum likely loss over the next 20 days, and uses the term 'daily earnings at risk' (DeaR) to refer to the maximum likely loss over the next day. However, outside Morgan the term 'value at risk' is used as a generic term for the maximum likely loss over whatever horizon is under consideration. It would perhaps cause less confusion if Morgan adopted the same practice, and used the term 'monthly earnings at risk' (MeaR) or some other similar phrase to refer to the VaR over a monthly horizon.

39.   See, e.g., the exchange between Longerstaey and Zangari (1995a) and Lawrence and Robinson (1995a) on the safety or otherwise of RiskMetrics. The various issues covered in this debate – the validity of underlying statistical assumptions, the estimation of volatilities and correlations, the inability of the RiskMetrics system to cope with options positions, and similar issues – will be dealt with in more detail in later chapters.

40.   Morgan continued to develop the RiskMetrics system after its public launch in October 1994. By and large, these developments consisted of expanding data coverage, improving data handling, broadening and improving the instruments covered, and various methodological refinements. These further developments are explained in the fourth edition of the *RiskMetrics Technical Document* (Longerstaey *et al.*, 1996). In June 1996, Morgan teamed up with Reuters in a partnership to enable Morgan to focus on the risk management system while Reuters handled the data, and in April 1997, Morgan and five other leading banks launched their new CreditMetrics system, which is essentially a variance-covariance approach tailored to credit risk.

41.   There is already a very large literature on VaR. Some good article-length overviews of the main issues involved can be found in Beder (1995), Meegan (1995), Frain and Meegan (1996), Hendricks (1996), Holton (1996a), Hopper (1996) and Simons (1996). There are also many excellent shorter pieces on the subject, most particularly in *Risk*, but also in other publications such as *The Treasurer*, *Derivatives Strategy*, *Capital Market Strategies*, and other trade journals, many of which are listed in the bibliography. There are also many discussions of VaR issues in the *RiskMetrics Technical Document* and the *RiskMetrics Monitor*, published by JP Morgan and Reuters, and also at least three other books specifically on the subject (Beckström and Campbell, 1995, Jorion, 1996 and Best, 1998). Much of this literature is also listed in Barry Schachter's on-line bibliography on VaR.

42.   There is a clear trend towards increased reporting of VaR information. A joint Basle Committee-IOSCO survey of 67 banks and 12 securities houses published in November 1996 reported that 36 of the institutions covered reported VaR figures in their 1995 annual reports, up from 18 for their 1994 reports and only three the year before (Basle Committee on Banking Supervision and Technical Committee of IOSCO, 1996, p. 6). Moreover, the same report also indicated a tendency not just towards more institutions reporting VaR, but towards them reporting VaR information in more detail.

43.   Most of the critical discussion about VaR relates to how best to measure VaR, the limitations of particular VaR systems, and so forth, and there are few people who are antagonistic to the basic principles of VaR. One prominent exception is Taleb (1997a,b), whose main objection to VaR systems (and to other high-powered systems for measuring and managing risks) is that they make their users worse off by lulling them into a false sense of security. The response to this position is that no system is perfect, but VaR (and other risk measurement) systems can still be very useful *if* users understand their limitations and make allowances accordingly (see, e.g., Jorion (1997)). VaR systems are useful, but the people who use them must know what they are doing. Nonetheless, Taleb is right to worry about the dangers of VaR and other systems being abused.

44.   As noted earlier, there is also a short appendix to this chapter that gives a brief overview of derivatives issues for readers who might want it.

APPENDIX TO CHAPTER I: A QUICK PRIMER ON DERIVATIVES

I. Classification

Derivatives are contracts whose values or pay-offs depend on those of other assets. They can be classified according to (a) the type of contract, (b) the type of underlying asset, and (c) whether the contract is traded in an organised market or traded over-the-counter (OTC).[A1]

1.1. Types of Contract

The basic types of derivative contract are *forwards, futures, swaps* and *options*:

- Forward contracts are agreements to buy or sell a particular commodity or asset at a particular future time for a price agreed now, but paid on the arranged future date.
- Futures contracts are standardised, exchange-traded forward contracts. Those who take futures positions must satisfy the exchange's margin requirements, and positions are marked to market daily, so profits and losses are realised every day.
- A swap contract is an agreement to swap specified cash flows at particular times. It is, in effect, a series of forward contracts. The most common swaps are interest rate swaps, but swap payments can also be cross-currency or tied to commodity prices or price indices.
- Options give the holder the right but not the obligation to buy or sell an asset for some particular price, known as the strike price. A standard *call option* gives the holder the right to buy, and a standard *put option* gives the right to sell. *European* options give the holder the right to exercise the option at a particular future date, while *American* options give the holder the right to exercise at any time over a particular period. A call option is *at the money* when the price of the underlying asset is equal to the option's strike price, *in the money* when the underlying price exceeds the strike price, and *out of the money* when the underlying price is less than the strike price.

More complex derivatives, sometimes known as hybrid derivatives, can be constructed from combinations of these basic derivatives and other simple contracts (such as equity holdings and riskless bonds).[A2] The process of constructing these complex derivatives from more primitive building blocks is known as financial engineering.

1.2. Underlying Assets

The underlying assets are foreign exchange (FX), equities, fixed-income securities (e.g. bonds), commodities, or baskets of any of these (e.g. baskets of stocks).

1.3. Exchange-traded vs. OTC Derivatives

Many derivatives, such as futures and some options, are traded on organised exchanges. The terms of these contracts are highly standardised. Credit risk is eliminated by the exchange itself standing as counterparty to every transaction, and by it imposing rules about margin requirements (i.e., down payments to keep positions open), daily marking to market (so that market operators realise their profits and losses at the end of each day), the financial health of member firms, and contingency rules to suspend trading if prices hit certain limits. These limits allow for margins to be topped up, where necessary, to protect the exchange against default losses. Non-member firms and the public can get access to the exchange market by making appropriate arrangements with member firms. The combination of standardised contracts and absence of default risk makes these contracts highly liquid.

Other derivatives contracts are traded OTC. These include forward contracts, certain options contracts, swaps, and many hybrid derivatives. The great advantage of these OTC contracts is that they are tailor-made by derivatives providers to suit the needs of individual user-clients. However, the resulting lack of standardisation means that OTC contracts are often very illiquid. They are therefore difficult and/or costly for end-users to unwind. Since there is no exchange involved, OTC contracts also involve credit risk: each party bears the risk that the other might default. Those who deal in OTC contracts therefore have to put a considerable amount of time and energy – and ingenuity – into finding ways of ameliorating and/or living with this credit risk.

2. Uses of Derivatives Contracts

Derivatives have three main uses:

- They can help users to economise on transactions and/or financing costs. The use of derivatives instead of underlying cash market securities can lead to transactions cost savings of up to 95%.[A3] Derivatives such as swaps can also reduce firms' funding costs by giving them access to sources of funds that would otherwise be closed to them.
- They can be used to hedge (i.e., decrease) risks. A firm might be exposed to the risk of loss from a fall in the exchange rate, say, so it might protect itself by taking an appropriate offsetting position (e.g. a foreign currency forward or option contract) as a hedge. Models of derivatives can also assist us in determining the size of hedge positions and in pricing derivative instruments.
- They can help users to speculate (i.e., to increase risks). The greater leverage of derivatives positions enables us to make more profits than we would make if we speculated with positions in the underlying cash assets, but also leads to greater losses if we misjudge the market.

3. Distinguishing Features of Derivatives Contracts

3.1. Leverage

Derivatives contracts can be distinguished from other contracts by one or more of three different features. These of course provide the reasons – or the legitimate ones, at any rate – why there is so much concern about derivatives and the risks associated with them.[A4] One feature is much greater leverage. Leverage is what enables us to make large bets with small amounts of money. The leverage of any position is therefore the gain or loss in its value relative to (i.e., divided by) the change in the underlying risk factor. This risk factor might be a price, an interest or exchange rate, or an index such as a stock index. The bigger the leverage, the bigger the profit if the underlying price moves the right way – and the bigger the loss if it moves against us.

The concept of leverage is an old one, and it has long been understood that the shares of debt-issuing firms are leveraged against the firm's cash flows.[A5] However, the leverage of traditional contracts is usually limited by balance-sheet factors. The leverage of a firm's shares is limited by the willingness of other investors to buy debt, for example, and the willingness of investors to buy debt is limited in turn by the collateral the firm can offer and the firm's prospective cash flows.

Derivatives leverage differs from older forms of leverage in that it is less constrained and often much greater:

- The leverage of a futures position, say, is limited by the margin requirement imposed by the futures exchange. If the margin requirement is 10% of notional contract value, an investor can control $100 000 with a margin down payment of $10 000, making for a leverage ratio of 100 000/10 000, or 10. If the margin requirement goes down to 5%, an investor can control $100 000 in futures contracts with only $5 000, and the leverage ratio goes up to 100 000/5 000, or 20, and so on. The leverage ratio is 1 divided by the margin requirement expressed as a percentage of notional contract value. The limit to leverage is therefore the margin ratio, not a balance-sheet variable as such.
- Similarly, the leverage of a long option position is limited by the option's price, or premium. The leverage is the ratio of the percentage change in the option price to the percentage change in the underlying price. Since the option price can be very low for an option that is deep out of the money, such options enable us to obtain very high leverage.[A6] Again, leverage is not constrained by balance-sheet factors.
- The leverage of OTC contracts is potentially even less constrained, since there are no exchange-imposed rules about margin requirements or premium payments to contend with. The leverage of OTC contracts is therefore constrained only by the willingness and/or ability of both counterparties to the contract: the willingness of the end-user to bear the risk, combined with the willingness and ability of the provider to extend necessary credit and bear (or hedge) its side of the risk. To give one highly publicised example, Procter and Gamble took out a swap with Bankers Trust in 1994 that had a notional value of $200 million, and yet BT was said to have offset this position with a hedge worth at least $3 billion.[A7] The leverage implicit in this derivatives position can be gauged by looking at the ratio of the notional value of the offsetting hedge to the notional value of the derivatives position. It also illustrates the important point that knowledge of the notional values of derivatives positions on their own may give little indication of the risk exposures they entail.

Their potential for greater leverage is one of the attractions of using options – the greater leverage makes them better vehicles for speculation – but their greater leverage also makes them much more dangerous.

3.2. Opacity

Derivatives also differ from other contracts in their lack of transparency. Traditionally, one could usually form some idea of the risks a firm was taking by looking at its balance sheet. One would look at the firm's capital structure, its costs, and the like, and also how these factors changed over time. A certain amount of judgement and background knowledge (e.g., about the industry in which the firm operated) would then suffice to create a reasonable picture of the risks the firm was running (see Chew (1996, pp. 64–65)). A prospective investor would then have enough information on which to make (relatively) informed investment decisions.

Derivatives make it much more difficult to infer a firm's risk exposure, for a number of reasons:

- Derivatives are off-balance-sheet, so balance sheets as such give little idea of derivatives risks.
- Derivatives positions can be changed very rapidly and drastically, so past financial statements rapidly become out of date as indicators of financial risks, even if they were adequate when first produced.
- Even when derivatives positions have been reported in precise quantitative terms, they have often been set out in notional-value terms that revealed little of their true leverage and therefore little of their real risk exposures. This means that a derivatives position might be reported in what appears to be considerable detail, and yet still give little real indication of risk exposure.
- In any case, disclosure of derivatives positions has tended to be fairly rudimentary.[A8] Until recently, US firms were required to disclose derivatives positions only by notes attached to their financial statements, and these were often relatively uninformative. Accounting disclosure requirements in other countries were even less demanding.

This lack of transparency can create serious problems. One problem is the creation of a conflict of interest between the firm and its financial managers. A firm might use bonuses or other means to encourage its financial managers to seek cheaper costs of funding or higher rates of return on the firm's assets. Such incentives are often very beneficial if the firm's risks are transparent, but can be counter-productive if those managers commit the firm to hidden risks that their managers or shareholders don't see:

> To achieve a cheaper cost of funding or a better rate of return than those offered by existing market rates, some end-users will agree to structures whose risks are not apparent to the mathematically-untrained eye, or to take on more excessive risks than they should. The extra risks often boil down to the end-user selling simple or complex options and leveraging his exposure to future market moves. (Chew, 1996, p. 59)

A good example of this type of problem is the case of the Orange County Treasurer, Bob Citron, who adopted an investment strategy for the County in 1993–4 that was able to generate very high returns for a while by investing in highly leveraged structured notes. Unfortunately, these notes fell drastically in value as US interest rates started to rise in February 1994. Citron's superiors focused on the high returns he was generating prior to the interest-rate hike and overlooked the risks he was taking to obtain them. The consequence was County bankruptcy when interest rates rose and an ultimate loss of almost $1.7 billion.

A related transparency problem is the danger that derivatives providers might entice unwitting end-users into contracts that are not in their interest. A case in point is that of Gibson Greetings, which got itself embroiled in a series of highly leveraged contracts with Bankers Trust over the period from October 1992 to March 1994 and ended up with losses of $27 million. A subsequent investigation by the US Commodity Futures Trading Commission concluded that BT had materially misrepresented the contracts it sold to Gibson and deceived the firm at various stages about the losses it had accumulated. BT was later fined and prodded by regulators into accepting a code of conduct to prevent such episodes occurring again.

3.3. Curvature

Some derivatives, most particularly options, also differ from other contracts in the degree of their curvature. The curvature of a contract is the rate at which its price sensitivity – or the slope of a curve plotting the contract price against the price of the underlying variable – changes in response to changes in the underlying price. The localised curvature of an option contract is known as its gamma, and the slope itself is known as its delta. The gamma can therefore be regarded as the change in the delta as the underlying price changes. The delta and gamma of a long (European) call option are given in Figure 1A.1.

The option delta varies from just over zero, when the underlying price is very low, to almost one, when the underlying price is very high. If the underlying price is very low, there is relatively little chance that the option will end up in the money (and so be valuable). A small change in the underlying price will then have little effect on the option price, and so the option will have a small delta. If the underlying price is very high, there is a very good chance of the option ending up in the money. A small change in the underlying price therefore implies an almost equal change in the likely option pay-off, and so the option has a delta close to one. The option's gamma – the change in its delta – is just over zero if the underlying price is very low, rises as the underlying price rises, peaks when the underlying price equals the option's strike price, and then gradually falls back again towards zero as the underlying price continues to rise. The shape of the gamma curve reflects the fact that the option price is relatively insensitive to the underlying price if the option is deep out of the money or deep in the money, but becomes more sensitive to the underlying price as the latter moves towards the strike price. The gamma of an option is therefore at its maximum when the underlying price is equal to the option's strike price (i.e., when the option is at the money).

Moreover, the gamma also rises as the option moves towards maturity, particularly if the underlying price remains close to the strike price. If the option is very near the money, the option price becomes increasingly sensitive to minor changes in the underlying price. With little time to go, changes in the underlying price are less likely to be reversed, so such changes become increasingly influential in deciding whether the option is likely to end up in the money (and so be valuable on expiry) or out of the money (and be worthless). The option's price sensitivity, its gamma, therefore rises as the option approaches its maturity. Indeed, the gamma of an at-the-money option will approach infinity as maturity becomes imminent.

The existence of positive or negative gamma implies a corresponding gamma risk, the risk that the option's delta will change. Gamma risk matters because it undermines a delta hedge and makes hedging more difficult:

- Whenever there is gamma risk, a change in the underlying price implies a change in the delta and, hence, a change in the delta hedge ratio (see Box 1A.1). The hedge position then needs to be rebalanced if it is to continue to offset the risk we wish to hedge. Gamma risk therefore forces us to readjust the hedge position periodically in the light of changes in the underlying price, a process known as dynamic hedging. The greater the gamma, the more unbalanced a delta hedge will become in response to any given change in the underlying price, and the more frequently the hedge will need rebalancing.
- The existence of gamma risk also means that a delta hedge will only protect us fully against small changes in the price of the underlying asset, even if we use the correct (i.e., current) delta to construct our hedge position.

Those who engage in delta hedging must therefore be on their guard for gamma risk. If there is significant gamma risk, they may need to use gamma hedges or scenario analyses.[A9]

FIGURE 1A.1   Delta and Gamma of a Long Call Option

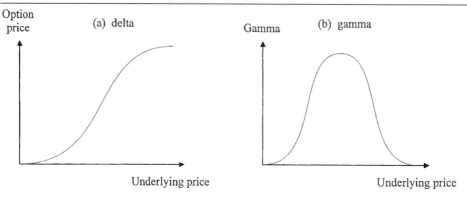

FIGURE 1A.1   Delta and Gamma of a Long Call Option

Box 1A.1:   Delta hedging

The concept of delta is very useful in hedging. Suppose that we wish to hedge a certain equity position, and wish to do so using an offsetting option position. If the equity position is long, we therefore wish to take a short option position to offset it. If the equity price rises, we gain on the equity position but lose on the options; if the equity price falls, we lose on the equity position but gain on the options. The two positions therefore offset each other. However, we also have to determine the size of our hedge if the two positions are to offset each other equally and give us the hedge protection we seek. But how do we choose the size of the hedge?

A solution is to use the option delta. If we let S be the price of the underlying stock, c be price of the call option, and δ be the option's delta, we know from the definition of delta that

$$\delta \approx \Delta c / \Delta S$$

where Δc is a small change in c and ΔS is a small change in S. We now rearrange this equation by multiplying through by ΔS and dividing by δ:

$$\Delta S \approx \Delta c / \delta$$

This tells us that we need $1/\delta$ options contracts to hedge one unit of stock. Our hedge ratio is therefore $1/\delta$. If $\delta = 0.5$, say, we would need to sell $1/0.5$, or 2, options to hedge our stock position. The option's delta thus tells us how to construct the hedge.

However, this hedge will need to be revised if δ should change. If δ fell from 0.5 to 0.33, say, the hedge ratio would change to $1/0.33$, or 3, and we would need to sell an additional option to maintain the hedge. The hedge therefore needs to be a dynamic one (i.e., one that needs regularly rebalancing in the light of changes in the option delta). Note, too, that the hedge is only good against small changes in the price of the underlying asset. The bigger the change in the underlying price, the less accurate the hedge will be. As the saying goes, the only perfect hedge is in a Japanese garden.[A10]

Endnotes

A1.   Dale (1996, p. 153)

A2.   Indeed, the four contract types specified in the text can themselves be built up from combinations of other contracts. A swap is a series of forward contracts, as noted already, but we can also build up futures contracts as combinations of options (i.e., one call minus one put equals one futures contract, more or less), and options themselves can be built up from combinations of the underlying asset and a riskless debt contract.

A3.   Merton (1996, p. *xiii*)

A4.   It cannot be emphasised enough that there is nothing about derivatives that is especially different from earlier or more familiar financial contracts. Much of the hype about derivatives is therefore just that – hype – and there is nothing about derivatives as such that justifies the fear they evoke or justifies new legislation or political intervention to cure some derivatives 'problem'. Companies make and lose money every day, but no one seriously suggests that that constitutes some new problem that requires some public policy 'solution'. As one observer commented about Procter and Gamble's derivatives losses in the early 1990s, 'if they had come in with a Pampers line that flopped, you wouldn't have hearings in Congress, would you?' (Quoted in *Derivatives Strategy*, 16 May 1994, p. 7).

A5.   To illustrate, suppose we denote a firm's equity by E, its assets by A, and its debt by D. The balance sheet constraint tells us that $E = A - D$. Treating D as constant and differentiating with respect to A then tells us that $\delta E/\delta A = 1$, and the leverage of E with respect to A – the proportional change in E over the proportional change in A – is A/E or $1 + D/E$. The bigger the ratio of A to E (or D to E), the bigger the leverage.

A6.   Put another way, the leverage of a call option is 1 divided by the option's delta, as shown in Box 1A.1. Since the delta can be very low, the leverage can rise to very high levels.

A7.   Chew (1996, p. 48)

A8.   As Chew writes,

Generally, only financial institutions (which mark their trading activities to liquidation value) bring derivative positions onto the balance sheet. For these, big losses cannot be deferred to later periods. Western corporates as a whole try to disguise or delay reporting derivatives positions that have gone sour until the potential losses are large enough to materially impact future profit and loss statements or when the losses are realized. But they look like paragons of honesty compared with their Japanese counterparts. Many of these have dragged their feet for ten years and more before telling the world, and their shareholders, about losses that they have made on forward currency transactions (Chew, 1996, p. 66).

A9.   Each of these also has its drawbacks. Gamma hedges require considerable skill to construct because they attempt to match the broad curvature, and not just the localised slope, of the position being hedged. Gamma hedges also need to be updated frequently, and they tend to become increasingly ineffective as the gamma gets bigger (and, therefore, as the option approaches expiry). Scenario analyses are useful for indicating what we stand to lose from stipulated scenarios, but don't actually tell us what hedges to put in place or how to construct them.

A10.   Quoted from Chance (1995a, p. 3)

2

VaR Basics

THIS chapter provides a general introduction to VaR. We begin with a simple numerical illustration of VaR, and then define VaR formally and show how to estimate it. Having introduced the concept, we then set out a probabilistic framework to analyse VaR in more depth. There are a number of such frameworks to choose from, but one in particular is very important: the normal framework based on the assumption that our portfolio return is normally distributed. This normal approach has a certain plausibility and is also very convenient in practice.

We then consider a number of conceptual, practical and managerial issues that arise in any VaR system:

- Since a reported VaR figure is an estimate, and 'true' VaR is usually unknown, we have to deal with the issue of estimation error in VaR.
- Since a portfolio return is only a weighted average of the returns of the individual assets (or liabilities) included in it, we need to examine how the VaR of a portfolio relates to the return volatilities, return correlations and relative sizes of the various positions that make up the portfolio. In other words, we need to relate the VaR of a portfolio to the individual components that make up that portfolio.
- We need to consider the issue of incremental VaR – the extent to which an individual asset position (or purchase) contributes to (or, indeed, reduces) overall portfolio VaR. This is a crucial issue, since information about incremental VaRs has a variety of very important uses (e.g. in setting position limits or determining capital requirements).
- We then discuss the choice of VaR parameters – the holding period and confidence level on which a VaR figure is predicated.
- Finally, since any VaR system generates results on which we are in effect betting money, we need some process of ongoing validation to check for, and, where possible, correct, major biases or other problems that might undermine the reliability of our VaR forecasts. This model validation issue is addressed in the appendix to this chapter.

1. NUMERICAL VaR

The best introduction to VaR is a numerical illustration. Consider the following histogram of daily trading revenues for JP Morgan over 1995, given in Figure 2.1.[1] As we can see, daily revenues fluctuate in a somewhat uneven manner around a mean of $7.6 million. From a risk management perspective, we are most concerned about the revenues, or rather losses, in the extreme left-hand side. There were many days on which the bank

FIGURE 2.1   Histogram of Daily Revenues, JP Morgan 1995

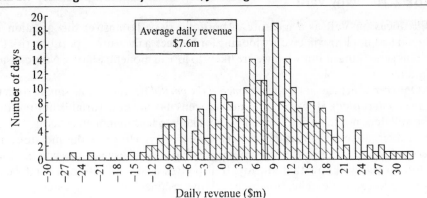

made losses of up to $10 million, there were a much smaller number of days on which there were losses in the range from $10 to $15 million, and on two really bad days there were losses of $23 million and $26 million each.

We begin by first choosing a confidence level to give us a cut-off point to delineate the left-hand tail from the rest of the distribution. We might choose a 99% confidence level, in which case our VaR estimate covers all but the largest 1% of losses, or we could choose a 95% confidence level, in which case the VaR would cover all but the highest 5% of losses, and so on. If we choose the 95% confidence level, the revenue level that delineates the lowest 5% of revenues from the rest is about $-\$11.4$ million (i.e., a loss of $11.4 million). We can therefore say that 1 time out of 20 we would expect a loss greater than $11.4 million. Alternatively, we could say that the maximum loss we would expect on 19 days out of 20 is $11.4 million. This maximum expected loss is the daily value at risk for the selected confidence level.

We can now formally define the value at risk: *the value at risk (VaR) is the maximum expected loss over a given horizon period at a given level of confidence.* Observe, therefore, that the concept of VaR involves two arbitrarily chosen parameters: the horizon period, which might be daily, weekly, monthly, quarterly, or whatever; and the level of confidence, which might be 90%, 95%, 99%, 99.9%, or any other probability we choose. We shall take these parameters as given for the moment.

We can also define VaR in terms of absolute dollar loss, or in terms of loss relative to the mean revenue. The former is simply the maximum amount we expect to lose with a given level of confidence, measured from our current level of wealth. In the case of JP Morgan's daily trading revenues over 1995, the VaR in terms of absolute dollar loss is the figure of $11.4 million given previously. Alternatively, we can also define VaR in terms of the maximum amount we expect to lose with a given level of confidence, measured relative to what we expect our wealth to be at the end of the holding period. This latter VaR is thus measured relative to our mean expected revenue over the period. This relative VaR figure is therefore obtained by adding the daily mean revenue to the absolute dollar loss figure just derived. For JP Morgan over 1995, the relative VaR is $7.6 million plus $11.4 million, or $19 million. These two VaR figures – absolute VaR, and VaR relative to the mean – are shown in Figure 2.2.

VaR can also be represented in terms of the rate of return on the portfolio. The return[2]

Box 2.1: Why VaR?

Why focus on VaR as a measure of portfolio risk? To answer this question, we should first be clear what we are looking for: we seek a measure of portfolio risk that tells us something about what we are likely to lose in monetary terms. Now consider the alternatives.

One common measure is the *variance of the portfolio return* (or its square root, the *standard deviation*). However, this measure tells us only how variable our return is, and still does not tell us how much we are likely to lose in monetary terms.

An alternative measure is the *maximum possible loss*. However, this measure is not very informative, since the maximum possible loss is usually the whole of our portfolio and we know that already. It also gives us no indication of what we are likely to lose, and no indication of the relative riskiness of different assets.

A more promising route is to search among *shortfall measures*, i.e., measures that focus on the worst $c\%$ of outcomes, the so-called *tail outcomes*. Amongst such measures, there are two that meet our criteria of telling us something about likely losses in monetary terms. These are: the *VaR*, the maximum likely loss to occur in $1 - c\%$ of cases; and the *expected loss if a tail event occurs* (i.e., the probability-weighted average of tail losses).[3]

Of these two shortfall measures, the VaR is often easier to calculate and has the advantage that it can be calculated without having to rely on assumptions about the underlying probability distribution. If we had to focus on one of these measures, we would therefore usually prefer the VaR.

Nonetheless, it is usually unwise to focus on one risk measure alone, and the expected tail loss (and other measures) can be useful supplementary statistics.

on the portfolio can be regarded as the revenue divided by the initial value of the portfolio. If we denote the return by R, the initial portfolio value by W, and the revenue by REV, and if we denote the cut-off returns and revenues by R^* and REV^* respectively, the VaR in absolute dollar terms is[4]

FIGURE 2.2   Absolute and Relative VaR, JP Morgan 1995

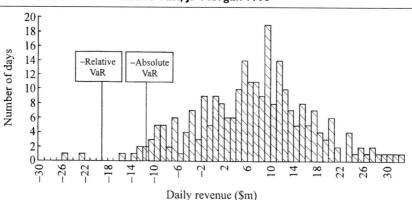

$$\text{VaR (absolute)} = -REV^* = -R^*W \qquad (2.1)$$

The negative sign arises because we can assume that the extreme tail revenues and returns with which we are dealing are losses, but the VaR is positive. Similarly, if the mean revenue is $\overline{REV}$, and the mean return μ, the VaR relative to the mean is[5]

$$\text{VaR (relative)} = -REV^* + \overline{REV} = -R^*W + \mu W \qquad (2.2)$$

These expressions allow us to transform VaR figures in terms of revenues into VaR in terms of returns, which are often more convenient to deal with.

Box 2.2:   Arithmetic or geometric returns?[6]

Returns can be expressed in either arithmetic or geometric form. The most straightforward is the arithmetic return R_t^A, usually defined as:

$$R_t^A = (P_t + D_t - P_{t-1})/P_{t-1}$$

where P_t is the price of the asset at the end of time t, P_{t-1} is the price of the asset a period earlier, and D_t is any interim payment, such as a dividend or coupon, made to the holder over period t. This expression accords with common sense, but has the drawback that it often suggests the possibility of returns of less than -100% (or, put another way, suggests that asset prices can become negative) when we try to model returns by fitting probability density functions (PDFs) to them. The alternative definition is the geometric mean:

$$R_t^G = \ln[(P_t + D_t)/P_{t-1}]$$

The geometric mean has certain other advantages over the arithmetic mean: (1) When returns are fitted with any reasonable PDF, the geometric formulation respects the constraint that returns cannot be less than -100%. (2) The geometric mean makes calculations much easier (e.g. the n-month geometric mean is simply the sum of the n successive one-month geometric means, while the corresponding n-month arithmetic mean is more involved).

Nonetheless, in practice the difference between the two return measures is often very small. To see why, note that

$$R_t^G = \ln[(P_t + D_t)/P_{t-1}] = \ln(1 + R_t^A)$$

If R_t^G is small, we can take a Taylor series approximation of R_t^G:

$$R_t^G = R_t^A + (R_t^A)^2/2 + \dots$$

which is approximately R_t^A if the latter term is sufficiently small. In other words, provided the returns are sufficiently small – which they would usually be if we were dealing with returns over periods as short as a day – the two returns will be fairly close to each other and we can use whichever we prefer. In practice, this means we would normally use the more tractable geometric mean.

2. PARAMETRIC VaR

We can make further progress if we focus on the random process that describes the behaviour of the portfolio's daily return (i.e., if we make some assumptions about the probability density function of the portfolio return). Suppose then that the return has a density function $f(R)$ and we are dealing at a level of confidence of $1 - c$. The probability of a return less than R^* is therefore:

$$\text{Prob}\,[R < R^*] = \int_{-100\%}^{R^*} f(R)dR = c \qquad (2.3)$$

There is now a three-stage procedure for determining VaR: we make some assumption about $f(R)$; we make use of this assumption, substituted in (2.3), to tell us the cut-off return R^*; we then substitute this cut-off return R^* into (2.1) or (2.2) to solve for the VaR.

The critical issue is what assumption to make about $f(R)$. In practice, it is often assumed that $f(R)$ represents a normal distribution. (We could, of course, also assume other distribution functions, and will have more to say on alternative functions presently.) The assumption of normality has a certain (although limited) plausibility, but also has the great advantage of making VaR estimations much simpler. A normal distribution with mean μ and standard deviation σ is given in Figure 2.3.

If R is normally distributed, we can always describe the confidence level in terms of a single parameter, α, which tells us how far away the cut-off values of the two tails are from the mean, μ, in terms of units of the standard deviation, σ. To find the precise value of α, we start with the observation that the probability of a return less than R^* is given by the area in the left-hand tail of the probability density function, say, 5%:

$$\text{Prob}\,[R < R^*] = 0.05 \qquad (2.4)$$

We then transform the random return R in (2.4) into a standard normal variate Z with mean 0 and standard deviation 1. (2.4) therefore becomes:

$$\text{Prob}\,[R < R^*] = \text{Prob}\,[Z < (R^* - \mu)/\sigma] = 0.05 \qquad (2.5)$$

FIGURE 2.3   Normal Distribution

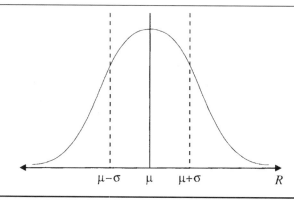

$$\mu-\sigma \quad \mu \quad \mu+\sigma \qquad\qquad R$$

The purpose of the transformation is to enable us to read off the implied value of $(R^* - \mu)/\sigma$ from standard normal tables. It turns out to be equal to -1.65. Hence $(R^* - \mu)/\sigma$ equals -1.65 and

$$R^* = \mu - 1.65\sigma \tag{2.6}$$

More generally, (2.5) would be replaced by

$$\text{Prob}\,[R < R^*] = \text{Prob}\,[Z < (R^* - \mu)/\sigma] = c \tag{2.5'}$$

where c again represents the probability of a lower-tail event (e.g. 5% for our 95% confidence level), and (2.6) would be replaced by

$$R^* = \mu + \alpha\sigma \tag{2.6'}$$

where α reflects the selected confidence level (e.g. -1.65 for a 95% confidence level).

We now plug (2.6') into (2.1) or (2.2) to solve for the implied VaR:

$$\text{VaR (absolute)} = -\mu W - \alpha\sigma W \tag{2.7a}$$

$$\text{VaR (relative)} = -\alpha\sigma W \tag{2.7b}$$

We have replaced the earlier numerical expressions for VaR (i.e. (2.1) and (2.2)) with expressions for VaR in terms of the parameters μ and σ of the probability distribution function assumed to represent the behaviour of portfolio returns. The absolute VaR depends on both μ and σ, while the relative VaR depends only on σ. Both of course depend on the confidence level parameter α.

In practice, instead of working with two different types of VaR, we would usually work with only one, the relative VaR. If we are using a parametric approach to VaR, the relative VaR is easier to handle because it does not require that we know the mean return μ, which could otherwise be a problem. In any case, if we are dealing with a short time period, the difference between absolute and relative VaRs will be fairly small anyway, so we may as well use whichever VaR is more convenient.

3. VaR ESTIMATION ERROR

Having arrived at an estimate of VaR, we should not forget that all we have is just that – an estimate – and it is useful to have some idea of how precise the estimate is. Suppose that we have a daily VaR estimate of, say, $15 million. The question then arises:

> How confident is management in this estimate? Could we say, for example, that management is highly confident in this figure or that it is 95 per cent sure that the true estimate is in a $14–16 million range? Or is it the case that the range is $5–25 million? The two confidence bands give quite a different picture of VaR. (Jorion, 1996, p. 96)

The former range gives us a reasonably precise idea of what the 'true' VaR probably is, but the latter tells us that our VaR estimate is very imprecise, and therefore tells us, in effect, that we don't really know much about the 'true' VaR at all. The usefulness of any VaR estimate is thus dependent on its precision, and an estimate can vary from being highly precise (and therefore highly informative) to being so vague as to tell us almost nothing.

Box 2.3: A *t*-distribution approach to VaR

A *t*-distribution provides a natural alternative to the normal distribution for modelling VaR. (1) It provides an easy and intuitively plausible way of capturing uncertainty about the portfolio standard deviation. In particular, it captures the idea that the less information we have about the portfolio standard deviation, the wider the VaR confidence interval should be. (2) A number of studies have reported that it appears to fit observed returns better than the normal distribution. For example, Wilson (1993, p. 38) compared the two by examining how frequently actual losses for a sample portfolio exceeded predicted VaR, where the VaR itself was based on a 99% confidence level. If the PDF is properly chosen, we would expect losses to exceed predicted VaR on 1% of occasions, and yet Wilson found that actual losses exceeded predicted normal VaR on 2.7% of occasions but exceeded predicted *t*-VaR on only 0.7% of occasions. These results therefore clearly suggest that the *t*-distribution is a better fit than the normal distribution. (3) The distribution is very easy to use in practice, since its properties are well understood and its values can be looked up in standard tables.

The *t*-distribution also has fatter tails than the normal distribution (see figure). These fat tails imply that there is more chance of extremely high losses than under the normal distribution, and that the *t*-VaR for any given confidence level is likely to be higher than the corresponding normal VaR.

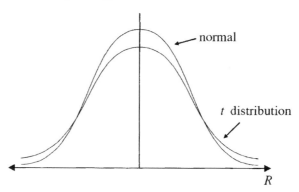

If the *t*-distribution *is* a better representation of returns than the normal one, as suggested by the Wilson results as well as by many others, then normal-based VaR will understate 'true' VaR *and* understate the losses that can be expected when extreme losses actually occur. Users of VaR systems should therefore *not* take normality for granted.

The most natural way to gauge the precision of a VaR estimate is to construct a confidence interval for it, and there is a very simple way to do this, at least under conditions of normality. Recall that under normality the 'true' VaR will be $-\alpha\sigma W$, where α reflects the level of confidence on which the VaR is predicated (so that a 95% confidence level implies that α is -1.65, and so on) and σ is the standard deviation of daily returns. The problem is that σ is unknown, and we wish to gauge the precision of our estimate of σ, and therefore of our estimate of VaR.

Our starting point is the observation that, if we draw a random sample of size n from a normal distribution, the variable $(n-1)s^2/\sigma^2$ will be distributed as a chi-squared with $n-1$ degrees of freedom, where s^2 is the (known) sample variance and σ^2 is the (unknown) population variance (see, e.g., Kendall and Stuart (1973, p. 118)). There will therefore be, say, a 2.5% probability that this variable will fall below the 2.5% chi-squared quantile, denoted by $\chi^2_{0.025}$, and a 2.5% probability that it will fall above the corresponding 97.5% chi-squared quantile, denoted by $\chi^2_{0.975}$. In other words, there is a 95% probability that this variable will fall between these two chi-squared values. It follows that the 95% confidence interval for σ^2 must be:

$$(n-1)s^2/\chi^2_{0.975} < \sigma^2 < (n-1)s^2/\chi^2_{0.025} \qquad (2.8)$$

Given a sample value of s, the confidence interval for the standard deviation σ is then:

$$s\sqrt{(n-1)/\chi^2_{0.975}} < \sigma < s\sqrt{(n-1)/\chi^2_{0.025}} \qquad (2.9)$$

This in turn yields the confidence interval for the VaR:

$$-\alpha s W \sqrt{(n-1)/\chi^2_{0.975}} < \text{VaR} = -\alpha \sigma W < -\alpha W s \sqrt{(n-1)/\chi^2_{0.025}} \qquad (2.10)$$

To give a concrete example, the standard error of daily revenues (i.e., sW) for JP Morgan over 1995 was \$11.52 million. (Recall that VaR was \$19 million, and sW is VaR/1.65.) With 254 daily observations, the lower bound $\alpha s W \sqrt{(n-1)/\chi^2_{0.975}}$ becomes $\$1.65 \times 11.52 \times [253/299.6]^{1/2}$ million or approximately \$17.5 million, and the upper bound $\alpha s W \sqrt{(n-1)/\chi^2_{0.025}}$ becomes $\$1.65 \times 11.52 \times [253/211.3]^{1/2}$ million or approximately \$20.8 million. The 95% confidence interval for the VaR is therefore [\$17.5 million, \$20.8 million]. In other words, we can be 95% confident that the true VaR lies within a range of about \$3.3 million around its estimated mean value.

We can use this approach wherever we have a sample of VaR estimates (or forecasts) and can assume that the distribution of portfolio profit and loss (from which the sample is drawn) is stable and normal. It also has the beauty of being simple to derive, since it depends on only one estimated parameter (i.e., the estimated standard deviation). Some alternative approaches to VaR estimation error are discussed in Box 2.4.

4. DECOMPOSING THE PORTFOLIO INTO ITS CONSTITUENTS

We can gain further insights into what lies behind VaR by decomposing a portfolio into its constituent elements. To take the simplest case, suppose our portfolio consists of two assets, 1 and 2, with a relative amount, w_1, held in asset 1, and relative amount, w_2, held in asset 2 (i.e., so $w_1 + w_2 = 1$). If asset i has a return with variance σ_i^2, the variance of the portfolio, σ_p^2, is:

$$\sigma_p^2 = [w_1^2 \sigma_1^2 + w_2^2 \sigma_2^2 + 2 w_1 w_2 \rho_{1,2} \sigma_1 \sigma_2] \qquad (2.11)$$

where $\rho_{1,2}$ is the correlation coefficient between the returns to the two assets. The VaR of the portfolio is therefore:

$$\text{VaR} = -\alpha \sigma_p W = -\alpha [w_1^2 \sigma_1^2 + w_2^2 \sigma_2^2 + 2 w_1 w_2 \rho_{1,2} \sigma_1 \sigma_2]^{1/2} W \qquad (2.12)$$

$$= [\text{VaR}_1^2 + \text{VaR}_2^2 + 2\rho_{1,2} \text{VaR}_1 \text{VaR}_2]^{1/2}$$

> **Box 2.4:** Alternative approaches to estimating VaR confidence intervals
>
> The approach to VaR estimation error outlined in the text is good if the underlying profit/loss distribution is normal, but is otherwise unreliable. But how do we construct VaR confidence intervals if we do not assume normality? The answer depends on how we estimate the VaR:
>
> *Non-parametric VaR.* If we use a non-parametric approach to VaR (i.e., one that does not specify any particular profit/loss distribution), we can estimate a confidence interval for any particular quantile (i.e., VaR) by using the standard theory of order statistics (Kupiec, 1995, and Pritsker, 1996, p. 44). Alternatively, we can use kernel theory to estimate the precision of any quantile or VaR estimate and infer the confidence interval from that (see, e.g., Butler and Schachter (1996)).
>
> *Monte Carlo simulation.* Monte Carlo simulation (MCS) is a very powerful approach to VaR that can accommodate virtually any instrument or underlying probability distribution. An MCS approach to VaR also allows us to derive explicit confidence intervals using order statistic theory (see Pritsker (1996, pp. 45–47)). However, since we can estimate the accuracy of any given MCS procedures for any given number of simulations, we can also infer the VaR estimation error directly from the particular simulation procedure we use and the number of simulations we run. We shall have more to say on this issue in Chapter 5.

where VaR_1 is the undiversified value at risk associated with holdings of asset 1 (i.e., $-\alpha w_1 \sigma_1 W$, or the value at risk of the asset 1 holding considered on its own), and VaR_2 is the undiversified value at risk associated with holdings of asset 2 (i.e., $-\alpha w_2 \sigma_2 W$). (2.12) gives us the VaR of the portfolio both in terms of underlying portfolio factors (i.e., individual variances, portfolio weights and the correlation coefficient) and in terms of the undiversified VaRs of the component assets.

The key point is the role of the correlation coefficient $\rho_{1,2}$ and there are three important special cases, corresponding to $\rho_{1,2}$ taking its maximum, middle and lowest values of $+1$, 0 and -1:

- If $\rho_{1,2}$ takes its maximum value of $+1$, the portfolio VaR also reaches its maximum and boils down to $[VaR_1 + VaR_2]$, i.e., the sum of the individual asset VaRs. If asset returns are perfectly correlated, the portfolio VaR is simply the sum of the individual undiversified VaRs and there is no diversification of risks.
- If $\rho_{1,2}$ is 0, the portfolio VaR boils down to $[VaR_1^2 + VaR_2^2]^{1/2}$, which is less than the sum of the individual VaRs. This result simply reflects the well-known idea that if returns are independent, a portfolio of two assets will be less risky than a portfolio consisting of either asset on its own.
- If $\rho_{1,2}$ takes its minimum value of -1, the portfolio VaR boils down to $|VaR_1 - VaR_2|$, i.e., the absolute value of the difference between the two VaRs. If returns are perfectly negatively correlated, the two individual VaRs offset each other in their impact on aggregate VaR, and if they are also of the same size, they knock each other out completely and the portfolio VaR is zero.

More generally, the main points are that the portfolio VaR falls as the correlation coefficient falls, and except for the special case where the correlation coefficient is 1, the VaR of the portfolio is less than the sum of the VaRs of the individual assets (i.e., the portfolio VaR is reduced by risk diversification within the portfolio).

These insights extend naturally to portfolios with more than two assets. Suppose, then, that we have a portfolio of n assets, with a relative amount w_i held in each asset i. Given that the return to asset i has a variance σ_i^2, the portfolio variance, σ_p^2, is:

$$\sigma_p^2 = [w_1, w_2, \ldots, w_n] \begin{bmatrix} \sigma_1, 0, \ldots, 0 \\ 0, \sigma_2, \ldots, 0 \\ \cdots \cdots \cdots \\ 0, 0, \ldots, \sigma_n \end{bmatrix} \begin{bmatrix} 1, \rho_{1,2}, \ldots, \rho_{1,n} \\ \rho_{2,1}, 1, \ldots, \rho_{2,n} \\ \cdots \cdots \cdots \\ \rho_{n,1}, \rho_{n,2}, \ldots, 1 \end{bmatrix} \begin{bmatrix} \sigma_1, 0, \ldots, 0 \\ 0, \sigma_2, \ldots, 0 \\ \cdots \cdots \cdots \\ 0, 0, \ldots, \sigma_n \end{bmatrix} \begin{bmatrix} w_1 \\ w_2 \\ \cdots \\ w_n \end{bmatrix} \tag{2.13}$$

where $\rho_{i,j}$ is the correlation coefficient between the returns to assets i and j, and $\rho_{i,j} = \rho_{j,i}$. Now let w represent the $1 \times n$ weight vector $[w_1, w_2, \ldots, w_n]$, σ the $n \times n$ diagonal standard deviation matrix in (2.13), C be the $n \times n$ correlation matrix, and w^T the transpose of w. This notation allows us to write (2.13) in shorthand form as:

$$\sigma_p^2 = w\sigma C\sigma w^T \tag{2.14}$$

$w\sigma C\sigma w^T$ in turn can be shortened to $w\Sigma w^T$ where Σ (which is identical to $\sigma C\sigma$) is the variance-covariance matrix of the returns to the different assets. Using (2.7b), the portfolio VaR, VaR_p, is:

$$\text{VaR}_p = -\alpha\sigma_p W = -\alpha[w\sigma C\sigma w^T]^{1/2} W = -\alpha[w\Sigma w^T]^{1/2} W = [\mathbf{VaR}*C*\mathbf{VaR}^T]^{1/2} \tag{2.15}$$

where $\mathbf{VaR}$ is the $n \times 1$ vector of individual undiversified VaRs, $[\text{VaR}_1, \text{VaR}_2, \ldots, \text{VaR}_n]$, and $\mathbf{VaR}^T$ is its transpose. The portfolio VaR depends on the whole array of the individual undiversified VaRs in the vector $\mathbf{VaR}$ (and therefore the vector $\mathbf{VaR}^T$), and on the complete matrix of return correlations, C. The portfolio VaR still has much the same diversification properties as the two-asset special case just discussed: if all returns are perfectly correlated, the C matrix becomes a matrix of ones, and the portfolio VaR becomes the sum of the undiversified VaRs; otherwise, the portfolio VaR is less than this sum (because some terms in the C matrix will be less than one) and we get some degree of portfolio risk diversification.

Looked at another way, (2.15) also tells us how portfolio VaR depends on underlying 'primitive' factors (i.e., the volatilities embodied in σ and the correlations embodied in C, or, if one prefers, these factors combined in the variance-covariance matrix Σ) and relevant scale factors (i.e., the weights embodied in w, and overall portfolio size, W). This decomposition is useful because it also suggests how we might go about estimating portfolio VaR in practice. It tells us that all we need to estimate portfolio VaR are, on the one hand, volatilities and correlations, given by σ and C, which we need to forecast, and, on the other, the portfolio weights w, which we know already. Once we have our forecasts of σ and C (or, alternatively, of Σ) estimating the VaR for *any* portfolio involving these assets is easy, at least in theory.

5. INCREMENTAL VaR

5.1. A 'Before' and 'After' Approach

The next logical step is to decompose our portfolio VaR to examine the impact of individual component positions on overall VaR. We might wish to investigate each individual asset's contribution to overall VaR or investigate the contribution of some collection of assets (e.g., stocks in a particular sector or a certain type of bond) to overall VaR. We might want this information to identify the major sources of overall risk exposure, to get information with which to adjust returns for risk, to get information on which to monitor position limits, or to evaluate the performance of individual traders or asset managers. It can also be helpful to assess the impact on portfolio VaR of a prospective asset purchase or disposal. Such information is essential if we are to make appropriate allowances for the risks associated with individual asset decisions and determine the internal capital requirements implied by such decisions.

But how do we determine the effects of individual positions on aggregate VaR? Perhaps the most clear-cut approach is to calculate the VaR of the portfolio including the asset in question, and then subtract from that the VaR of the otherwise identical portfolio without that asset. The incremental VaR associated with a position in asset A – the extent to which that position contributes to overall portfolio VaR – is therefore:

Incremental VaR for position in asset A = VaR (portfolio with marginal position in asset A)

$$- \text{VaR (portfolio without marginal position in asset } A)$$
$$(2.16)$$

In theory, (2.16) gives us a straightforward way to calculate the incremental VaR, IVaR. We can assume that we already know the overall VaR of our current portfolio, so we already have one of the two VaRs we need. It therefore remains to calculate the VaR for the other portfolio (i.e., the portfolio minus the asset, if we are dealing with the incremental VaR for an asset we already own; or the portfolio plus the asset, if we are dealing with the incremental VaR for an asset we are considering purchasing). In theory this second portfolio can always be calculated in the same way as we calculated the first portfolio VaR. The incremental VaR would then be the difference between the VaR of the second portfolio and the VaR of the first one, and can be positive (if the asset contributes significantly to portfolio risk), negative (if the new asset is a hedge against existing portfolio risks) or zero (if it adds nothing to overall portfolio risk).

However, any method of calculating incremental VaR that involves before and after calculations of portfolio VaRs is open to a serious practical objection: if the number of assets involved is large, even a fast computer would take time to carry out the necessary matrix operations. Calculating incremental VaR could become slow and cumbersome, and it could be difficult to use IVaR in real-time decision making.[7]

5.2. A Short Cut to Incremental VaR

5.2.1. An Approximate Solution for IVaR

Fortunately, there is an alternative and computationally much easier way to estimate the IVaR. This approach starts from the standard statistical result that allows us to infer the variance of the new portfolio from the variances and covariance of the old portfolio and the new asset, viz.:

$$\sigma_{p^{new}}^2 = (1 + a)^{-2}[\sigma_p^2 + a^2\sigma_A^2 + 2a\sigma_{A,p}] \tag{2.17}$$

$$\Rightarrow \sigma_{p^{new}} = (1 + a)^{-1}\sqrt{\sigma_p^2 + a^2\sigma_A^2 + 2a\sigma_{A,p}}$$

where $\sigma_{p^{new}}$ is the second portfolio standard deviation, σ_p is the old portfolio standard deviation, σ_A is the new asset's volatility, $\sigma_{A,p}$ is the covariance between the new asset and old portfolio, and a is the size of the new asset position relative to the existing portfolio (i.e., so the new portfolio is $(1 + a)$ times the size of the old one). For most trades, a would be small, and a^2 (and therefore $a^2\sigma_A^2$) would be negligible. It follows that:

$$\sigma_p \approx (1 + a)^{-1}\sqrt{\sigma_p^2 + 2a\sigma_{A,p}} \tag{2.18}$$

So (given that we already know σ_p^2 and a), the only additional information we need to estimate the second portfolio standard deviation is the covariance, $\sigma_{A,p}$. The VaR of the second portfolio is then found by multiplying both sides of (2.18) by $-\alpha(1 + a)W$, where W is the size of the old portfolio. Hence:

$$VaR^{new} \approx \sqrt{(VaR^{old})^2 + 2a\alpha^2\sigma_{A,p}W^2} \tag{2.19}$$

and the incremental VaR follows from plugging (2.19) into (2.16). The key point is that each of the operations involved is simple, so we can estimate what we need quickly, without having to estimate the new VaR in the same laborious way we estimated the old one.[8] We can therefore use this procedure interactively, in real-time decision making.

It can also be useful to derive an analytical solution for the IVaR. To obtain such a solution, we first square each side of (2.19) and then subtract $(VaR^{old})^2$ from both sides:

$$(VaR^{new})^2 - (VaR^{old})^2 \approx 2a\alpha^2\sigma_{A,p}W^2 \tag{2.20}$$

We now rearrange the left-hand side of (2.20):

$$(VaR^{new})^2 - (VaR^{old})^2 \approx (VaR^{new} + VaR^{old})(VaR^{new} - VaR^{old}) \tag{2.21}$$

$$= (\Delta VaR + 2VaR^{old})\Delta VaR = (\Delta VaR)^2 + 2VaR^{old}\Delta VaR$$

where of course $\Delta VaR = VaR^{new} - VaR^{old}$ is the IVaR. If a is small, we can presume that $(\Delta VaR)^2$ is small relative to $2VaR^{old}\Delta VaR$, and the right-hand side of (2.21) is approximately $2VaR^{old}\Delta VaR$. We now equate this expression to the right-hand side of (2.20) and rearrange to obtain:

$$\Delta VaR \approx a\alpha^2\sigma_{A,p}W^2/VaR^{old} \tag{2.22}$$

This expression gives us the incremental VaR in terms of the old portfolio VaR, the size of the new asset position (a), the size of the old portfolio (W), the VaR confidence parameter (α) and the covariance ($\sigma_{A,p}$). However, we can also substitute out the old portfolio VaR using (2.7b) and simplify to derive:

$$\Delta VaR \approx -a W\alpha\sigma_{A,p}/\sigma_p \Rightarrow \Delta VaR = a\beta_{A,p}VaR^{old} \tag{2.23}$$

where $\beta_{A,p} \approx \sigma_{A,p}/\sigma_p^2$ is the new asset's portfolio beta. (2.23) gives us a very simple approximate expression for the IVaR: the IVaR is equal to the relative size of the new position (a) times the asset's portfolio beta ($\beta_{A,p}$) times the old portfolio VaR.[9] Given that we already have a and VaR^{old}, the only additional information we need to estimate the IVaR is the beta coefficient (or, if one prefers, the covariance between the new asset and the existing portfolio), which can easily be estimated.[10] Once we have these data, we can plug them into (2.23) and obtain the IVaR without having to recalculate the portfolio VaR from scratch. Again, the simplicity of the calculations means that they can be done instantaneously, and can therefore be used in real-time situations.[11]

5.2.2. A Confidence Interval for IVaR

Having estimated IVaR, there then arises the question of how precise the estimate is. In particular, can we put a confidence interval around this estimate, as we did earlier with our VaR estimate? To answer this question, we should first note that the IVaR estimate just derived involves the product of two random variables – $\hat{\beta}_{A,p}$, the estimate of $\beta_{A,p}$, and $\widehat{VaR}^{old}$, the estimate of VaR^{old} – and both of these have very simple distributions. Since $\hat{\beta}_{A,p}$ is just the coefficient of the portfolio return in an ordinary least squares regression of the return to A against the portfolio return, we know that $\hat{\beta}_{A,p}/se(\hat{\beta}_{A,p})$ is distributed as a t-statistic, where $se(\hat{\beta}_{A,p})$ is the standard error of this estimate. We already know that the square of VaR^{old} is distributed as a chi-squared, assuming that returns are normal.

Unfortunately, we cannot easily construct a confidence interval for the product of two such statistics. However, we *can* construct a confidence interval for our estimate of IVaR *if* we are prepared to make it conditional on our estimate of one or other of these statistics. We could therefore construct a confidence interval for estimate of IVaR conditional on $\widehat{VaR}^{old}$, or one conditional on $\hat{\beta}_{A,p}$. Of these two, the former confidence interval focuses on statistical information specific to the asset in question, and therefore *highlights* differences between different assets, while the latter focuses on statistical information related to the overall VaR, and so *downgrades* differences between different assets. The former is therefore likely to be more useful in practice when comparing different assets. Our preferred conditional confidence interval – our confidence interval conditional on our estimate of VaR^{old} – is therefore simply the confidence interval for $\hat{\beta}_{A,p}$ times $a\widehat{VaR}^{old}$:

$$[\hat{\beta}_{A,p} - t_{df}\, se(\hat{\beta}_{A,p}), \hat{\beta}_{A,p} + t_{df}\, se(\hat{\beta}_{A,p})]a\widehat{VaR}^{old} \qquad (2.24)$$

where t_{df} is our t-statistic conditional on our chosen confidence level and the number of degrees of freedom, df.[12]

Estimating confidence intervals for IVaR estimates is thus extremely easy, if we are prepared to live with conditional intervals.[13]

6. CHOICE OF VaR PARAMETERS

There is also the issue of how to choose the parameters on which VaR figures are based: the holding period and the level of confidence.

6.1. Choice of Holding Period

The usual holding periods are one day or one month, but institutions can also operate on longer holding periods (e.g. one quarter or even one year) and the new BIS capital adequacy rules to come into effect by the end of 1997 stipulate a holding period of two weeks (or ten business days). At the moment, the shortest feasible holding period is one day, although it is theoretically possible for institutions to work with holding periods of less than a day, and we should expect to see intra-day holding periods develop as global securities firms settle into operating around the clock.

There are four main factors that affect the choice of holding period. The first is the liquidity of the markets in which the institution operates: other things being equal, the holding period appropriate in any given market is, ideally, the length of time it takes to ensure orderly liquidation of positions in that market.[14] If a position can be liquidated quickly in an orderly fashion, we might prefer to base that position's VaR on a short target period; but if orderly liquidation takes time (e.g., because the market is thin and it takes time to find counterparties), a longer holding period might be more appropriate. However, the time it takes to liquidate a position in an orderly manner will generally vary from one market to the next (and also vary over time), and a bank has little choice in practice but to work with a common holding period across all its markets. Hence, the most an institution can do in these circumstances is to choose a holding period that best reflects trading horizons in the markets in which it is most involved. A securities house that trades actively in the major financial markets would therefore work with a daily holding period, since it already works with a daily trading horizon, but a bank that trades in thinner markets, particularly OTC ones, may want a longer holding period, such as a month.

The other three factors all suggest a very short holding period. One reason is to justify a normal approximation. The typical situation is where we have a portfolio that includes some options – which means that the portfolio return is not actually normal – but we still want to work with a normal approximation. We therefore take a normal approximation, but this approximation will provide a reasonable fit to our real position only if the observation period is kept short. In other words, a shorter holding period helps make the normal approximation more defensible.

A second reason is to accommodate changes in the portfolio itself. The longer the holding period, the more likely portfolio managers are to change the portfolio, particularly if it is making losses. If a portfolio persistently makes losses, managers will shift out of the loss-making positions into others. To quote Kupiec and O'Brien:

> Typically, the trading departments of major banks are closely monitored by senior management and operate under risk management systems. When these systems are operating properly, they allow the bank to contain losses within management guidelines with a high degree of certainty by making frequent adjustments to exposures.
>
> For example, a bank might set an objective to keep losses on a monthly basis within some predetermined limit with a very low probability of greater losses. In monitoring daily profits and losses, the bank can achieve its objective by making daily adjustments in one-day exposures. If losses begin to occur, exposures would be reduced. If there are profits, the bank might allow its traders to take larger exposures. (Kupiec and O'Brien, 1995a, p. 45)

Yet our analysis of VaR often implicitly requires that the portfolio remains the same over the holding period. The assumption of an unchanging portfolio can therefore be defended more easily if we assume a shorter rather than longer holding period.

We might also want a short holding period for validation purposes. The fact is that reliable validation requires a large data set, and a large data set requires a short holding period. (We shall have more to say on this issue in the appendix to this chapter.) If a reliable test requires, say, 1000 (non-overlapping) observations to be reliable, we would need a data period of at least four years (at 250 business days a year) if we used a daily holding period; we would need 20 years of data to get the same number of non-overlapping observations if we had weekly data, and we would need 80 years' data if we had monthly observations. Not only are such long data sets obviously impractical, but they are also so long that, even if we had the data, the earlier observations would be too old to make meaningful comparisons (because the world would have changed too much). The need for large data sets for validation exercises compels us to work with daily observations, at least for validation purposes.

6.2. Choice of Confidence Level

There is also the choice of confidence level. Is there any reason to prefer one confidence level to another? The answer depends in part on the purpose at hand – which could be to validate VaR systems, determine internal capital requirements or provide inputs for internal risk management, or to report VaR or make comparisons among different institutions – and in part on whether we assume normality or some other well-behaved probability distribution (e.g. a t-distribution).

6.2.1. System Validation

As far as system validation is concerned, we should generally avoid VaR predicated on high confidence levels. The problem with high confidence levels is that they make losses in excess of VaR relatively rare: the higher the confidence interval, the rarer these excess losses, and the longer we must wait to accumulate a data set with enough excess loss observations to give us reliable results (see, e.g., Kupiec (1995) and the appendix to this chapter). The need to accumulate sufficient data for system validation imposes a limit on how high the confidence level can be.[15]

However, the choice of confidence level for validation purposes is really only a matter for the team working on internal system validation (or the regulatory supervisor who is trying to test an institution's VaR system), and there is no strong reason why the same confidence level has to be used when VaRs are produced for other purposes.

6.2.2. Capital Requirements

The appropriate confidence level when assessing capital requirements depends on the management's overall aversion to the risks associated with extreme events. The more risk averse they are, the more importance they would attach to having enough capital to cover specified very low returns. They would obtain higher capital levels by choosing higher confidence levels when using VaR to determine their capital requirements.[16]

6.2.3. Accounting and Comparison Purposes

Finally, there is the issue of the confidence level for accounting or comparison purposes.

Different institutions report their VaRs using different confidence levels: Bankers Trust report VaR based on a 99% confidence level, JP Morgan use a 95% confidence level, Citibank a 95.4% confidence level, and so on. The central issue is whether we can compare different institutions' VaRs, based on different confidence intervals, by means of a common yardstick. If we are comparing BT's VaR to JPM's, we obviously cannot compare a VaR based on a 99% confidence level directly with a VaR based on a 95% confidence level. The confidence level of one or the other would have to be altered to make the VaRs directly comparable at the same confidence level.

Translating VaR from one confidence level to another is no problem if we assume normality. In that case, VaRs can easily be translated across confidence levels and the choice of confidence level for reporting purposes becomes entirely arbitrary: it does not matter whether we report VaRs based on 99%, 95% or any other particular level of confidence. (More will be said on this issue in the next chapter.) Whatever the confidence level on which a VaR is reported, we can always transform the figure into a VaR based on some other confidence level. The choice of VaR for accounting or comparison purposes is therefore irrelevant.

However, all this depends on the normality assumption. Without this assumption or something similar, a VaR figure based on one confidence level tells us very little about VaRs at other confidence levels. Translating a VaR from one confidence level to another is therefore straightforward *only* if we can make convenient assumptions about the underlying probability distribution.

6.2.4. VaR Confidence Levels: Conclusion

Different VaR confidence levels are appropriate for different purposes: a low one for validation, a high one for risk management and capital requirements, and perhaps a medium or high one for accounting/comparison purposes. However, there is no compelling reason for an institution to work with one confidence level alone: there is no need for an institution to choose a low confidence level when assessing its capital requirements, say, just because model validation requires a VaR based on a low confidence level. Within reason, the institution could use a high confidence level when determining capital requirements and a low one when conducting validation exercises. In short, an institution should generally use whatever confidence level is appropriate to the task at hand.

ENDNOTES

1. The data in Figures 2.1 and 2.2 are taken from JP Morgan's 1995 *Annual Report*.
2. Since the term 'rate of return' figures repeatedly in the discussion, it soon becomes tedious to keep repeating the phrase in full. I therefore prefer to use the term 'return' as a shorthand.
3. As many readers will be aware, there are also a number of other statistical measures of risk, but there is no point delving into them here, since our focus will be on VaR and, to a lesser extent, expected tail losses. For more on such measures, Artzner *et al.* (1996) and Bassi, Embrechts and Kafetzaki (undated) are recommended.
4. See Jorion (1996, p. 88)
5. See Jorion (1996, p. 87)
6. The discussion in this Box is based on that of Jorion (1996, pp. 76–79).
7. For more on this point, see the Garman papers cited elsewhere.

8. Estimating incremental VaR is more awkward if we do not assume normality. If we use a non-parametric approach to VaR (such as the historical simulation (HS) approach considered in Chapter 4) or a Monte Carlo approach to VaR (discussed in Chapter 5), then we appear to have little option but to estimate incremental VaRs the long way, as the difference between the 'before' and 'after' portfolio VaRs. In view of the fact that each of these could take time to carry out, these approaches can make it difficult to estimate incremental VaR in real-time situations. One of the under-appreciated advantages of normality is that it gives us a reasonable approach to incremental VaR that other approaches cannot easily provide.

9. Note, too, that the beta we are dealing with here is the portfolio beta (i.e., the slope coefficient in a regression of the asset return against the portfolio return), *not* some CAPM-type market beta. All that matters here is the relation of our asset return to that of our existing portfolio.

10. It was apparently Garman who first identified the incremental VaR issue and proposed solutions to it that avoided the need to carry out 'before' and 'after' VaR calculations for each candidate trade (see, e.g., Garman (1996a, b, c, d)). Garman has also explored a number of further implications of IVaR that are not pursued here, and particularly recommended is the discussion in Garman (1996c), which goes further into the intuition of IVaR and into various practical issues related to it (such as mapping and normalisation). However, the explicit solution for IVaR contained in (2.23) is, I believe, simpler and more explicit than any of Garman's solutions, even if they all give the same numerical answers.

11. Thanks to the mapping procedures discussed in the next chapter, the IVaR approach not only enables us to estimate the relevant beta parameters for each asset *actually in* our portfolio, but also enables us to estimate these parameters for *almost any other assets that we might wish to add* to our portfolio. To understand why, we need to recognise that in practice we don't usually estimate the VaRs of the different instruments in our portfolio. Instead, we 'map' all instruments onto a set of core assets and estimate the VaRs of their mapped equivalents in terms of these core assets. So the only beta parameters we really need are those of the core assets. These 'core' beta parameters then enable us to infer the corresponding beta parameters for all other assets, including those that we may not currently hold in our portfolio.

12. The degrees of freedom, in turn, will equal the number of observations minus the number of estimated parameters, of which there would be two (i.e., the intercept and slope parameters) in the present context.

13. Conditional confidence intervals *are* useful (and, in any case, we should remember that all confidence intervals are conditional in some way or other). The point about the conditional interval is that it takes VaR to be given and therefore understates the 'true' unconditional [sic] confidence interval to the extent there is any imprecision in our estimate of this VaR: the more precise our estimate of VaR^{old}, the closer the conditional confidence interval (2.24) will be to the unconditional confidence interval we would prefer to have. Furthermore, (2.24) should also give us some indication of the *relative* precision of the IVaRs estimated for different positions, even if the estimate of VaR^{old} is imprecise. Lastly, if our conditional IVaR confidence interval is very loose, it tells us that our estimate of IVaR is very imprecise: if the conditional confidence interval is loose, the unconditional one will, in general, be even looser.

14. Lawrence and Robinson (1995b), p. 52

15. There is, however, a cost to having a low confidence level. The lower the confidence level, the bigger the tail, and the less chance we have of detecting any abnormality in the more extreme regions of the tail.

16. The appropriate confidence level also depends on what management regard as the extreme events against which the institution holds capital in the first place. Are they the kind of extreme events that occur every 20 days, every 100 days, every year, or every 10 years? The less common (and therefore more catastrophic) the extreme events, the higher the bank's confidence interval and the higher the resulting capital requirement.

APPENDIX TO CHAPTER 2: VERIFYING VaR SYSTEMS

One of the most important points to appreciate about any VaR system is simply that the figures it produces are subject to error. There are many sources of error. Besides sampling error, errors can also arise because of data problems (e.g. the use of inadequate proxies or incompatible data processing systems), inappropriate models, inappropriate dynamic specifications, inappropriate implementation decisions, or just plain human error. These factors also mean that our best estimate of VaR will often be biased (i.e., systematically too high or too low) as well as subject to random error. It is therefore essential that we monitor our VaR forecasts on a regular basis.

However, any monitoring of VaR forecasts must also grapple with the fact that we never actually observe any realised VaR value after the event: the model forecasts an unobservable variable. We therefore have to monitor VaR forecasts not by checking if VaR forecasts as such are subsequently realised, but by checking whether our VaR forecasts are consistent with subsequently realised returns given the confidence level on which the forecasts are constructed.

1. A Frequency of Excessive Losses Test

Perhaps the most obvious way to do this is to investigate how frequently losses are realised in excess of VaR. Do such losses occur significantly more frequently than predicted by the chosen confidence level? For instance, if the chosen confidence level is 95%, we would expect losses in excess of VaR to occur 5% of the time. However, for any given sample, it would be something of a coincidence if the actual loss exceeded VaR on exactly 5% of occasions. The practical issue is how to tell if the realised frequency of such excessive losses – 5.1%, 6%, 16%, or whatever – is sufficiently different from the predicted frequency of 5% to be statistically significant.

One test is suggested by Kupiec (1995).[A1] Imagine that a bank provides VaR figures based on a confidence level of $1 - p^*$. Predicted VaRs and realised losses are observed over T days and we find that the losses exceed predicted VaRs on N days. The frequency of losses in excess of VaR is therefore N/T. We want to know whether this frequency is significantly different from its predicted value of p^*. The point is that the probability of observing N failures in a sample of size T is governed by a binomial process and given by:

$$(1 - p)^{T-N} p^N \tag{2A.1}$$

Kupiec goes on to argue that the most appropriate test of the null hypothesis that $p = p^*$ against simple alternate hypotheses is a likelihood ratio (LR) test given by:

$$-2 \ln[(1 - p^*)^{T-N} p^{*N}] + 2 \ln[(1 - N/T)^{T-N} (N/T)^N] \tag{2A.2}$$

and this test statistic is distributed as a chi-squared with one degree of freedom under the null hypothesis.

The test becomes more powerful as the sample size T increases. As the sample size gets bigger, any given discrepancy between N/T and p^* (i.e., between the actual and expected frequencies of excess losses) becomes less likely if the model is correct. Discrepancies are therefore more significant when they do occur and more likely to lead us to the conclusion that the model is flawed.[A2] Unfortunately, Kupiec also finds that the power of his test statistic is generally poor (i.e., the test has difficulty discriminating among competing alternatives). As he puts it,

> Even when tests are based on daily performance comparisons [i.e., are frequent], small sample test statistics have extremely low power for detecting a model or institution that habitually underestimates potential loss amounts. If only a small history of performance is available, moreover, a model or institution can substantially underestimate the magnitude of its potential losses with little probability of detection either internally by the bank's risk management staff or externally by a supervisor using a performance-based verification test. Reliable performance-based verification techniques require a relatively long comparison sample period. (Kupiec, 1995, p. 74)[A3]

Box 2A.1:   A time of first failure test

If the bank is monitored continuously, Kupiec (1995) also proposes a test of the null hypothesis that the true probability of failure is 5% (or whatever) on the basis of how long it takes fore the first failure to occur. We therefore carry out a test whenever a failure actually occurs rather than wait to accumulate a run of failures in our sample. Intuitively, the more quickly the failure occurs, the higher our estimate of the 'true' probability of failure. Let $\tilde{T}$ be a random variable denoting the number of days until the first failure. If the true probability of failure on any one day is p, the probability of observing the first failure in the period up to and including day $\tilde{T}$ is $p(1 - p)^{\tilde{T} - 1}$.

   Given a realisation of $\tilde{T}$, the likelihood ratio (LR) test for the null hypothesis that $p = p^*$ is:

$$\text{LR}(\tilde{T}, p^*) = -2 \ln[p^*(1 - p^*)^{\tilde{T} - 1} + 2 \ln[(1/\tilde{T})(1 - 1/\tilde{T})^{\tilde{T} - 1}]$$

Under the null hypothesis, $\text{LR}(\tilde{T}, p^*)$ is distributed as a chi-squared with one degree of freedom, and Kupiec reports its critical values. These indicate that the test statistic has relatively little power to discriminate among alternative hypotheses. For example, if the first failure occurs on day 7, the ML estimate of p is 14.3%, and yet the test will not reject the null hypothesis that $p^* = 0.01$ (Kupiec, 1995, p. 77). It can therefore be very difficult to detect a systematic underestimation of failure probabilities.

   This test is best used as a preliminary to the frequency of excessive losses test discussed in the text, and should be carried out every time we observe a loss in excess of predicted VaR.

---

2. The Crnkovic-Drachman VaR Percentile Test

An alternative test has been suggested by Crnkovic and Drachman (1995).[A4] This test can be viewed as a generalisation of the frequency of excessive losses test. The difference is that while the previous approach considers only losses that exceed VaR with a particular probability p^*, their approach considers losses that exceed VaR for all possible values of p^*. Their approach also has the attraction that it makes minimal assumptions about the probability distribution that generates losses.

The idea is simple. At each day we start with a PDF forecast and we end with a realised profit or loss. Regardless of whether the distribution is stationary over time or not, we can always classify the realised profit or loss into some percentile of the forecasted distribution. The key step is then to realise that these percentiles should be uniformly distributed, more or less regardless of what happens to the probability density function from one day to the next.

The actual approach is therefore as follows. Each day a forecast is made of the PDF of our portfolio. The actual profit or loss is then realised, and this profit or loss is classified by its relevant percentile in terms of the forecasted PDF. This percentile is denoted by p, where $0 \leq p \leq 1$, and we keep a record of the daily values of p that occur. If the forecasting method is up to scratch, the recorded percentiles should look like drawings from a sample uniform distribution and be independent of each other. All that remains is then to test these two predictions. Crnkovic and Drachman suggest that the former be tested by means of Kuiper's statistic,[A5] and the latter be tested by means of a BDS statistic that tests whether a variable is independently and identically distributed.[A6]

This approach is straightforward to implement, makes few assumptions about underlying PDFs, and can be applied to any type of VaR system. It is therefore ideal for comparing different VaR systems with each other. However, it also has a serious drawback: its data intensity. Crnkovic and Drachman observe that in their experience, results begin to deteriorate with fewer than 1000 data points to work with, and the deterioration becomes serious when there are fewer than 500 (Crnkovic and Drachman, 1995, p. 5). Their approach therefore requires relatively long data sets to give reliable results. And, as with Kupiec's tests, their tests also have less power as p^* falls (i.e., the tests have more difficulty with smaller tail probabilities).[A7]

3. Christoffersen's Interval Forecast Test

Another useful test for model validation is the interval forecast test proposed by Christoffersen (1996). This procedure provides a fairly general test for the efficiency of any interval forecast, including a VaR forecast. (An interval is any dispersion of outcomes, and a VaR is simply a one-sided interval figure.) The procedure also takes account of any conditionality in our forecast (e.g., if volatilities are low in some periods and high in others, the interval forecast should be smaller in low-volatility periods and bigger in high-volatility periods). The Christoffersen procedure takes account of this type of conditionality and also enables us to separate the effects of these dynamic factors from the effects of assumptions about the probability distribution governing returns. If our interval forecasts fail, this procedure will indicate whether it fails because of inadequate treatment of dynamic factors or because of inappropriate distributional assumptions, or both, and this information is potentially very helpful when deciding how to improve forecasts.

4. A Size of Excessive Losses Test

We can carry out further tests if we are prepared to make particular assumptions about the return PDF. If returns follow a specified distribution, we can use this distribution to infer the losses to expect when tail events occur, and can then compare these expected losses with realised losses to assess the validity of our VaR system. Expected tail losses would be a probability-weighted average of tail losses, conditional on a tail event occurring. For a normal distribution, these expected losses are given by:

$$E[R_t \,|\, R_t < -\alpha\sigma_t] = -\sigma_t f(\alpha)/F(\alpha) \tag{2A.3}$$

where $f(\alpha)$ is the standard normal density function evaluated at α, and $F(\alpha)$ is the standard normal cumulative density function also evaluated at α, both of which can be looked up in standard tables for any chosen value of α (see, e.g., Zangari (1995, p. 92)). We can then test this prediction by taking observations of actual tail losses, estimating their sample standard deviation, and carrying out a t-test of the hypothesis that the sample mean is equal to the predicted mean given by (2A.3). A rejection of this test would constitute evidence against the joint hypothesis that the underlying distribution is normal and that the VaR model is generating figures consistent with the confidence level on which it is predicated.[A8]

5. The Lopez Probability Forecasting Approach

A major problem with all the above procedures, and indeed, with all statistical procedures, is that they tend to have low power (i.e., they are often likely to misclassify a bad model as good). And, as we have already seen from the work of Kupiec and others, this problem of low power is particularly difficult when the data set is small. Lopez (1996) suggests getting around this problem of low power by using a procedure that gauges the accuracy of VaR models, not by testing hypotheses, but by using a standard (i.e., non-statistical) forecast evaluation criterion. The idea is that we specify a forecast loss function and gauge the accuracy of our VaR forecasts (and, hence, the validity of the model that generates these forecasts) by how well they score in terms of this loss function. The higher the score, the poorer the model, and we reject the model if the score is too high.

   We start by specifying the event of interest (i.e., in our case, the occurrence in any period of a loss in excess of VaR). We then predict the probability of this event over the next period (which, in theory, should be one minus the confidence level on which the VaR is constructed) and collect a sample of such probability forecasts, along with a record of whether the event actually took place or not. We also choose a loss function by which to evaluate the goodness of these forecasts against subsequently realised outcomes. The model's score is then obtained by plugging our data into this loss function. The particular loss function Lopez uses is the quadratic probability score (QPS) due originally to Brier (1950). The QPS for a model over a sample of size T is

$$QPS = 2 \sum_{t=1}^{T} (p_t^f - I_t)^2 / T \tag{2A.4}$$

where p_t^f is the forecasted probability that the event happens in period t, and I_t is an indicator variable that takes the value one if the event occurs and zero if it does not. The QPS index generates lower scores for more accurate forecasts and also has the useful property that forecasters must report their true forecasts to the model validator if they wish to minimise their QPS score. This eliminates any incentive for forecasters to fiddle their reported forecasts in order to manipulate their score: if they wish to do well, they must report their best forecasts.[A9]

Lopez went on to compare the accuracy of this approach against the accuracy of statistical approaches – specifically, Kupiec's binomial test, Crnkovic and Drachman's VaR percentile test, and Christoffersen's interval forecast test – by means of a simulation experiment. The simulations specified a number of alternative 'true' statistical processes and then investigated how well each validation approach rejected the (incorrect) null hypothesis. His results suggested that the power of the statistical procedures was generally rather low and that such tests were likely to be inaccurate.[A10] His results also showed that his loss function correctly identified the 'true' model in a large majority of simulated cases,[A11] a result that seems to confirm Lopez' claim that the loss function approach is likely to be quite reliable.

Endnotes

A1.   Jackson, Maude and Perraudin (1997) and Mahoney (1996, p. 12) suggest similar tests, but ones which translate into standard normal Z tests rather than chi-squared ones.

A2.   His results also suggest that we will have more difficulty rejecting a bad model if the VaR figures are based on high levels of confidence. With a confidence level of 90% we would expect to see losses in excess of predicted VaR on one day in ten and it would not take too long before we had accumulated a reasonable number of excess-loss observations. With a confidence level of 99%, however, we would expect to wait for 100 days before observing one loss in excess of VaR, and with such infrequent extreme observations, it obviously takes that much longer to accumulate enough observations for a reliable test. In other words, the higher the confidence level (and, therefore, the lower the probability of extreme events), the more observations are needed to carry out reliable tests. For purposes of model validation, we should avoid basing VaR on excessively high confidence levels.

A3.   This problem also leads to others: once a problem has been detected and corrective action taken, the data collection process begins again and the institution will have to wait a considerable time before it has enough data to tell whether the problem has been corrected or not (see, e.g., Kupiec (1995, p. 74)). The institution therefore gets no real chance to fine tune its corrections: it has to take a stab in the dark and wait in the hope that it gets the correction right, with no or little feedback until it has accumulated enough new observations on which to mount a new test. Furthermore, if the institution has to wait a long time for feedback, there is also the danger that external factors will change and make it even more difficult to tell whether any changes have been good ones or not.

A4.   Mahoney (1996) suggests a similar approach. He breaks the distribution of forecasted returns into K percentiles, where each fractile has the same probability ($= 1/K$) of occurring. If the forecasted distribution is equal to the subsequently realised distribution, then the same fractile of the latter distribution should fall into each of the K 'buckets'. The significance of the difference between the two distributions can then be tested by a chi-squared test (see Mahoney (1996, p. 13)) which should be zero under the null hypothesis that the two distributions are the same. A significantly positive test statistic therefore indicates that the realised and forecasted distributions are different.

A5.   There are a number of ways to test for uniformity. Let $F(t)$ be the number of observed percentiles p that are less than or equal to t, divided by the number of observations N. We can then define Kuiper's statistic in this context:

$$K(F(t),t) = \max\{F(t) - t\} + \max\{t - F(t)\}$$

where $0 \leq t \leq 1$. This statistic gives a measure of how far away the observed cumulative distribution $F(t)$ is from being a cumulative uniform distribution. The lower the statistic, the better the fit. The actual test is then carried out by comparing the test value of $K(F(t),t)$ with the (known) critical values at our desired level of confidence. The Kuiper statistic is equally sensitive for all values of t, but can also be modified to place more weight on the extreme percentiles. This modification is useful, because it is the tails that usually concern us. Details of this procedure are given in Crnkovic and Drachman (1995, pp. 5–6).

A6.   For more on this test, see Brock, Dechert and Scheinkman (1987), Crnkovic and Drachman (1995, pp. 6–7) or Chappell (1997).

A7.   There is some controversy between Kupiec and Crnkovic-Drachman on these tests. Kupiec argues that the verifier will practically never have enough data on which to mount a successful check, and therefore concludes that model verification is nearly impossible in practice. He also points out that the symmetric weighting of all percentiles implicit in the Kuiper statistic approach is usually unreasonable for financial data, since financial data tend to be skewed, and that the weighting modification suggested by Crnkovic and Drachman to correct for this type of problem requires even more data. Crnkovic and Drachman accept these points in principle, but still insist that their approach is feasible. The main issue revolves around how much information is used in the test. Kupiec uses relatively little – merely whether losses exceed VaR or not, on any given day – while Crnkovic and Drachman use all the information in their data set. They argue that this gives them a better picture of the quality of the overall VaR system, and therefore of any individual VaR figure as well. They also buttress this argument with some concrete examples that suggest that errors are relatively small (e.g., no more than 7–10%) provided we do not base VaRs on confidence levels higher than 95%.

A8.   As noted in the text, once we assume a particular distribution such as the normal, we are testing the joint hypothesis that returns are normal and that the VaR model is correct. We can then apply all the usual battery of normality tests, the failure of which would indicate that we could reject the normal VaR approach. These include, among others, BDS tests, tests for zero skewness and zero excess kurtosis (e.g., Bera and Jarque (1980)), and the Q-Q test that examines quantile deviations from normality (see, e.g., Zangari (1995, pp. 51–2)).

A9.   See Lopez (1996, p. 12).

A10.   Lopez (1996, p. 16)

A11.   Lopez (1996, Table 2)

PART TWO

Different Approaches to Measuring VaR

3

The Variance-Covariance Approach

THIS chapter examines further the normal approach to VaR introduced in the last chapter.[1] Our point of departure is the archetypal normal case where all risks are normal and the portfolio is a linear function of these normal risks. This case is easy to handle because the VaR is a multiple of the portfolio standard deviation, and the portfolio standard deviation is a linear function of individual volatilities and covariances. Estimating VaR is therefore a simple matter of using the variance-covariance matrix and information on the sizes of individual positions to determine the portfolio standard deviation; we then multiply this standard deviation by a confidence level parameter and a scale variable reflecting the size of the portfolio. All this is familiar from the last chapter.

However, before we can use this approach we must first deal with certain other issues. Perhaps the main one is what to do when returns are non-linear functions of risk variables, as is often the case with derivatives and fixed-income instruments, or when the risk variables themselves are non-normal. One response is to take a first-order or linear approximation to the returns to these instruments, and then use the linear approximation to work out the VaR. This first-order approximation, known as the delta-normal approach, restores the linear normality of the standard case and makes VaR estimation easy again. However, it also has the drawback that it may not produce VaR estimates that are accurate enough for our purposes. If we want more accurate VaR estimates, we need to investigate ways in which we can make some adjustment for non-linearity or non-normality whilst still retaining at least some of the convenience of working with a variance-covariance matrix. There are two general approaches we can adopt, depending on whether we wish to focus on non-linearity or non-normality. If we wish to focus on non-linearity, we can take a more refined (i.e., second-order) approximation for our non-linear positions, and there are a number of these second-order or delta-gamma procedures to choose from. Alternatively, we can focus on non-normality and adopt one of several non-normal approaches that use the variance-covariance matrix as their primary input, but also make use of certain additional parameters to allow for the fat tails that characterise the observed distributions of many financial returns.

There are also two other issues we must attend to. (1) Since the VaR formula for an equity position will, in general, be different from that for a bond position, and so on, we need formulas for the VaRs of *specific* positions (e.g., positions in equities, bonds, foreign currencies, derivatives, and so on). (2) We may also face the problem of not having volatility and correlation data for all the different instruments we might wish to deal with. Moreover, even if we had such data, we may not be able to use them anyway because our variance-covariance matrix might become too unwieldy. We may therefore have to find proxies for some positions to reduce our information requirements, and we may wish to cut down our variance-covariance matrix to a more manageable size.

I. ADVANTAGES OF NORMALITY

I.I. Tractability of Normality

The first and perhaps most obvious attraction of normality is that it facilitates VaR calculations. As we have already seen, if the portfolio return is normal, the VaR is just a multiple of the portfolio standard deviation. Normality gives us a very simple and tractable expression for VaR. Furthermore, normality also leads to simple and tractable expressions for the confidence interval around our VaR estimate, for incremental VaR, and for the confidence interval around our IVaR estimate.

I.2. Informativeness of Normal VaR

A second major attraction of normality is that it makes VaR figures very informative. Recall that any VaR figure is conditional on two parameters: a holding time period, and a confidence level. However, as we have seen from the last chapter, there is no single best set of values for these two parameters and different institutions might use VaRs based on different parameter values. This raises the important issue of informativeness: does a VaR figure based on one set of parameter values enable us to infer the corresponding VaR figures based on alternative parameter values? For example, can we infer the VaR figure based on a 99% confidence level from a VaR figure based on a 95% level, or can we infer a monthly VaR figure from a daily one?

The answer depends on what we assume about the PDF. If we assume nothing about the PDF, a VaR figure conditional on one set of VaR parameters will not tell us anything bout VaRs conditional on other parameter values, and VaR figures alone would be of little use unless they happened to be based on the particular parameter values we were specifically interested in. We must therefore make some assumption about the PDF if a VaR figure is to be informative about corresponding VaR figures based on other holding periods or confidence levels.

I.2.I. Translatability Across Confidence Level

A normal distribution is particularly attractive in this context because it makes VaR informative about all possible confidence levels and holding periods. Suppose we are given a VaR figure based on a 95% confidence level, but we really want a figure based on a 99% confidence level instead. If we assume normality, then the VaR is equal to $-\alpha\sigma W$, where α in this case equals -1.65 corresponding to the 95% confidence level. If the VaR at a 95% confidence level is $VaR_{0.95}$, we can infer that the portfolio standard deviation is equal to $VaR_{0.95}/(1.65W)$. However, we can also infer from normality that the VaR at the 99% level, $VaR_{0.99}$, is equal to $2.33\sigma W$, or $(2.33/1.65)VaR_{0.95}$. We can therefore readily infer the VaR based on a 99% confidence level from the VaR based on a 95% confidence level. The same logic also applies to *any* two confidence levels. Knowledge of the VaR at any one level of confidence enables us to infer the VaR at any other level of confidence, *if* we assume normality.

1.2.2. Translatability Across Holding Period

The same applies if we are given VaR information based on one particular holding period, but want VaR information based on a different holding period. Imagine we are still dealing with daily revenues or returns, but are now interested in a longer horizon period of, say, 20 days (i.e., one business month). Provided that daily returns are independently distributed from one day to the next, the mean return over the 20-day period is:

$$\mu_{\text{monthly}} = 20\mu_{\text{daily}} \tag{3.1}$$

where μ_{daily} is the daily mean return and μ_{monthly} is the monthly mean return. Similarly, the variance of the 20-day return is:

$$\sigma^2_{\text{monthly}} = 20\sigma^2_{\text{daily}} \tag{3.2}$$

The latter implies that the standard deviation of returns over the 20-day period is:[2]

$$\sigma_{\text{monthly}} = \sigma_{\text{daily}}\sqrt{20} \tag{3.3}$$

The VaR for the longer holding period is then found by using (3.3) to replace the old (daily) standard deviation, σ_{daily}, with $\sigma_{\text{daily}}\sqrt{20}$ in the expression for VaR. The (relative) monthly VaR is therefore:

$$VaR = -\alpha\sigma_{\text{daily}}\sqrt{20}.W \tag{3.4}$$

The VaR figure thus rises as the holding period increases, but this rise is a function of the longer holding period on which the VaR is based and *not* a reflection of any greater risk-taking on the part of the institution that owns the portfolio whose risk we are considering.[3] When comparing VaR figures, we must allow for differences in the holding periods on which the VaRs are predicated.

More generally, if we have VaR based on a holding period of length t_1, normality means we can always translate it into a corresponding VaR for a holding period of length t_2. The first VaR, VaR_{t_1}, is equal to:

$$VaR_{t_1} = -\alpha\sigma\sqrt{t_1}.W \tag{3.5}$$

The second VaR, VaR_{t_2}, is then equal to:

$$VaR_{t_2} = -\alpha\sigma\sqrt{t_2}.W = \alpha[VaR_{t_1}/(\alpha\sqrt{t_1}.W)]\sqrt{t_2}.W = \sqrt{(t_2/t_1)}.VaR_{t_1} \tag{3.6}$$

In other words, we can adjust VaR for different holding periods by rescaling by the ratio of the square root of the two holding periods.

The bottom line is that under normality any VaR figure based on any particular combination of confidence level and holding period implicitly tells us *all* other VaR figures for *all* other combinations of confidence level and holding period. Normality makes VaR *very* informative.

I.2.3. Normality Informative about Expected Tail Losses

Specifying a particular PDF also means that a VaR figure can give us the expected loss if a tail event occurs. The reader will recall from the appendix to the last chapter that this loss is the probability-weighted average of tail losses, conditional on a tail event occurring. If we assume normality, this expected loss is:

$$E[R_t \mid R_t < -\alpha\sigma] = -\sigma f(\alpha)/F(\alpha) \tag{3.7}$$

where $f(\alpha)$ and $F(\alpha)$ are the standard normal and standard normal cumulative density functions evaluated at α.[4] This expected loss is a nice complement to the VaR figure. It tells us what we are likely to lose if a tail event *does* occur, while the VaR tells us the maximum loss if a tail event does *not* occur.

In addition to telling us the expected loss if a tail event occurs, a single normal VaR figure also tells us the expected loss for *any* tail we choose. Recall that a normal VaR figure predicated on one set of parameters implicitly gives us the corresponding VaRs predicated on all other sets of parameters. Hence, if the VaR also gives the expected loss for the particular tail on which it is predicated, that same VaR figure must also give us the expected losses for all other possible tails (i.e., for all possible VaR parameters). Normality thus gives us a complete picture of what we are likely to lose over all possible confidence levels and holding periods.

2. THE DELTA-NORMAL APPROACH

As we have seen, if all positions are linear in underlying risks, the portfolio standard deviation (and, hence, portfolio VaR) is a simple linear transformation of individual risk factors. The difficult issue is therefore what to do with positions that are *not* linear in the underlying risk factors. Such non-linearity is very common when dealing with options, but is also common with positions in fixed-income instruments (i.e., where a bond's price-yield relationship exhibits convexity).

How do we handle such positions? One possible response is to work with linear approximations: we replace the 'true' positions with these linear approximations, and we handle the linearly approximated positions in the same way as other linear positions.[5] This is the delta-normal approach. In using this approach, we are effectively assuming that the non-linearity in our position is sufficiently limited that we can ignore it and still get VaR estimates that are sufficiently accurate to be useful.

Imagine we have a straightforward equity call option of value c. The value of this option depends on a variety of factors (e.g., the price of the underlying stock, the exercise price of the option and the volatility of the underlying stock price), but in using the delta-normal approach we ignore all factors other than the underlying stock price, and we handle that by taking a first-order Taylor series approximation of the change in the option value:

$$\Delta c \approx \delta \Delta S \tag{3.8}$$

where $\Delta c = c - \bar{c}$ and $\Delta S = S - \bar{S}$, S is the underlying stock price, δ is the option's delta, which is assumed here to be given, and the dashes above c and S refer to the current values of these variables. We now rearrange (3.8) to obtain an expression for c as a simple linear function of S:

$$c \approx \bar{c} - \delta\bar{S} + \delta S = k + \delta S \tag{3.9}$$

where $k = \bar{c} - \delta\bar{S}$ can be treated as a constant. The option value at risk, $\text{VaR}^{\text{option}}$, is then:[6]

$$\text{VaR}^{\text{option}} \approx \delta\text{VaR}^S = -\delta\alpha\sigma S \tag{3.10}$$

where $\text{VaR}^S = -\alpha\sigma S$ is the VaR of a one-unit position in the underlying stock.

This approach has a number of attractions: (1) It keeps the linearity of the portfolio without adding any new risk factors. Moreover, the new parameter introduced into the calculation, the option's δ, is readily available for any traded option. Hence, it requires minimal additional data. (2) It gives us an eminently tractable way of handling option positions that retains the benefits of linear normality. (3) It relies on a premise – normality – that is often plausible, and particularly so

> if the time horizon is very short, e.g., intra-day, and if the products themselves have a relatively linear pay-off profile, or, because it is easy to calculate, if a quick and dirty method is required. Thus, it may be very well suited for measuring and controlling intra-day risks of a money market or foreign exchange book with few option positions. (Wilson, 1996, p. 220)

We can handle bonds in a similar way. The holding period returns from a bond depend on changes in the bond's price over the holding period, and the bond price changes with changes in interest rates or yields. The bond price/yield relationship is generally non-linear, but we can always take a linear approximation around the current combination of price (P) and yield (y):

$$P(y + \Delta y) \approx P(y) + (dP/dy)\Delta y \tag{3.11}$$

where Δy is some small change in yield. However, we also know that

$$dP/dy = -D^m P \tag{3.12}$$

where D^m is the bond's modified duration. The percentage change in bond price is then

$$\Delta P/P \approx -D^m\Delta y = -D^m y(\Delta y/y) \tag{3.13}$$

and the volatility of bond prices (and, hence, the volatility of holding return R) is approximately:

$$\sigma_R = \sigma_p \approx D^m y\sigma_y \tag{3.14}$$

Assuming that the yield is normally distributed, the approximate VaR for the bond holding is therefore

$$\text{VaR}^{\text{bond}} = -\alpha\sigma_R B \approx -\alpha D^m y\sigma_y B \tag{3.15}$$

where B is the bond's present price. (3.15) allows us to estimate the bond VaR as a linear function of the bond's yield volatility (σ_y). The only additional information we would need are the bond's modified duration (D^m), yield (y), and price (B), all of which are easily obtained.[7]

However, the delta-normal approach is likely to be reliable only when our portfolio is close to linear in the first place, since only then can a linear approximation be expected to produce an accurate VaR estimate.[8] We can therefore get away with delta-normal techniques if there is limited non-linearity (e.g., some but not much optionality in our portfolio), but we should be wary of resorting to such techniques when dealing with positions with considerable optionality or other non-linear features.

Box 3.1: A duration-convexity approximation to bond portfolios

The second-order approximation approach used to handle non-linearity in options positions can also be used to handle non-linearity in bonds. Suppose we take a second-order approximation of a bond's price-yield relationship:

$$P(y + \Delta y) \approx P(y) + (dP/dY)\Delta y + (1/2)(d^2P/dy^2)\Delta y^2$$

We know from standard fixed-income theory that

$$dP/dy = -D^m P \quad \text{and} \quad dP^2/d^2y = CP$$

where D^m is the bond's modified duration and C its convexity (see Tuckman (1995, pp. 122, 126)). The percentage change in bond price is therefore

$$\Delta P/P \approx -D^m \Delta y + (1/2)C(\Delta y)^2$$

which is the second-order approximation for bond prices corresponding to the delta-gamma approximation for option prices given by (3.12).

---

3. DELTA-GAMMA APPROACHES

3.1. The Delta-Gamma Approximation

But what do we do if these checks suggest that normality is inappropriate? One response is to take a second-order approach: to accommodate non-linearity and resulting portfolio non-normality (e.g., as arises from option positions) by taking a second-order approximation rather than a first-order one.[9] This second-order approximation is usually known as a delta-gamma approximation, and taking such an approximation for a standard European call option gives us the following:[10]

$$\Delta c \approx \delta \Delta S + \gamma(\Delta S)^2/2 \tag{3.16}$$

This second-order approximation takes account of the gamma risk that the delta-normal approach ignores (cf. (3.8)).[11] The improvement over the delta-normal approach is particularly marked when the option has a high (positive or negative) gamma (e.g., as would be the case when dealing with at-the-money options that are close to maturity).[12] The only problem is that it is then no longer clear how to estimate VaR, and this is a more difficult problem than it might at first seem.

Box 3.2: Instruments with embedded optionality

Many otherwise straightforward instruments have embedded optionality. Many bonds have embedded call options that allow the issuer to call (i.e., repurchase) them before maturity on prespecified terms. Bonds can also be convertible, giving the holder the right to convert them into the issuer's equity on certain prespecified terms, or puttable, giving the holder the right to sell back to the issuer.

The existence of an embedded option can have a major impact on an instrument's price and volatility behaviour. Where a call option is embedded in a bond, the bond price cannot rise too far without leading the issuer to call the bond. (The issuer would call the bond to profit from the difference between the high market price and the (low) call price.) Similarly, if the issuer's share price rose too high, the holder of a convertible bond would have an incentive to exercise his or her option to convert. Hence, the price/volatility behaviour of a callable or convertible bond can be quite different from that of a corresponding straight bond.

Handling instruments with embedded options is fairly straightforward, at least in theory. The rule of zero arbitrage should ensure that the price of any instrument with an embedded option, a callable bond, say, is the same as the price of the corresponding straight instrument minus the price of the embedded option, viz.:

$$p_B^{callable} = p_B - c$$

where $p_B^{callable}$ is the price of the callable bond, p_B is the price of its straight equivalent, and c is the price of the option. In theory, we can therefore handle the callable bond by working with its synthetic equivalent consisting of a long straight bond and a short call.

3.1.1. The Delta-Gamma Normal Approach

One common but highly flawed response to non-linearity is the delta-gamma normal approach, the essence of which is to regard the extra risk factor $(\Delta S)^2$ as equivalent to another independently distributed normal variable to be treated in the same way as the first one (i.e., ΔS). We can then regard the change in option value as if driven by two risk factors, ΔS and ΔU:

$$\Delta c \approx \delta \Delta S + (\gamma/2)\Delta U \tag{3.17}$$

where ΔU equals $(\Delta S)^2$. When estimating VaR, we now treat the option position as equivalent to a portfolio in both the underlying stock and a hypothetical instrument of price U:

$$c \approx k + \delta S + (\gamma/2)U \tag{3.18}$$

where $k = \bar{c} - \delta\bar{S} - (\gamma/2)\bar{U}$. This option position is now treated as approximately linear in normal risk factors, so we can estimate its VaR by applying the delta-normal approach. The option VaR is therefore equal to $-\alpha$ times the 'portfolio' standard deviation, where the latter is found by applying the usual formula. Hence:

$$\sigma_p = \sqrt{\delta^2\sigma^2 + (\gamma/2)^2\sigma_U^2} = \sqrt{\delta^2\sigma^2 + (1/2)\gamma^2\sigma^4} \qquad (3.19)$$

where σ, as before, is the volatility of the stock and σ_U is the volatility of the hypothetical instrument U. Consequently, the option VaR is:

$$\text{VaR}^{\text{option}} = -\alpha\sigma_p S = -\alpha S\sqrt{\delta^2\sigma^2 + (1/2)\gamma^2\sigma^4} = -\alpha\sigma S\sqrt{\delta^2 + (1/2)\gamma^2\sigma^2}$$
$$> -\alpha\sigma\delta S = \text{delta-normal VaR}^{\text{option}} \qquad (3.20)$$

The delta-gamma normal approach thus salvages tractability by forcing the model back into the confines of linear normality, so that we can then apply the delta-normal approach to it. Unfortunately, it also suffers from a glaring logical problem: ΔS and $(\Delta S)^2$ *cannot* both be normal. If ΔS is normal, then $(\Delta S)^2$ is chi-squared, and Δc, as given by (3.16), is the sum of a normal and a chi-squared, and therefore another chi-squared.[13] The delta-gamma normal approach consequently achieves tractability by compromising its logical coherence, and its lack of logical coherence can in turn also lead to seriously flawed estimates of VaR.[14]

3.1.2. Wilson's Delta-Gamma Approach

An alternative approach was proposed by Tom Wilson (1994b, 1996). This procedure goes back to the definition of VaR as the maximum possible loss with a given level of probability. Wilson observed that this definition implies that the VaR is the solution to a corresponding optimisation problem, and his suggestion is beguilingly obvious: that we estimate VaR by solving this problem. In the case of a single call option, the VaR can be formally defined as the solution to the following problem:[15]

$$\text{VaR} = \underset{\{\Delta S\}}{\text{Max}} -[\Delta c], \quad \text{subject to } (\Delta S)^2\sigma_S^{-2} \leqslant \alpha^2 \qquad (3.21)$$

In words, the VaR is the maximum loss (i.e., the maximum value of $-[\Delta c]$) subject to the constraint that underlying price changes occur within a certain confidence interval. The bigger the chosen confidence level, the bigger α is and the bigger the permitted maximum price change ΔS.[16] In the present context we also take the option price change Δc to be proxied by its delta-gamma approximation:

$$\Delta c \approx \delta\Delta S + \gamma(\Delta S)^2/2 \qquad (3.22)$$

In general, this approach allows for the maximum loss to occur with $(\Delta S)^2$ taking any value in the range permitted by the constraint, i.e.

$$0 \leqslant (\Delta S)^2 \leqslant \alpha 2\sigma_S^2 \qquad (3.23)$$

which in turn implies that

$$\alpha\sigma_S \leqslant \Delta S \leqslant -\alpha\sigma_S \qquad (3.24)$$

However, in this particular case, we also know that the maximum loss occurs when ΔS takes one or other of its permitted extreme values, i.e., where $\Delta S = \alpha\sigma_S$ or $\Delta S = -\alpha\sigma_S$. We therefore substitute each of these two values of ΔS into (3.24) and see which one produces the bigger loss. The VaR is then the bigger of the two losses, i.e.

$$VaR = -\alpha\sigma_S[\delta - \gamma\alpha\sigma_S/2]S \qquad (3.25)$$

Incidentally, one might note that the gamma effect in (3.25) means that this VaR estimate is less than the corresponding delta-normal estimate (i.e., $-\alpha\sigma_s S$). Given that the delta-normal estimate is too high, we therefore know that the Wilson delta-gamma estimate is on the right side of the delta-normal estimate, at least for this particular option.

The Wilson approach also applies to portfolios with more than one instrument, but unfortunately loses its easiness. In this more general case, the VaR is given by the solution to the following optimisation problem:

$$\text{VaR} = \underset{\{\Delta S\}}{\text{Max}} -[\delta^T \Delta S + \Delta S^T \gamma \Delta S/2], \quad \text{subject to } \Delta S^T \Sigma^{-1} \Delta S \leqslant \alpha^2 \qquad (3.26)$$

where we use the ^{T} to indicate a transpose and again use bold face to represent the relevant matrices.[17] This problem is a standard quadratic programming problem. One way to handle it is to rewrite the problem in Lagrangian form:

$$L = -[\delta^T \Delta S + \Delta S^T \gamma \Delta S/2] + \lambda[\Delta S^T \Sigma^{-1} \Delta S - \alpha^2] \qquad (3.27)$$

We then differentiate L with respect to each element of ΔS to arrive at the following set of Kuhn-Tucker conditions:

$$[-\gamma - \lambda \Sigma^{-1}]\Delta S = \delta$$

$$\Delta S^T \Sigma^{-1} \Delta S \leqslant \alpha^2 \qquad (3.28)$$

$$\lambda(\Delta S^T \Sigma^{-1} \Delta S - \alpha^2) = 0 \quad \text{and} \quad \lambda \geqslant 0$$

where λ is the Lagrange multiplier associated with the constraint, which indicates how much the VaR will rise as we increase the confidence level.[18] The solution, ΔS^*, is then

$$\Delta S^* = A(\lambda)^{-1}\delta \qquad (3.29)$$

where $A(\lambda) = [-\gamma - \lambda\Sigma^{-1}]$. Solving for ΔS^* therefore requires that we search over each possible λ value and invert the $A(\lambda)$ matrix for each such value. We also have to check which solutions satisfy our constraint and eliminate those that don't satisfy it. In so doing, we build up a set of potential ΔS^* solutions that satisfy our constraint, each contingent on a particular λ value, and then we plug each of them into (3.26) to find the one that maximises L.

In theory this procedure should give us our VaR, but it also means that we have to invert bigger and bigger matrices as the number of risk factors gets larger. We can then get into difficulties because carrying out these calculations can be very time-consuming and give rise to other computational problems (e.g., matrices failing to invert). However, we can ameliorate these problems if we are prepared to make some simplifying assumptions, and one useful simplification is to assume that the $A(\lambda)$ matrix is diagonal. If we make this assumption, (3.29) then gives us closed-form solutions for ΔS^* in terms of λ without any need to worry about matrix inversions. Computations become much faster, especially when we have a big $A(\lambda)$ matrix.[19] However, even this improved procedure can be tedious, and the diagonal $A(\lambda)$ simplification still does not give us the convenience of a closed-form solution for VaR.[20] In addition, such empirical evidence as there is suggests that this approach can be very inaccurate and, indeed, sometimes more so than the delta-gamma normal approach.[21]

3.1.3. Delta-Gamma Approaches Using Estimates of Delta and Gamma

Fortunately, there are also more recent approaches that work much better. One line of attack is to estimate the VaR directly from the PDF of the position whose VaR we seek, using estimates of the delta and gamma parameters.[22] The point is that we already know (or think we know) the PDF of the underlying variable. If we know the delta and gamma parameters, we can easily work out the PDF of our derivative position, and from that we can infer the VaR we want. It therefore remains only to get estimates of these parameters and feed them into the VaR calculations.

There are two ways of obtaining such estimates: (1) We can obtain them using market delta and gamma data. Jamshidian and Zhu (1996, pp. 29–30) took this approach and found that their delta-gamma approximations gave fairly accurate estimates of VaR, and that these estimates were considerably better than delta-normal estimates. (2) Alternatively, since we may not have such data for the positions we are interested in, we can also obtain them (as Fallon (1996) does) by estimating the non-linear relationship (e.g. (3.22)) directly, using an appropriate non-linear econometric procedure. Fallon's results suggest that his delta-gamma procedures can significantly improve VaR estimates relative to delta-normal procedures, but even his delta-gamma approaches can perform poorly when options are very out of the money.[23]

3.1.4. Higher-Moment Delta-Gamma Approaches

Alternatively, we can forget about deltas and gammas and focus instead on the higher moments of the portfolio return distribution. Recall the delta-gamma approximation for a call option:

$$\Delta c \approx \delta \Delta S + \gamma (\Delta S)^2/2 \tag{3.22}$$

Other things being equal, the presence of gamma risk implies that the option pay-off will be greater, and losses less, than indicated by a delta approximation.[24] Gamma risk therefore leads the profit/loss distribution to become skewed to the right, as shown in Figure 3.1. As is apparent from the figure, the VaR percentile is now pushed to the right. The 'true' VaR is therefore somewhat less than suggested by a normal estimate. The distribution is now obviously non-normal, and the normal estimate of VaR is therefore clearly inappropriate.[25]

Zangari then suggests two ways we can proceed: a moment-correction approach or a moment-fitting approach.

A Moment-correction Approach   The first is to adjust the confidence interval parameter (i.e., α) for the skewness and other distortions from normality created by the presence of the gamma factor (Zangari, 1996a).[26] We can make this adjustment using an approximation formula known as the Cornish-Fisher expansion, which is based on the underlying statistical principle that one distribution (e.g. a chi-squared) can always be described in terms of the parameters of another (e.g. a normal). The actual adjustment is

$$v \approx (1/6)(z_\alpha^2 - 1)\rho_3 + (1/24)(z_\alpha^3 - 3z_\alpha)\rho_4 - (1/36)(2z_\alpha^3 - 5z_\alpha)\rho_3^2 \tag{3.30}$$

where Z_α is the distribution's lower α-percentile (i.e., -1.65 for α equal to 5%), ρ_3 is a

FIGURE 3.1   Normal and Skewed Distributions

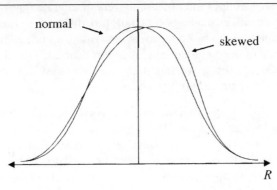

measure of the distribution's skewness, and ρ_4 a measure of its kurtosis.[27] All we need to estimate this adjustment factor are estimates of the skewness and kurtosis parameters ρ_3 and ρ_4, and these are readily obtainable.[28] We apply the adjustment simply by using $-(\alpha - v)$ instead of $-\alpha$ as our confidence parameter and then proceed as if the distribution were normal.

This particular delta-gamma procedure is easy to carry out and readily extendable to portfolios of more than one instrument, and does not require too much computer time even for large portfolios. Its potential weakness is that it is dependent on our estimates of its various parameters, so errors in these estimates will carry over to our estimated VaR. Nonetheless, some simulation results presented by Zangari (1996a, pp. 10–12) suggest that the approximation usually leads to more accurate VaR estimates than the delta-normal approach, and that the improvement can sometimes be quite substantial.

A Moment-fitting Approach   The other procedure is even simpler. Zangari (1996d) suggests that we estimate the first four moments of the profit/loss (or return) distribution and then fit those moments to a known distribution. He actually suggests matching moments to one of a family of distributions known as Johnson distributions. This hypothetical distribution will have the same moments as the 'true' profit/loss distribution, but (unlike the true distribution) will also have a known form. We then estimate the VaR of this known distribution – again, not a difficult task – and take the resulting figure to be an estimate of the 'true' VaR. Zangari goes on to present some simulation results that suggest that this procedure usually produces reasonably low errors, but errors can still be quite substantial for options with high gamma.[29] The procedure therefore appears to work quite well, provided the second-order (i.e., gamma) effects are not too large.[30]

3.1.5. Conclusions about Delta-Gamma Approaches

We should pause at this point to pull our discussion together. We have examined four main approaches to delta-gamma VaR. The first, the delta-gamma normal approach, is clearly inadequate, being both logically incoherent and unreliable. It should therefore be ruled out of court. The second is the Wilson approach, which is essentially an exercise in quadratic programming. This approach is theoretically sound but is awkward to implement, potentially time-consuming and potentially very inaccurate. The other approaches have reasonable theoretical groundings, are not too difficult or time-consuming to implement, and are often (though by no means always) quite accurate. They are therefore almost certainly the best of the delta-gamma procedures currently available.

Whichever particular approach we might choose, we must also recognise certain limitations common to all delta-gamma approaches:

- They rely on second-order approximations, and such approximations might not be sufficiently accurate for our purposes.[31]
- Whatever improved accuracy we get comes at the cost of at least some reduced tractability relative to the linear normal (or delta-normal) procedure.
- In using any delta-gamma approach, we also lose normality in our portfolio return. Even though the underlying risk factors might be normal, the non-linearity of their impact on the portfolio return leads that to have a chi-squared rather than a normal distribution. The incidental benefits of normality – the ability to translate VaR figures easily from one set of VaR parameters to another, the ability to infer expected tail losses without any difficulty, and the general intuitive ease of normality – are compromised or lost altogether. However, we must recognise that this loss is inevitable once the portfolio return ceases to be normal, and the loss of normality is inevitable once we move to a second-order approximation. It is therefore a problem that would occur with *any* delta-gamma approach.

When trying to handle gamma effects, we need to either accept the limitations of our chosen delta-gamma procedure or else abandon delta-gamma approaches altogether.

4. ADJUSTING FOR FAT TAILS

4.1. The Normal Mixture Approach

Besides adopting a delta-gamma approach, the other avenue open to us within the variance-covariance paradigm is to make some adjustment for fat tails, and two approaches have been suggested that could make such adjustments. The first is the normal mixture approach proposed by Zangari (1996c, e) and Venkataraman (1997). To understand this approach, we should go back to the standard normal approach with which we started. This approach assumes that standardised returns (i.e., returns R_t divided by standard deviation σ_t) are generated by

$$R_t/\sigma_t = \varepsilon_t \tag{3.31}$$

where ε_t is a normal random variable with mean 0 and variance 1. We can say that standardised returns are normal or that the returns are normal, conditional on σ_t.

However, this conditional normal distribution implies that extreme standardised returns – very large, or very low or negative standardised returns – should be considerably less frequent than they often appear to be (i.e., the normal distribution generates tails that are not fat enough to match the observed frequency of extreme returns). We therefore need some way to adjust the normal distribution to fatten the tails. Zangari's suggestion is that we do this by adding a new term to (3.31) that reflects a drawing from another normal distribution with a higher standard deviation. Hence

$$R_t/\sigma_t = \varepsilon_{1,t} + \delta_t\varepsilon_{2,t} \tag{3.32}$$

where $\varepsilon_{1,t}$ is the equivalent of ε_t in (3.31) (i.e., is distributed as standard normal) and $\varepsilon_{2,t}$ is a normal variable with mean $\mu_{2,t}$ and $\sigma_{2,t}^2 > 1$. (For convenience, we also assume that the parameters of the two distributions are independent.) The variable δ_t is a binary variable that takes the value 0 most of the time, but occasionally takes the value 1, which it does with some small probability p. In 'normal' circumstances, the distribution of (3.32) is therefore the same as in the standard normal approach, but in a small proportion of occasions δ_t takes the value 1 and the standardised return is more volatile. The result is that extreme values are that much more frequent than under the previous unadjusted normal distribution: we therefore have our fat tails.

Although the standardised return distribution is not normal, we can nonetheless work out the relevant VaR percentile (and, hence, estimate the VaR itself) if we have estimates of the key parameters: the 'old' volatility σ_t, the probability p of the new return distribution kicking in, and the mean and variance of the new distribution, $\mu_{2,t}$ and $\sigma_{2,t}^2$. We then assume that we can approximate σ_t by means of the old linear normal estimate of standard deviation. This assumption is very convenient because it allows us to use the volatility estimate (and, in the case of multi-instrument positions, the variance-covariance estimates) we already have, and the approximation will be fairly close because p is small. Estimating the other parameters is more difficult, and perhaps the best way to estimate them is by means of the quasi-Bayesian framework proposed by Venkataraman. This procedure estimates these parameters conditional on our data and our initial prior beliefs about parameter values.

The last remaining issue is to extend this approach to deal with portfolios of more than one instrument. With two instruments, the return to the portfolio would then be

$$R_{pt} = w_A\sigma_{At}R_{At} + w_B\sigma_{Bt}R_{Bt} \tag{3.33}$$

where each of R_{At} and R_{Bt} would be decomposable into expressions comparable to (3.32). The various volatility and mean terms would then be replaced by their matrix equivalents. This means that the old volatility σ_t would be replaced by the standard variance-covariance matrix, and the old $\mu_{2,t}$ and $\sigma_{2,t}^2$ terms would be replaced by matrices. This raises the awkward issue of how to deal with the off-diagonal terms in these matrices, but Venkataraman proposes a simplifying algorithm that handles these terms in a computationally straightforward way.[32]

This approach has a number of attractions. (1) It incorporates observed fat tails. (2) It makes use of standard linear normal estimates of variances and covariances (i.e., the ones we already have). (3) It is intuitively simple, and not too difficult to operationalise. (4) It requires a relatively small number of additional parameters to be estimated.

4.2. A Generalised Error Distribution

The other way to accommodate fat tails is by means of a generalised error distribution (GED) (Zangari, 1996e). The GED is a family of distributions which takes a variety of particular forms depending on the value of a parameter v, and which includes the normal as a special case. The GED can therefore be regarded as a more flexible generalisation of the normal distribution. According to this model, standardised returns are generated according to the process

$$R_t/\sigma_t = \varepsilon_t \tag{3.34}$$

but ε_t now follows a GED, i.e., has a fearsome-looking PDF, $f(\varepsilon_t)$, given by

$$f(\varepsilon_t) = v \exp[-(1/2)|\varepsilon_t/\lambda|^v]/[2^{(1+v^{-1})}\Gamma(v^{-1})] \tag{3.35}$$

where $\Gamma(v^{-1})$ is the standard gamma function and

$$\lambda = [2^{-(2/v)}v\Gamma(1/v)/3]^{1/2} \tag{3.36}$$

This process becomes a normal distribution when $v = 2$. However, it has fatter tails than the normal when $v < 2$, and the probability of large extreme events rises as v gets smaller. We can then proxy just about any observed frequency of extreme events by selecting an appropriate value of v.

To assess the relative performance of the standard-normal, normal mixture and GED approaches in forecasting VaR, Zangari (1996e, pp. 25–31) applied each of them to a sample of 15 FX and equity time series from nine emerging market countries. If a model is accurate, then 1% of losses should occur in the first percentile, 5% of losses in the fifth percentile, and so on. Zangari's results suggested that all three procedures performed reasonably well at the 5% level, but the normal mixture and GED procedures did considerably better at the 1% level. Both of these approaches are therefore considerable improvements over the traditional standard normal, although even they still under-estimate VaR by a sizeable amount.

5. MAPPING POSITIONS

We now turn to a different set of issues. We have assumed up to now that every instrument in our portfolio is one for which we have ready risk and correlation data, and the availability of this information enabled us to proceed directly to estimating VaR. However, in practice it is very unlikely that we would have such information for every instrument in our portfolio. One reason is the huge number of real-world securities, and the fact that this number is growing very rapidly. We would need data not only on each security's own volatility, but also on its correlations with *all other* instruments. If we have n different securities, we would need data on n separate volatilities, one for each security, plus data on $n(n-1)/2$ cross correlations – a total altogether of $n(n+1)/2$ pieces of information. As new series are added, the additional amount of correlation data needed grows geometrically. Obviously, as n gets large, the amount of data needed becomes enormous. For practical purposes, it is clearly impossible to collect and process such information for any but a very small proportion of possible securities.

In any case, we would not normally want to work with very high dimension matrices, even if we had all the data. The point is that our estimated variance-covariance matrix Σ must be positive semi-definite to ensure that the estimated variances are always non-negative regardless of the relative amounts (given by the x vector) of different instruments in our portfolio.[33] However, this condition will be satisfied only if two other conditions hold, both of which put limits on the size of the variance-covariance matrix. One is that the number of observations from which the variance-covariance matrix is estimated must be at least as large as the number of dimensions in the matrix itself. If the volatilities and correlations are calculated with 100 observations, this condition therefore requires that the variance-covariance matrix has a dimensionality of no more than 100. The other condition (and the one that usually most constrains us) is that none of the included time series – asset prices, returns or whatever – be linearly correlated with other series or groups of series (i.e., each series must have some independent movement of its own, distinct from the movements of other series). In practical terms, this means that we frequently get problems when including groups of assets that, whilst not perfectly correlated, are sufficiently closely correlated with each other that our estimated variance-covariance matrix fails to be positive semi-definite due to rounding errors.[34]

The problem, then, is to overcome the lack of positive semi-definiteness associated with large variance-covariance matrices. The usual solution is to scale down the dimensionality of the matrix, and the most common way to do that is to 'map' our assets onto benchmark assets for which we do have the required data.[35] In other words, we describe the instruments we hold 'approximately as combinations of standard building blocks' (Zangari, 1995, p. 107). Mapping positions enables us to estimate VaR, albeit with error, in situations that would otherwise be informationally extremely demanding or even impossible.

5.1. Alternative Mapping Procedures

There are two ways we can map positions, which we can broadly distinguish as 'representative' and 'quantitative'.

5.1.1. The 'Representative' Approach to Mapping

The 'representative' approach is to select a set of core instruments (e.g., key money market and equity instruments, key currencies, etc.) that can be regarded as representative of the broad types of instruments actually held. The ideal is to have a rich enough set of core instruments to be able to provide good proxies for the instruments in our portfolio whilst not having so many core assets that we run back into the high-dimensionality problems from which we wish to escape.

The best-known representative approach – that used by RiskMetrics – maps individual positions to the following set of core instruments (Longerstaey, 1995a, p. 107):

- Foreign exchange (FX) positions are represented by the relevant amounts in terms of a certain number of 'core' currencies, and FX forward positions are mapped as equivalent fixed-income positions in their respective currencies.
- Equity positions are represented by equivalent amounts in terms of equity indices in each of the core currencies.
- Fixed-income positions are represented by combinations of cash flows in a given currency of a limited number of specified maturities.[36]

- Commodity positions are represented by amounts of selected standardised futures contracts traded on organised exchanges.

RiskMetrics uses a broad set of core instruments to be able to map a correspondingly broad range of different positions. However, most users of VaR have more specialised portfolios and would therefore work with some subset of the RiskMetrics cores to reduce dimensionality problems and speed up calculations. If they wanted, they could also add new cores of their own (e.g., fixed-income instruments with new maturities, or sector-specific equity indices) and collect the data themselves or pay a specialist firm to collect them on their behalf.

The process of mapping involves three stages. The first is to construct a set of benchmark assets and collect data on their volatilities and correlations. The benchmark assets might include key bonds, equities, commodities, and so on. (As an aside, the selection of benchmark assets and the collection and processing of data might be done by a central service provider, as JP Morgan does with the RiskMetrics database.) Having established a set of core assets and collected the necessary data, the next step is to derive synthetic substitutes for each asset we hold, where these substitutes are made up of positions in the core securities. This synthetic substitution is the actual mapping (and can be done locally by the user-client). The final stage is to calculate VaR using the mapped assets (i.e., the synthetic substitutes) instead of the actual assets we hold. Put differently, we pretend that we are holding the synthetic portfolio composed only of core assets, and we estimate its VaR which we take to be an estimate of the 'true' VaR that we are otherwise unable to estimate.

5.1.2. The 'Quantitative' Approach to Mapping

The second, 'quantitative' approach is to identify key factors by principal components analysis (PCA) or factor analysis (FA), both of which are quantitative procedures that identify the independent sources of movement within a group of time series (such as historical return data). Principal components (or factors) are hypothetical variables that are constructed to 'explain' the movements in a group of time series. These series in our case would be a set of prices or returns.[37] Each principal component/factor is constructed to be independent of the others, so all have zero covariance with each other. In addition, we will usually find that a relatively small number of principal components or factors is sufficient to explain a very large proportion of the movement in our price or return series. This procedure can therefore cut down drastically on the dimensionality of our system. Moreover, because the principal components (or factors) are independent of each other, the only non-zero elements of the principal components (or factor) variance-covariance matrix will be the volatilities, which cuts down even further on the number of parameters we would need to work with.

PCA and FA procedures are generally suited to portfolios with a large number of different instruments that tend to be closely correlated with each other, reflecting the presence of common influences. Perhaps the best examples of such portfolios are port-folios of money market instruments and bonds, which typically show very high degrees of correlation with each other. If we had 50 different instruments in a bond portfolio and were to work with those instruments directly (i.e., without mapping), we would need to handle a 50×50 variance-covariance matrix with $50(51)/2 = 1275$ separate volatility

---

Box 3.3: Principal component mapping

To illustrate principal component mapping in more detail, imagine we have a portfolio of n instruments to map, and this portfolio has an $n \times 1$ vector of prices p. Mapping in this context means that we wish to proxy the prices p in terms of their principal components. Let us assume that p is distributed normally with mean 0 and an $n \times n$ variance-covariance matrix Σ. We therefore seek to estimate m principal components, where m is presumably small and very much less than n. The $m \times 1$ vector of principal components Π has a diagonal $m \times m$ variance-covariance matrix Ω. Since it is diagonal, this matrix only has m non-zero terms, these being the m volatilities along the diagonal. The mapped prices, p^{map}, are then a linear function of the m principal components:

$$p^{\mathrm{map}} = B\Pi$$

where p^{map} is an $n \times 1$ vector corresponding to p and B is an $n \times m$ matrix that transforms the principal components into mapped values of the original prices. If we have the price data p, we can estimate Π from a standard principal components procedure, and we can estimate B by regressing the prices on the principal components. The B matrix is then the matrix of resulting coefficients. Once we have estimates of B and Π we apply a position vector x to the vector of mapped prices to give us the value of our mapped portfolio, and from that we can estimate the VaR.

Note that the estimated VaR now depends on Ω rather than Σ. In other words, we now need an estimate of the smaller Ω matrix (which has only m non-zero terms) rather than the bigger Σ matrix (which has up to $n(n + 1)/2$ separate non-zero terms) – a potentially huge reduction in the number of estimated parameters.

---

and correlation parameters.[38] However, if we used a principal components analysis, we could expect to proxy the overwhelming proportion of bond price movements by three principal components, and the only variance-covariance parameters needed would be the volatilities of the three principal components.[39] These three components can usually be identified as specific types of movement in the underlying yield curve: the first principal component, the most important one, represents a parallel shift in the yield curve, the second represents a twist of the yield curve (i.e., a change in its slope); and the third, the least important, represents a butterfly movement in the yield curve (i.e., short and long rates going in one direction, and intermediate rates going in another). Once we have our principal components, each individual instrument can then be mapped as a linear combination of these components, and the values of the linear parameters can be found by regressing each instrument on the principal components.

6. VaR FOR SPECIFIC POSITIONS

We now turn to consider how to map and estimate VaR for specific portfolios. There are of course a huge variety of different financial instruments, but the task of mapping them

---

Box 3.4: Principal components vs. factor analysis

Wilson (1994a) shows how both FA and PCA can be understood in terms of how they break down the variance-covariance matrix of our prices/returns (i.e., Σ) into an 'explained' component Ω and an 'unexplained' or residual component Σ^u, i.e.,

$$\Sigma = \Omega + \Sigma^u$$

PCA and FA differ in how they handle the residual matrix Σ^u: PCA minimises the diagonal terms of the residual matrix, while FA tries to minimise its off-diagonal elements. This suggests that PCA will do a better job explaining the volatility of prices/returns, while FA will be better at explaining their correlation structure. There is therefore a trade-off between explaining variance and explaining correlation, and the difference between these two approaches is not necessarily minor.

In the end, the choice of PCA or FA should depend on the features of the problem at hand. We would choose PCA if our applications are mainly volatility dependent (e.g., as with pricing simple options) and FA if our applications are mainly correlation dependent (e.g., as with pricing swaps and, significantly, calculating VaR).

---

and estimating their VaRs can be simplified tremendously by recognising that most instruments can be decomposed into a small number of more basic, primitive instruments. Instead of trying to map and estimate VaR for each specific type of instrument, all we really need to do is: (a) break down each instrument into its constituent building blocks – a process known as reverse engineering – to give us an equivalent portfolio of primitive instruments; (b) map this portfolio of primitive instruments; and (c) estimate the VaR of the equivalent mapped portfolio.

6.1. The Basic Building Blocks

6.1.1. VaR for Straight FX Positions

Our first tasks are therefore to identify these primitive instruments, show how to map them, and then estimate their VaRs. There are four types of basic building block, and the first of these is straight FX positions (e.g., holdings of non-interest-bearing foreign currency). FX positions are particularly simple to handle where the currencies involved (i.e., our own and the foreign currency) are included as core currencies in our mapping system.[40] We would then already have the exchange rate volatilities and correlations that we require for variance-covariance analysis. If the value of our position is x in foreign currency units and the exchange rate is E, the value of the position in domestic currency units is xE. Since there is no foreign interest rate being paid, x is constant, and so the only risk attaches to E. If the exchange rate is normally distributed, with standard deviation σ_E, then the VaR is

$$VaR^{FX} = -\alpha\sigma_E xE \tag{3.37}$$

The VaR is the confidence level parameter $(-\alpha)$ times the standard deviation of the exchange rate (σ_E) times the size of the position in domestic currency units (xE).

6.1.2. VaR for Equity Positions

The second type of primitive position is straight equity, and handling equity positions is slightly more involved. Imagine we hold an amount x_A invested in the equity of firm A, but lack this particular firm's volatility and correlation data. However, we do know that the firm's return to equity, R_A, is related to the equity market return, R_m:

$$R_A = \alpha_A + \beta_A R_m + \varepsilon_A \tag{3.38}$$

where α_A is a firm-specific constant, $\beta_A R_m$ is the market-specific component of the firm's return, and ε_A is a firm-specific random element. The variance of the firm's return is then:

$$\sigma_A^2 = \beta_A^2 \sigma_m^2 + \sigma_{\varepsilon_A}^2 \tag{3.39}$$

where σ_A^2 is the variance of R_A and so on. The variance of the firm's return therefore consists of a market-based component, $\beta_A^2 \sigma_m^2$, and a firm-specific component, $\sigma_{\varepsilon_A}^2$. Assuming normality, the VaR of the equity position is therefore:

$$VaR_A = -\alpha \sigma_A x_A = -\alpha x_A \sqrt{(\beta_A^2 \sigma_m^2 + \sigma_{\varepsilon_A}^2)} \tag{3.40}$$

Estimates of both σ_m^2 and β_A should be publicly available, so we can easily estimate $\beta_A^2 \sigma_m^2$. We will not usually have data on the firm-specific variance σ_ε^2. However, if our portfolio is well diversified, the firm-specific risks will largely net out in the aggregate portfolio and we could estimate VaR as if $\sigma_{\varepsilon_A}^2$ were zero. Our VaR would then be:

$$VaR_A = -\alpha \beta_A \sigma_m x_A \tag{3.41}$$

We could therefore proxy the firm's VaR by using volatility information about the market equity return, and the only specific information we would need about the firm itself would be its market beta. The only real problem is that if we hold an undiversified portfolio, the estimate of VaR given in (3.41) will understate true VaR because it ignores the firm-specific risk.[41] However, we can also improve the VaR estimate by using an adjustment that takes account of how well diversified the portfolio is. This adjustment is explained in Box 3.5.

6.1.3. VaR for Zero-coupon Bonds

The third type of primitive instrument is a zero-coupon bond (known as a zero). Let us assume for the time being that we are dealing with instruments that have no default risk. (We shall deal with default risk in Chapter 9.) The first task is therefore to map a default-free zero-coupon bond against (default-free) reference instruments. Let us also suppose that we are using a representative mapping procedure of the RiskMetrics sort. The core or reference assets might be one-month zeros, three-month zeros, and so on. Remember that we will have volatility and correlation data on zeros of these particular maturities, but not on zeros of other maturities. We will therefore generally lack volatility and correlation data for the particular bonds we hold, except in the unusual (and fortuitous) special cases where our instruments happen to be reference ones. We might hold bonds with maturities varying from 10 to 100 days, and yet the nearest reference bonds might be 30-day and 90-day bills. We would have the data we want for any 30-day or 90-day bonds in our portfolio, but not for any of the others. But how then do we

Box 3.5:   Adjusting equity VaRs for firm-specific risk

The drawback with the market beta approach to estimating the VaRs of equity positions is that it ignores firm-specific risk and thereby leads to an underestimate of true VaR. One way to adjust for this bias is to multiply the beta-based VaR (i.e., $-\alpha\beta_A\sigma_m x_A$) by an adjustment factor that reflects the degree to which the portfolio is *imperfectly* diversified. This adjustment factor is

$$A = \phi + (1 - \phi)\sigma_p^u/(\beta_A\sigma_m)$$

where σ_p^u is a hypothetical portfolio variance that assumes that risks are completely undiversified (i.e., perfectly correlated) and ϕ is a diversification index given by

$$\phi = (\sigma_p^u - \sigma_p)/(\sigma_p^u - \sigma_m)$$

where σ_p is an estimate of the portfolio variance as it is. If the portfolio is perfectly diversified, then $\sigma_p = \sigma_m$ and $\phi = 1$. The adjustment factor A is therefore also 1, and the VaR is exactly as given in (3.41). At the other extreme, if the portfolio is not diversified at all, then $\sigma_p = \sigma_p^u$ and $\phi = 0$. The adjustment A is therefore $\sigma_p^u/(\beta_A\sigma_m)$ and the VaR is $-\alpha\sigma_p^u x_A$, which is easily verified as the correct expression in the absence of any diversification.[42] Finally, if the portfolio is imperfectly diversified, ϕ takes a value between 0 and 1 and we get a VaR somewhere between $-\alpha\beta_A\sigma_m x_A$ and $-\alpha\sigma_p^u x_A$. We thus have an adjustment factor that leads to correct VaRs at the extremes of perfect and zero diversification, and at least makes some allowance for the extent of diversification of intermediate portfolios.

It only remains to find ways of estimating σ_p^u and σ_p when we have very little information about the volatilities and correlations of specific assets. However, if the portfolio is totally undiversified, then σ_p^u is just the average standard deviation of the individual assets. We can therefore estimate σ_p^u by taking such an average. Estimating σ_p is only slightly more involved. The portfolio variance can be written as

$$\sigma_p^2 = \sum_{i=1}^{N} w_i^2\sigma_i^2 + \sum_{i=1}^{N}\sum_{j=1}^{N} w_i w_j\sigma_{ij}^2$$

where w_i is the weight of stock i in the portfolio. If the portfolio is equally weighted in the different assets (i.e., $w_i = 1/N$), the portfolio variance becomes

$$\sigma_p^2 = (1/N)\bar{\sigma}_i^2 + [(N - 1)/N]\bar{\sigma}_{ij}$$

which means that we can approximate the portfolio variance if we have data on the average variance and average covariance of the individual stocks in our portfolio. Provided we have these data, we can estimate both σ_p^u and σ_p and make our adjustment for the effect of imperfect portfolio diversification.[43]

estimate the VaR of, say, an 80-day bond? The answer is that we estimate the 80-day VaR from the mapped equivalent of our 80-day bond, that is to say, from its equivalent in terms of some combination of 30-day and 90-day bonds. We can then estimate the volatility and whatever other parameters we need from the relevant parameters for the 30-day and 90-day bonds.

Unfortunately, there is no simple way to map such bonds. We therefore need to begin by deciding on criteria that the mapping procedure should satisfy, and the best criteria seem to be those used by the RiskMetrics team. They suggest that the mapped position should have the same value and same variance as the old one, and should also consist of cash flows of the same sign.[44] We can illustrate this procedure with an example adapted from the 1996 edition of the *Technical Document*, pp. 117–121. Suppose we have a cash flow coming in six years' time, but the nearest reference instruments are comparable bills maturing in five and seven years. The mapped six-year instrument (I_6^{mapped}) is then a combination of the five-year and seven-year instruments, I_5 and I_7:

$$I_6^{mapped} = \alpha I_5 + (1 - \alpha)I_7 \tag{3.42}$$

The problem is then to find some way of choosing α. Since the mapped asset is a linear combination of the other two, we know that the variance of its return, σ_6^2, is:

$$\sigma_6^2 = \alpha^2 \sigma_5^2 + (1 - \alpha)^2 \sigma_7^2 + 2\alpha(1 - \alpha)\rho_{5,7}\sigma_5\sigma_7 \tag{3.43}$$

where $\rho_{5,7}$ is the correlation coefficient and the other variances are obvious. We could solve α if we knew all the other terms, and the only one we don't know is σ_6^2. Longerstaey *et al.* now suggest estimating a proxy for σ_6^2 from a simple linear average, viz.:

$$\sigma_6 = \hat{a}\sigma_5 + (1 - \hat{a})\sigma_7, \quad 0 \leqslant \hat{a} \leqslant 1 \tag{3.44}$$

where the weight $\hat{a}$ is proportional to the relative distance between the maturity of the mapped instrument and the maturities of the reference ones (i.e., in this case, 0.5). We then substitute (3.44) into (3.43) and solve the resulting equation for α. Since this equation is quadratic, there are two solutions for α, i.e.[45]

$$\alpha = [-b \pm \sqrt{b^2 - 4ac}]/2a \tag{3.45}$$

where

$$a = \sigma_5^2 + \sigma_7^2 - 2\rho_{5,7}\sigma_5\sigma_7$$
$$b = 2\rho_{5,7}\sigma_5\sigma_7 - 2\sigma_7^2 \tag{3.46}$$
$$c = \sigma_7^2 - \sigma_6^2$$

We choose the solution that satisfies our earlier criteria (i.e., in practice, the one that gives us an α value between 0 and 1). We then substitute this value into (3.42) to give us our mapped position.[46]

Once our bond is mapped, we estimate its VaR by estimating the VaR of the mapped bond (i.e., the portfolio of five-year and seven-year zeros, with weights α and $1 - \alpha$). This latter VaR is estimated in the same way we would estimate the VaR of any other zero-coupon bonds for which we have adequate volatility and correlation data (e.g., by using a duration approximation).[47]

6.1.4. VaR for Forwards/Futures

The fourth building block is a forward/futures position. A forward contract is an agreement to buy a particular commodity or asset at a specified future date at a price agreed now, with the price being paid when the commodity/asset is delivered. A futures contract is a standardised forward contract traded on an organised exchange. There are a number of differences between these contracts, but for our purposes here these differences are not especially important. We can therefore run the two contracts together and speak of a generic forward/futures contract. To illustrate what is involved, suppose we have a forward/futures position that gives us a daily return dependent on the movement of the end-of-day forward/futures price. If we have x contracts each worth F, the value of our position is xF. If F is normal with standard deviation σ_F, the VaR of our position is approximately[48]

$$VaR^F \approx -\alpha\sigma_F xF \tag{3.47}$$

The VaR is approximately $-\alpha$ times the standard deviation of the forward/futures price (σ_F) times the value of our position (xF).

The only problem is that we may need to map the forward/futures position. How we map depends on the reference data available, but if we are using a RiskMetrics type of approach, we would have data on a number of points along a forward/futures maturity spectrum: the spot price, the one-month forward/futures price, the three-month forward/futures price, and so on. We would then map the particular position we have against these reference assets. If our position had a four-month maturity, say, we might map it against reference contracts with maturities of three months and six months, and do so in much the same way as we previously mapped zero-coupon bonds. The mapped four-month contract (I_4^{mapped}) would be a combination of the three-month and six-month instruments, I_3 and I_6:

$$I_4^{mapped} = \alpha I_3 + (1 - \alpha)I_6 \tag{3.48}$$

We then map this position as we did the earlier zero-coupon bonds and take the position's VaR to be the estimated VaR of its mapped equivalent.

6.2. VaR for More Complex Positions

Having set out our building blocks, we can now show how other positions can be regarded as being built up from combinations of these building blocks. The VaRs of these more complex positions can then be found by taking the VaRs of equivalent positions made up of these building blocks.

6.2.1. VaR for Fixed-rate Bonds

We begin with fixed-income instruments. In general, these instruments promise a variety of fixed-cash flows at different future times, and the price of any such instrument will be the discounted present value of these future cash flows. In the case of a standard coupon bond, the bond price, B, will be:

$$B = \sum_{i=1}^{N} [C_i/(1 + y_i)^i] \qquad (3.49)$$

where C_i is the cash flow in period i (i.e., the various interim coupons plus the final coupon and principal payment at $t = N$) and y_i is the discount rate on zero-coupon bonds of the same maturity, which can be taken as given for present purposes. A coupon bond can therefore be regarded as a portfolio of zero-coupon bonds, each maturing at a different maturity date, where the ith one pays C_i at date i and has a current price $C_i/(1 + y_i)^i$. We then map coupon-paying bonds by regarding them as portfolios of zero-coupon bonds and mapping each individual zero-coupon bond separately. The VaR of our coupon-paying bond is then equal to the VaR of its mapped equivalent in zero-coupon bonds.

6.2.2. VaR for Floating-rate Instruments

We can also use the zero-coupon building block to derive the VaR of floating rate instruments. The usual floating-rate instruments are coupon-paying bonds in which the coupons are reset periodically (usually every six months) in line with market interest rates. These reset dates also coincide with the dates when coupons are paid.[49] Since coupons are reset in this way, the bond price is also restored to par on each coupon date, so we know that the bond price will be restored to par when the next coupon payment is made. We can therefore think of our floating-rate bond as being equivalent to a hypothetical zero-coupon bond, the final payment on which is equal to the next coupon payment plus the par value. We can then handle this hypothetical zero-coupon bond in the same way we would any other zero-coupon security (i.e., we map it and estimate the VaR of its mapped equivalent).

6.2.3. VaR for Interest-rate Swaps

Once we can handle fixed-rate and floating-rate bonds, we can easily handle standard interest rate derivatives such as interest-rate swaps. An interest-rate swap is an agreement between two parties to exchange future cash flows at predetermined dates. In the basic 'plain vanilla' variety, one party pays a fixed interest rate and the other pays a variable one. The party paying the fixed rate makes the same payments as it would make if it were paying off a comparable coupon bond of the same size, and the party paying the floating rate makes the same payments it would make on a floating-rate bond. We can then regard an interest-rate swap as equivalent to a portfolio that is long a fixed-coupon bond and short a floating-rate bond, or vice versa, and we already know how to map these instruments. All we therefore need to do is map a portfolio that is long one instrument and short the other, and the VaR follows in the usual way.

6.2.4. VaR for Structured Notes

The same approach also allows us to handle structured notes. Thus, an inverse floating-rate note (i.e., a floating-rate note whose return moves inversely with market yields) can be produced synthetically by a combination of interest-rate swaps and conventional floating-rate notes: more specifically, an inverse floater with a given notional principal has the same pay-out structure as *two* plain vanilla swaps in which the investor receives fixed/pays floating, plus a long position in a conventional floater, all with the same notional principal.[50] The investor's net return is then equal to twice the fixed rate minus the floating rate, which is the same as that of the original inverse floater. We can also leverage up both floaters and inverse floaters by entering into more swaps. A leveraged floater would be equivalent to entering into more swaps as the fixed-rate receiver, and a leveraged inverse floater would be equivalent to entering into more swaps as the fixed-rate payer. Given that we can produce these instruments synthetically, we can then map them and estimate their VaRs as before.[51]

6.2.5. VaR for FRAs

Zero-coupon building blocks also allow us to handle forward rate agreements (FRAs). An FRA is a contract made now to lock in a future interest rate for a loan of a given size, future start date and maturity. Suppose an FRA stipulates that the loan will start at some future date t and end at some later future date T. The party taking out the loan can be thought of as issuing a zero-coupon bond that matures at T and simultaneously using the proceeds to buy a zero-coupon bond that matures at t. He or she experiences no net cash flow when the contracts are agreed, gets a net cash inflow at t, and experiences a final net outflow at T. We can therefore regard an FRA as equivalent to a position that is long in the zero-coupon bond with the longer maturity and short in the zero-coupon bond with the shorter maturity. We then proceed to map and estimate VaR in the usual way.

6.2.6. VaR for FX Forwards

A foreign exchange forward is an agreement to exchange a specified amount of one currency for a specified amount of another at an agreed exchange rate and future date. The party buying the foreign currency forward gets a fixed amount of foreign currency in the future, and pays a fixed amount of his or her own currency in the future. He or she therefore has the equivalent of a long position in a foreign currency zero-coupon bond and a short position in a domestic currency zero-coupon bond.

We already know how to map the domestic bond and estimate its VaR. However, the long position in the foreign bond is complicated by its exposure to exchange rate risk. If the amount of foreign currency he or she gets in the future is x, its future value will be xE, where E is the exchange rate, and its net present value will be $xE/(1 + r^f)$ where r^f is the foreign interest rate. To estimate the VaR of this second bond, first let $y = xE/(1 + r^f)$ and then take a first-order Taylor approximation around its current value:

$$dy \approx (\partial y/\partial E)dE + (\partial y/\partial r^f)dr^f \tag{3.50}$$

$$= [y/E]dE - [y/(1 + r^f)]dr^f$$

$$\Rightarrow dy/y \approx dE/E - [r^f/(1 + r^f)]dr^f/r^f$$

It follows that

$$\sigma_y^2 \approx \sigma_E^2 + [r^f/(1 + r^f)]^2\sigma_{r^f}^2 - 2[r^f/(1 + r^f)]\rho\sigma_{E,r^f} \tag{3.51}$$

where all variables have the natural interpretations. Hence, under normality, the VaR of the foreign currency bond is

$$-\alpha\sqrt{\sigma_E^2 + [r^f/(1 + r^f)]^2\sigma_{r^f}^2 - 2[r^f/(1 + r^f)]\rho\sigma_{E,r^f}}.xE/(1 + r^f) \qquad (3.52)$$

We can then estimate this VaR provided we have estimates of σ_E^2 and σ_{E,r^f} (i.e., provided we have the foreign bond mapped).

6.2.7. VaR for Commodity, Equity and FX Swaps

The earlier approaches now make it easy to deal with more sophisticated commodity, equity or FX swaps. These are swap agreements in which one party agrees to make payments to another based on the realised value of some commodity price, commodity price index, equity index or exchange rate, whilst the other commits to make payments based on some other schedule. These other payments might be fixed, interest-rate contingent, or contingent on the realised value of some other commodity price or price index. Moreover, one or more of the scheduled set of payments may also be denominated in a foreign currency. However, it should be clear by now that this type of contract can easily be dealt with by breaking it down into its two constituent components: some form of forward/futures contract on the one hand, and some other forward/futures contract or bond contract on the other. We then map these contracts and estimate their VaRs in the standard manner.[52]

6.2.8. VaR for Options

Finally, options can be mapped by reverse-engineering them into their building blocks, and then mapping the building blocks separately. For example, if we are dealing with a standard European equity call option, we can use the Black-Scholes equation to give us the equivalent synthetic option, which will consist of δ shares in the underlying stock and a short position in zero-coupon bonds (see (1.6)). We can then map the equity and bond positions separately, and the combination of the two gives us our mapped option position. The only novel point to watch for here is that the components of the synthetic option will change with changes in the underlying price – and, indeed, other factors as well – so the mapping itself needs to be regularly updated to reflect current market conditions. Mapping options is therefore a dynamic process.[53] Other options can be mapped in the same sort of way, provided only that we can synthesise them into components that we can already map.

7. ARE PORTFOLIO RETURNS NORMAL?

The appropriateness or otherwise of these procedures depends on the assumption that portfolio returns can be described by a normal distribution. We must therefore investigate whether this is a reasonable assumption.

To some extent, the answer clearly depends on the distributions of the individual instruments in our portfolio. There is a huge amount of empirical literature on this issue, and whether or not normality is an adequate empirical description of individual portfolio returns varies from one case to another. In many cases, the assumption of normality is not too unreasonable, at least as an approximation. However, there is also a very large amount of evidence that many individual return distributions are *not* normal.[54] The most important departure from normality from our point of view is that many return distributions have fat tails (i.e., there are more occurrences far away from the mean than is consistent with a normal distribution, a characteristic sometimes known as excess kurtosis). Fat tails are particularly worrying because they imply that extraordinary losses will occur more frequently and be larger than the normal distribution would lead us to expect. Estimates of VaR based on an assumed normal distribution could therefore underestimate 'true' VaR quite considerably. In addition, asset returns are often negatively skewed (i.e., there are more observations in the left-hand-side tail than the right-hand-side one). Negative skewness is unfortunate, because it means that we get more bad tail events than good ones, and also because it makes VaR estimation considerably more complicated.[55]

However, even if we conclude that individual returns are not normal, it would be premature to jump to the conclusion that portfolio returns must also be non-normal. The central limit theorem tells us that independent random variables of any well-behaved distribution will have a mean that converges in large samples to a normal distribution.[56] In practical terms, this result implies that the assumption of a normal portfolio return will often work quite well provided the portfolio is fairly well diversified and individual returns are sufficiently independent of each other, *even if the individual returns are not themselves normally distributed*. In other words, we might still be able to get by on the assumption that portfolio returns are normal, despite evidence that individual returns are non-normal.[57]

So the answer to the question of whether the normal distribution is an adequate description of the portfolio return really depends on our portfolio. The normal distribution is clearly adequate if our portfolio is linear in normal risks, and it may or may not be adequate if our portfolio is non-linear in such risks or if some of the risks are not normal. Whether normality is an adequate description for the portfolio return therefore depends on the distributions of the individual instruments in the portfolio, the nature and extent of any non-linearity, and the particular ways in which individual risks interact to affect the overall portfolio return.[58]

If we assume normality, we should always run checks to satisfy ourselves that normality is an adequate description of the particular portfolio at hand.

8. CONCLUSIONS

The bottom line is that normal VaR is excellent for handling portfolios that have normal returns. It is intuitive and easy to implement, and can also accommodate large portfolios, although we will usually have to use mapping approximations to reduce the dimensionality of the variance-covariance matrix. It is therefore ideal for handling straightforward positions that are largely linear in normal risks and which have little or no optionality.

Unfortunately, the flip side is that the normal approach loses both accuracy and tractability when dealing with positions that are non-linear in risk factors (e.g., because of options positions) or when the risk factors themselves are not normal. If these non-linear or non-normal factors are not too large, it may be possible to estimate VaR with one of

---

Box 3.6: The problem of system risk

A major concern with any risk management system is the issue of system risk, i.e., the risk of different answers arising from differences in the way a particular model is implemented in practice. This problem is a different and more subtle one than model risk (i.e., the risk of different answers arising from the choice of particular models, such as the choice of a variance-covariance model over a historical simulation one). The point is that no general model (such as RiskMetrics) can ever specify all possible implementation issues in advance. A certain amount of operational discretion is therefore inevitably left to the systems developer. This means that we cannot expect the same basic model applied to the same portfolio to produce exactly the same results in every case: our results will be contaminated by various firm-specific operational decisions made by each systems developer.

To assess how serious this problem might be, both Beder (1995) and Marshall and Siegel (1997) examined how different firms estimated their VaRs, and both studies found major differences among procedures used. Marshall and Siegel also found that there were sometimes extensive differences between different firms' estimates of the same portfolio's VaR, even when firms were using approaches that should have been similar. These results are disturbing, to say the least.

---

the modified variance-covariance approaches considered in this chapter and still get estimates that are sufficiently accurate to be useful. However, if departures from portfolio normality are serious, we should really use some alternative procedure such as Monte Carlo simulation.

ENDNOTES

1. Strictly speaking, the key assumption is that returns are conditionally rather than unconditionally normal. Conditional normality means that the return is normal at any point in time, given the standard deviation. When the mean return is negligible, conditional normality implies that the standardised return (i.e., the ratio of return to standard deviation) is distributed as approximately standard normal (i.e., mean zero and variance one). Unconditional normality simply means that the return is normal, with the same standard deviation applying to all data points in the sample period. Conditional normality is therefore a more general distribution, since it allows the standard deviation to change from one period to another. Except for the discussion in section 4 of this chapter, the distinction between conditional and unconditional normality is of no importance to us, so for convenience the distribution will be referred to as simply being normal.
2. As discussed in the appendix to this chapter, the variance/standard deviation would usually be estimated around an assumed mean of zero. This avoids compounding our VaR estimates with additional errors due to our not knowing the true mean return, but also means that our estimates of variance and standard deviation will be biased upwards. Nonetheless, this bias should be negligible for any but very long holding periods.
3. However, this procedure implicitly assumes that the portfolio does not change over the holding period. In practice, short holding period VaRs extrapolated to longer holding periods will probably overstate 'true' VaR over the longer holding period because the portfolio holder will tend to move out of loss-making instruments as losses build up. Extrapolations from shorter holding periods to longer ones ignore this tendency and therefore overstate true VaR.
4. See, e.g., Zangari (1995, p. 92).

5. It also helps working with a short holding period such as a day. Large changes in underlying variables and awkward non-linear/non-normal jumps in options prices are less likely for a shorter holding period. As Linsmeier and Pearson (1996, p. 17) observe, 'As a result, the variance-covariance method works well even for positions with moderate options content provided the holding period is short. However, over longer holding periods, for example, two weeks or one month, larger changes in underlying rates and prices are likely and value at risk estimates produced using the variance-covariance method cannot be relied upon for positions with moderate or significant options content.'

6. If the option position was a short one, however, the δ would negative and the option VaR would be $\delta\alpha\sigma S$. More generally, the option VaR is $-|\delta|\alpha\sigma S$.

7. Of course, taking a modified duration approach is not the only way to estimate the bond's VaR, but it is the only way to estimate the bond's VaR that is linear in risks and is therefore the only way compatible with the delta-normal approach being considered here. The natural non-linear extension to the duration approach, the duration-convexity approach, is discussed in Box 3.1.

8. This supposition is confirmed by the simulation results of Estrella *et al.* (1994, p. 39), which suggest that linear approximations can 'seriously underestimate' the VaRs of option positions precisely because they ignore second-order risk factors (i.e., gamma risks).

9. This conjecture is confirmed by the simulation evidence of Estrella *et al.* (1994, pp. 27, 39–40). They examined the usefulness of delta-gamma approximations for a variety of options positions and concluded that allowing for gamma risk by a second-order approximation 'significantly enhanced' the accuracy of their VaR estimates.

10. The goodness of the delta-normal approximation also depends on the time period over which we are considering changes. The smaller the time period, the smaller the change dS and, hence, the smaller the squared change $(dS)^2$. We can therefore often get away with the delta-normal approximation when dealing with relatively short holding periods, but it is more difficult defending this assumption with longer holding periods. This proves the point, made in Chapter 2, that we can often defend normality over short periods whilst being unable to defend it over longer ones.

11. As is clear from the Black-Scholes equation, both delta-normal and delta-gamma approximations can also run into problems from other sources of risk. Even if the underlying price S does not change, a change in expected volatility will lead to a change in the price of the option and a corresponding change in the option's VaR. Similarly, the option's value will also change in response to a change in the interest rate (the ρ effect) and in response to the passing of time (the θ effect). However, these effects are not particularly difficult to handle because they do not involve higher-order (e.g. squared) terms. We can therefore easily tack these additional terms onto the basic delta-normal or delta-gamma approximations if we wish to.

12. There are, nonetheless, some difficult problems lurking beneath the surface here. (1) We might be dealing with instruments with more awkward pay-off functions than simple call options. Their pay-off profiles might then make second-order approximations very inaccurate (e.g., as is potentially the case with certain options such as knockout options or range forwards) or just intractable (as is apparently the case with the mortgage-backed securities considered by Jakobsen (1996)) when estimating VaR. (2) Even when dealing with simple instruments such as call options (and, a fortiori, even more so when dealing with more complex instruments), the second-order approximation might still be inaccurate. Estrella (1996, p. 360) points out that the power series for the Black-Scholes approximation formula does not always converge, and even when it does, we sometimes need higher-order approximations to obtain results of sufficient accuracy to be useful. However, Mori, Ohsawa and Shimizu (1996a, p. 9) and Schachter (1996) argue on the basis of plausible-parameter simulations that Estrella is unduly pessimistic about the usefulness of Taylor series approximations, but even they do not dispute Estrella's warning that results based on Taylor series approximations can be unreliable.

13. Longerstaey (1995a, p. 136)

14. Indeed, a good example is the option position just considered, since the delta-gamma estimate of VaR is actually *worse* than the delta-normal one. (3.20) tells us that the delta-gamma normal procedure gives an estimate of VaR that is even higher than the delta-normal estimate, and the delta-normal estimate is already too big. (Why? If the underlying stock price falls, the corresponding fall in the option price is cushioned by the gamma term. The true VaR of the option position is then less than would be predicted by a linear delta approximation that ignores the gamma effect.

Hence, the delta-normal approach overestimates the option's VaR.) Since the delta-normal estimate is already too high, the delta-gamma one must be even higher. In this particular case, we would have a better VaR estimate if we ignored the gamma term completely. This example highlights very clearly how treacherous the delta-gamma normal approach can be.

15. See, e.g., Wilson (1996, pp. 205–7).

16. In the case of our call option, the constraint could equally have been written in the more intuitive form $(\Delta S)\sigma_S^{-1} \leqslant \alpha$. However, more generally, the maximum loss could occur for positive or negative values of ΔS depending on the particular position. Writing the constraint in squared form is a convenient way to capture both positive and negative values of ΔS in a single constraint.

17. See Wilson (1996, p. 207).

18. See Wilson (1996, p. 208).

19. Wilson (1996, p. 210)

20. Wilson (1994; 1996, pp. 210–12) goes on to show that a closed-form solution can be derived if we make a further simplification and assume that delta-gamma option price approximations can themselves be approximated by piece-wise linear expressions (i.e., linear expressions that allow for asymmetrical upward and downward movements) in ΔS. However, in going this extra step one has merely forced the model back into linearity again. Except perhaps in unusual cases, it is difficult to see why we would be happy with piece-wise linearity when we are (presumably) not happy with delta-normal linearity. After all, if we were satisfied with linearity, we would not usually be bothering with delta-gamma in the first place.

21. See, e.g., Pritsker (1996, pp. 3, 39).

22. See also, e.g., Rouvinez (1997, p. 58).

23. Fallon (1996, p. 24)

24. This claim is correct for a long position in a standard European call option. For a short position in such an option, the gamma factor will have a negative rather than a positive effect on pay-off. However, the key point here is simply that the gamma factor makes the PDF of the option return asymmetric, and it is this asymmetry that we are seeking to address.

25. The loss of symmetry associated with skewness can also lead to other problems. One difficulty is that even if the underlying asset has a zero mean, the derivative position will generally not. Another implication of lack of symmetry is that the VaR now depends on whether one is long or short in the option. If we are long, the return distribution is skewed to the right and the VaR percentile will be pushed to the right. VaR will therefore be pushed downwards. If we are short, the distribution will be skewed to the left and the VaR will be pushed upwards.

26. Where there is only one instrument in a portfolio, we can estimate delta-gamma VaR directly, because the delta and gamma are readily available. However, we run into problems with more than one instrument, because there is no easy way to combine the delta, gamma and other risks of individual positions into the resulting delta, gamma and related risks of the portfolio as a whole (Zangari, 1996c, p. 16). We therefore need a method of handling gamma risk that works for portfolios with more than one instrument, and this is what Zangari's procedures provide.

27. Zangari (1996a, p. 9)

28. See Zangari (1996a, p. 9).

29. Zangari (1996d, p. 19)

30. If we wish to save ourselves some work, we can also resort to various results in the theory of moments (such as Chebyshev's inequality or Rohatgi's inequality) to compute upper bounds for VaR. These are easy to compute, but whether they would be accurate enough for any given purpose can, of course, be problematic. For more on these issues, see Rouvinez (1997, pp. 57–58).

31. See, e.g., Estrella (1996). Again, as Rouvinez points out, 'although delta-gamma methods improve the reliability of the computation in most cases, the margin of accuracy is highly dependent on the composition of the portfolio. Moreover, one should never forget that it is very simple to design a portfolio emphasising the weaknesses of any approximation'. (Rouvinez, 1997, p. 65).

32. Zangari (1996c, e) had earlier recommended that we estimate these parameters using Monte Carlo simulation. We simulate as much data as we want, and then estimate the required parameters from the simulated data. The data are simulated by assuming a particular distribution, and the only constraint is that this distribution must have fat tails reflecting those of observed distributions (see Zangari (1996b, p. 11)). However, the work of Venkataraman strongly suggests that the quasi-

Bayesian technique is computationally easier, particularly when dealing with portfolios of multiple positions.

33. An $n \times n$ matrix Σ is positive semi-definite if the product $x\Sigma x^T$ is non-negative, where x is any $n \times 1$ vector with one or more positive terms and the remaining terms, if any, are zero, and x^T is its transpose.

34. See, e.g., Longerstaey (1995b, p. 10), Jorion (1996, p. 244).

35. Scaling down the dimensionality of our system not only restores positive semi-definiteness, but also reduces the amount of noise in calculations (which helps in the estimation of the remaining parameters) and speeds up computations. These are not inconsiderable benefits. As Jorion observes, 'This is why the design of the experiment, including the number of variables to estimate, is critical' (Jorion, 1996, p. 244).

36. Positions are also differentiated by their credit standing, i.e., government (which is assumed to be free of default risk) and non-government (which is not). This categorisation fails to do any real justice to credit risk, but discussions of credit risk will be postponed to Chapter 9.

37. The first principal component would be a linear function of the different price (or return) series constructed to explain as much price movement as possible. It will therefore leave behind a certain residual price movement that it cannot 'explain'. The second principal component is then constructed to explain as much as possible of this residual movement. This exercise will also leave a residual, and this residual will be that price movement that neither of the first two principal components can explain. We can then construct a third principal component that will explain as much as possible of the movement of this second residual and so leave a third residual that none of the first three principal components can explain, and we can carry on producing more principal components in the same way. Details on how the procedure is carried out can be found in a good econometrics textbook such as Koutsoyiannis (1977, pp. 424–36).

38. PCA appears to be more widely used than FA in this context, but we cannot assume that it always provides good fits. As Wilson (1994a) points out, PCA can sometimes produce considerable errors, particularly if underlying stochastic processes are unstable. Moreover, it does not always follow that adding more factors produces better fits, because new factors can have so much noise of their own that that they add more error than they remove. The comparative merits of the two procedures are discussed in Box 3.4.

39. See, e.g., Jorion (1996, p. 162).

40. Where currencies are not included as core currencies, we need to proxy them by basket equivalents in terms of core currencies. Typically, non-core currencies would be either minor currencies (e.g., the Hungarian forint) or currencies that were closely tied to some other major currency. The latter category might include, for example, the Dutch guilder, because the guilder has for a long time been tied very closely to the mark. Including the guilder and the mark as separate core currencies would lead to major collinearity problems: the variance-covariance matrix would fail to be positive semi-definite, etc. The mapping of non-core currencies to baskets is much the same in principle as the mapping of individual equities to equity indices as described in the next section. However, for the reader who wants more specific material on mapping currencies, a good reference is Laubsch (1996).

41. The minimum number of assets the portfolio must reach to be considered diversified depends on the precise make-up of the portfolio, but the usual rule of thumb in US equity markets is that portfolios of 25 or more stocks are usually well diversified. However, if in doubt, we can always resort to the tracking error approximation procedure outlined in Box 3.5.

42. Remember that under zero diversification all risks are perfectly correlated. The individual asset variance is therefore the same as the portfolio variance and the result follows.

43. Another way to reduce the degree of understatement of VaR that arises from a portfolio being imperfectly diversified is to use more than one price index. Instead of using the overall stock market index, we might use more specific indices such as those for energy stocks, manufacturing stocks and so on. These sector-specific indices would pick up more of the movement in each stock return, and thereby reduce the amount of risk left unaccounted for as firm-specific. σ_ε^2 would then be lower and so result in a smaller understatement of VaR.

44. See Zangari (1996f, p. 118). The more common criteria used in financial institutions are that the mapped position have the same value and same duration as the old one. However, the duration approach only gives an exact measure of bond price volatility if the yield curve is horizontal and

movements of the yield curve are strictly parallel. A mapped position that has the same duration as the original position will therefore have a different exposure to changes in the slope or shape of the yield curve (see Zangari (1996f, pp. 107–8)).

45. See, e.g., Zangari (1996e, p. 120).

46. This description of mapping zero-coupon bonds ignores certain complications peculiar to bonds. One of these is the tendency of bond prices to move towards par as maturity approaches (the 'pull to par' effect). The other is the associated tendency of bond price volatility to decline as a bond approaches maturity (the 'roll down' effect). These effects imply that the standard rules – outlined in section 1.2 – to infer VaR over longer horizons from VaR figures over shorter horizons will tend to overstate the true amounts at risk, and some illustrative exercises carried out by Finger (1996, p. 7) suggest that the errors involved can be quite substantial, especially for longer holding periods. However, Finger (1996, pp. 6–9) also suggests some simple modifications to correct for these errors.

47. With zero-coupon bonds, there is also the additional simplification that the duration is just the remaining term to maturity and, if we wish to take a duration-convexity approximation, the convexity is the term to maturity squared.

48. One reason for the approximation is that, with either contract, the investor is likely to face collateral or margin requirements, and the cost of maintaining these margin positions will usually be interest-sensitive. With forward markets, a second source of approximation is the illiquidity of secondary forward markets. A forward VaR is based on a price in a very thin market, and any estimated forward price/VaR is therefore subject to considerable illiquidity risk.

49. The minor complication that real-world coupon rates are set to reflect the market interest rate of the previous period is ignored here. Ignoring this complication does not affect the main argument that floating-rate bonds can be reverse-engineered into equivalent zero-coupon bonds.

50. See, e.g., Chew (1996, p. 183).

51. There is a very small amount of embedded optionality in these particular instruments which we can ignore. However, more sophisticated structured notes can have a great deal of optionality – an example is the accrual super-floating rate note which revolves around an embedded digital option (see Chew (1996, pp. 184–7)) – and such positions can be dealt with properly only by coming to terms with their embedded options.

52. The particular instruments discussed in this section are by no means exhaustive, but we have discussed enough of them to demonstrate the basic approach, and other instruments (e.g., more fancy structured notes, exotic derivatives and so on) can be mapped in similar ways (i.e., by reverse-engineering the instrument into more basic instruments that we can map, and mapping those).

53. The obvious analogy here is with hedging. Option mapping is dynamic for exactly the same reasons as option hedging (i.e., because changes in other factors lead to changes in hedge ratios).

54. See, e.g., Fama (1965), Hsieh (1988), Hendricks (1996), or the summaries in Meegan (1995, pp. 23–4) or Zangari (1995, p. 47).

55. Other frequently recorded departures from normality are not necessarily trivial either. For example, asset returns often show some small amount of serial correlation (i.e., high asset returns in one period tend to imply somewhat higher than average returns in the next), which contradicts the assumption that returns are independent over time (see, e.g., Fama (1965), Fama and French (1988) or Meegan (1995, pp. 19–21)).

56. See, e.g., Freund (1972, p. 206).

57. This line of inquiry takes us to the portfolio-normal approach (see, e.g., Wilson (1994b) or Frain and Meegan (1996, pp. 7–9)), which is based on the assumption that the portfolio return is normal, but does *not* assume that individual asset returns are normal. It is to be distinguished from the asset-normal approach, outlined earlier in the text, which assumes that individual assets in our portfolio have normal returns and that the portfolio is a linear function of these normal risk variables, and which therefore *implies* that the portfolio return must be normal. The portfolio-normal approach is clearly less restrictive, because it does not require individual returns to be linear and normal, and there will be clearly be cases where the asset-normal approach is not valid but where the portfolio-normal approach is (e.g., due to the operation of the central limit theorem in a well-diversified portfolio).

58. The empirical evidence is also mixed on the issue of whether portfolio returns are normal, and some of this evidence is summarised in the second appendix to Chapter 6. Suffice it here to note that the normality assumption is reasonable for some portfolios but not for others.

APPENDIX TO CHAPTER 3: FORECASTING VOLATILITIES AND CORRELATIONS

Forecasts of volatilities and correlations are of crucial importance in risk management. One reason for this is that good volatility (and correlation) estimates are essential if we are to price derivatives properly: if we underestimate the volatility of a stock, say, we will also underestimate the 'correct' (i.e., zero arbitrage) price of a call option on that stock, and will then expose ourselves to arbitrage attack in the call option market. A poor volatility estimate can also lead to poor estimates of the various Greek parameters – the deltas, gammas, and so on – and therefore lead to the construction of poor hedge positions.

However, we also need volatility forecasts for another reason, specific to VaR: we need them as inputs into the variance-covariance approach discussed in Chapter 3. The quality of our VaR estimates (and, of course, of anything else that depends on these estimates) therefore depends on the quality of our volatility and correlation forecasts.[A1]

I. Forecasting Volatilities

I.I. Sample Variance

The simplest measure of volatility is the sample variance. If r_t is the return in period t, and there are T observations, the variance is taken to be:

$$\hat{\sigma}^2 = \sum_{i=1}^{T} (r_i - \bar{r})^2/(T-1) \qquad (3A.1)$$

Since $\bar{r}$ is itself usually unknown, our volatility estimate (3A.1) will be affected by errors in our estimation of $\bar{r}$. To eliminate such errors, it is common practice to estimate volatility around an assumed mean return of zero. This procedure introduces a slight upward bias in the volatility estimate, but evidence indicates that the bias is likely to be very small, especially when dealing with returns over very short periods (see, e.g., Figlewski (1994) or Longerstaey and Zangari (1995b, pp. 16–21)).

The sample variance has the attraction of being easy to estimate, but is, in practice, almost always inadequate:

• The biggest problem is that it assumes that the underlying 'true' variance is constant, and so cannot accommodate any changes in the variance over time. In particular, it fails to allow for the well-established phenomenon of volatility clustering – the tendency of high-volatility observations to be clustered with other high-volatility observations, and low-volatility observations with other low-volatility observations – which was first observed by Mandelbrot (1963) and has been confirmed by many studies since.

• The fact that it ignores the temporal order of observations implies that it ignores the dynamic information in our return series and (inappropriately) gives earlier and more recent observations equal weight.[A2]

1.2. Exponentially Weighted Moving Average (EWMA)

A more promising alternative is the exponentially weighted moving average (EWMA), which takes the volatility forecast to be a weighted average of the previous period's forecast volatility and the current squared return:

$$\sigma_t^2 = \lambda \sigma_{t-1}^2 + (1 - \lambda) r_t^2 \tag{3A.2}$$

with the weight λ chosen to minimise the error between the forecast and measured volatilities over some sample period. This approach allows the volatility to vary from one period to another, and also explains volatility clustering, since a higher than average volatility in one period is likely to lead to a higher-than-average volatility in the next. This formula also implies that we can write the volatility forecast in the form of the exponentially weighted moving average that gives it its name, assuming we have the observations:

$$\hat{\sigma}_t^2 = (1 - \lambda) \sum_{i=0}^{\infty} \lambda^{i-1} r_{t-i}^2 \tag{3A.3}$$

The EWMA volatility estimator is easy to use, requires only one parameter value (i.e., λ), and appears to work quite well in practice.[A3]

The EWMA is used in the RiskMetrics system, which uses a λ value of 0.94 for daily observations and one of 0.97 for monthly observations.[A4]

1.3. GARCH

A more general class of volatility estimators is the generalised autoregressive conditional heteroskedastic (GARCH) estimator. The generic GARCH model posits a volatility estimator that depends on both lagged values of squared returns and lagged volatility estimates:

$$\sigma_t^2 = \alpha_0 + \sum_{i=0}^{p} \alpha_i r_{t-i}^2 + \sum_{i=1}^{q} \beta_i \sigma_{t-i}^2 \tag{3A.4}$$

where all parameters are assumed to be positive. For example, if $p = q = 1$, we get the GARCH (1,1) estimator:

$$\sigma_t^2 = \alpha_0 + \alpha_1 r_t^2 + \beta \sigma_{t-1}^2 \tag{3A.5}$$

The GARCH framework allows for both time-varying volatility and volatility clustering. It has proven to be a very flexible model that performs well empirically. The GARCH framework also encompasses a variety of specific models. These include: the (relatively) simple ARCH model, which dispenses with the lagged volatility terms in (3A.4); the asymmetric GARCH (or AGARCH) model, which allows for skewness and kurtosis in the return distribution; and the exponential GARCH (or EGARCH) which formulates the conditional variance equation in logarithmic terms. The GARCH model also includes the EWMA as a special-case GARCH (1,1) model in which the intercept is zero and the sum of the two remaining parameters is one.

However, the GARCH model also has its drawbacks. (1) It can be difficult to implement. (2) It needs a large number of observations to get reliable estimates, and these might not be available. (3) GARCH models can be unstable, and therefore produce unreliable forecasts when forecasting out of the period used to estimate the model's parameters.[A5]

1.4. Implied Volatilities

A fifth estimator is implied volatility, the volatility forecast implied by observed option prices. The idea is that since the prices of options depend on market operators' forecasts of volatility, we can use observed option prices to infer their (unobserved) forecasts. Chance (1993) and Corrado and Miller (1996) discuss various ways of doing this and the procedures they recommend appear to be very accurate.[A6]

The major attraction of implied volatilities is that market operators have sufficient confidence in them to bet real money on them. They also have the attraction over historically-based forecasts that they can move rapidly in response to changes in market expectations (e.g., if a change is suddenly expected in a previously stable exchange rate, the implied volatility will move immediately, but historically based forecasts will not). The empirical evidence of Jorion (1995; 1996, pp. 180–81) also suggests that implied volatility forecasts are better than historically based ones.

The main drawback of implied volatilities is that they are available only for the prices of assets on which options are traded (i.e., they are available for a small subset of the assets for which we might seek volatility estimates).[A7]

2. Forecasting Correlations

The estimation of correlations involves many of the same issues as the estimation of volatilities, and the only additional issues are (1) that the number of correlation coefficients grows very rapidly with the number of different returns involved and (2) that correlation forecasts must lie in the range from minus to plus one. As with volatilities, we also need forecast procedures that allow for the fact that correlations can change quite suddenly (e.g., in a crisis).

We can therefore forecast correlations using similar procedures to those we might use to forecast volatilities.

2.1. Sample Correlations

One way to forecast correlations is by means of sample correlations. However, sample correlations suffer from the same basic drawback as sample volatilities (i.e., they presuppose that the 'true' correlation is constant).

2.2. EWMA Correlations

We can also forecast correlations using an EWMA rule. The correlation forecast would be given by:

$$\sigma_{i,j;t} = \lambda\sigma_{i,j;t-1} + (1 - \lambda)r_{i,t-1}r_{j,t-1} \tag{3A.6}$$

where i and j refer to assets i and j. This correlation forecast rule is simple, and (if we use the same λ value for all volatility and correlation forecasts, as RiskMetrics does) is guaranteed to produce a correlation coefficient in the permissible range from minus to plus one.

2.3. GARCH Correlations

We can also use forecast correlations using multivariate GARCH procedures, but the number of parameters involved grows exponentially with the number of correlations.[A8] The number of parameters makes estimates potentially unreliable and there comes a point where there are so many parameters we cannot estimate them. Multivariate GARCH procedures are therefore ill suited to estimates of high-dimension variance-covariance matrices. In addition, multivariate GARCH methods can easily produce correlation estimates that are outside the permissible range.

2.4. Implied Correlations

We can also forecast correlations using implied correlations from the prices of options whose pay-offs are dependent on the prices of both the underlying variables whose return correlation we are trying to forecast. The main drawback of using implied correlations is, of course, that such options are few and far between relative to the number of correlations we might want to forecast.[A9]

2.5. Principal Component/Factor Analysis

A final approach to forecasting correlations is to finesse the issue by working with principal components or factor analysis. If we work with these, the variance-covariance matrix will be diagonal by construction, and will thereby relieve us of the need to estimate or forecast any correlations. For obvious reasons, this approach is very attractive when dealing with high-dimension problems. With large numbers of correlations, principal components/factor analysis is the only feasible alternative to simple approaches to volatility and correlation such as the RiskMetrics one.

Endnotes

A1. For more on this literature, see, e.g., Alexander (1996) or Jorion (1996, Chapter 9).
A2. This equal weighting also implies that a given observation has the same effect on our volatility estimate from the time it occurs until the time it eventually drops out of the period covered by our sample, at which point its effect suddenly drops to zero. This pattern of effect is difficult to rationalise, to say the least.
A3. See, e.g., Zangari (1995, p. 76).
A4. There are, however, some problems with these weights (see, e.g., Alexander (1996, p. 238)). Perhaps the main problem is that the two weights are mutually inconsistent. Against this, there is a good argument that we should be pragmatic with the selection of weights, and that each weight should be the best one for the relevant horizon: the fact that the two weights might be inconsistent with each other would then be one of the prices we pay for tractability.
A5. A related model is the stochastic variance (SV) model. This model is similar to GARCH, but assumes that volatility is a stochastic rather than a deterministic function of historical volatilities.

SV models can also explain volatility clustering. Multivariate SV models are more parsimonious (i.e., have fewer parameters) and there is some evidence that they perform better than multivariate GARCH models (see Danielsson (1996)), but they are also more difficult to estimate.

A6.   The major issue here is that out-of-the-money options imply higher volatilities for the same underlying price than near-the-money options. This is the phenomenon of the 'volatility smile' and is something of a puzzle because all implied volatilities for the same underlying price should be the same under the conditions on which the option-pricing models are based. The explanation appears to have something to do with the non-normality of the underlying price, and different ways of handling the volatility smile are discussed in the references mentioned in the text.

A7.   There are also other approaches we could use to estimate volatilities. For example, Tompkins (1995) suggests forecasting volatility by dividing historical data into low-volatility and high-volatility regions. The volatility forecast is then the proportion of highly-volatility periods times average high volatility plus the proportion of low-volatility periods times average low volatility. His evidence suggests that this approach works very well, and, indeed, even better than implied volatility.

We can also forecast volatility using neural networks, and there is some evidence that neural networks are at least as good as more traditional procedures. For more on neural networks and evidence on their performance, see González Miranda and Burgess (1997).

A8.   For more on the use of GARCH models to forecast correlations, see Alexander (1996, pp. 247–9) and Engle and Mezrich (1996).

A9.   There are also other problems with correlation forecasting. One problem is that underlying relationships are sometimes very unstable (as one would expect if there are periodic crises in which correlations move very suddenly). Another problem is that correlations can be biased by non-synchronous data (i.e., by data collected at different times; see Longerstaey (1995b)). There is also some evidence that we should also be worrying not just about correlations between returns, but about correlations between volatilities as well (Louis, 1997, p. 54).

4

The Historical Simulation Approach

THE idea behind the historical simulation (HS) approach is to use the historical distribution of returns to the assets in our portfolio to simulate the portfolio's VaR, on the hypothetical assumption that we held this portfolio over the period of time covered by our historical data set.

To apply this approach, we first identify the different instruments in our portfolio and collect a sample of their historic returns over some observation period. We now use the weights in our current portfolio to simulate the hypothetical returns we would have had if we had held our current portfolio over the observation period. We then assume that this historical distribution of returns is also a good proxy for the distribution of returns we face over the next holding period. The relevant percentile from the distribution of historical returns then leads us to the expected VaR for our current portfolio.

Suppose we have t observations running from period 0 to period T. If $R_{i,t}$ is the return to asset i over period t, w_i is the relative weight of asset i in our portfolio, and there are n assets in our portfolio, the portfolio return R_t^p over period t is:

$$R_t^p = \sum_{i=1}^{n} w_i R_{i,t}, \quad t = 0, \ldots, T \tag{4.1}$$

Each observation t gives us a particular portfolio return R_t^p. The sample of historical observations therefore gives us a sample distribution of (hypothetical) portfolio returns. We then translate from portfolio returns to portfolio profits and losses, and we read off the VaR from the histogram of profits and losses. For example, if we have a sample of 1000 daily observations, and our VaR is based on a 95% confidence level, we would expect the actual loss to exceed the VaR on 5% of days, or 50 days in total, and the VaR would be the 51st highest loss.

I. ADVANTAGES OF THE HISTORICAL SIMULATION APPROACH

The HS approach has a number of attractions. It is conceptually simple, a feature that not only helps risk managers but also makes it easier to report results to senior management. Much of the necessary data should be available from public sources or already stored in-house (e.g., data will often be collected as a by-product of daily marking to market).

Historical simulation is also easy to implement and can usually be implemented on a spreadsheet. Once an estimation period is chosen and the data collected, all that remains is to use our data sample and (4.1) to simulate the returns we would have had over the sample period and infer the VaR from the distribution of profits and losses. The calculations involved are tedious but straightforward, so a good computer should be able to produce answers fairly quickly.[1]

Another major attraction is that it does not depend on assumptions about the distribution of returns. We do not have to assume that returns are distributed as normal, t, or any other particular distribution. Nor do we even have to assume that they are independent over time. In this regard, the HS approach is less restrictive than approaches based on specific distributional assumptions such as normality: it allows the data free rein to determine the distribution of returns. The HS approach therefore has no problem accommodating the fat tails that plague normal approaches to VaR (see also, e.g., Allen (1994, p. 78) or Jorion (1996, p. 195)).

The non-parametric nature of the HS approach also obviates the need to estimate volatilities, correlations or other parameters. There is therefore no danger of incorrectly estimating parameters because there are no parameters to estimate. Historical volatilities and correlations are already reflected in the data set, and all we need to calculate are the actual returns. There is therefore no need to deal with variance-covariance matrices, and no need for fancy matrix operations. There is also no need to make assumptions about underlying models, since the HS approach as such does not use models. Our VaR estimates are therefore free of the model risk that attaches to normal approaches or Monte Carlo simulation.

The HS approach applies to any type of position and any type of market risk. It therefore accommodates the gamma risks, volatility risks and similar risks that the parametric approaches have difficulty with. The HS approach can also be used to carry out full valuations (i.e., to value the portfolio properly without using simplifying and possibly inaccurate assumptions such as those implied in the use of Taylor series approximations).

HS also yields other useful statistics as by-products. Since HS involves reading off the VaR from an estimated distribution, that same distribution will also yield other useful statistics. These include measures of skewness and excess kurtosis, expected tail losses for any given size of tail, and VaR estimates based on alternative confidence levels.[2] These can be very useful in arriving at a more complete picture of the risks associated with a portfolio (e.g., to check for normality).[3]

Moreover, while the conventional HS approach does not generate an indication of the accuracy of our VaR estimate (e.g., a VaR standard error), a recently developed modification of the HS approach, the historical kernel approach of Butler and Schachter (1996), now allows us to derive precision estimates for HS models. This procedure uses a kernel estimator to estimate the PDF of portfolio returns. This kernel estimator can be thought of as a means of smoothing the histogram of returns by fixing a PDF to each data point. We then derive the VaR from the returns histogram in the usual way, but the kernel estimator now gives us an indication of the precision of our VaR estimate as well.[4] We can then use this precision estimator to put confidence intervals around our VaR estimate.

It is also now fairly easy to estimate incremental VaRs using an HS approach. We do so by calculating both 'before' and 'after' VaR figures from scratch and derive the incremental VaR as the difference. While there is no short cut (as there is under normality) that avoids the need to calculate the second VaR, the calculations involved are straightforward and a good computer should be able to produce rapid answers in real time.[5]

Finally, there is also some evidence that the HS approach works better than normal approaches. Mahoney (1996) found evidence that the HS approach yields unbiased estimates of VaR for all confidence levels up to (at least) 99%, while normal approaches start to underestimate VaR for confidence levels higher than 95%. The superiority of HS over normal approaches was also supported by Mahoney's chi-squared goodness of fit tests. Similarly, Jackson, Maude and Perraudin (1997) found evidence that HS VaR estimates were generally superior to normal ones, particularly when it came to forecasting tail probabilities. In short, both studies found that HS was superior to normal approaches because there were fat tails that HS could allow for but normal approaches could not. On the other hand, Kupiec (1995) presented simulation evidence that HS is inferior to a normal approach, so these findings are controversial.

2. PROBLEMS WITH THE HISTORICAL SIMULATION APPROACH

2.1. Obtaining Data

Naturally, the HS approach also has its problems. One problem is simply obtaining the data. In particular, all an institution's positions would need to be accessible by the risk management team, which can create problems if units are geographically dispersed or handle data in incompatible ways.[6] However, this issue arises with any approach to VaR, and not just HS. (In fact, it arises with any centralised approach to risk management.)

The HS approach also requires adequate runs of data for each instrument we hold, and yet the instruments might be new ones with little or no history (as with those from emerging markets).[7] The only practical response to this problem is to resort to proxy data of some sort.

2.2. Complete Dependence on a Particular Historical Data Set

A more serious problem is the complete dependence of HS results on the *particular* historical data set used.[8] The underlying assumption is that the past (as captured in the historical data set) is sufficiently like the future to give us a reliable idea of future risks, which implicitly presumes that the risks we face in the future are similar to those we have faced in the past. While this assumption is often reasonable, it can lead to seriously distorted estimates of VaR in a number of circumstances:

- The data in our estimation period may be unusual. They may be unusually quiet, in which case our estimates of risk (and hence of VaR) are likely to be too low. Alternatively, they may be unusually volatile, in which case our estimates of VaR are likely to be too high.
- Our estimation period may incorporate unusual events (e.g., a major stock market crash or exchange rate crisis) that we would not expect to recur in the foreseeable

future, in which case our estimates of VaR are likely to be too high. Moreover, our estimates of VaR would remain too high until the effects of the event in question had dropped out of our estimation period. If we had an estimation period of five years, say, a major, one-off shock (and therefore one unlikely to be repeated) not only would influence our VaR forecasts immediately after it happened, but would also exert the *same* influence on our VaR forecasts for the next five years. Once the five years had passed, the shock would drop out of the estimation period and its influence would suddenly go to zero. Our forecasts of VaR would be distorted for a full five years, and distorted in a very odd way.

- The HS approach also has difficulty dealing with permanent changes in risk factors. If a permanent change takes place (e.g., there is a change in exchange rate policy which largely eliminates a particular exchange rate risk), the exchange rate risk will still be present in the historical data set and will dissipate only gradually as time passes and old data are replaced. The change will be fully reflected in VaR estimates only after all the old data observations have been replaced (i.e., after a full five years or whatever).[9]

- No way of forecasting VaR based on historical data can accommodate plausible events that may occur in the future but did not actually occur in the historical data period. Hence the HS procedure deals only with risks as reflected in the particular historical estimation period. For instance, if no devaluation occurred in a historical data period, the HS procedure would implicitly regard exchange rate risk as very low. Yet 'true' exchange rate risk may be very much higher, particularly in cases where the market expects the exchange rate to change after a long period of stability. A case in point is the period preceding the crisis of late 1992: ERM exchange rate risk would have appeared low using historical data, and yet markets were (correctly) expecting major exchange rate movements. Real exchange rate risk was therefore much greater than an HS approach would have suggested.

2.3. Problem of Estimation Period Length

There are also problems relating to the length of the historical estimation period. On the one hand, we clearly want a reasonable run of data to have enough observations from which to draw reliable inferences about the tail of our distribution. Since tail events are by definition unusual, we therefore need quite a long run of data to get reliable results. This is particularly the case if we are dealing with VaRs based on high confidence levels. If we base our VaR on a 95% confidence level, we would have to wait, on average, 20 days to expect a single loss in excess of VaR; if we had a 99% confidence level, we would expect to wait 100 days to get a single loss in excess of VaR; and so forth. The more extreme the tail, the longer the estimation period must be. Assuming the underlying data processes remain the same over the whole estimation period, we would presumably want the longest possible period to maximise the accuracy of our results.

However, it is likely that even well-behaved data will exhibit some systematic changes over time, and this might lead us to prefer a somewhat shorter estimation period. Volatilities and correlations will change, and so on. If this is the case, the information contained in more recent observations would be more useful than the information

---

Box 4.1: Weighted historical simulation

An odd feature of HS is that any observation is given a weight of one if it falls within a certain past period, and a weight of zero when it falls out of that period. Some chance event that is unlikely to be repeated therefore haunts our VaR estimates for a long time after it has occurred and then suddenly disappears a long time later. Another awkward feature of HS is that it presupposes that the process generating the profit and loss remains the same. If we have a ten-year estimation period, we have to make the heroic assumption that the profit and loss distribution remains the same over that whole period.

One way to avoid both these implications is to discount our observations according to how far back they occurred: the further back they are, the lower the weight they would have. We could then construct our histograms (and thence infer our VaR) from weighted observations of profit and loss. Any given observation would then have its maximum effect on estimated VaR just after it occurred; thereafter its influence would decline and gradually go to zero. This weighted HS therefore has the intuitively desirable property that events further back in time are given less importance than recent events. Moreover, the declining weight attached to older events can be interpreted as a way of allowing the profit and loss distribution to change slowly over time. Indeed, we could say that it is the changing distribution that actually motivates the declining weight in the first place: the older the event, the less relevant it is to the present, because it comes from a PDF that differs so much more from the PDF that generates our current VaR.

We could choose a weight by making some a priori decision as to how quickly the distribution changes. Alternatively, we could try out different weights on past data sets and select the one that seems to give the best VaR forecasts by some criterion.

---

contained in older observations. A long estimation period would lead the newer, more useful information contained in more recent observations to be drowned out by the older, stale information in the earlier observations. Our VaR estimate would then be insensitive to new information and reveal little about changes in risk factors over time (and Hendricks (1996, p. 54) provides evidence that this is exactly what happens with long estimation periods, i.e., ones of 1250 days).

We can thus end up in something of a dilemma: if the estimation period is too short, we will not have enough historical observations from which to draw reliable inferences, but if it is too long, the estimate can place too much emphasis on stale data and be insufficiently sensitive to new information.

2.4. Potentially Unreliable VaR Estimates

There are also some concerns about the reliability of VaR estimates under the HS approach. There are two main issues here. (1) The empirical results of Butler and Schachter (1996, Table 2) indicated that VaR estimates varied considerably in their accuracy and were usually quite inaccurate: the standard errors varied from 6.5% of estimated VaR to 23.8%. Furthermore, their results also suggested that the distribution of returns might be skewed, in which case the true confidence intervals would not be centred around estimated means and the VaR estimates would be even less reliable than their standard errors alone would suggest. (2) The other concern is that the HS approach might generate unreliable VaR estimates when confidence levels are high (i.e., when tails are small). The source of this unreliability is largely an issue of sample size. For any given sample size, as we know, tail events will be rarer when VaRs are based on higher confidence levels. The greater rarity of tail events then means that VaR estimates hinge on a smaller number of observations, and are therefore less reliable. Consequently, unless sample sizes are particularly large, VaR estimates are likely to be unreliable when based on high confidence levels.[10]

3. CONCLUSIONS

HS is a useful and straightforward approach to VaR. It is simple and easy to explain, and compared with other approaches, relatively easy to implement. It also has a number of other attractive features. (1) It is non-parametric (i.e., does not depend on assumptions about underlying probability distributions) and can easily accommodate fat tails and other non-normal features. (2) It accommodates correlations and volatilities implicitly (i.e., from our point of view, painlessly) in so far as they are reflected in market-price data. (3) It largely avoids model risk. (4) It is a full valuation approach, and therefore (usually) avoids the need to rely on approximations that may turn out to be inaccurate. (5) It can accommodate all types of instruments, at least in theory. (6) It can produce a range of useful statistics, including estimates of VaR at other confidence levels, estimates of the precision of our VaR figures and estimates of incremental VaR. (7) It has a reasonable empirical record compared with normal or variance-covariance approaches to VaR.

However, HS also has its disadvantages, mainly relating to data problems. Perhaps the main disadvantage of HS is its total dependence on the particular data set used: any plausible events not represented in the data set will therefore be completely ignored. This underlines the need to use HS with discretion, and also suggests the importance of complementing HS with stress tests or scenario analyses to pick up plausible risks that are not well represented – or not represented at all – in our data set.

Box 4.2: The bootstrap approach

An alternative to HS is the bootstrap approach in which we take samples from some set of historical data and replace each observation after we register it to keep our data set the same size.[11] The HS approach is equivalent to drawing from the historical data set without replacement, with observations taken in their historical order. The bootstrap approach draws from the same sample, but drawings are taken in random order and, because they are replaced, we can take as many drawings as we wish. The bootstrap approach has a number of attractions:

- As with HS, the bootstrap implicitly incorporates historical volatilities and correlations, since these are already reflected in the historical price/return data.
- It has the advantage, relative to the normal distribution, that it incorporates fat tails or extreme events in the historical data that are never, or almost never, allowed for under normality. For example, a US data set that included October 1987 would incorporate a stock market fall of about 23 standard deviations – an event that would almost never occur under a normal distribution.
- The bootstrap has the advantage, relative to the HS approach, that the sample size can be as large as we want, so we don't have the model validation problems that arise under HS due to lack of enough historical data. The ability to work with a larger sample size should also mean that we can estimate VaR more accurately and also have a better idea of the accuracy of our estimates.[12]

However, these attractions come at a price:

- As with the HS approach, any results will depend entirely on the historical data set, and both these approaches are hopeless at dealing with events that are not included in their data sets. Everything hinges on the data set, and any given data set may or may not provide a good basis for dealing with prospective future risks.
- Again, as with the HS approach, the bootstrap approach will be reliable only if we have a sufficiently large data set. If the data set is too small, we run into small-sample bias and cannot assume that the bootstrapped distribution will be a good approximation to the 'true' distribution we are trying to model.
- The bootstrap approach depends critically on the assumption that returns are independent over time. If this assumption does not hold, then it makes no sense to resample at random (i.e., independently of the original date of each sample observation) and the whole basis of the bootstrapping procedure is undermined.

ENDNOTES

1. If speed is an issue, we can also resort to short cuts such as mapping instruments to reduce the number of calculations or taking random samples from within the historical data set to reduce the number of observations used in each VaR estimation (e.g. Beckström (1995, p. 3)). However, improvements in computing power mean that we can now make calculations much faster than we used to and there is much less pressure to take short cuts to speed up calculations.
2. The HS procedure allows us to infer VaRs at any level of confidence we choose, simply by reading the relevant quantile off the histogram. For disclosure purposes, we need only report the histogram and readers can infer VaR at whatever confidence level they choose. Used in this way, the HS approach can be very informative, regardless of the distribution of underlying risk factors.
3. The HS approach does not generate any formula to infer a VaR based on one holding period from a VaR based on another, but we can always estimate VaRs for longer holding periods by aggregating returns accordingly and then reading off the VaR from the histogram of returns for the longer holding period. There are, however, two limitations. (1) We lose observations in aggregating the data, so the histogram becomes coarser and the longer-holding-period VaR less accurate. (2) The VaR estimate still assumes that the portfolio does not change, and as we have already seen, the assumption of an unchanging portfolio is harder to maintain over a longer holding period (e.g., because institutions will move out of loss-making positions).
4. See Butler and Schachter (1996, pp. 4–7).
5. Beckström (1995) objects that estimating incremental VaR will be a slow process because of the number of calculations that need to be carried out. I do not accept this argument. While no one denies that carrying out such calculations could be a slow process in the past, the calculations involved are straightforward and a good computer now should be able to race through them in no time at all. I believe that speed is no longer a major issue with HS.
6. Wilson (1996, p. 221)
7. See Wilson (1996, pp. 221–2). The extent to which this problem is unique to HS is unclear. The variance-covariance and MCS approaches as such do not need long data periods, but they still need enough data to estimate volatilities, correlations and other relevant parameters. All VaR approaches therefore require *some* historical data in practice. However, all things considered, the HS approach probably requires more historical data than the other approaches do.
8. Advocates of Monte Carlo simulation are fond of putting this problem another way, which also highlights the attraction of the Monte Carlo approach. The HS approach estimates VaR on the basis of only one price path – the particular historical price path actually followed. The quality of its results therefore depends entirely on the set of unique historical accidents and other factors that produced this particular historical price path. In so doing, the HS approach makes no allowance for the infinite number of alternative price paths that could have been followed but didn't actually materialise. If we are concerned with future risks, they argue, quite rightly, that these alternative paths also have something to tell us. This, they argue, is what makes Monte Carlo simulation superior to historical simulation. I have a lot of sympathy with this argument, but one must also take other factors (e.g., the precise MC procedure, the presence of model risk in MC simulation, the difficulty and cost of carrying out MCS, whether we have staff qualified to carry out MCS, how quickly we need the calculations, and so on) into account when judging whether Monte Carlo is superior to historical simulation.
9. See also, e.g., Holton (1996a, section 5).
10. There are two specific issues here. (1) To what extent does the reliability of HS deteriorate with the confidence level? (2) How is reliability related to the length of data period used? Unfortunately, the evidence is somewhat mixed on both issues.

As regards the first issue, Hendricks (1996, p. 49) found evidence that the accuracy of VaR estimates deteriorates as the confidence level increases, and yet Mahoney (1996, p. 17) found no such evidence even when confidence levels went as high as 99.9%.

As regards the second, both Kupiec (1995, p. 82–3) and Hendricks (1996, p. 50) found evidence that the reliability of HS VaR simulations increases with the length of the data set. However, their evidence gives conflicting impressions of how long the data set must be for results to be reliable when VaRs are based on high confidence levels, Hendricks (1996, p. 50) finding that HS gave reliable results with only five years of daily data, and yet Kupiec (1995, p. 19) finding that estimates could still be unreliable even with nearly ten years of daily data.

11. See Efron (1979).

12. However, a comparison of the historical kernel and bootstrap approaches by Butler and Schachter (1996) suggests that the superiority of the bootstrap over HS approaches cannot be taken for granted. Their historical kernel results were based on 12 real trading positions, with data for the previous 100 days, while their bootstrapped results involved 1000 bootstrapped simulations from the same data set. They found not only that bootstrapped results were less accurate (the standard errors of the VaRs were considerably higher) but also that the bootstrapped distributions were more prone to skewness and kurtosis. To the extent there is significant skewness, the bootstrapped results would therefore be even less accurate than their standard errors suggest, since the true confidence interval would not be centred around the estimated mean VaR.

5

Monte Carlo Simulation and Related Approaches

I. INTRODUCTION

THIS chapter deals with Monte Carlo and related methods that estimate VaR on the basis of simulation results derived from statistical or mathematical models. The idea is to simulate repeatedly the random processes governing the prices of the financial instruments we are interested in. Each simulation gives us a possible value for our portfolio at the end of our target horizon. If we take enough of these simulations, the simulated distribution of portfolio values will converge to the portfolio's unknown 'true' distribution, and we can use the simulated distribution to infer the VaR of the 'true' one.

This simulation process involves a number of specific steps. The first is to select a model for the price(s) of interest. Having chosen our model, we estimate its parameters – volatilities, correlations, and so on – on the basis of whatever historical or market data are available. The next step is to construct fictitious price paths for the random variables involved. In the case of Monte Carlo simulation (MCS), we construct these price paths using random numbers – or, strictly speaking, pseudo-random numbers – produced by a (so-called) 'random number generator'. In the case of quasi-Monte Carlo (QMC) methods, we construct these paths using 'quasi-random' numbers that do not pretend to mimic real random numbers as such, but instead attempt to fill the domain interval more uniformly and avoid the clusters that occur with pseudo-random numbers. Each set of 'random' numbers produces a hypothetical terminal price for the relevant instrument, and we carry out similar exercises for the other instruments in our portfolio to produce a hypothetical terminal value for the portfolio as a whole. We then repeat these simulations enough times to be confident that the simulated distribution of portfolio values is close enough to the 'true' (but unknown) distribution of actual portfolio values to be a reliable proxy for it. Once that is done, we can read off the VaR from this proxy distribution.

MCS and QMC are very powerful tools for estimating VaR and can handle virtually any type of portfolio, however complex or exotic. They can easily handle the price risks associated with non-linear positions which, as we have seen in Chapter 3, pose serious problems for normal-based approaches. They can also accommodate prices that depend on more than one stochastic variable, path-dependent pricing (e.g., as in Asian options), time variation in parameters (e.g. in volatilities or correlations) and non-normal distributions (and therefore fat tails, skewness and the like). As well as handling standard call and put options, they can also handle more difficult derivatives, including ones that do not have analytic solutions (such as certain American-style options).

Box 5.1:   The use of Monte Carlo simulations for managing derivatives positions

The use of MCS to price derivatives positions and manage derivatives risks was suggested by Boyle (1977) and is now fairly common among financial institutions with major derivatives positions. It tends to be used for exotic derivatives for which alternative approaches such as lattice procedures are computationally too intensive (e.g., when handling certain types of interest-rate derivatives) or inaccurate (e.g., when handling options with discontinuous pay-offs, such as barrier options).

MCS is used both to price derivatives and to estimate particular risks, such as delta, gamma, volatility and similar risks. These risks can be estimated by pricing the derivative on the basis of one value of the relevant underlying factor (e.g., the underlying price, in the case of the delta risk), and then pricing the derivative again on the basis of another underlying factor value close to the original one. The difference between the two derivative prices then enables us to estimate the delta, gamma or whatever risk parameter we are looking for. (Recall that $\Delta c \approx \delta \Delta S$, so our delta, δ, is approximately $\Delta c / \Delta S$, and so on.) However, over the last decade or so, new MCS procedures have been developed – so-called direct methods, using the techniques of infinitesimal perturbation analysis – that allow these parameters to be estimated on the basis of a single set of simulations, without the need to carry out resimulations at perturbed parameter values.[1] These new techniques can cut down drastically on the number of calculations needed, particularly when we want estimates of a number of different risk parameters (such as delta, gamma, rho, vega, etc.).

Institutions that already have the capability to carry out MCS for their derivatives positions should therefore have little difficulty building up an MCS capability to estimate VaR. Indeed, they will almost certainly have to: the very fact that they already use MCS to handle their derivatives positions implies that those positions must be both large and complex, which implies that MCS is almost certainly the appropriate way for them to estimate their VaRs.

---

2. THE MONTE CARLO SIMULATION APPROACH

Perhaps the first point to appreciate about MCS is that it is to be used when simpler approaches are inappropriate. MCS is not easy to use; if simpler approaches are satisfactory, we should therefore use them instead. For example, if we had a simple normal position, there would be no point going through MCS because we could work out the VaR easily and directly: we already know that the VaR is $-\alpha \sigma W$, so we need only estimate σ and plug this estimate into our VaR formula. We would therefore use MCS only in more difficult situations where more direct approaches are unavailable, computationally too intensive, or insufficiently accurate for our purposes. MCS approaches are particularly useful when dealing with multidimensional problems (i.e., where outcomes depend on more than one risk variable) and, as a rule, become relatively more attractive as the dimensionality of a problem increases.

2.1. Monte Carlo Simulation for Portfolios with Single Assets

The MCS procedure is best explained in the context of an illustrative example. Suppose we are interested in forecasting the VaR of a position in a particular stock. Our first task is to choose some model to describe the behaviour of the stock price over time. For convenience, let us assume that the price of this stock is described by the following continuous process:[2]

$$dp_t = \sigma dZ_t \tag{5.1}$$

This equation gives the change in the current price dp_t in terms of a volatility parameter σ (which is assumed to be known, or at least estimated) and a standard normal variable Z_t. Equations of this type are usually made more tractable by taking a discretised approximation over some short time interval Δt. Let us therefore take such an approximation whilst also choosing our time units so that $\Delta t = 1$. Hence:

$$p_t = p_{t-1} + \sigma Z_t \sqrt{\Delta t} = p_{t-1} + \sigma Z_t \tag{5.2}$$

which gives the current price p_t in terms of the price for the previous period p_{t-1}, as well as σ and Z_t. We now wish to simulate the stock price over the interval from t to T. (If Δt is a minute long, for instance, the interval from t to T might represent a day.) We do so by first leading (5.2) by one period to give us an expression for p_{t+1} in terms of p_t and Z_{t+1}; we then substitute (5.2) into this equation to give:

$$p_{t+1} = p_t + \sigma Z_{t+1} = p_{t-1} + \sigma[Z_t + Z_{t+1}] \tag{5.3}$$

We repeat the exercise to get an expression for p_{t+2}, then one for p_{t+3}, and so on, until we have an expression for p_T:

$$p_T = p_{t-1} + \sigma \sum_{i=t}^{T} Z_t \tag{5.4}$$

The price at T depends on the initial price (p_{t-1}) and the sum of the realised values of Z from t to T.

We now use a random number generator to produce a series of realised values of Z_t, $Z_{t+1}, \ldots,$ to Z_T, and substitute these into (5.4) to produce a final simulated price, p_T. We then multiply this price by the number of shares we have to determine the portfolio value. If we repeat the process enough times, the distribution of simulated portfolio values produced in this way will converge to the 'true' PDF underlying the portfolio value process.[3] We can then use the simulated portfolio-value histogram to construct the corresponding profit and loss histogram and thence infer our VaR.

2.2. Monte Carlo Simulation for Portfolios with Multiple Assets

Now suppose we are interested in a portfolio involving more than one stock, so that the portfolio return depends on more than one stock price. Portfolios with more than one asset generally require us to simulate more than one Z-path, except for two special cases in which the procedure is much the same as with a single asset. The first of these is where the prices are independent, in which case we have equations analogous to (5.4). With two prices, we have:

$$
p_{1,t} = p_{1,t-1} + \sigma_1 Z_{1,t} \quad \text{or} \quad \begin{bmatrix} p_{1,t} \\ p_{2,t} \end{bmatrix} = \begin{bmatrix} p_{1,t-1} \\ p_{2,t-1} \end{bmatrix} + \begin{bmatrix} \sigma_1, 0 \\ 0, \sigma_2 \end{bmatrix} \begin{bmatrix} Z_{1,t} \\ Z_{2,t} \end{bmatrix} \tag{5.5}
$$

The value of the portfolio in period t, PV_t, is found by multiplying (5.5) by $[x_{1,t}, x_{2,t}]$, the vector of positions in the two assets, to get:

$$
PV_t = [x_{1,t}, x_{2,t}] \begin{bmatrix} p_{1,t} \\ p_{2,t} \end{bmatrix} = [x_{1,t}, x_{2,t}] \begin{bmatrix} p_{1,t-1} \\ p_{2,t-1} \end{bmatrix} + [x_{1,t}, x_{2,t}] \begin{bmatrix} \sigma_1, 0 \\ 0, \sigma_2 \end{bmatrix} \begin{bmatrix} Z_{1,t} \\ Z_{2,t} \end{bmatrix} \tag{5.6}
$$

which depends on period t's drawings of $Z_{1,t}$ and $Z_{2,t}$. The portfolio value at period T is:

$$
PV_T = \sum_{i=1}^{T} PV_i \tag{5.7}
$$

which depends on the drawings of both Z variables from t to T. All we now need to do is run enough iterations to simulate the true distribution of portfolio values, switch over to the profit/loss distribution and infer the VaR. Note that this exercise does not require any fancy matrix operations.

The other case is where the prices are perfectly correlated with each other, either positively or negatively. In this case,

$$
p_{1,t} = p_{1,t-1} + \sigma_1 Z_{1,t} \quad \text{or} \quad \begin{bmatrix} p_{1,t} \\ p_{2,t} \end{bmatrix} = \begin{bmatrix} p_{1,t-1} \\ p_{2,t-1} \end{bmatrix} + \begin{bmatrix} \sigma_1, 0 \\ \pm\sigma_2, 0 \end{bmatrix} \begin{bmatrix} Z_{1,t} \\ Z_{2,t} \end{bmatrix} \tag{5.8}
$$

We now multiply (5.8) by the position vector $[x_{1,t}, x_{2,t}]$ to solve for the portfolio value PV_t, use (5.7) to solve for the final portfolio value PV_T, and proceed as before to repeat the exercise as many times as required to produce a reliable VaR estimate.

The difficulties arise when the two prices are imperfectly correlated with each other. In this case, we have

$$
\begin{bmatrix} p_{1,t} \\ p_{2,t} \end{bmatrix} = \begin{bmatrix} p_{1,t-1} \\ p_{2,t-1} \end{bmatrix} + \begin{bmatrix} a_{1,1}, a_{1,2} \\ a_{2,1}, a_{2,2} \end{bmatrix} \begin{bmatrix} Z_{1,t} \\ Z_{2,t} \end{bmatrix} \tag{5.9}
$$

where the $a_{i,j}$ are functions of the underlying variances and correlations. We now have to solve for these, and the usual procedure is by means of a Choleski decomposition.[4] To see what is involved, let us first rewrite (5.9) in first-difference form by subtracting the lagged p terms from each side:

$$
\begin{bmatrix} \Delta p_{1,t} \\ \Delta p_{2,t} \end{bmatrix} = \begin{bmatrix} a_{1,1}, a_{1,2} \\ a_{2,1}, a_{2,2} \end{bmatrix} \begin{bmatrix} Z_{1,t} \\ Z_{2,t} \end{bmatrix} \tag{5.10}
$$

Now denote the vector of $\Delta p_{i,t}$ terms by Δp_t, the matrix of $a_{i,j}$ terms by A and the vector of $Z_{i,t}$ terms by Z_t. We then multiply each side of (5.10) by its transpose, denoted by $Z_t^T A^T$:

$$
\Delta p_t \Delta p_t^T = A Z_t Z_t^T A^T \tag{5.11}
$$

However, the left-hand side of (5.11) is the variance-covariance matrix Σ and, since the $Z_{i,t}$ variables are independent standard normal, the expectation of the matrix $Z_t Z_t^T$ is the identity matrix consisting of ones along the diagonal and zeros everywhere else. Running an expectations operator through (5.11) then gives:

$$\Sigma^e = AA^T \tag{5.12}$$

which tells us that A, the matrix of $a_{i,j}$ terms in (5.9), is the 'square root matrix' of the expected variance-covariance matrix Σ^e. The actual values of the terms in A then turn out to be:

$$A = \begin{bmatrix} 1, 0 \\ \rho, (1 - \rho^2)^{1/2} \end{bmatrix} \tag{5.13}$$

(The reader can easily verify this result by postmultiplying (5.13) by its transpose to give (5.12).) Once we have the A matrix, (5.9) gives us the prices in period t and the analogues to (5.6) and (5.7) give us the portfolio value in period T, conditional on the Z variables. We then do repeated iterations as before, estimate the histogram of portfolio values and infer the VaR.

The Choleski decomposition approach also works for portfolios with n assets. Whatever the number of assets involved, the A matrix is still the matrix square root of the matrix Σ^e, as defined in (5.12). Provided all variables are independent, this matrix will have the same dimensions as Σ itself: it will be a 3×3 matrix if there are three independent variables, a 4×4 matrix if there are four independent variables, and so on. Whatever the dimension, the relevant n-dimensional version of (5.13) will tell us what A actually is.

2.3. Some Practical Issues with Monte Carlo Simulation

2.3.1. Generating Random Numbers

Monte Carlo simulations depend on drawings from a random number generator. However, strictly speaking, these 'random' numbers are not random at all. They are pseudo-random numbers generated from an algorithm using a deterministic rule (i.e., a rule that does not have any random elements). These rules take some initial value, a 'seed' number, and then generate a series of numbers that *appear* random and ought, if the number generator is well designed, to pass the standard tests for randomness (and, among these, especially the tests for independence). However, if a random number generator is poorly designed, the 'random' numbers it produces will not have the properties that we assume them to have (e.g., they may not be independent of each other) and our results could be compromised. It is therefore critical to use a good random number generator.

There is also another problem. A random number generator will always generate the same sequence of numbers from the same initial 'seed' number. Eventually, the seed number will recur and the sequence of 'random' numbers will repeat itself. All random number generators therefore cycle after a certain number of drawings, and the only issue is how long they take to cycle: good ones will cycle after perhaps billions of draws, but bad ones will cycle after only a few thousand.[5] If the cycle is too short relative to the number of drawings we want, the extra accuracy we think we are getting from taking so many drawings is spurious and we may fool ourselves into thinking that our results are more accurate than they actually are. It is therefore important to use a random number generator with a long cycle.

Box 5.2: Full, grid and other MC procedures

There are a number of ways of applying MCS. The most elaborate and (usually) most demanding is full MC, which involves the exact valuation of (i.e., the computing of price paths for) every instrument in our portfolio.

However, there are approximation procedures that can cut down on the calculations required. One of these is grid MC, which is essentially MCS applied to a mapped position. We therefore map our portfolio onto a grid of factor values and then carry out a full valuation of the mapped portfolio. The number of calculations grows geometrically with the number of primary factors, however, so if the number of factors is large, we would need to use some other method or simplify the grid procedure further. One possible way to do this – a modified grid MC approach – is suggested by Pritsker (1996, p. 24). An alternative is to apply full valuation to an approximation of the actual portfolio, the typical case being a delta-gamma approximation. This is the delta-gamma MC approach.

Simulation results by Pritsker (1996) suggest that full MC generates the most accurate VaR estimates, but is also the most computer-time-intensive procedure. The slowness of this procedure leads him to conclude that it is probably not much use in practice. The other two approaches were comparable in accuracy, but the delta-gamma MC approach was eight times faster. The best procedure would therefore appear to be the delta-gamma MC one.

2.3.2. Ensuring a Positive Semi-definite Variance-covariance Matrix

Another practical problem is the one familiar from Chapter 3 of ensuring that the estimated variance-covariance matrix Σ is positive semi-definite. If this condition is not met, the A matrix cannot exist and the MC procedure outlined above cannot be applied. The reader will recall from Chapter 3 that this condition will be satisfied only if two other conditions hold, both of which put limits on the size of the variance-covariance matrix. One of these is that the number of observations from which the variance-covariance matrix is estimated must be at least as great as the number of dimensions in the matrix itself, and the second is that none of the included time series – asset prices, returns or whatever – be perfectly linearly correlated with other series. However, in practice, we usually have problems not so much with assets that are perfectly correlated with each other (we usually have a good idea where to expect such problems, so we can eliminate one or more assets accordingly), as with assets that are sufficiently closely correlated with each other that the *estimated* variance-covariance matrix will not be positive semi-definite because of rounding errors. This is often a major problem, especially when dealing with high dimension matrices.[6] The solution is to reduce the dimensionality of the variance-covariance matrix, which we can do by mapping our assets onto a smaller number of 'core' equivalents or by resorting to principal components or factor analysis. Reducing the size of the variance-covariance matrix also has the not insignificant benefit of speeding up the calculations.[7]

2.3.3. How Many Iterations?

For most MCS procedures, the accuracy of any estimated parameter will be proportional to $1/\sqrt{n}$, where n is the number of iterations. Increasing the number of paths by a factor of 100 therefore cuts the error by (about) a factor of 10. The MCS approach is thus very computer-intensive, particularly when we need a high level of accuracy. In addition, the number of calculations required also depends on the number of random drawings we take in each iteration. A simple linear position in n imperfectly correlated assets will typically depend on the realisations of n random variables, and non-linear or more complex positions will often depend on even more. Hence, the value of a position with 50 assets would generally depend on the realisations of *at least* 50 random variables, so an iteration to produce a single hypothetical portfolio value would require us to construct hypothetical paths for at least 50 random variables. If we have to carry out, say, 10 000 iterations to get results of acceptable accuracy, we would therefore have to construct at least 500 000 hypothetical price paths. If we wish to use MCS when operating under real-time constraints, we may therefore have to sacrifice accuracy for speed.[8]

However, it is possible to obtain great improvements in accuracy (and/or speed) by using one of a number of variance-reduction techniques.[9] One such technique is the Martingale Variance Reduction (MVR) procedure proposed by Clewlow and Carverhill (1994),[10] and they produce an example of a lookback option pricing exercise in which the MVR technique leads to the same level of accuracy as conventional MCS for only about 0.5% of the number of simulations needed with MCS. Even more dramatic improvements were reported by Boyle, Broadie and Glasserman (1997, p. 1282), who present an example of an arithmetic Asian option pricing exercise in which a variety of other variance-reducing techniques produced the same level of accuracy as conventional MCS using as little as 0.01% of the number of simulations – an astonishing fall in the computational burden.

2.3.4. Model Risk

Results from any MCS procedure also depend critically on the models used to describe the relevant price processes. The use of MCS therefore exposes us to model risk, the risk of misleading results due to the choice of inappropriate pricing models. It is therefore important to get the models right. This task is relatively straightforward for positions where there is a single well-established model available, but more difficult for others (such as certain interest-rate derivatives) where there may be a number of alternative models to choose from, each of which might have its own advantages and disadvantages. Hence, if we are still concerned about model risk even after making an informed choice of models, we might wish to check our results by comparing them to simulation results based on other models.

But what models should we use? The answer depends on the instrument whose price we wish to model and, sometimes, on other factors such as how accurate we want our results to be. For equity positions we can often get by on the assumption of geometric Brownian motion, which is a generalisation of (5.1). This model assumes that the stock price is governed by the process:

$$dS_t/S_t = \mu dt + \sigma dW_t \tag{5.14}$$

where $dW_t = \sqrt{\Delta t} \cdot Z_t$. As with (5.1), changes in the stock price are driven by the random standardised normal variable Z_t. The standard deviation of the stock price also decreases as the length of the time interval, Δt, gets smaller, a feature which rules out big jumps to the stock price and characterises the process as Brownian. In addition, the change in stock price is allowed to have a non-zero drift term that captures expected changes in the stock price. If we like, we can also allow the instantaneous drift (μ) and volatility (σ) to change over time.[11]

Modelling the prices of fixed-income instruments is, by contrast, a much more difficult business, and one that has been the subject of a huge amount of intellectual effort over the past 15 years or so. The more traditional approach to this problem is to go down the duration-convexity route, i.e., to avoid trying to model the bond price as such, but to work with a duration-convexity approximation instead:

$$\Delta p/p \approx -D^m \Delta y + (1/2)C(\Delta y)^2 \tag{5.15}$$

All we then need to do is derive the values of the modified duration (D^m) and convexity (C) parameters – both of which can be calculated fairly easily – and plug them into (5.15) to give us the approximate bond price movement in response to a given change in interest rates. The VaR then follows fairly easily given some assumed PDF for the bond yield process. This duration-convexity approach is simple to use, but also has a number of well-known drawbacks (e.g., the approximation might not be close, the basic modified duration measure does not allow for changes in the shape of the yield curve, and so on). It also has the additional drawback that it is not much use for many kinds of interest-rate derivatives, particularly some of the more exotic ones.

Because of these problems, financial industry practitioners usually prefer the alternative, but potentially far more difficult, approach of actually modelling the relevant security price. We then have to choose a particular model, and there are a large number to choose from. If we are satisfied with a simple model, we might choose something like the Cox-Ingersoll-Ross (1985) bond pricing model:

$$dr_t = \kappa(\mu - r_t)dt + \sigma\sqrt{r_t}dW_t \tag{5.16}$$

This model has the attraction that it captures the stylised fact that interest tends to revert to its mean: if r_t is very high, the first term is negative and the interest rate will tend to come down, and vice versa. However, since this model allows only one factor to drive interest rates, it has implausible implications for the yield curve that can create problems if the model is used for pricing purposes. This weakness can be ameliorated to some extent by using a model, such as the Longstaff-Schwartz (1992) model, that allows the interest rate to depend on two factors instead of one, but even two-factor models are still excessively restrictive for real-world pricing purposes. Most industry practitioners therefore now use more sophisticated 'no arbitrage' models, of which the best known are those of Heath, Jarrow and Morton (1990a, b, 1992). As the name implies, these models are constructed to rule out arbitrage attack, and are theoretically more attractive and empirically more flexible than earlier models. The HJM model in particular has now become an industry standard, and few if any specialists in interest-rate contingent claims will now work with anything less.

3. QUASI-MONTE CARLO APPROACHES

One of the major drawbacks of conventional MCS is its relative slowness. This slowness arises in large part because the pseudo-random numbers it uses tend to be clustered along their domain interval. This clustering effectively wastes observations, since sets of closely clustered observations convey little more information than single observations around the same points. Ideally, it would therefore be better to place our 'random' observations more evenly, and this notion has since given rise to a number of alternatives to MCS – sometimes known as quasi-Monte Carlo or low-discrepancy techniques – that seek to do just this. These approaches produce 'quasi-random' numbers that fill the domain interval nearly uniformly and thereby avoid the clusters that occur with pseudo-random numbers. Prices or parameters estimated by averaging over such a nearly uniform set should then be more accurate than those estimated by taking averages over more clustered sets of pseudo-random numbers.[12]

A number of studies have produced results indicating that QMC procedures are considerably more accurate than MCS procedures for modelling financial instruments. Boyle, Broadie and Glasserman (1997) obtained such a result for a simple call option, Owen and Tavella (1996) obtained similar results for a simple bond and an interest rate cap, and Brotherton-Ratcliffe (1994), Joy, Boyle and Tan (1995), Paskov and Traub (1995) and Papageorgiou and Traub (1996) found similar results for more exotic positions. The actual gains in accuracy are also very impressive. For example, Boyle, Broadie and Glasserman (1997, p. 1297) found that the best of their QMC procedures was able to improve on the accuracy of a 10 000-observation MCS call option estimate using only 192 observations (i.e., with less than 0.02% of the number of observations of MCS), and Papageorgiou and Traub (1996) found that QMC approaches were a number of times more efficient than MCS with small sample sizes and as much as 1000 times more efficient with very large sample sizes.[13]

More recently, some new QMC-based techniques have been developed that are even more accurate. For example, Moskowitz and Caflisch (1995) show how the performance of QMC techniques can be improved by reducing the effective dimensionality of the problem, and some new QMC techniques have been developed by Niederreiter and Xing (1995) and Tezuka (1994) that appear to be considerably faster than previous QMC procedures. There is also the scrambled nets approach – a kind of randomised QMC procedure – developed by Owen (1995) and Owen and Tavella (1996). This procedure avoids the clustering of observations one gets with MC procedures, but delivers results at least as accurate as QMC. The scrambled nets approach also has the advantage over QMC procedures that it allows for data-based estimation of accuracy (as opposed to the usual resort to order-of-magnitude rules), and Owen and Tavella find that the VaRs estimated using scrambled nets have errors that are less than 0.1% of the estimated VaR. Scrambled nets thus appear to deliver very precise VaR estimates.

4. SCENARIO SIMULATION

Another alternative to MCS is the scenario simulation methodology (SSM) proposed by Jamshidian and Zhu (1996, 1997). The idea behind SSM is that we use the distribution of principal factors to approximate the distribution of the prices or rates that determine the value (and hence the VaR) of our portfolio. In other words, we work with principal factors rather than final derivative prices or rates. Working with principal factors produces gains in efficiency, not just because there are fewer of them to handle, but also because they are by construction independent of each other. A principal-factors-based simulation can then give us results of comparable accuracy to MCS, but for far fewer calculations.

To see how SSM works, suppose we are dealing with a fixed-income portfolio, and we decide that we want to work, say, with three principal components. We then decide how many paths we want for each principal component. Since the first principal component is more important than the second, and the second more important than the third, we would therefore choose more paths for the first, fewer for the second, and even fewer for the third principal component. Jamshidian and Zhu give an example in which they choose seven paths for the first principal component, five for the second, and three for the third. A yield curve scenario is then a combination of paths for each of the three principal components and, since the principal components are independent, there are seven times five times three, or 105, yield curve scenarios in all. Each yield curve scenario also has its own distinct (and easily computable) probability. The PDF of our portfolio can then be inferred from the portfolio values associated with, and probabilities of, each scenario, and the VaR can be inferred from the PDF.

Were we to use MCS to estimate the VaR of this same portfolio, we would have to generate a very large number of yield curve paths, with each yield curve proxied by a number of key factors. We would then have to value our transactions on each path, construct the PDF of final portfolio values, and infer the VaR from that. This MCS approach would typically require a much larger number of calculations, for two reasons. One is that we would be working with a larger number of key factors. For example, if we were dealing with a fixed-income portfolio, we would normally want to deal with at least six to twelve key rates along the yield curve. Each yield curve simulation would then require us to simulate paths for each of these six to twelve or more key rates. The other reason is the familiar one that MCS requires us to carry out a very large number of runs (each run is one yield curve simulation) to get results of sufficient accuracy. The combination of these two factors means that MCS will often require vastly more computations than SSM to produce results of the same accuracy. Moreover, the relative computational efficiency of SSM over MCS also increases very rapidly as the dimensionality of our portfolio increases (e.g., as we move from single-currency fixed-income portfolios to multi-currency ones).[14]

These conjectures are borne out by the results of simulation exercises carried out by Jamshidian and Zhu on a variety of different derivatives portfolios. In a nutshell, these indicate that SSM delivers results of the same accuracy as MCS, but for a very small fraction of the number of calculations that MCS requires.

Besides its superior computational efficiency, SSM also has several other advantages over MCS:

- It is better at handling low-probability events, and therefore at estimating tail parameters such as VaR. Since MCS scenarios all have equal probability, MCS procedures can require very large numbers of runs to produce enough tail observations to give us VaR estimates of adequate accuracy. By contrast, we can design SSM scenarios to give us more tail observations and thereby get more accurate VaR estimates. SSM thus gives us better as well as quicker estimates of VaR.

● The ability of SSM to target tail events also makes it easier to play with tails by conducting 'what if' experiments in which we make certain changes and see how they affect the VaR.[15] This makes SSM very useful for stress-testing purposes. Furthermore, since one type of 'what if' experiment is to make incremental changes to our portfolio, SSM is also better than MCS for estimating incremental VaR.

5. CONCLUSIONS

MCS and related approaches offer powerful and flexible approaches to VaR. They have a number of major advantages over other approaches and, in theory, there is little that they cannot do. Indeed, they not only generate VaR figures, but can also generate other useful statistics as by-products. After all, if a VaR is obtained from a simulated distribution, that same distribution can also generate a variety of other useful statistics as well. Amongst these are VaR figures based on alternative confidence levels, expected tail losses for any given size of tail, and measures of skewness or kurtosis. These approaches also give us some idea of the accuracy of our results, so we can construct confidence intervals or other indicators of the precision of our VaR estimates.

However, the complexity of these procedures inevitably creates problems. These approaches tend to be intensive, both in terms of computing time and in terms of the intellectual/human resources needed to run them. Calculations usually take time, and can be done successfully only if staff have the appropriate expertise and computing resources. The difficulty and opacity of these procedures also make it harder for senior management to keep abreast of what modellers and risk managers are doing.[16]

These are serious drawbacks, but there are nonetheless good reasons to expect these VaR procedures to become much more widely used than they are at present. We have already seen how the more recent techniques can lead to very large increases in computational efficiency over conventional MCS. These new techniques are only now catching on, and they will make simulations much more feasible than they used to be. This theoretical/technical progress is likely to continue and produce even more gains in future computational efficiency. We can also expect further large improvements from the ongoing rapid improvement in the state of information technology, bearing in mind that IT costs have been falling at a rate of some 25–30% a year for decades, and improvements in computing power have been even more rapid.

These improvements, in turn, will help make MCS and related technology more widely available and more user-friendly. At the moment, such systems are still costly to set up from scratch, and they need highly qualified staff to operate them. To some extent, they are therefore still largely the preserve of larger financial institutions that can get a large amount of use out of them. However, this state of affairs is rapidly changing, and institutions are increasingly purchasing simulation expertise from larger institutions or specialist consultants. Such partnerships give the client-firm access to simulation technology for VaR purposes without the set-up and operating costs of having their own in-house simulation units, whilst the wider client base gives the specialists a good return from their investments in simulation capability. More importantly, perhaps, we are also starting to see 'off the shelf' software packages become available that allow complex simulations to be run by smaller financial institutions and corporates with staff who are specialist risk managers rather than experts in simulation per se. These 'expert systems' make simulation technology much more accessible, and will in time make simulation exercises as easy for users to carry out as many of the other 'black box' techniques they already use.

ENDNOTES

1. For more on these techniques, see, e.g., Glasserman (1991), Broadie and Glasserman (1996), or Boyle, Broadie and Glasserman (1997, pp. 1306–9).

2. Of course, if we believed that a price really was described by such a simple process, we could derive the VaR directly without the need to go through an MCS process. I assume this process here merely to illustrate the Monte Carlo procedure with the minimum of mathematical baggage.

3. See, e.g., Jorion (1996, pp. 232–4, 239).

4. The Choleski decomposition procedure is efficient when the matrix Σ^e is positive definite, and more details on the approach and on its application are given in Zangari (1996e). The main alternatives to Choleski decomposition are the eigenvalue decomposition and singular value decomposition approaches, but these are more computationally intensive. However, they have the advantage over the Choleski decomposition approach that they also work when the Σ^e matrix is positive semi-definite, while the Choleski decomposition procedure does not.

5. See Jorion (1996, pp. 236–7).

6. Zangari (1995, p. 101), Jorion (1996, p. 244)

7. Jorion (1996, p. 244)

8. We can also improve the speed of calculations by making the time interval Δt longer, so that there are fewer drawings of Z to take over the period from t to T. However, there are limits to how far we can increase Δt without running into trouble. As Δt increases, the discretised equation (e.g. (5.2)) will provide a less accurate approximation to the 'true' continuous-time process (e.g. (5.1)) and the quality of the approximation will deteriorate. How far we can go also depends on the nature of our position, and we need to be particularly careful with derivatives (e.g. barrier options) in which the pay-off is a non-continuous function of the underlying price.

9. The two classic ones are the control variate approach and the antithetic approach, but a number of new techniques – the moment-matching method, the importance sampling method, and various others – have been developed more recently. These techniques are discussed further in Boyle, Broadie and Glasserman (1997, pp. 1270–90).

10. The idea behind this approach is to simulate not so much a price path as such, but a price path adjusted for the effects of other variables on which the price may depend. These additional variables are constructed to have zero value, so that the value of the adjusted price is equal to the value of the unadjusted one. These variables can then be interpreted as self-financing hedges of the underlying price (which, by the way, the MVR procedure will estimate as an added side benefit). The first might be the delta hedge, the second the gamma hedge, and so on. We can think of these additional variables as mopping up systematic movements in the price, leaving the simulation process to focus on the remaining unsystematic movement which it can then predict more rapidly and/or accurately than standard, unadjusted MCS.

11. See, e.g., Chance (1994) or Jorion (1996, p. 232). The GBM model is widely used for equity prices because it is simple and it accommodates the main stylised features of equity prices, namely, that stock prices are non-negative, random, tend to drift upwards (which we can accommodate by letting μ be positive), and become harder to predict over longer horizons. Chance (1994) has an excellent discussion of the GBM model in this context.

12. For more on these techniques see, e.g., Niederreiter (1992), Boyle, Broadie and Glasserman (1997) or Moro (1995). The basic point to appreciate is that these methods have different convergence properties from MCS. While MCS produces estimates with errors of the order of n^{-1}, QMC

techniques generally produce estimates of the order of $([\log n]^d/n)$, where d is the dimensionality of the problem (see Boyle, Broadie and Glasserman (1997, p. 1293)). This means that QMC clearly dominates MCS if d is low, and MCS procedures should dominate QMC if d is very high. However, for most practical finance applications, d appears to be sufficiently low that the QMC techniques win out.

13. Papageorgiou and Traub also report another advantage of QMC procedures: MCS results were sensitive to the initial 'seed' number, indicating that their results are not as reliable as they purport to be. Quasi-random number approaches are free of this problem because they do not depend on an initial seed number.

14. See, e.g., Jamshidian and Zhu (1997, p. 55).

15. See Jamshidian and Zhu (1997, p. 50).

16. Linsmeier and Pearson (1996, p. 18)

6

Stress Testing

WE now take a break from VaR and turn to consider stress testing, a variety of different procedures that attempt to gauge the vulnerability of our portfolio to hypothetical events. These exercises are useful primarily because they give us an idea of the loss we would suffer in a hypothetical future state of the world. This information can be very useful when we come to make capital allocation, hedging, investment, pricing and other decisions.

I. SCENARIO ANALYSIS

Broadly speaking, there are two main approaches to stress testing. The first of these focuses on the impact of particular specified scenarios – typically a fairly limited number of such scenarios – that we feed into an analytical process. This approach to stress testing is usually known as scenario analysis.[1] Note that scenario analysis only tells us what we stand to lose in a particular state of the world, and does not tell us – and is not designed to tell us – how likely any particular state is to occur. It is therefore a natural complement to VaR approaches that tell us something about the probability of a clearly defined bad event (i.e., a loss in the lower tail of the PDF), but do not as such tell us what we would lose if a tail loss actually occurred.

I.I. Choosing Scenarios

Stress testing begins with a set of hypothetical scenarios, and scenarios can come in various forms: stylised scenarios, actual extreme events and hypothetical one-off events.

I.I.I. Stylised Scenarios

One type of scenario is a stylised scenario: a simulated movement in one or more major interest rates, exchange rates, stock prices or commodity prices. These scenarios can range from relatively moderate changes to quite extreme ones, and the movements considered can be expressed in terms of absolute changes, percentage changes, or standard-deviation units (i.e., the price change divided by the historical standard deviation of the relevant price). For example, the traditional approach to scenario analysis would typically consider a change of 100 basis points in interest rates over the coming month or a sudden adverse exchange-rate movement of something like 30%.[2] Some other scenarios have been suggested by the Derivatives Policy Group (1995), and include parallel yield curve shifts of plus or minus 100 basis points, yield curve shifts of plus or minus 25 basis points, stock index changes of plus or minus 10%, currency changes of plus or minus 6%, and volatility changes of plus or minus 20%. If the institution is concerned about more extreme events (e.g., because it is concerned about gamma risks), it might also want to consider such relatively extreme events as a five- or ten-standard deviation change in the relevant underlying price.

Box 6.1:   Traditional scenario analysis

Sensitivity analysis has been used for a long time in asset-liability management where it is suited to handling portfolios that are exposed to a small number of risk factors. The idea is to imagine hypothetical changes in the value of each risk factor and then use pricing equations (e.g., simple linear equations for straightforward positions, duration or duration-convexity approximations for bonds, or delta or delta-gamma approximations for options) to determine the change in the portfolio value resulting from the market factor change. We might assume that the exchange rate rises by x%, interest rates fall by y%, and so on. Each particular combination of risk factor movements leads to a particular new portfolio value and hence a particular profit or loss. Combined with some assessment of the likelihood of these changes, these computations give a good picture of the risks confronting our portfolio. However, the main limitation of this approach is that it becomes un-manageable when there is more than a small number of risk factors. If there are too many risk factors or too many different scenarios for each factor, then the risk manager can easily end up with thousands of loss figures, each for a different combination of risk factor movements. He or she will then be overwhelmed by a mass of information and have great difficulty getting any overall sense of portfolio risk (Linsmeier and Pearson, 1996, p. 23).

1.1.2.   Actual Extreme Events

We can also choose our scenarios from actual extreme events (e.g., the stock market crash of October 1987, the ERM exchange rate movements in late 1992, or the bond price falls of 1994). The best guide here is to choose scenarios of much the same order of magnitude as the worst-case historical events we are using as our model scenarios. All we really need to do is collect time-series data, identify the biggest fall, and use that fall as the basis of our model scenario. For example, if we were looking at the US equity market we would consider a stock price fall of about 23% or 22 standard deviations, which of course reflects the fall that occurred on 19 October 1987; if we were looking at US bond yields, we would be looking at a fall of about 9.5%, or just over 12 standard deviations, and so forth.[3]

1.1.3.   Hypothetical One-off Events

Scenarios can also come from imagining certain one-off surprises and then thinking through their implications. We might want to examine the consequences of a major earthquake in Tokyo or San Francisco, or of a major terrorist attack on London or New York. Alternatively, we might want to examine the impact of a major bankruptcy or important legal ruling, or of a major political event, such as North Korea launching another attack on South Korea. Some of these hypothetical events are not always that obvious, and the only way to spot them is to try to be aware of what is going on in the world at large. Moreover, it is not enough just to think up a particular initiating event (e.g., a military attack by North Korea); one also has to develop its further potential consequences (e.g., the military response by other powers, and the impact of the event on various exchange rates, interest rates and stock market indices). Each particular combination of events constitutes a distinct scenario, and it does not take much imagination to realise that these scenarios are not only difficult to think through clearly, but can also proliferate at a mind-boggling rate. This last sort of scenario is therefore anything but easy to analyse.

1.2. Evaluating the Effects of Scenario Changes

Having developed each scenario as fully as we can, we then need to consider the effect of each scenario on the prices of all instruments in our portfolio. The key task is to get an idea of the sensitivities of our various positions to the underlying risk factors whose hypothetical changes we are considering. This is very easy for some positions. Thus, a straight FX position changes one for one in value with changes in the exchange rate, and the value of a diversified stock portfolio changes (roughly) one for one with changes in the stock market index. Many other positions also change one for one (or thereabouts) with changes in the underlying market risk factor. Some other positions have less straightforward sensitivities, but we can usually handle them by using approximations. For example, we could obtain the approximate sensitivities of option prices to changes in underlying risk factors from estimates of their deltas, gammas, vegas and other risk parameters, all of which should be readily available; and where bonds are concerned, we can proxy their sensitivities to changes in market interest rates by taking duration or duration-convexity approximations.

Once we have determined the effect of each scenario on all relevant prices, we can infer the effect of each scenario on the portfolio value as a whole. The portfolio loss is then found by subtracting the portfolio's existing value from its post-scenario value.

In evaluating the effects of scenarios on our portfolio, we should also consider the impact of our hypothesised events on the markets in which we operate. In particular, it is very unwise to assume that markets will continue to function 'normally' when subjected to extreme stress. For example, under normal stock market conditions we could expect to see sell orders executed within a matter of minutes; yet, on 19 October 1987, stock markets were so overwhelmed that it could take hours to get orders executed. Sell orders either expired because of time or price limits, or were executed at much lower prices than the sellers had expected. Market liquidity dried up just when sellers were most dependent on it. Firms whose risk management strategies are based on dynamic hedging or an assumed ability to rebalance portfolios quickly should therefore pay considerable attention to the impact of extreme events on market liquidity.[4] In addition, we also have to watch out that volatility and correlation assumptions that may appear reasonable in 'normal' times don't break down when markets are stressed and leave us with much bigger exposures than we thought we would have.

Companies that use futures contracts to hedge illiquid positions should also take into account the funding implications of their hedge positions. Gains or losses in futures positions must be settled on a daily basis, while changes in other positions (e.g. forward ones) will not be settled until the position is finally closed out. Hence, even otherwise well designed hedges can lead to mismatches between the timing of receipts and the timing of the payments that theoretically cover them.[5] If the hedges are large, these interim funding requirements can also be large. Indeed, it was the failure to consider just this point that brought the German industrial giant Metallgesellschaft to its knees in 1993–94.[6]

1.3. Benefits of Scenario Analysis

Scenario analysis is ideal for showing up the vulnerability of our portfolio (and of our VaR calculations) to a variety of otherwise hidden risks. In the words of the President of the New York Fed, William McDonough, 'One of the most important functions of stress testing is to identify hidden vulnerabilities, often the result of hidden assumptions, and make clear to trading managers and senior management the consequences of being wrong in their assumptions'.[7]

A case in point is the danger of a large market move. We might have an options position that is hedged against a small market move, but very exposed to a large one. Given the leverage involved in options positions, a firm that delta hedges could therefore be covered against a very small market move and destroyed by a very large one, and the only way to detect this sort of exposure is to run scenario analyses based on very large hypothesised market moves (e.g., moves of five to ten standard deviations, or more). Similarly, we would also use scenario analyses to examine some of the other potential consequences of a large market move. These include the consequences of a possible drying up of market liquidity, or the possible funding consequences if positive-value derivatives positions suddenly become major liabilities and force us to put up collateral or meet margin calls.

Scenario analysis is also good for examining the consequences of a change in volatility. Estimates of volatility based on historical data can be unreliable, and reliance on them can, on occasion, lead to much bigger losses than we might have expected. For example, prior to the ERM crisis of September 1992, any historically based estimate of the risk (or VaR) of a pound-denominated portfolio would have indicated relatively little risk from changes in the pound-DM exchange rate. The exchange rate had been stable for a considerable time, and so no historical approach would have had any reason to indicate major exchange rate risk. The exchange rate then changed very abruptly and anyone who had relied on historical indicators of risk and been on the wrong side of the market would have taken major losses. Yet this vulnerability could easily have been picked up by a simple stress test. Similarly, stress tests would have also shown equity market investors what they stood to lose in 1987 or shown investors in US bond markets what they stood to lose in 1994.[8]

Scenario analyses are also good for highlighting our potential dependence on particular correlation as well as volatility assumptions. Since the risk associated with any portfolio depends on the expected correlations of the various positions included in it, a major change in correlation could leave our portfolio much more exposed than we thought it was going to be. Moreover, historical correlations can be very volatile and, when correlations change suddenly, it is sometimes during crises such as market crashes.[9] If we wish to survive such events, it is therefore important that we not only examine our exposure to large market moves, but also examine what we stand to lose if normal correlations break down and markets all move against us.

Scenario analyses can also be very useful for highlighting other weaknesses in our risk management set-up. The process of actually going through a stress-testing exercise should also force risk managers and senior managers to think through the ramifications of bad scenarios as well as help them to pinpoint weaknesses that they have under-estimated or overlooked. If it is done well, it should not only give some indication of where the institution is vulnerable, but also show up flaws in contingency planning. Indeed, what risk managers learn about these hidden weaknesses is often as valuable for risk management purposes as the loss figures that the exercise finally produces.[10]

1.4. Problems with Scenario Analysis

Perhaps the most noticeable problem with scenario analysis is that it is totally dependent on the chosen scenarios and, hence, on the judgement and experience of the people who carry out the stress tests. This is a serious drawback because, as we all know, the negative events that we want to guard against can often be very hard to predict. Choosing the 'right' scenarios is therefore an important, but sometimes very difficult, task. There have been many cases in the last few years of large companies being severely embarrassed or bankrupted by events that their management did not see coming (and, in some cases, by events that they clearly *should* have seen coming). When portfolios are complex, it can also be very difficult to identify the risk factors to look at. As Litterman (1996, p. 59) says, 'in complex portfolios...it may be virtually impossible to know which among many risk factors need to be considered'. And, even when risk factors are identified, how bad risks look also depends on the perspective we adopt – the direction of our view and how far back we stand – and there is no uniquely best perspective to take. The usefulness of scenario analyses consequently boils down to the skill, good sense and intuition of those who carry out the stress tests. In the final analysis, this is why good risk management is still as much craft as science.

The other glaring problem with scenario analysis is the sheer difficulty of working through scenarios in a consistent, sensible way, *without* being overwhelmed by a mass of different possibilities. There are three main issues here:

- We need to be able to follow through scenarios, and the consequences of some scenarios can be very complex. For example, if the Italian lira were allowed to float, 'one could surmise that...short-term rates could likewise drop and the stock market rally. Beyond the effect on Italian interest rates and equity prices, it is not easy to come up with plausible scenarios for other financial variables. Thus, stress testing is not well-suited to large, complex portfolios' (Jorion, 1996, p. 198). We therefore face an awkward choice. We could just ignore some of the secondary effects and assume that the devaluation affects only interest rates and the stock market index, and nothing else.

This is the simplest option and makes scenario analysis straightforward, but we also know very well that there will be other effects, so a scenario that ignores them will occur with zero probability. Alternatively, we can just guess the follow-on effects, but then we have to guess from a vast number of possibilities with little to tell us how to choose among them, and it becomes very difficult to avoid being knocked senseless by a plethora of possibilities that make the whole exercise effectively meaningless.

- In working through scenarios, we will often (though not necessarily always) also want to take account of the interactions of different risks. While it is sometimes very useful to carry out scenario analyses in which all correlations are assumed to move in the most damaging ways, the fact is that we will not always want to make such assumptions and will often want to take account of the interrelationships between different variables. Our scenario analysis might indicate that the maximum loss could occur when one price rises and the other falls, and yet the prices of the two assets might be very strongly correlated. The scenario analysis then ignores the likelihood that the two prices are likely to move up or down together, and may produce a loss estimate much higher than any loss that could plausibly occur.[11] In using scenario analysis, we must therefore decide when and, if so, how, to allow for correlations.

- In designing our scenarios, we must also recognise that there are often situations where prices cannot move independently of each other because doing so would violate a zero-arbitrage condition. To carry out scenario analysis sensibly, we need to eliminate all co-movements that are inconsistent with zero arbitrage.

One other objection sometimes made to scenario analysis is that it doesn't give us any indication of the likelihood of different scenarios actually occurring. The claim is perfectly correct, but as an objection to scenario analysis it is somewhat misplaced. The fact is that scenario analyses are not *designed* to tell us how likely particular scenarios are. Instead, their purpose is to provide a different indication of vulnerability: to tell us what would happen *if* a particular event or scenario actually occurred. We should not criticise scenario analysis for not doing what it is not designed to do.

2. MECHANICAL APPROACHES TO STRESS TESTING

The other main approaches to stress testing are more mechanical approaches that go through a number – typically, a very large number – of different possibilities to determine the most damaging combinations of events and the losses they would produce. These approaches differ from scenario analysis in that they emphasise a range of possibilities rather than particular specified scenarios as such. They can therefore be more thorough than scenario analysis in the range of possibilities considered, but are also computationally more intensive. Some mechanical stress-testing procedures also differ from scenario analysis in that they are able to give some (albeit sometimes rather vague) indication of the likelihood of different outcomes occurring, and this information can obviously be useful when trying to decide how seriously to take particular outcomes.

2.1. Factor Push Analysis

The simplest of these procedures is factor push analysis, the idea of which is to 'push' the price of each individual security (or, if we use mapping procedures, the relevant underlying risk factor) in the most disadvantageous direction and work out the combined effect of all such changes on the value of the portfolio.[12] We have already met this type of approach in Chapter 3 in the shape of Wilson's delta-gamma approach to VaR. We start by specifying a level of confidence, which gives us a confidence level parameter α. We then consider each price on its own, 'push' it by α times its standard deviation and select that price movement (i.e., up or down) that has the worst effect on the portfolio value. Collecting these worst price movements for each instrument in our portfolio gives us our worst-case scenario, and the maximum loss is equal to the current value of our portfolio minus the portfolio value under this worst-case scenario.

Factor push analysis has a number of attractions. (1) It is relatively easy to program computers to carry it out, at least for simple positions. (2) It identifies the worst-case outcome from the range of possibilities put into it, which can be very useful in showing up where and how we are most vulnerable. (3) It is not restricted to some of the assumptions that tie down, say, some VaR approaches (e.g., we are not restricted to linear normal portfolios). (4) We can plug whatever correlations we like into the model to see what impact they have on our maximum loss. For example, Page and Costa (1996) developed a very quick algorithm that allows us to estimate maximum loss figures for a multi-position portfolio, based on whatever correlation assumptions we care to make. (5) If we are prepared to make certain assumptions, we can also say something useful about likelihood, and hence, make the jump from maximum loss to VaR. For instance, if we just had a single normally distributed random variable, then the α-parameter by which we push our risk factor immediately gives us the probability of the relevant tail event occurring, as well as the tail event itself. If there is more than one risk factor then our α-parameters are those of the relevant multivariate rather than univariate normal distribution, but we can still infer the probability of maximum loss and, hence, the VaR, provided we have some means of handling any correlations between risk factors.[13]

However, FP analysis also has its difficulties. One complication is the need to take account of the differing sensitivities of different prices to different underlying risk factors. Pushing all prices by the same multiple of their standard deviation, say, ignores the sensitivity of each position to the underlying risk factor.[14] For example, an option that is deeply out of the money will be very insensitive to any change in the underlying price, particularly if it is close to expiry, but an option that is deeply in the money could be very sensitive to it. Consequently, it does not make much sense to push all prices by the same number of standard deviations, when the probability of such a change varies, possibly very considerably, from one position to another. The solution is not to push the individual prices by any particular multiple, but to push the underlying risk factors instead.[15] However, this requires that we work with appropriate delta, delta-gamma or other approximations.[16]

A second problem is that FP rests on the not always appropriate assumption that the maximum loss occurs at extreme values of the underlying risk variables (i.e., it assumes that the maximum loss occurs when the price moves up or down by α times its standard deviation). However, this assumption is appropriate only for certain relatively simple types of portfolio (e.g., uncomplicated equity, fixed-income or FX positions), but there are many other positions for which this assumption does not hold. A particularly good example is a long straddle – a combination of a long call and a long put written against the same underlying asset. The profit on a straddle depends on movements in the underlying variable, either up or down – the greater the movement, the bigger the profit – and the maximum loss on a straddle actually occurs when the underlying price does not move at all. A factor push methodology applied to a straddle position would then give a very misleading picture of maximum loss, since it would assume that the maximum loss occurred in exactly those circumstances where it would in fact make its maximum profit!

2.2. Maximum Loss Optimisation

The solution to this latter problem is to search over the losses that occur for intermediate values as well as extreme values of the risk variables.[17] This procedure is known as maximum loss optimisation.[18] Maximum loss optimisation is essentially the same as factor push analysis, except for the fact that it also searches over intermediate values of the risk variables. There are therefore more computations involved, and MLO will take longer if there are many risk factors involved and a lot of intermediate values to search over. The choice between FP and MLO therefore depends on pay-off characteristics of our portfolio. If the portfolio is made up of straightforward positions, each of which takes its maximum loss at extreme values of the underlying risk factors, then FP and MLO will deliver exactly the same results and we may as well use the computationally simpler FP approach. However, if the portfolio has fewer straightforward pay-off characteristics (as with many options positions), then it may make sense to use MLO.[19] As a general rule, if the portfolio is complex or has significant non-linear derivatives positions, it is best to play safe and go for MLO.[20]

2.3. Worst-case Scenario Analysis

While factor push analysis and MLO deal with bad scenarios that *may* occur, we can also examine the worst case that we actually *expect to* occur. This is the idea behind the worst-case scenario analysis of Boudoukh, Richardson and Whitelaw (1995). Imagine we are concerned about losses over a particular horizon period (e.g. ten days) and expect to realise some profit or loss over each sub-period (e.g. each day). The worst-case scenario is the loss associated with the most adverse daily outcome. If each daily outcome is a random variable Z_i and there are n sub-periods in our horizon, then the worst-case scenario is

$$Min[Z_1, Z_2, \ldots, Z_n] \tag{6.1}$$

We can now estimate the actual worst-case scenario by running simulations of the random Z variables. BRW produce tables comparing the VaR, the expected WCS and the lower percentiles of the distribution of the WCS. If we take a horizon of 100 sub-periods (i.e., $n = 100$) and a confidence level of 99%, then the VaR is 2.33, the expected WCS is -2.51, and the lowest percentile of the WCS distribution is -3.72. The lowest percentile of the WCS distribution is thus (minus) 160% of the VaR.

If an institution uses VaR to determine its capital, it will have enough capital to avoid distress – a loss exceeding VaR – in 99% of cases, and it will face distress in the other 1% of cases. However, the management might want to be more conservative and have a capital level that can withstand the worst-case scenario loss without distressing the institution. In that case it would want a level of capital that could withstand losses up to the lowest percentile of bad scenarios. In the context of the example above, this criterion would then imply a capital level of 3.72, which is 160% of VaR. WCSA thus gives us a more prudent approach to capital requirements than VaR analysis.

3. CONCLUSIONS

Stress tests have three main uses. (1) They are ideal complements to VaR exercises. While VaR approaches tell us what we might lose with a certain maximum probability, stress tests give us an idea of what we stand to lose if a worst-case event actually occurs. The two approaches – VaR and stress tests – are therefore natural complements to each other. (2) Stress tests can highlight weaknesses (such as awkward assumptions or failures in contingency plans) in our risk management procedures. If we don't engage in stress tests, it is only a matter of time before we become seriously unstuck by something or other: we will delta hedge, say, and take a big negative gamma hit when the underlying price crashes, or correlations will alter suddenly and leave us much more exposed than we thought we would be. Stress testing is therefore essential for sound risk management. (3) The information provided by stress tests can be very useful in determining capital allocation within an institution, and we shall have more to say on this issue in Chapter 11.

ENDNOTES

1. There is a certain amount of terminological ambiguity in the literature, and not all writers use the same terms in the same way. To avoid any confusion on this issue, the term 'stress testing' is used here to apply to any procedures that attempt to evaluate the impact on us of hypothetical future events. The term 'scenario analysis' is used to apply to that type of stress testing that focuses on particular specified scenarios, as distinct from the second type of stress testing (to be discussed shortly) that specifies classes of mathematical or statistical possibilities and then cranks through these possibilities in a mechanical way.
2. Jorion (1996, p. 196)
3. The figures come from S. Allen (1996, p. 12), who also gives a number of comparable figures for other market rates. There are two striking features about these sorts of figures. (1) The maximum price falls vary enormously from one market to another, and could hardly be predicted in advance. (2) The maximum price falls are often very much bigger than the next biggest fall. Take out the last quarter of 1987, for example, and the maximum fall in the US stock market is only 7% or seven standard deviations. These features therefore strongly suggest that we should not rely too much on historic movements alone to provide our scenarios.
4. Linsmeier and Pearson (1996, p. 21)
5. Linsmeier and Pearson (1996, p. 21)
6. The problem with Metallgesellschaft was that a US subsidiary, MG Refining and Manufacturing, had written long-term forward fuel contracts, which it hedged by buying oil futures contracts and rolling them over. However, the oil price then fell and MGRM was hit by major margin losses on its futures positions which it had difficulty meeting. In the end, the German parent company

intervened to liquidate the futures contracts and the company ended up losing about $1.3 billion. For more on this episode, see, e.g., Chew (1996, pp. 119–26).

7. Quoted in Chew (1994, p. 70).

8. Historical volatilities can themselves be fairly volatile. Mori, Ohsawa and Shimizu (1996a, chart 2) present some charts of the volatilities of major US and Japanese market rates over the first quarters of 1994 and 1995, and several of these are very volatile. For example, the daily volatility of the Nikkei 225 in early 1995 varies from just over 0.6% to 1.8%, and there were five occasions in this quarter on which the volatility jumped suddenly, in one case from under 0.7% to 1.2%.

9. Correlations can also be very volatile. For example, in the first quarter of 1993, the average correlation between the Nikkei 225 and the FT-SE 100 stock market indices varied from $+0.9$ to -0.9 (Jackson, 1996, p. 181). Similarly, over the first quarter of 1995, correlations between the Nikkei 225 and the US$/yen exchange rate varied from less than -0.4 to about $+0.7$ (Mori, Ohsawa and Shimizu, 1996a, chart 3). Moreover, the evidence also indicates that correlations can jump very suddenly, and not just when there is a major market crash.

10. In order to make the best use of stress tests, a good practice is to specify a threshold beyond which the loss would be regarded as a serious problem. This threshold would be set in terms of the institution's capital or in terms of the capital allocated to the business unit concerned. If a stress test threw up a loss that exceeded this threshold, the institution would respond with a formal review to examine the circumstances under which a very high loss could occur. This process would look closely at the co-movements leading to the loss and assess how likely the outcome is. An informed decision can then be made as to whether and, if so, how, to cover the risk.

11. See, e.g., Wilson (1996, p. 226).

12. For more on this approach, see, e.g., Frye (1996), Meegan (1995, pp. 25–6), Rouvinez (1997, pp. 60–62), Studer (1995) or Wilson (1996, pp. 224–7).

13. There are three ways we can do this. (1) We can estimate probabilities and VaRs conditional on particular estimates of or assumptions about correlations between risk factors. (2) We can ignore correlations and regard our maximum loss figures as upper bound estimates of VaR (e.g., as in Page and Costa (1996)). (3) If we work from principal components, these will be independent of each other and therefore have zero correlations, and we can then infer the maximum-loss probabilities and VaRs easily, as in (1) above. This is the approach adopted by Frye (1996) and Studer and Lüthi (1996). Note also that once we make the jump from maximum loss to VaR, our factor push analysis becomes effectively indistinguishable from the scenario simulation analysis (i.e., à la Jamshidian and Zhu) discussed in the last chapter.

14. Wilson (1996, pp. 225–6)

15. Frye (1996) uses just such a procedure. However, there are a number of further issues involved in this type of approach and the reader is referred to Frye's article for further details.

16. Of course, to do factor push analysis properly, we should also take account of relevant constraints, such as zero-arbitrage conditions. As explained in the text, we might also want to push the risk factors rather than individual instrument prices, and also want to work with mapped positions, delta-gamma approximations and so on. None of these modifications alters the basic nature of factor push analysis. For more on factor push, see, e.g., Frain and Meegan (1996), Lawrence (1996, p. 178) or Wilson (1996, pp. 224–7).

17. There is also good reason to believe that this is a serious problem in practice. As Beder recently observed:

> In our experience, portfolios do not necessarily produce their greatest losses during extreme market moves…portfolios often possess Achilles' heels that require only small moves or changes between instruments or markets to produce significant losses. Stress testing extreme market moves will do little to reveal the greatest risk of loss for such portfolios. Furthermore, a review of a portfolio's expected behavior over time often reveals that the same stress test that indicates a small impact today indicates embedded land mines with a large impact during future periods. This trait is particularly true of options-based portfolios that change characteristics because of time rather than because of changes in the components of the portfolio. (Beder, 1995, p. 18)

18. For more on maximum loss optimisation, and on the difference between it and factor push analysis, see Frain and Meegan (1996, pp. 16–18). Many writers use the two terms synonymously,

but Frain and Meegan are quite right to distinguish explicitly between them. I have therefore adopted their terminology which uses the term 'factor push' to refer to those procedures that assume that the maximum loss occurs only when risk factors take their extreme values, and 'maximum loss optimisation' to refer to those procedures that allow for maximum loss to occur when risk factors take intermediate values.

19. See Frain and Meegan (1996, pp. 16–18).

20. Such procedures can also pick up interactions between different risks that we might otherwise have overlooked. This can be very useful, particularly for more complex portfolios whose risks might interact in unexpected ways that portfolio managers might not otherwise be aware of.

FIRST APPENDIX TO CHAPTER 6: THE EXTREME VALUE APPROACH

A final, quite different, approach to VaR is the extreme value (EV) approach.[A1] This approach starts from the premise that it is the extreme values of the profit/loss distribution that we are mostly concerned about, and then uses the statistical theory of extreme values to determine maximum extreme losses with a determined degree of confidence.

In practice we do not know the distribution of extreme values, but the key insight of EV theory is that this distribution converges in large samples to a limiting distribution of a particular known form. An analytic solution for the VaR can then be found from this distribution once we specify our desired confidence level. For example, Daníelsson and de Vries (1997, appendix A) show that for most heavy tailed data, the large sample distribution of the tail return x is:

$$F(x) \approx 1 - ax^{-\alpha}[1 + bx^{-\beta}], \quad \alpha, \beta > 0 \tag{6A.1}$$

for given parameters a, b, α and β. The important parameter is α, which is usually known as the tail index and gives the thickness of the tails (e.g., for a t distribution, α is the number of degrees of freedom). We now choose a threshold index M which determines where our tail begins. We can think of this index as the number of observations in the tails. X_{M+1} then determines where the tail begins, and we estimate our tail using values of x bigger than X_{M+1}. Daníelsson and de Vries (1997) now show that we can estimate the probability p of a tail event by:

$$\hat{F}(x) = p = (M/T)(X_{M+1}/x)^{\hat{\alpha}}, \quad x > X_{M+1} \tag{6A.2}$$

where T is the number of observations and $\hat{\alpha}$ is our estimate of α. The tail itself is obtained by inverting this expression to yield:

$$\hat{x} = \hat{F}^{-1}(x) = X_{M+1}(M/Tp)^{1/\hat{\alpha}} \tag{6A.3}$$

To estimate the tail (i.e., the VaR), we need the values of X_{M+1}, M, T, p and $\hat{\alpha}$, and we already have all of these except $\hat{\alpha}$. All that remains therefore is to estimate $\hat{\alpha}$ (and there are a number of ways we can do so)[A2] and plug this estimate and the other necessary data into (6A.3).

The EV approach improves on both variance-covariance and HS approaches to VaR:[A3]

- It improves on VC procedures in so far as these procedures make use of volatility estimation techniques (such as GARCH) that are good for common events, but poor for tail ones.

- It improves on HS in that it gives more reliable estimates of VaR, bearing in mind that lack of data makes it difficult for HS to estimate tails accurately. It also improves on HS in so far as it allows easier sensitivity analysis, and avoids (or at least mitigates) some of the awkward consequences for HS of having unusual events (e.g. stock market crashes) in our historical sample.

Danielsson and de Vries (1997, Table 8) present some empirical evidence on the relative performance of the RiskMetrics approach (which is, as we have seen, a particular version of the more general VC approach), HS, and their own EV approach. They find that the RiskMetrics approach is good for estimating VaR at the 5% level, but increasingly underpredicts the occurrence of tail events (and, by implication, underpredicts VaR) as the tails become more extreme. The HS approach tends to overpredict the occurrence of tail events, and the underprediction gets worse as tails become more extreme. The EV approach, by contrast, performs well overall, and is especially good at handling tails.[A4]

The EV approach has various attractions. (1) It deals directly with the extreme values, which is what we are particularly concerned about. (2) It provides a firm methodological basis for the estimation of VaR. (3) It does not impose any particular form on the underlying return distribution, but instead allows this distribution to take any well-behaved form, including an asymmetric (i.e., skewed) one. (4) It produces a simple analytical formula for VaR. (5) The approach is robust, flexible and easy to use.

Endnotes

A1.   This approach was developed in various papers by Longin (1994), Bassi, Embrechts and Kafetzaki (undated), Embrechts, Klüppelberg and Mikosch (1997), and Danielsson and de Vries (1996, 1997). Strictly speaking, Longin deals not with VaR explicitly, but with the superficially different but essentially similar problem of how futures clearing houses should determine their margin requirements. In both cases, the relevant problem boils down to how much the relevant party (the institutional risk manager/supervisor on the one hand, or the clearing house on the other) should allow for occasional extreme losses. Longin's margin requirements are therefore essentially the same as our VaR.

A2.   See, e.g., Danielsson and de Vries (1997) for more on these estimation procedures.

A3.   See, e.g., Danielsson and de Vries (1997, pp. 10–15).

A4.   The results of Longin (1994) also suggest that the EV approach predicts much larger VaRs than a normal or VC approach. The explanation is a familiar one: once again, normal-based VaR is undermined by the thickness (i.e., non-normality) of the tails.

SECOND APPENDIX TO CHAPTER 6: DIFFERENT APPROACHES COMPARED

Attractions and Limitations of Main Approaches to Measuring VaR

Approach	Attractions	Limitations
Variance–covariance approaches	Intuitive. Easy formula for VaR. Tractable. Informativeness of normal VaR. Easy to handle incremental VaR. Ideal for linear positions in normal risk factors. Because of central limit theorem, applies if risks are not normal, provided they are numerous and independent. Can handle 'small' departures from normal linearity by delta-gamma, normal mixture and GED approaches.	Dependence on normality assumption, and evidence that returns are not normal (fat tails, etc.). Can be very misleading if returns are not normal – VaR underestimated, etc. Not suited to handling optionality or non-linearity. Possible problems ensuring variance-covariance matrix is well behaved. Need to map. Delta-gamma approaches difficult to implement and not necessarily much better than delta-normal. Problems with extreme events.
Historical simulation	Very intuitive and easy to explain. Non-parametric – not dependent on normality. Straightforward to implement – no need for correlations, volatilities, etc. Applies to almost any type of position. Little or no exposure to model risk. Full valuation. Not (usually) necessary to map. Yields other useful statistics as by-products. Some empirical evidence that it works at least as well as normal VaR.	Possible problems obtaining data (e.g., for emerging markets). Complete dependence on particular data set: risks not represented in data set are completely ignored. Problems with length of estimation period: results unreliable if too short; results insensitive to news if too long. Potentially unreliable, especially in the face of structural changes.
Monte Carlo simulation and quasi-MC approaches	Extremely powerful and flexible: can handle virtually any position. No problem with non-linearity, non-normality, etc. Ideal for complex and exotic positions.	Unintuitive, opaque and hard to explain. Computer-time intensive, but can be speeded up by using grid or delta-gamma approximations, variance-reducing or quasi-random-number techniques. Requires considerable human and financial investments.

Attractions and Limitations (cont.)

Approach	Attractions	Limitations
	Yield other useful statistics as by-products. Can be simplified to speed up calculations. Speed and efficiency of MCS and related procedures rapidly improving.	Dependence of results on specified models and stochastic processes.
Stress testing	Can handle any specified scenario. Excellent for handling extreme events. Ideal for 'what if' experiments. Highlights hidden vulnerabilities (e.g., to changes in volatilities or correlations). Process of carrying out stress testing very useful for risk management and contingency planning. Excellent complement to proper VaR approaches.	Scenarios can be difficult to identify. Only as good as specified scenarios – garbage in, garbage out. Analysis sometimes difficult to carry out.
Extreme value approach	Deals directly with the extreme values. Provides firm methodological basis for VaR estimation. Allows return distribution to take any well-behaved form. Produces a simple analytical formula for VaR. Robust and easy to use.	

Summary of Evidence on Main Approaches to Measuring VaR

Study	Description	Major findings
Allen (1994)	Compared HS and normal approaches to VaR, using various equity and FX portfolios.	Circumstantial evidence that HS estimates better than normal ones.
Beder (1995)	Applies eight common VaR methodologies to three hypothetical portfolios to estimate their VaRs.	Results showed very large variations in VaRs estimated for the same portfolio, with smallest and greatest VaRs varying by a factor of 14. Results indicate VaR's 'extreme dependence on parameters, data, assumptions, and methodology'.
Butler and Schachter (1996)	Compared normal, bootstrapped and historical-kernel approaches to VaR at 95% confidence level, using data on 12 real trading positions.	VaR estimates closely correlated, although differences between VaR estimates are not necessarily negligible. The normal model generates more stable and generally lower estimated standard errors than the other two. However, also suggests that the normal model may give misleading impression of VaR accuracy. Evidence of skewness indicates that VaR estimates may be less accurate than their estimated standard errors might suggest.
Crnkovic-Drachman (1995)	Compared normal and HS approaches to VaR for stock index portfolios, using Crnkovic-Drachman procedure.	HS approach generally better than normal VaR approaches.
Danielsson and De Vries (1997)	Compares RiskMetrics, HS and EV approaches.	Risk Metrics approach good for low-confidence-level VaR but increasingly underpredicts losses as tails become more extreme. HS approach overpredicts tails, and overpredicts more as tails become more extreme. EV approach good overall, and particularly good as tails become more extreme.
Estrella et al. (1994)	Examines delta and delta-gamma approaches to estimating the VaR of a variety of options positions.	Finds that delta-gamma adjustment leads to significantly better VaR estimates.

Summary of Evidence (cont.)

Study	Description	Major findings
Fallon (1996)	Compares various delta-normal and delta-gamma approaches using hypothetical equity option portfolios.	Delta-normal approaches perform very poorly. Delta-gamma approaches perform significantly better, but even they sometimes perform poorly.
Frye (1996)	Assesses his own 'factor-based scenario' (i.e., factor-push) procedure on a sample of randomly generated portfolios, including portfolios with options.	Finds that his procedure is usually conservative (i.e., overstates risk) at 99th percentile.
Hendricks (1996)	Compares 12 HS and variance-covariance approaches, based on varying assumptions about volatility and the length of period used to estimate VaR.	Some evidence that HS approaches might be better than VC ones, although no one single model dominates the rest. Choice of confidence level – 95% or 99% – can make a substantial difference to relative model performance. All the models produced accurate VaR estimates at the 95% percentile, but VaR estimates at the 99% percentile were less accurate and generally too low – on average, something over 10% too low. Different approaches produce substantial discrepancies in VaR: differences of 30–50% in estimated daily VaR not uncommon. Average tail losses tended to be higher – sometimes considerably higher – than the tail losses we would expect under normality (i.e., evidence of fat tails).
Jackson, Maude and Perraudin (1997)	Uses data on actual trading book of a large bank, with interest rate and FX exposures. Comparisons made on three real portfolios at different dates, plus one hypothetical portfolio. VaRs have confidence level of 99%. Historical data periods vary from 3 to 24 months.	HS forecasts of VaR generally superior to normal ones. Superiority of HS forecasts particularly apparent in forecasting tail probabilities, as normal approaches suffered from fat tails. HS approach also slightly better at coping with unexpected 'spike' losses. Superior volatility forecasting techniques lead to economically insubstantial improvements in the ability of normal approaches to forecast VaR. Substantial biases when short data sets are used: long data sets recommended.

Jamshidian and Zhu (1996)	Compares delta-normal approach, delta-gamma approach using market estimates of delta and gamma, and full scenario simulation approach, for three derivatives positions.	Delta-normal approach performs poorly in presence of gamma risk. Both delta-gamma approach and scenario simulation approaches handle gamma risk well. Approximation error in delta-gamma approach about 2%.
Jamshidian and Zhu (1997)	Compares MCS and scenario simulation approaches on a variety of swap positions.	Both approaches give very similar results, but SS approach is much faster.
Longin (1994)	Compares normal and EV approaches to estimation of VaR (or, strictly speaking, clearing-house margin requirements).	Normal approach leads to considerably lower VaR than EV approach.
Mahoney (1996)	Compares HS and normal approaches using various FX and equity index positions. Focuses on ability to forecast VaR and on size of measurement error problem that arises when same data set is used to construct hedges and estimate VaR. Deals with VaR confidence levels varying from 90% to 99.9%.	The HS approach using a long data period yields unbiased VaR estimates at various confidence levels. Parametric approaches work well for confidence levels below 95%, but understate frequency of large extreme losses (i.e., fat tails). If a portfolio is the result of intentional hedging activity, simple VaR calculations may understate true VaR due to measurement error problem, and this error is particularly acute for short sample periods. HS approaches therefore apparently better than VC approaches.
Mori, Ohsawa and Shimizu (1996a)	Examines performance of variance-covariance VaR estimation procedures given alternative treatments of volatility and correlation, using hypothetical portfolio and real data.	Finds that VC procedures with historical volatility/correlation estimates give excess losses considerably more frequently than they should. VC procedures with no allowance for historical correlation give results more consistent with VaR confidence level, but also give considerably higher VaR estimates. Implication is that usual VC procedure with historical correlation does not work well.
Mori, Ohsawa and Shimizu (1996b)	Compares HS, MCS and VC procedures using hypothetical portfolios and real (mainly Japanese) data.	VC procedure leads to losses in excess of VaR that are considerably more frequent than they should be. HS and (some) MCS procedures lead to excess losses of about right frequency. Evidence of excess kurtosis.

Summary of Evidence (cont.)

Study	Description	Major findings
Pritsker (1996)	Focuses on trade-off between accuracy and computational time for hypothetical options positions. Compares six different approaches: delta-normal, delta-gamma-normal, Wilson's delta-gamma, delta-gamma MC, modified grid MC, and full MC.	MC approaches most accurate, but also most computer-time-intensive. Of these, full MC most accurate and most intensive. Delta-gamma MC and modified grid MC of comparable accuracy, but delta-gamma MC much faster. Delta-gamma-normal and delta-gamma-normal next most accurate, but also faster (and delta-normal very much faster) than MC approaches. Wilson's delta-gamma approach slower and less accurate than delta-gamma-normal and delta-normal. Hence, dominated. Given real-world time constraints, Pritsker suggests that delta-gamma MC is best, but even that can produce substantial errors.
Rouvinez (1997)	Compares different methods for estimating the VaRs of portfolios with option positions	Finds delta-gamma methods much better than delta-normal ones. Not easy to rank alternative delta-gamma procedures because their accuracy is portfolio-dependent. Wilson approach good for small number of risk factors, but accuracy falls as number of risk factors increases.
Venkataraman (1997)	Examines normal and normal mixture approaches using various FX portfolios.	Normal approach leads to significantly more excess losses than consistent with confidence level on which VaR is based. Normal mixture approaches produce excess losses consistent with VaR confidence level. Normal mixture approaches therefore clearly superior to normal ones.
Zangari (1996c, e)	Assess the relative performance of the standard-normal, normal mixture and GED approaches in forecasting VaR percentiles. Apply each to a sample of 15 FX and equity time series from nine emerging market countries. Examine both fifth and first percentiles.	Results suggest that all three procedures performed reasonably well at the 5% level. Normal mixture and GED procedures do considerably better than standard normal procedure at the 1% level, but even they still underestimate VaR by a sizeable amount.

PART THREE

Risk Management

7

Risk-Adjusting Returns and Evaluating Performance

THIS chapter deals with the problem of how to adjust returns to allow for risk. This problem has two aspects.

- The first is adjustment before we take on the relevant risk, the typical case being that of investment managers choosing between alternative risky investment opportunities. How do we choose between investment A, which has a high expected return but is also a high risk, and investment B, which has a low expected return but is relatively safe? We can answer this question only if we have some means of adjusting expected returns for risk.
- The second side of the problem is that of evaluating *actual* investment performance *after* the event, when decisions have already been made and the results of those decisions are apparent. We may need to compare trader A, say, who made a high profit but took a lot of risks, with trader B, who made a low profit but took few risks. Besides evaluating individual traders or asset managers, we might also wish to evaluate the performance of a particular individual investment or a portfolio of investments, such as those made by a particular business unit.

To distinguish between these two aspects of risk adjustment, we normally use the term risk adjustment to refer to the first, *ex ante*, aspect, and we usually refer to the second, *ex post*, aspect, as performance evaluation.

I. THE NEED FOR RISK ADJUSTMENT AND PERFORMANCE EVALUATION

Measures of risk adjustment and performance evaluation have a number of important uses. The first is the obvious one of enabling us to compare the returns associated with different levels of risk, either those returns expected *ex ante* or those actually made *ex post*. Risk adjustment gives us a metric that enables us to choose between investment opportunities of differing expected returns and risks. Similarly, performance evaluation gives us a metric to compare the performance of units or portfolios that made different returns but also took different risks.

A second use is to guide management in allocating internal capital and setting position limits, and also in developing strategic plans. If unit A is persistently producing higher risk-adjusted profits than unit B, where A and B are particular traders, asset managers, business units or lines of business, then management should reallocate capital towards A and away from B. A's position limit should therefore increase and B's should fall. We can apply these measures at different levels throughout the organisation, from the larger business units (e.g., fixed-income investments, equity investments, and so on), down through their component business units (e.g., UK fixed-income, US fixed-income, etc.), and on down to the level of the individual manager or trader. At each level, the relevant unit is allocated capital and subjected to position limits that are determined on the basis of its risk-adjusted profitability relative to other business units in the organisation.

Performance evaluation measures are also very important in framing appropriate compensation rules. If management wish to maximise risk-adjusted profits, as they should, it is essential that they use compensation rules based on risk-adjusted rather than raw profits. If management reward traders on the basis of actual profits, traders and other decision makers will seek to maximise profits to boost their bonuses, and they will do so with relatively little concern for the risks they are taking.[1] Those who read the financial press will need no reminding of this particular problem. It makes no sense for management to reward traders for taking excessive risks and *then* worry about how to control their excessive risk-taking. Instead, management should manage their risk-taking in the context of incentive structures that *encourage* traders to take account of the risks they inflict on the institution. Traders will then seek to maximise risk-adjusted profits, and the conflict of interest between the institution and its traders will be significantly ameliorated.

2. GENERAL ISSUES

The process of risk adjustment can be illustrated by an example. Imagine we have a number of traders, A to E, who generate the risk-return combinations shown in Figure 7.1. Trader E makes the highest return, but also takes more risk than the other traders. Trader A makes the lowest return, but also takes the lowest risk, and other traders produce various intermediate combinations of return and risk. If we were to rank traders by their returns alone, we would therefore rank E first, followed by D, B, C, and finally A. On the other hand, if we were to rank traders by their risks alone, we would rank A first, followed by B, C, D and E: a very different ranking. Obviously, the first ranking places too much attention on return, and the second places too much attention on risk. We therefore need to take both risk and return into account in a single ranking (i.e., we need to risk-adjust the return), and the impact of risk-adjustment can be seen from the third column in Table 7.1.[2] If we rank by risk-adjusted return, it turns out that trader B has done best. Trader E, who made the highest profit, now ranks third, and trader A, who ranked top by risk alone, now comes bottom. The risk-adjusted ranking is thus very different from both the return-alone and risk-alone rankings.

FIGURE 7.1 Adjusting for Risk

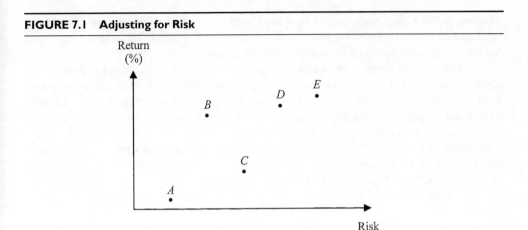

Table 7.1 Rankings of Traders

By return	By risk	By risk-adjusted return
E	A	B
D	B	D
B	C	E
C	D	C
A	E	A

3. THE SHARPE RATIO APPROACH

3.1. The Traditional Sharpe Ratio[3]

How do we carry out the risk adjustment? There are a number of risk-adjustment procedures to choose from, but perhaps the best-known is the traditional Sharpe ratio approach. Suppose we have a portfolio, p, with a return R_p. We also observe a benchmark portfolio, denoted by b, with return R_b. Let d be the differential return $R_p - R_b$, and let $\bar{d}^e$ be the expected differential return. We can now define the *ex ante* Sharpe Ratio:

$$SR^{ante} = \bar{d}^e / \sigma_d^e \tag{7.1}$$

where σ_d^e is the predicted standard deviation of d. This ratio captures the expected differential return per unit of risk associated with the differential expected return, and thereby takes account of both the expected differential between two portfolios and the associated differential risk. Since it gives risk estimates before decisions are actually taken, the *ex ante* Sharpe Ratio can be very useful for decision making (e.g., choosing investments) and, therefore, for *ex ante* risk adjustment. We can also define the *ex post* Sharpe Ratio:

$$SR^{post} = \bar{d} / \sigma_d \tag{7.2}$$

where σ_d is the standard deviation of d over a sample period. This version of the ratio takes account of both the *ex post* differential return and the variability of that return, and can be used for performance evaluation after the event.

The Sharpe ratio captures both risk and return – actual or expected depending on the circumstances – in a single measure. A rising return differential or a falling standard deviation – both 'good' events – lead to a rise in the Sharpe ratio; conversely, a falling return differential or a rising standard deviation – both 'bad' events – lead to a fall in the Sharpe ratio. Hence, a higher Sharpe ratio is good, and a lower one is bad. When comparing or choosing between two alternatives, we prefer the one with the higher Sharpe ratio. If we are deciding on investments before the event, we would choose that investment with the highest *ex ante* Sharpe ratio; if we are trying to evaluate traders after the event, we would give higher marks to the trader with the higher *ex post* Sharpe ratio.

It is important to appreciate that the Sharpe ratio always refers to the *differential* between two portfolios. We can think of this differential as reflecting a self-financing investment portfolio, with the first component representing the acquired asset and the second reflecting the short position – in cash or in some other asset – taken to finance that acquisition. As Sharpe explains,

> Central to the usefulness of the Sharpe Ratio is the fact that a differential return represents the result of a zero-investment strategy. This can be defined as any strategy that involves a zero outlay of money in the present and returns either a positive, negative, or zero amount in the future, depending on circumstances. A differential return clearly falls in this class, because it can be obtained by taking a long position in one asset (the fund) and a short position in another (the benchmark), with the funds from the latter used to finance the purchase of the former. (Sharpe, 1994, p. 52)[4]

The Sharpe ratio gives us sufficient information to choose between two investment options *ex ante* or evaluate the better of two trading units *ex post*, provided the returns to the two assets in question (or the two traders' portfolios) are uncorrelated with the returns to the rest of the institution's portfolio.

The Sharpe ratio therefore enables us to compare any pair of investments, *provided* they are uncorrelated with the portfolio. If we are choosing between alternatives, we pick the alternative with the higher Sharpe ratio; if we are ranking investments, we rank the investment with the higher Sharpe ratio ahead of the investment with the lower one.[5] However, if we can compare investments on a bilateral basis, we can also compare investments within a larger group, subject to the qualifier about zero correlation with the portfolio. If investment A has a higher Sharpe ratio than investment B, and B has a higher Sharpe ratio than C, and so on, we rank investment A first, followed by B, C, and so on. The relevant bilateral comparisons between different investments enable us to rank all our investments on a risk-adjusted basis. The higher the Sharpe ratio, the higher the risk-adjusted return. In effect, we can take the Sharpe ratio to be a proxy for the risk-adjusted return.

However, we should not lose sight of the restriction that the use of the Sharpe ratio presupposes that the return is uncorrelated with the rest of our portfolio. The implication is that the Sharpe ratio may not give a reliable ranking if one or more of the assets involved *is* correlated with the rest of our portfolio. If asset A has a lower Sharpe ratio than asset B, the Sharpe ratio criterion would suggest that we prefer B to A. However, if A's return is negatively correlated with the rest of our portfolio and B's is positively correlated with our portfolio, then the purchase of asset A would reduce portfolio risk while the purchase of B would increase it, and it is possible that we would prefer A over B if we took these correlation effects into account. Correlations between the assets in question and the rest of our portfolio mean that the Sharpe ratio cannot always be relied upon to give the right answer.

Box 7.1: Alternatives to the Sharpe ratio: the information ratio and the Treynor-Black ratio

One obvious question with the Sharpe ratio is why we should apply it only to *differentials* between two returns. Why not simply use the ratio of a portfolio's return (or expected return) to its standard deviation, without reference to any benchmark? The answer is that this latter ratio – sometimes referred to as the *information ratio* – may give misleading answers. This can be demonstrated by an example borrowed from Sharpe (1994, p. 52). An investor has a choice of two funds, X and Y, to be financed by cash borrowing. Fund X has an expected return of 5% and a standard deviation of 10%, and fund Y has an expected return of 8% and a standard deviation of 20%. Fund X therefore has an information ratio of 0.5 and fund Y one of 0.4, and so the information ratio criterion would lead us to prefer X to Y. Now suppose that the riskless interest rate is 3%. Fund X therefore has a Sharpe ratio of $(5 - 3)/10$ or 0.2, and fund Y has a Sharpe ratio of $(8 - 3)/20$ or 0.25. The Sharpe ratio criterion would therefore lead us to prefer Y to X – and it is easy to show that this latter answer is correct. The information ratio is misleading because it fails to make proper allowance for the cost of funds.

Another alternative is the *Treynor-Black ratio*, which is the Sharpe ratio squared. The problem with this ratio is that the process of squaring obscures information: if two funds had differentials relative to the benchmark that were equal but opposite in sign, the Sharpe ratio would regard them as very different, and yet the Treynor-Black ratio would regard them as equivalent since the sign of the differential would be lost in squaring.[6]

3.2. A Generalised Sharpe Rule

3.2.1. Derivation of the Generalised Sharpe Rule

Fortunately, this problem with the traditional Sharpe ratio is easily put right. Suppose we have a current portfolio and are considering buying an additional asset. To get around this correlation problem all we need to do is construct two Sharpe ratios, one for the old (or current) portfolio taken as a whole, and one for the new portfolio (or the portfolio we would have if the proposed trade went ahead), also taken as a whole. If we denote the old Sharpe ratio by SR^{old}, and the new one by SR^{new}, the decision rule is very simple:

Buy the new asset (i.e., go from old to new) if and only if $SR^{new} \geqslant SR^{old}$ (7.3)

We go for the new portfolio if and only if it has a Sharpe ratio greater than that of the old portfolio. The optimality of this rule follows from the previous discussion, which told us that we should choose the position with the highest Sharpe ratio if two positions are uncorrelated with the rest of our portfolio – and this condition is now automatically satisfied.[7]

This generalised Sharpe rule avoids the correlation problem we encountered with standard applications of the Sharpe ratio. The correlation of any new position to the old portfolio can take any value, not just zero, and its value is already allowed for in the denominator of SR^{new}. *This rule is therefore generally valid, unlike traditional applications of the Sharpe ratio, which are valid only if the correlation is zero.*

It remains to spell out the details. Suppose we are deciding whether to make an investment decision involving the purchase of a new asset A with a short position in the benchmark b, and we assume for simplicity that the benchmark asset is cash. (We shall relax the assumption of a cash benchmark in due course.) We shall also drop the expectation superscripts to keep the notation from becoming too cumbersome. As before, let R_p^{old} be the return to the old portfolio and note that the return to the cash benchmark is zero. The differential return, d^{old}, is therefore simply R_p^{old} and the standard deviation is $\sigma_{d^{old}}$. The ratio of d^{old} to $\sigma_{d^{old}}$ then gives us our existing (old) Sharpe ratio. Now suppose that the prospective new portfolio consists of the new asset A and the existing portfolio, in relative proportions a and $1 - a$. (We assume here that the new instrument has a positive market value, so $a > 0$. The alternative is a position of zero current value (i.e., where $a = 0$), which is discussed in Box 7.2.) The expected return on the new portfolio is:

$$R_p^{new} = aR_A + (1 - a)R_p^{old} \tag{7.4}$$

and the expected differential for the new portfolio, d^{new}, is:

$$d^{new} = R_p^{new} = aR_A + (1 - a)R_p^{old} \tag{7.5}$$

The cash benchmark asset implies that $\sigma_{d^{old}}$ is equal to $\sigma_{R_p^{old}}$ and $\sigma_{d^{new}}$ is equal to $\sigma_{R_p^{new}}$. Using (7.3), we should therefore make the investment if:

$$SR^{new} = d^{new}/\sigma_{R_p^{new}} \geqslant d^{old}/\sigma_{R_p^{old}} = SR^{old} \tag{7.6}$$

Substituting (7.5) into (7.6) and rearranging, our criterion becomes:

$$R_A \geqslant R_p^{old} + [\sigma_{R_p^{new}}/\sigma_{R_p^{old}} - 1]R_p^{old}/a \tag{7.7}$$

(7.7) tells us that the expected return on asset A must be at least as great as the expression on the right-hand side if the asset is to be worth acquiring. The expression on the right-hand side of (7.7) can therefore be interpreted as the required return on asset A. This required return consists of the expected return on the existing portfolio plus an adjustment factor that depends on the risks involved, and, more specifically, rises with the ratio of new to old portfolio standard deviations. This tells us, as we would have expected, that the more the new asset contributes to overall portfolio risk, the greater the expected return required to make its acquisition worthwhile. There are also some other implications:

Box 7.2: The generalised Sharpe rule: some illustrative figures

We can get some further feel for the generalised Sharpe rule (7.7) by plugging in some illustrative figures. Let us therefore assume the following:

$$R_p^{old} = 0.12, \ a = 0.01, \ \sigma_{R_A} = \sigma_{R_p^{old}}$$

Our decision rule (7.7) then becomes:

$$R_A \geqslant 0.12 + [\sigma_{R_p^{new}}/\sigma_{R_p^{old}} - 1]0.12/0.01$$

and the ratio of standard deviations, $\sigma_{R_p^{new}}/\sigma_{R_p^{old}}$, becomes $\sqrt{a^2 + (1-a)^2 + 2\rho a(1-a)}$, where ρ is the correlation coefficient between σ_{R_A} and $\sigma_{R_p^{old}}$. The required return then depends on the correlation coefficient:

$$\rho = 1 \text{ implies } R_A \geqslant 0.12$$
$$\rho = 0 \text{ implies } R_A \geqslant 0$$
$$\rho = -1 \text{ implies } R_A \geqslant -0.12$$

The value of the correlation coefficient therefore makes a very big difference to the required return on the new asset. If $\rho = 1$, there is no diversification of risks and the new asset is worth acquiring only if it promises a return at least as high as the existing portfolio return (as we would have expected). If $\rho = 0$, the independence of the new risk implies a more stable portfolio return and the new asset is worth acquiring if its expected return exceeds the much lower threshold of 0%. Finally, if the new asset is negatively correlated with the current portfolio, the new asset reduces overall portfolio risk (i.e., has a negative risk) and is worth acquiring even if its return is negative, provided it is not too negative. This last result highlights the value of assets that are negatively correlated with our portfolio and illustrates why we might pay to hedge our risks.

- The new asset's risk is only relevant to the decision whether to acquire the new asset in so far as it affects overall portfolio risk: the volatility of the new asset's return does not enter the decision rule other than through the portfolio risk $\sigma_{R_p^{new}}$. This reflects the well-known result in portfolio theory that the risk that matters is not an asset's own individual volatility, but its contribution to the risk of the portfolio as a whole.
- In the special case where the new asset adds nothing to overall portfolio risk (i.e., where $\sigma_{R_p^{new}}$ is equal to $\sigma_{R_p^{old}}$), the right-hand side of (7.7) boils down to R_p^{old} and the decision rule merely requires that the new asset have a net return at least as great as that from the existing portfolio. This makes intuitive sense: if there are no risk factors involved, we should purchase the new asset if and only if it has an expected net return at least as great as that we can attain with our existing portfolio.

If the new asset makes a positive contribution to portfolio risk (i.e., if $\sigma_{R_p^{new}}$ is greater than $\sigma_{R_p^{old}}$), we should expect it to earn a net return greater than R_p^{old} for it to be worth acquiring. We need the greater return as compensation for the greater portfolio risk its purchase would involve. And, conversely, if the asset makes a negative contribution to portfolio risk, we might be willing to purchase it even if its net expected return is less than that of our existing portfolio. We might be willing to accept the lower expected return because of the risk-reducing benefits of acquiring the new asset.

3.2.2. The Generalised Sharpe Rule in VaR Form

We can also write (7.7) in an equivalent form using VaR instead of portfolio standard deviation. Assuming normality, and noting that the overall portfolio size remains unchanged, then we immediately know that:

$$VaR^{new}/VaR^{old} = \sigma_{R_p^{new}}/\sigma_{R_p^{old}} \tag{7.8}$$

Our decision rule (7.7) becomes:

$$R_A \geqslant R_p^{old} + [VaR^{new}/VaR^{old} - 1]R_p^{old}/a \tag{7.9}$$

Noting that $\Delta VaR = VaR^{new} - VaR^{old}$ and rearranging, the above rule now becomes:

$$R_A \geqslant R_p^{old} + [\Delta VaR/VaR^{old}]R_p^{old}/a \tag{7.10}$$

$$= [1 + \eta_A(VaR, a)]R_p^{old}$$

where $\eta_A(VaR, a)$ is the percentage change in VaR occasioned by the acquisition of the position in asset A divided by the percentage change in the portfolio, or the elasticity of the VaR with respect to a. We can regard this elasticity as a measure of the increase in the risk of our portfolio, adjusted for the size of the change in the portfolio.

We therefore acquire the new position if its return is at least equal to its required return, given by the right-hand side of (7.10). This required return is equal to one plus the VaR elasticity, times R_p^{old}. The required return on the new asset will be bigger than the expected return on the existing portfolio if the VaR elasticity is greater than zero (i.e., if the VaR increases), and the required asset return will be less than the expected portfolio return if the VaR elasticity is less than zero.

3.2.3. Computational Speed

There is also the practical issue of computing time. Can we evaluate the terms in (7.7) or (7.10) in real time, without cumbersome matrix operations? The answer is that we can, provided we have the necessary information. We can assume that we already know (or can estimate) R_p^{old}, a, and the existing portfolio variance $\sigma_{R_p^{old}}$. We can also easily estimate R_A. All we then need is $\sigma_{R_p^{new}}$, and we can obtain that from the standard formula for the variance of two variables:

$$\sigma^2_{R_p^{new}} = a^2 \sigma^2_{R_A} + (1 - a)^2 \sigma^2_{R_p^{old}} + 2a(1 - a)\sigma_{R_A, R_p} \qquad (7.11)$$

$$\Rightarrow \sigma_{R_p^{new}} = \sqrt{a^2 \sigma^2_{R_A} + (1 - a)^2 \sigma^2_{R_p^{old}} + 2a(1 - a)\sigma_{R_A, R_p}}$$

where σ_{R_A, R_p} is the covariance between the return to asset A and the return to the portfolio. The only missing information is data on $\sigma^2_{R_A}$ and the covariance σ_{R_A, R_p}. However, for most trades, a would be small and a^2 negligible, in which case the volatility term $a^2 \sigma^2_{R_A}$ would also be negligible. So unless a is particularly large, the only additional information we would really need to estimate the new portfolio standard deviation would be σ_{R_A, R_p}. Estimating the factors that go into the decision rule (7.7) is therefore straightforward, and calculations can be done instantaneously without awkward matrix operations.[8]

However, in practice it is likely to be even easier to work with (7.10). We presumably already know or have estimates of R_p^{old}, a and VaR^{old}, and the only missing information is the incremental VaR, ΔVaR, which we can estimate using one of the procedures discussed in Chapter 2. We then simply plug our various parameters or estimates into the right-hand side of (7.10) to check whether the inequality in (7.10) holds. Once again, the calculations involved can be done instantaneously without any complex matrix operations.

Box 7.3: The generalised Sharpe rule with zero-value positions

Some positions, such as forwards and conventional swaps, have zero value when contracts are first made. Applying the generalised Sharpe rule to such cases involves a minor modification to the procedure for positive-value positions. As in the text, our basic rule is to agree to the contract if and only if:

$$SR^{new} \geqslant SR^{old}$$

In this case, $d^{new} = R_p^{new}$ and $d^{old} = R_p^{old}$. Substituting these into the above and rearranging, we then get:

$$R_p^{new} \geqslant (\sigma_{R_p^{new}} / \sigma_{R_p^{old}}) R_p^{old}$$

Assuming normality, we can replace the standard deviations with corresponding VaRs and rearrange again to obtain:

$$R_p^{new} \geqslant R_p^{old} VaR^{new} / VaR^{old}$$

We therefore obtain a simple and intuitively appealing decision rule: we agree to the contract if it promises to increase the return on our portfolio by proportionately more than it increases the VaR on our portfolio.

3.3. The Generalised Sharpe Ratio with a Risky Benchmark

We have assumed so far that the benchmark asset is cash, but firms will in practice be more likely to use a risky benchmark such as the opportunity cost of funds.[9] We can then no longer treat R_b as zero, and the standard deviation of the differential, σ_d, would no longer be equal to σ_{R_p} but instead be given by:

$$\sigma_d = \sqrt{\sigma_{R_p}^2 + \sigma_{R_b}^2 + 2\rho_{R_p,R_b}\sigma_{R_p}\sigma_{R_b}} \qquad (7.12)$$

where the 'old' and 'new' superscripts are dropped for convenience. With a risky benchmark, the analysis of (7.3) to (7.7) becomes a bit more complicated and we end up with a version of (7.7) in which R_b appears explicitly and the σ_{R_p} terms are replaced with σ_d terms. Nonetheless, the calculations involved are still straightforward and a computer would have no problem carrying them out in real time.

However, the benchmark asset may also be endogenous as well as risky. An endogenous benchmark is one that alters (or may alter) in response to the decision under consideration. Our generalised Sharpe ratio rule (7.3) then implies that we acquire the new asset if and only if:

$$(R_p^{new} - R_b^{new})/\sigma_{dnew} \geqslant (R_p^{old} - R_b^{old})/\sigma_{dold} \qquad (7.13)$$

We now substitute out R_p^{new} using:

$$R_p^{new} = aR_A + (1 - a)R_p^{old} \qquad (7.14)$$

Substituting (7.14) into (7.13) and rearranging gives us:

$$R_A \geqslant R_p^{old} + [(\sigma_{dnew}/\sigma_{dold} - 1)(R_p^{old} - R_b^{old})/a] + \Delta R_b/a \qquad (7.15)$$

where $\Delta R_b = R_b^{new} - R_b^{old}$.

(7.15) tells us that the required return on the new asset equals the existing portfolio return plus the adjustment for risk (which now depends on the expected old benchmark return R_b^{old}), plus the change in benchmark returns ΔR_b (i.e., the change in finance costs) due to the acquisition.

We now need to nail down the last term, ΔR_b. To do so, let us assume that our initial portfolio is financed by capital and debt, in relative proportions K^{old}/W^{old} and $(1 - K^{old}/W^{old})$. It follows that:

$$R_b^{old} = (K^{old}/W^{old})c^k + (1 - K^{old}/W^{old})c^d \qquad (7.16)$$

where c^k is the cost of capital and c^d ($< c^k$) is the cost of debt, and we shall assume that these costs are given. The change in financing cost is then:

$$\Delta R_b = (K^{new}/W^{new} - K^{old}/W^{old})(c^k - c^d) \qquad (7.17)$$

The financing cost rises if the capital/asset ratio rises, and falls if the capital/asset ratio falls. We therefore need to pin down the change in the capital ratio, which requires that we specify the institution's capital structure policy. To do this, we need to anticipate the discussion of Chapter 11, but there are two main possibilities.

3.3.1. Case 1: Capital Determined by Market Risk/VaR Analysis

The first case is where the level of capital is determined by market risk or VaR analysis. In this case, (11.9) tells us that the capital level can be written as a multiple of the VaR:

$$K = \varphi VaR \qquad (7.18)$$

This multiplier φ is broken down further in Chapter 11, but all that matters for present purposes is that we already know it. The capital/asset ratio K/W is therefore equal to $\varphi VaR/W$. Substituting out the K/W terms in (7.17) and rearranging then gives us:

$$\Delta R_b = \varphi(VaR^{new}/W^{new} - VaR^{old}/W^{old})(c^k - c^d) \tag{7.19}$$

We now substitute out W^{new} ($= (1 + a)W^{old}$) and rearrange again:

$$\Delta R_b = \varphi[VaR^{new} - (1 + a)VaR^{old}](c^k - c^d)/[(1 + a)W^{old}] \tag{7.20}$$

Finally, we divide by a and rearrange one more time to obtain:

$$\Delta R_b/a = [\eta(VaR, a) - 1](c^k - c^d)K^{old}[(1 + a)W^{old}] \tag{7.21}$$

where $\Delta VaR = VaR^{new} - VaR^{old}$.[10]

In practice, all we need to do is work out (7.21), substitute this term into (7.15) and then apply (7.15) to determine if the acquisition is worthwhile.

3.3.2. Case 2: Capital Determined by Stress Tests

The other case is where the level of capital is determined by the outcome of stress tests. In this case, the capital level is set to enable the institution to absorb the impact of unlikely but plausible shocks (like a stock market crash or an exchange-rate crisis) and still be strong enough to remain in business. If the capital level is set in this way, we would presume that our capital is well above the level needed to absorb day-to-day fluctuations in asset values (i.e., to absorb normal market risks). The level of capital would then be independent of market risks, at least at the margin, and this means that we can treat the level of capital as constant. Hence (7.16) implies:

$$\Delta R_b = (K^{old}/W^{new} - K^{old}/W^{old})(c^k - c^d) \tag{7.22}$$
$$= -aK^{old}(c^k - c^d)/[(1 + a)W^{old}]$$

We then substitute (7.22) into (7.15) and use the latter to test if a prospective acquisition is worthwhile.[11]

4. SOME FLAWED ALTERNATIVES

We now consider some common alternative decision rules.

4.1. The CAPM

The Capital Asset Pricing Model (CAPM) suggests that an investment i is worthwhile if its expected return exceeds a required return given by:

$$r_f + (r_m - r_f)\beta_i \tag{7.23}$$

where r_f is the risk-free rate of return, r_m is the expected rate of return on the market portfolio of risky assets, and β_i is the (hypothetical) market beta of the stock.

There are a number of well-known problems with the CAPM,[12] but for our purposes here the main one is that it fails to consider the impact on our investment decision of the specific portfolio we actually hold. The risks and returns of any prospective investment are instead judged against a hypothetical market portfolio that the CAPM implies we should all hold. However, in the real world, no one holds the CAPM market portfolio and – to state the obvious – the portfolios people actually hold differ enormously from each other. Our real portfolio will therefore usually be *very* different from the fictional CAPM market portfolio. Consequently, the relevance of the CAPM to any given investment decision is, to say the least, problematic.

4.2. The APT

The Arbitrage Pricing Theory (APT) suggests that the required rate of return on any investment is a linear function of a set of k factors.[13] It can also be regarded as a generalisation of the CAPM, but one that is free of the market portfolio and return distribution assumptions on which the CAPM depends. However, the APT still has the CAPM's weakness of not allowing for correlations between a prospective investment and the portfolio we actually hold.

4.3. The RAROC

The RAROC (Risk Adjusted Return on Capital) rule is an important and widely used alternative to the Sharpe rule.[14] The RAROC risk adjustment for any position is that position's realised returns divided by its VaR:

$$RAROC = R/VaR \tag{7.24}$$

The RAROC measure captures the most basic features of any sensible risk-adjustment procedure: it rises when returns rise, and falls when risk (in this case, VaR) rises, and vice versa.

But beyond that, it suffers from a number of drawbacks.[15] That there is something wrong with it can easily be seen by noting that the RAROC measure goes to infinity as the VaR goes to zero. This implies that any zero-risk investment has an infinite RAROC. All a trader therefore has to do to achieve an infinite RAROC is purchase riskless assets (e.g., short-term Treasuries) and hold them to maturity. The VaR of such a position would be zero, and the zero VaR would make RAROC infinite. The RAROC measure therefore incorporates a very pronounced over-adjustment for risk and any performance evaluation system based on a RAROC measure would provide excessive rewards to very safe traders (more particularly, to those who took no risks at all). As Wilson dryly observes,

> an institution's management might wake up one morning to find all its funds invested in overnight Treasuries, which would guarantee the risk managers an infinite RAROC. This is probably not the signal the board wants to send out. (Wilson, 1992, p. 114)

The incorrectness of the RAROC measure can also be demonstrated another way, which also provides more insight into what is wrong with the measure. Suppose we multiply (7.24) by VaR and then run an expectations operator through the resulting equation. We then get:

$$E(R) = E(RAROC)\,VaR = -E(RAROC)\alpha\sigma W \tag{7.25}$$

if we make the additional convenient assumption of normality.[16] (7.25) gives us the expected return from the asset/position in terms of expected RAROC, α (the confidence level on which the VaR is based), and σ (the standard deviation of the return to the asset/position). However, (7.25) is clearly incorrect:[17]

- If we move towards a safe position, (7.25) suggests that the expected return will go to zero. Yet we know very well that perfectly safe positions do not have zero returns. The underlying problem is that the RAROC measure considers only capital invested in risky positions. It ignores the fact that the market also rewards capital allocated to riskless positions.
- The RAROC measure makes the expected return a function of the confidence level on which the VaR is predicated. This implies that we can achieve more or less any expected return we want by an appropriate change in our (subjectively chosen) confidence level! This is obviously incorrect. The RAROC measure mixes up an objective, market-constrained factor, the expected return, with an arbitrarily chosen confidence parameter, α.[18,19]

5. CONCLUSIONS

The generalised Sharpe rule proposed here is superior to existing approaches to risk adjustment and performance evaluation: it is superior to the standard Sharpe ratio because it is valid regardless of the correlations of the investments being considered with the rest of our portfolio, and it is also free of the problems affecting the CAPM, the APT and the RAROC. The generalised Sharpe ratio is also straightforward to implement and can easily be programmed into packages for decision makers to use. In addition, it can also be readily extended to cover the financing as well as risk implications of investment and performance evaluation decisions.

ENDNOTES

1. The institution's interest is usually to have them take relatively moderate risks, since the institution (usually) has to bear the full losses that would occur if the risks turn out badly. The trader's interest is different, since he/she gets their share of profits if the risks turn out well, but does not bear their corresponding share of losses if the risks turn out badly. If the trader makes a loss, he/she loses their bonus, or at most their job. Hence, their personal downside risk is limited, regardless of the losses their risk-taking might inflict on their employer. The trader therefore faces an asymmetric pay-off – a share of the profits if risks pay off, and a limited loss if they do not – which encourages him/her to take more risks than the employer would like.
2. There are in fact a variety of ways to adjust for risk, and they don't (usually) give the same rankings. This is the main reason why the precise risk-adjustment procedure matters. The actual risk adjustment used in Table 7.1 – to divide return by risk – is not actually the best one, as we shall presently see, but it is simple and it helps to establish the main point being made here, namely, that risk adjusting can easily affect our ranking.
3. The analysis of this section draws heavily from Sharpe (1994) and presupposes a mean-variance world (i.e., one where mean and variance/standard deviation are sufficient to guide all relevant decisions). Extending the analysis to deal with skewness, excess kurtosis and other non-normal features would obviously complicate the analysis considerably.
4. An asset disposal can be thought of as a negative acquisition. The cash position then becomes a long one, reflecting the proceeds from the asset sale.

5. It is useful to understand why the Sharpe ratio gives us the best alternative, subject to the zero-correlation caveat. Suppose we are comparing two self-financing investment opportunities, one consisting of asset A and the other of asset B. (The fact that they are self-financing means that each investment opportunity also involves a short position in some benchmark, such as cash, which is used to finance the asset acquisition.) The Sharpe ratios for each investment then give the ratio of each position's net return over the standard deviation of that net return. However, if the net return is uncorrelated with the return to the rest of our portfolio, the standard deviation of net return also gives us the contribution of each position to overall portfolio standard deviation (i.e., its true risk, as opposed to its individual volatility). The Sharpe ratio therefore gives us the ratio of expected return to risk for each position. However, in a mean-variance world we would always choose the position with the highest return per unit risk. We would therefore always choose the one with the higher Sharpe ratio. This establishes that the Sharpe ratio is a sufficient statistic for investment (or evaluation) purposes, *provided* the two assets are uncorrelated with the rest of our portfolio.

6. Sharpe (1994, p. 52)

7. It is satisfied because the Sharpe ratio criterion requires that the return to each position be uncorrelated with the return to whatever else is in our portfolio, and the 'whatever else' (i.e., nothing) has a zero return. The required condition is therefore satisfied.

8. There are also related practical issues to consider. (1) When used for risk-adjustment *ex ante*, each decision to buy or sell an asset will change the whole portfolio, which implies that the next such decision is made against a (slightly) different portfolio. In other words, the portfolio changes in real time. However, in practice, the best we can hope for, at least for the foreseeable future, is to take periodic snapshots of the portfolio (e.g., at the end of every day). Individual traders and asset managers will therefore have to make their decisions against a hypothetical portfolio that will, strictly speaking, be out of date after the first trading decision is made. The use of this snapshot portfolio instead of the current portfolio introduces an additional source of error into our traders'/managers' decision making. Fortunately, the error itself is likely to be small unless the portfolio itself undergoes drastic changes throughout the day. (2) When evaluating performance after the event, we must recognise that this same error – the use of a snapshot portfolio instead of a changing one – means that estimates of risk-adjusted returns after the event based on, say, end-of-day portfolios can only be approximations to true performance evaluation. Again, we have to rely on the hope that the portfolio does not change too much over the day.

9. The choice of the benchmark to use in VaR calculations has caused a considerable amount of hand-wringing and there is no clear consensus in the literature on how to handle it. For example, Beckers (1996, pp. 179–84) emphasises that a benchmark is critical to risk analysis and gives a good account of the role it plays, but does not actually tell us how to choose it, Glaeser (1996) offers a few sensible, although vague, comments about the problem before acknowledging that the choice of benchmark is very difficult, and Shimko (1997) makes some suggestions about industry averages as benchmarks and about choosing benchmarks that promote shareholder value whilst meeting constraints about the interests of other stakeholders, but even he does not get to the bottom of the issue. However, in my view both Glaeser and Shimko make the problem out to be more difficult than it really is. The underlying issue is the familiar one of the cost of capital, and the best way to handle this issue is to resort to the firm's capital structure policy, as in the text. Referring to the firm's capital structure is the only way to resolve the choice of VaR benchmark consistent with the rest of the firm's financial policy. It not only provides the benchmark, but also (satisfying Shimko) gives us a benchmark that gives the appropriate balance between the conflicting interests of shareholders and other stakeholders.

10. The marginal cost of funds $\Delta R_b/a$ thus rises if the VaR rises proportionately more than the size of the portfolio (i.e., if the percentage change in VaR exceeds a). This is as we would expect: if the new asset is particularly risky, the percentage rise in VaR would be more than a, the capital/asset ratio would rise, and the cost of funds would be higher; if the new asset is of relatively low risk, the VaR would grow by less than a, the capital/asset ratio would fall, and the cost of funds would be less.

11. ΔR_b is negative because of the fall in the capital ratio. (Remember that the level of capital is constant but the asset base rises.) The fall in K/W implies that the weight attached to c^k in (7.16) falls and the weight attached to c^d rises. The benchmark cost of funds then falls because c^k is bigger than c^d.

12. See, e.g., Roll (1977) or Frankfurter (1995).

13. See Ross (1976).

14. This RAROC risk-adjustment *procedure* is not to be confused with the RAROC risk measurement/management *systems* used by Bankers' Trust (such as BT's RAROC 2020 system). The use of the RAROC terminology to describe both is unfortunate, at least for BT.

15. The RAROC suffers from the same zero-correlation limitation as the Sharpe ratio: it fails to allow for correlation between the asset or position in question and the rest of our portfolio. This limitation can presumably be overcome by replacing the VaR with the incremental VaR instead, but this improvement still does not correct the other problems with the RAROC measure discussed in the text.

16. See Wilson (1992, p. 114).

17. See again Wilson (1992, p. 114).

18. An alternative to the RAROC is the *Treynor ratio*, which boils down to the ratio of the profits earned by a trader or an asset position, divided by that trader's (or position's) incremental VaR. However, the Treynor ratio has the same drawback as the RAROC: a trader can always achieve a zero VAR and therefore an infinite Treynor ratio by buying overnight Treasuries (see, e.g., Jorion (1996, p. 289)).

19. One other risk-adjustment procedure is suggested by Modigliani and Modigliani (1997). Their procedure uses the 'market opportunity cost of risk . . . to adjust all portfolios to the level of risk in the unmanaged market benchmark (e.g., the S&P 500), thereby *matching* a portfolio's risk to that of the market, and then measuring the returns of this risk-adjusted portfolio' (Modigliani and Modigliani, 1997, p. 46, their emphasis). This procedure essentially boils down to a Sharpe rule in which the benchmark portfolio is taken to be a market portfolio. The Modigliani-Modigliani rule has the advantage over the traditional Sharpe ratio that it is expressed in terms of a metric – basis points – that investors can more easily understand, but is open to the same basic objection as that rule (i.e., it ignores correlations with our existing portfolio). However, in so far as it relies on a market portfolio, there are also questions as to its relevance to users who might prefer alternative benchmarks.

APPENDIX TO CHAPTER 7: DIFFERENT RISK-ADJUSTMENT RULES

Rule	Decision criterion/key points	Limitations/weaknesses
Traditional Sharpe rule	Choose position with higher Sharpe ratio, where SR is ratio of difference between return to position and return to benchmark, over standard deviation of this difference. Gives correct answer subject to limitations.	Applies to mean-variance world. Assumes zero-correlations of candidate positions with existing portfolio.
Information rule	Choose position with higher information ratio, where IR is ratio of return to standard deviation of return.	Misleading. Dominated by Sharpe rules.
Treynor-Black rule	Use Sharpe ratio squared.	Less informative than Sharpe rules. Dominated by Sharpe rules.
CAPM	Use CAPM 'market beta' to determine required return; make decision on the basis of a comparison of prospective and required returns.	Subject to generic weaknesses of CAPM. CAPM beta tells us little about actual IVaR.
APT	Use APT to determine required return; make decision on the basis of a comparison of prospective and required returns.	Subject to problems of APT. Risk estimate bears little relationship to IVaR.
Modigliani-Modigliani risk adjustment rule	Standardise risk to that of market portfolio; choose position with highest return. Boils down to traditional Sharpe rule with market portfolio as benchmark.	Same limitations as traditional Sharpe rule. Use of market portfolio as benchmark might be inappropriate.
Generalised Sharpe rule	Choose position with higher generalised Sharpe ratio, where GSR is Sharpe ratio applied to new position plus existing portfolio. Gives correct answer subject to limitations. Accommodates any correlations of candidate positions with existing portfolio; hence dominates traditional Sharpe rule.	Applies to mean-variance world.
RAROC	Choose position with highest ratio of return to VaR.	Very biased towards safe positions.
Treynor rule	Choose position with highest Treynor ratio, where TR is ratio of profits to incremental VaR.	Biased in a similar way to RAROC.

8

Decision Making

1. INTRODUCTION

THIS chapter considers the VaR approach to decision making. As explained in the last chapter, the core of this approach is the application of the generalised Sharpe rule in one or other of its various manifestations (e.g. (7.10) or (7.15)). We therefore begin by reviewing how the generalised Sharpe rule would be implemented in practice. We then look at the three main applications of this decision-making rule: to investment decisions, to hedging decisions, and to portfolio management.

2. USING THE GENERALISED SHARPE RULE TO MAKE DECISIONS

The reader will recall from the previous chapter that our generalised Sharpe rule tells a decision-maker to acquire a new position A if and only if its expected return, R_A, is at least as big as the required return given by the right-hand side of (7.10) or (7.15), depending on the precise assumptions we make about the benchmark return. Assume for convenience that we are dealing with the simpler condition, (7.10).[1] This rule tells us to acquire the new asset if its expected return satisfies:

$$R_A \geqslant [1 + \eta_A(VaR, a)]R_p^{old} \tag{7.10}$$

(7.10) gives us a decision rule in terms of the returns to the old portfolio and the new asset, and VaR elasticity associated with the new asset acquisition. The required return itself is equal to one plus the VaR elasticity, times the expected return to the existing portfolio. Clearly, the greater the incremental VaR, the bigger the risk associated with the new investment, and the higher the required return.

In theory, all our decision maker has to do is plug in the relevant parameter values and check whether (7.10) holds or not. He/she acquires the position if it does, and does not acquire it otherwise. The main requirement in using this rule is therefore to ensure that the decision maker has the relevant information and data processing capability to hand. He/she would presumably sit at a suitably programmed computer terminal and plug in the details relevant to the candidate position. The computer would then apply the decision rule (7.10) to its data bank and give a yes/no answer. If the answer were yes, the decision maker would authorise the deal, the transaction would be logged and records amended accordingly. If the answer were no, the deal would be rejected.[2]

3. INVESTMENT DECISIONS

This decision rule (and, where appropriate, its analogues) can be applied to any decision, large or small, that involves expected return and/or risk, and takes account of the incremental risks associated with those decisions in a theoretically correct way (i.e., taking account of the risks as they relate to our existing portfolio). One obvious use of this decision rule is in making investment and disinvestment decisions. Assuming we already have the necessary data about the old portfolio and the benchmark asset, we simply estimate R_A and the VaR elasticity for the asset in question (or, if one prefers, the incremental VaR), and check whether R_A exceeds its required return given by the right-hand side of (7.10) (or (7.15)). A disinvestment decision or a decision to take a short position can be handled in the same way by considering the decision as a negative acquisition. The generalised Sharpe rule is thus very helpful in deciding whether to acquire new assets, keep assets we already have, get rid of them, or take short positions in assets we don't have.[3]

Box 8.1: Are dealing rooms worthwhile?

Decision makers using the generalised Sharpe rule will find that some investments that currently appear to be poor ones are actually quite good, once they take proper account of their true risks. However, they are probably more likely to find that many investments that they previously thought were worthwhile are not in fact good investments at all. As one experienced observer recently put it,

I...guarantee to you, based on 20 years of experience, that large parts of the trading rooms around the world in and out of banks don't make money when risk adjusted...The vast majority of highly 'market active' non-financial institutions learn to reduce their use of financial markets very substantially within a short period of hitting their peak turnover levels. Sadly it is often not because they learn how to create risk offsets, but because they lose a lot of money...Many trading environments are expensive waste and shouldn't exist. (Simister, 1996, pp. 3–4)

Firms with large dealing rooms should therefore brace themselves for a rude awakening.

This decision rule tells us whether we would be better off making an investment (or disinvestment) decision of a particular given size, and is obviously well suited to situations where the size of the investment is given and where all we need to do is decide whether to proceed with it. However, it is frequently the case that we must decide not only whether to make an investment, but also how large the investment should be if we go ahead and make it (i.e., we must select the position size a as well). We therefore need to adapt the rule to handle investment problems where the investment size is itself a choice variable.

To do so, we begin by using the right-hand side of (7.10) (or (7.15)) to estimate the investment asset's required return, for a range of different values of a ranging from very small to large. This will produce one of two types of relationship between required return and position size, as given in Figure 8.1. Remember that required return increases with

FIGURE 8.1   Required Return and Position Size

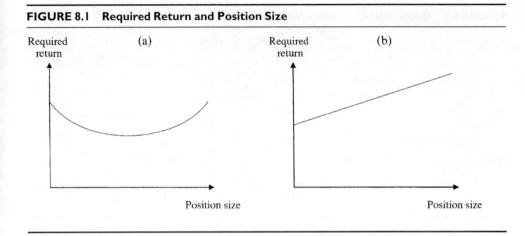

incremental VaR, so the shape of the required return curve reflects the shape of an underlying IVaR curve. The curve showing the relationship between required return and position size will therefore either fall initially and then start to rise (as in Figure 8.1a), or rise indefinitely (as in Figure 8.1b). Whether the curve initially falls or rises depends on the correlation of the required return on the asset with the return to the rest of our portfolio, but the curve *must* eventually rise, if only because at some point the new investment would become so large relative to our portfolio that it would start to dominate it; further increases in the size of the new investment would then add to overall risk and push up the IVaR and, therefore, the required return.

The answer to our decision problem now depends on the relationship between this required return and the expected return on the asset. Applying standard intermediate microeconomic theory, the optimal level of investment turns out to be where the required return curve cuts the expected return curve from below. Consider the two cases in Figure 8.2. In both cases we assume that the required return curve first falls with a and then rises.[4] The expected asset return curve is taken as horizontal, on the assumption that the expected asset return is given. Now note the two possible outcomes:

- In Figure 8.2a, the expected return to the new asset is always less than the required return, regardless of the size of the position in the new asset. It is then obvious from (7.10) that no amount of the new asset is worth acquiring.
- By contrast, in Figure 8.2b, the two curves cross at two points. The answer to our decision problem is therefore to invest in the new asset, with the size of our investment (given by a^*) determined where the required return cuts the expected return curve from below.[5] This level of investment is optimal because it maximises risk-adjusted expected return: at any investment level above a^*, marginal increases in investment have a required return that exceeds the return expected from the asset, which means that we would be better off cutting back on our investment; at any investment level below a^*, marginal increases in investment have a required return that is less than the return expected from the investment, which means we are better off increasing our investment. The optimal level of investment is therefore that at which the investment level actually equals a^*.

FIGURE 8.2   Optimal Investment Levels

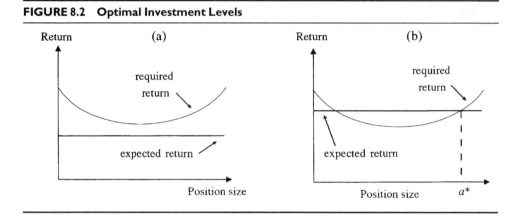

Our decision problem is now resolved: our decision rule not only tells us whether to invest, but also tells us how much to invest if we do.

4. HEDGE DECISIONS

The same approach can also be used to guide hedging and similar (e.g., insurance purchase) decisions. Indeed, the approach to hedging decisions is essentially the same as with the more general investment decisions just considered. This is as it should be, since hedging decisions are merely investment decisions taken with a primary objective of reducing overall risk. When considering hedges, we therefore apply (7.10), but with the proviso that we are considering a decision which reduces overall VaR and which, therefore, has a negative incremental VaR. However, (7.10) then tells us that the hedge position must have a required return that is less than zero.

Since hedge decisions are otherwise the same as investment decisions, we can represent hedges by appropriately modified versions of Figure 8.2. Hedge decisions can therefore be represented by Figure 8.3. The only difference between Figures 8.2 and 8.3 is that Figure 8.3 considers investment decisions with negative IVaR or, given the conditions underlying (7.10), a required return lower than the benchmark return of R_p. The story is otherwise the same as it was before:

- In Figure 8.3a, the expected return to the new asset is always less than the required return, regardless of the size of the position in the new asset. Therefore no hedge is worthwhile.
- In Figure 8.3b, the two return curves cross at two points. We should therefore acquire that amount of the hedge asset – given by a^* – determined where the required return cuts the expected return curve from below. This level of investment is optimal for exactly the same reasons as it was optimal for (other) investment decisions.[6]

This VaR approach to hedging therefore tells us whether to hedge and, if we do, also tells us the size of our hedge position. The VaR hedge position also hedges the exposure of the portfolio as a whole, not just the exposure of some particular part of it. It therefore allows

FIGURE 8.3   Hedging Decisions

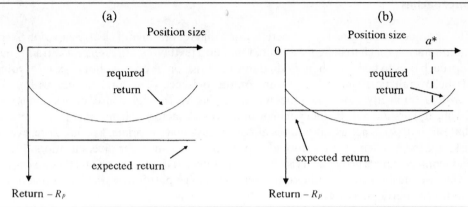

for the interaction of the hedge position with *all* the risks in our portfolio, and not just one of them. Furthermore, the hedge is based on a measure of the net exposure of our portfolio – namely, the IVaR – rather than the gross exposure. The net exposure is the theoretically correct exposure to cover, and is also often considerably less than the gross exposure (net exposures are often, in fact, only a fraction of gross exposures) due to the presence of natural hedges within the portfolio (between currency and equity positions, and so on).[7] One of the attractions of this approach is, therefore, that it helps protect us against spending a lot of money hedging micro-level risks that largely offset each other at the firm-wide level.

Box 8.2:   Finding a hedge portfolio

If we wish to hedge risks, it will often be the case that the best hedge is not a position in any single instrument, but a portfolio made up of a variety of different instruments. Litterman (1996, pp. 69–70) suggests a simple way to derive this hedge portfolio. All we need to do is specify the number of assets we want in this portfolio, and then search over different combinations of prospective assets to find that particular combination that best replicates the pay-off to the portfolio we wish to hedge. This 'best replicating portfolio' then mimics our real portfolio, and a short position in the best replicating portfolio is our hedge.

The fact that the replicating portfolio consists of a small number of assets also makes it easy to buy or sell the assets in our replicating portfolio when we wish to set up or change the hedge position.

Litterman (1996, p. 70) also notes that, since it provides an approximate replication of our portfolio, the best replicating portfolio also provides a simplified aid to understanding the risks in our 'real' portfolio: it is far easier to understand the risks in a replicating portfolio of, say, five assets, than it is to understand the risks in a 'real' portfolio of perhaps hundreds of assets.[8]

4.1. The VaR Approach to Hedging Compared to Traditional Approaches

The approach to hedging set out here is quite different from and clearly superior to the traditional approach to hedging set out in standard textbooks.[9] In essence, the traditional approach tries to hedge each individual source of risk on its own, without taking account of the overall portfolio risk exposure or the presence of natural hedges within the portfolio. Implicitly, it presumes that we are dealing with a single source of risk that is also (implicitly) assumed to be independent of other risk factors. The problem, of course, is that this independence assumption is almost always inappropriate. Furthermore, even if risks are independent, the traditional approach fails to allow for diversification of risks and requires that we hedge each risk factor separately. If there are n risk factors we wish to hedge, we must do so by taking out n separate hedge positions, rather than one hedge against the portfolio as a whole.

The new VaR approach is superior to the traditional approach in a variety of ways:

- The fact that the traditional approach looks at separate hedges for each risk factor often leads to excessive (and excessively costly) hedge positions. It will often be the case that different risks largely offset each other or diversify away, and so all that is really required is one particular small hedge position or possibly no hedge at all instead of a number of larger ones. The VaR approach is therefore better because it gives us the one cheaper, smaller portfolio hedge we actually need, while the traditional approach gives us a string of expensive micro hedges that to a greater or lesser extent offset each other.

- The traditional approach can easily lead to over-hedging in situations where the risks concerned are to a large extent already hedged naturally. The over-hedging arises because the traditional approach relates the size of the hedge position to the gross exposure of the new position (i.e., its exposure considered independently of the rest of the portfolio), instead of relating it to the (usually smaller) net exposure. The hedge might therefore be unnecessary, and the amount spent on it wasted. Indeed, if it knocks out an existing natural hedge, a new 'hedge' position can leave our portfolio even more exposed than it already is.

- The traditional approach gives us little help with basis risk. Hedges will rarely, if ever, be perfect and there will almost always be some mismatch between the position being hedged and the hedge itself. The resulting basis risk can be quite substantial, particularly when the hedging positions being used are standardised exchange-traded instruments. However, the traditional approach gives us no real quantitative guidance on how to manage the basis risk. Once we have 'hedged' our position – which, in reality, only means that we have swapped the original risk exposure for an exposure to basis risk – the traditional approach has little more to offer. By comparison, basis risk is simply not an issue with the VaR approach.

The VaR approach is thus clearly superior to the traditional approach to hedging. Yet the VaR approach to hedging is also exactly the same as the VaR approach to other investment decisions, and the only feature that distinguishes a hedge investment from any other (i.e., speculative) investment is that the hedge investment involves a negative IVaR: whatever the type of investment, we always apply the same approach. Having applied it, we can then classify the negative-IVaR investments as hedges and the positive ones as speculative investments, if we have any particular reason to make such a classification. There is therefore no need for a separate theory of hedging as such, as distinct from our more general theory of investment. VaR theory simplifies risk management by enabling us to collapse hedging theory into a more general theory of investment decision making.

5. MANAGING PORTFOLIOS

A VaR approach can also help with portfolio management. Perhaps the most important use is to assess the efficiency of our current portfolio and of any prospective changes to it. This efficiency check is based on the principle, embodied in (7.10) and its various analogues, that any position *included in* our portfolio should have an expected return at least as great as the required return. If we are using (7.10), we therefore require that R_A be at least as great as $[1 + \eta_A(VaR, a)]R_p^{old}$. Similarly, any position *excluded from* our portfolio should have an expected return that is *less than* the required return $[1 + \eta_A(VaR, a)]R_p^{old}$. If our portfolio is efficient, any position included in the portfolio should have an expected return at least as great as any position excluded from our portfolio. If this condition is not met, there will be some currently excluded asset with a greater expected return than some currently included asset, and we should acquire the former asset (or increase our holdings of it) and sell (or reduce our holdings of) the latter.

A simple way to implement this rule in practice is to give portfolio managers an efficiency score for each position they hold or are considering acquiring. This score would be the ratio of expected to required returns. An efficiency score of more than one indicates that a particular position has (or would have) an expected return greater than its required return; an efficiency score of more than one therefore indicates that the position in question is good for our portfolio. An efficiency score of less than one indicates that a position has (or would have) an expected return that is less than its required return; it indicates that the position is bad for our portfolio. And an efficiency score of about one indicates that the expected and required returns are about equal, and so indicates that the position is marginal. The efficiency scores of current and prospective positions therefore give portfolio managers easily comprehensible and very useful leads on where and how they should change their portfolios.[10]

6. CONCLUSIONS

The VaR approach to decision making has a number of very useful applications. However, it is also important to appreciate its limitations, and two limitations particularly stand out:

- The first is that the VaR approach always requires an estimate of IVaR. These estimates are required not only for decisions involving market risks, but for almost any decisions that impinge on risk and/or return. These include credit risk decisions, liquidity and operational risk decisions, and all manner of contingent-commitment decisions. Unfortunately, estimates of their IVaRs are not always easy to obtain or particularly accurate when we get them. We therefore need ways of imputing IVaRs to those positions for which we may not have good data and whose IVaRs cannot be estimated using other, more reliable ways.

- The other limitation is that all decisions need to be taken in a context determined by the firm's overall risk management policy. This policy will tell decision makers about any particular factors they should take account of and will also give them an indication of the range of options they are allowed to consider.[11] If the decision being considered is a major one, decisions should also be made taking account of their broader strategic ramifications.

ENDNOTES

1. The use of (7.10) implicitly presumes that the benchmark return is zero and that the incremental position size a is non-zero. As discussed in the last chapter, we can relax these assumptions either by using (7.15) or by using the slightly different procedure for zero-value positions outlined in Box 7.3. However, in the present context we shall stick with the one relatively simple condition, (7.10), since that makes the exposition easier.

2. In using this rule, we also have to decide how to estimate the IVaR. The answer is that given in Chapter 3: if the position being considered is small relative to the overall portfolio, we might be able to get by using the short-cut approach outlined in Chapter 3; however, if the position is large relative to our existing portfolio, we would have to estimate the IVaR using the longer but more accurate 'before-and-after' approach.

3. Where we are dealing with major investments, it obviously makes sense to use the most accurate approach available rather than skimp on computational time. We would therefore presumably use (7.15) instead of (7.10) to allow for a more sensible benchmark than cash, and would also estimate the IVaR using the 'before-and-after' approach.

4. It makes no major difference if the required return curve slopes upwards along its entire length. If the required return curve is upward-sloping, we will still invest, if we do at all, at that point where the required return curve cuts the expected asset return curve from below. If such a point does not exist (i.e., in the present context, if the two curves don't cross), we don't invest anything.

5. See also, e.g., Masters (1997, p. 32).

6. The optimal hedge position developed here is not to be confused with Litterman's (1996, p. 64) 'best hedge' (sic). Litterman's 'best hedge' is that position in any given asset that minimises the contribution of that asset to portfolio risk, i.e., it is the position that minimises the IVaR. However, as the text has (hopefully) made clear, the (correct) optimal position – assuming there is a non-zero optimal position – is where the required return curve crosses the expected asset return curve from below, and this position will in general be quite different from Litterman's 'best hedge'. Litterman's 'best hedge' is therefore generally not optimal.

7. See, e.g., Falloon (1995, p. 44).

8. Naturally, finding hedge positions also involves an element of judgement, but a good place to look for hedges is among positions that are negatively correlated with the main risk(s) in our portfolio, but which we also feel bullish about. Unless the new position is very large, the negative correlation with the major portfolio risk(s) will make the new position a hedge – more or less regardless of the volatility of the new position considered on its own – and our bullish outlook on this position implies that we expect to earn a positive return from it. A hedge that earns a positive return is a very attractive hedge. For more on this issue, see Litterman (1996, pp. 71–3).

9. It is also set out in, e.g., Campbell and Kracaw (1993, pp. 219–23).

10. Portfolio managers would also want to see the incremental VaRs from current and prospective positions, and such information is very useful for getting an idea of the main sources of risk in our (current or prospective) portfolio. However, data on IVaRs alone are not enough for portfolio managers to make sensible portfolio management decisions. What matters for portfolio efficiency is not the IVaR alone, but the relationship of the required return (which of course reflects the IVaR, among other factors) and the expected return from the position in question. Hence my advice to

portfolio managers is to use IVaRs to get some idea of the main risks of their portfolios, but to rely mainly on efficiency scores to identify the changes they may need to make.

11. For example, a decision maker might check out the firm's risk strategy documentation and realise that the firm has a clear policy against bearing a particular risk. His/her options would then be very clear: they could either reject any position that carries such a risk or (perhaps) consider it in conjunction with an insurance contract or hedging strategy to offset the risk involved. Alternatively, the firm might have a clear policy that it wants to bear particular risks and therefore does not want hedges taken out against those risks. If the firm produces oil, say, it may not want to hedge itself against oil-price risk, on the grounds that its shareholders bought their shares precisely because they wanted to bear such risk.

9

Credit Risk

1. CREDIT RISK MEASUREMENT

1.1. Overview

C REDIT risk can be defined as the risk of loss arising from the failure of a counterparty to make a contractual payment.[1] Some examples are the risk that a bondholder bears from the possibility that the bond issuer will default and the risk that an option holder bears from the possibility that the option writer might not honour the contract if called upon to do so. Credit risk has three main components:

- *Probability of default*: the probability that the counterparty will fail to make a contractual payment.
- *Recovery rate*: the proportion of our claim that we recover if the counterparty defaults.
- *Credit exposure*: credit exposure relates to the amount we stand to lose in default. This is usually interpreted as the replacement value of the contract in the event of default, net of whatever we expect to recover from the counterparty.[2]

We now have two main tasks: to analyse and measure these three components of credit risk, and to investigate how institutions can influence these factors to reduce their credit risk.

1.1.1. Historical Context

It is important to appreciate how credit risk has altered in recent years. Traditionally, credit risk was mainly the concern of bank lending managers, bondholders and specialist credit rating analysts. The basic question was whether to grant a loan or buy a bond, and the credit exposure from any transaction was readily related to the book value of the amount loaned plus any accumulated interest.

Credit risk has since become much more complex. Whilst loans and bonds are still significant, a great deal of credit risk now arises from derivatives transactions. Credit risk is therefore a major concern to many of the institutions that participate in derivatives markets, many of whom bore little credit risk in the past except for the trade credit they extended to their customers. Moreover, the newer credit risks are often less transparent and more difficult to assess than traditional credit risks. They are more difficult to assess for three main reasons:

- Notional amounts often give us little idea about derivative credit exposures. With a bank loan, we at least knew that the book value of the loan gave us an idea of the amount we could lose. We could then estimate our likely loss by applying some estimates of default probabilities and recovery rates to this notional amount. However, with derivatives contracts there is often no clear relation between a contract's value and its credit exposure. For example, swap or forward contracts will usually have zero initial values, and yet both contracts can produce large losses if the underlying variables move strongly in the wrong direction. Hence, when an institution engages in a derivatives deal, it is often not immediately obvious how much credit risk it is really taking on.
- The credit risks associated with derivatives positions can vary enormously (e.g., as with leveraged structured notes) and in complicated ways (e.g., as with cylinder options), with movements in underlying prices. In some cases, maximum losses can also occur when the underlying price does not move at all (e.g., as with a long straddle).
- Derivatives credit risk is further complicated by portfolio effects. With loans, we know that the total exposure is closely related to the total gross amount loaned. However, with derivatives there are no simple rules to relate total credit exposure to the gross size of a derivatives portfolio. If we have two zero-value FX forward contracts, say, and one contract gains in value when the underlying exchange rate rises but the other falls, then the credit exposures of the two contracts will move in opposite directions when the exchange rate changes. In general, we cannot get an accurate picture of overall credit exposure by adding up individual exposures, because the individual exposures may (and generally will) interact with each other.

Consequently, it is not surprising that institutions had difficulty when they first started to handle derivatives credit risks, and resorted instead to convenient rules of thumb. For example, when interest-rate swaps were first being used in the early 1980s, institutions tended to treat swaps as offsetting bond purchases because doing so implied that a swap had the same credit risk as a bond purchase from the same counterparty. Unfortunately, this procedure overlooks an important difference: while mutual bond purchases imply commitments to make both coupon and principal payments, an interest-rate swap involves no exchange of principal at maturity and only implies a commitment to make mutual coupon payments. Hence, an interest-rate swap involves a lower credit risk – typically, a much lower one – than a corresponding mutual bond purchase. The result was that companies tended to overstate the default risk of swaps. Yet, as time passed and defaults were seen to be relatively rare, there arose an opposite tendency to regard interest-rate swaps as having no default risk at all, and some of those who did so became unstuck in the early 1990s. Swap managers swung from one extreme to the other. The truth of the matter is that interest-rate swaps are risky, though not nearly as risky as bonds, but we can only assess their true credit risk if we abandon rules of thumb and resort to some decent credit risk analysis.

1.2. Assessing Default Risk

Traditionally, likely default rates were assessed by loan officers using information from financial statements, knowledge of the relevant firm's history, a view of the quality of the

---

Box 9.1:   Differences between credit and market risk

Credit and market risks differ in a number of ways:

(1) To handle credit risk we need to pay attention to default probabilities, recovery rates in default, and the identity of our counterparties – factors that are not directly relevant to market risks.

(2) When dealing with market risk, we tend to focus on risk over one, often relatively short, time horizon; when dealing with credit risk, we often tend to be concerned about risks over a much longer horizon, until the credit risk is eliminated.

(3) Assuming normality with credit risks is more problematic than assuming normality for market price risks. There are two reasons for this. (a) Normality is harder to justify over the longer horizons often relevant for credit risk. (b) When dealing with credit-related risks, the underlying risk variable – the occurrence or otherwise of default – is not itself normally distributed, and this makes it harder to treat the resulting credit risks as normally distributed.[3]

(4) When trying to control market risk, we usually try to impose position limits on *individual units* within *our* organisation. When trying to control credit risk, we try to impose limits on the *other* party (i.e., the counterparty) *taken as a whole.*

(5) While market risk issues are legally clear-cut, there are a number of major legal uncertainties surrounding credit risk (e.g., over the legal status of netting agreements and the ownership of collateral in default), and these uncertainties are a major source of concern for credit risk managers and corporate lawyers.

---

firm's management and an assessment of its prospects. More recently, Moody's and Standard and Poor's have published studies of bond defaults in the US that enable one to use current credit ratings to predict default rates over specified horizons.[4] These exercises indicate that there is a strong negative correlation between credit ratings and default rates, and this finding allows us to use current credit ratings to predict bond default rates.

Predictions of default rates can also be improved by using other observable factors. The work of Edward Altman in particular has examined the predictive power of a range of financial variables and uses the results to discriminate between those firms likely to fail and those that are not.[5] Altman's procedures are reasonably good at discriminating between these types of firm, and can therefore be used to fine-tune predicted failure probabilities. However, they are not well suited to predicting the failure rates of highly rated firms. Since highly rated firms are very unlikely to default, we can expect only a very small number of such firms to fail in any given sample. Hence, even a good discriminant rule that correctly predicts their failure will also incorrectly predict the failure of a large number of other firms that do *not* subsequently fail. The cost of these errors is therefore likely to be high relative to the benefits of being able to identify the small number of highly rated firms that do fail. Accordingly, Wakeman (1996a, p. 316) recommends that we do not bother with such methods when trying to predict the failure rates of highly rated firms. We should therefore concentrate our credit evaluation procedures on firms with lower credit ratings or no credit ratings at all.[6]

1.3. Recovery rates

The second major factor affecting credit risk is the amount recoverable in default: the greater the amount we expect to recover, the lower the credit risk, other things being equal. Not surprisingly, evidence indicates that recovery rates vary considerably. They depend on the seniority ranking of the creditor: recovery rates typically vary from 10–50% for subordinated debt, 30–70% for senior unsecured debt, and 40–90% for secured debt, and derivatives claims generally rank equally with senior unsecured debt.[7] Recovery rates also depend on the terminal value and credit rating of the defaulted firm, the bargaining power of different groups, the arbitrariness of the legal process, and other relevant factors.[8]

These figures also give a clear indication that courts tend not to apply absolute priority rules, so junior creditors often get some payment when senior ones are not paid off in full, despite absolute priority rules that should, in principle, require creditors to be paid off in strict order of seniority.

1.4. Credit Exposure

1.4.1. Credit Exposure as Replacement Cost

An institution faces credit exposure on a contract only if that contract has a positive market value to the institution. Its replacement cost is then equal to this positive value minus whatever is recovered from the defaulting counterparty (collateral, proceeds obtained through bankruptcy court, and so on). If a contract has a negative value, on the other hand, the institution is owed nothing and therefore has no current credit exposure. Hence, the replacement cost of a contract is the bigger of the market value of the contract minus its recovery value,[9] or zero.

In practice, we will usually be interested in fours sorts of exposure: the expected credit exposure and expected default loss, and the maximum likely credit exposure and maximum likely default loss, at given levels of confidence. We now consider each of these in turn.

1.4.2. Expected Credit Exposure and Expected Default Loss

The expected credit exposure can be found by specifying a PDF for our net replacement cost – either a theoretical one such as a normal distribution, or an empirical one based on real-world data – and taking its mean. Let x be the estimated replacement value of a contract at some future date t. If x has a PDF $f(x)$, the expected credit exposure (ECE) is:

$$\text{Expected credit exposure} = \int_{-\infty}^{\infty} Max(x, 0)f(x)dx \qquad (9.1)$$

This equation tells us that the ECE is the probability-weighted average of possible credit exposures, where each credit exposure is the maximum of the amount we are owed, if positive, and zero otherwise.[10] If $f(x)$ is normal with standard deviation σ, then[11]

$$\text{Expected credit exposure} = \sigma/\sqrt{2\pi} \qquad (9.2)$$

Box 9.2:   The BIS add-on approach to credit risk

During the last decade many institutions have attempted to allow for credit risk by the add-on procedure used by the BIS to determine minimum capital requirements. As revised in 1995, this procedure allows for credit risk by classifying instruments into categories and giving each category a fixed weight. With on-balance-sheet positions, the credit exposure is held to be the nominal value of the position times the relevant credit weight. For off-balance-sheet positions, the credit exposure is held to be a credit equivalent amount (CEA) times a relevant credit weight, and this CEA is equal to the absolute value of the mark-to-market value plus an add-on factor, itself taken to be a certain percentage of the effective notional amount. Different percentages are specified for different types of position, and positions are classified in terms of the type of contract (e.g., interest-rate, FX) and the time to maturity (e.g., less than one year). The total credit exposure is the sum of the credit exposures of the individual instruments, subject to some limited (and arbitrary) allowance for the netting of risks.

   This approach has the attraction of being simple to operate, but its drawbacks far outweigh any advantages. The most fundamental problem is that it does not tell us much about credit exposure at all, except for the most simple portfolios and only then if the weights just happen to be about right. More specifically: (1) The principle of allowing for credit risk by fixed 'add-ons' is intellectually indefensible, and makes no allowance for default risks, market volatilities, recovery rates, and so on. (2) The broad categories used – interest-rate contracts, and so forth – are far too broad to do any justice to the contracts involved. Two interest-rate derivatives can have very different risk exposures, and we cannot do justice to them by imposing the same exposure weights on each. (3) The weights chosen are completely arbitrary and do not reflect the diversity and complexity of real-world credit exposures. (4) The add-on approach makes no genuine allowance for portfolio factors, and the modifications used to allow for them do not really do so. This in turn usually leads to risk exposures being overestimated.

   These drawbacks have led many institutions to abandon the BIS model when assessing their credit risks and to develop their own models instead.

The expected credit exposure is therefore a multiple (i.e., $1/\sqrt{2\pi}$) of the standard deviation of the estimated replacement value.

   We can also estimate the expected default loss. This is the loss in the event of default times the probability that the contract is in the money and the counterparty defaults, and this latter probability is usually the probability of default times one-half. Hence:[12]

$$\text{Expected default loss} = ECE.prob[default]/2 \qquad (9.3)$$

The expected default loss under a normal distribution is then found by substituting (9.2) into (9.3):

$$\text{Expected default loss} = \sigma.prob[default]/\sqrt{8\pi} \qquad (9.4)$$

This expected default loss tells us how much we can expect to lose from our estimated credit exposure on a certain contract over a certain period. This is very useful cost information and should always be subtracted from the contract's expected revenue if we are to arrive at an appropriate estimate of the project's expected profit.[13] Such information is not only useful for budgetary purposes, but can also be useful to set up default reserves, rank prospective contracts, and guide purchase and sale decisions.

1.4.3. Credit at Risk and Default Value at Risk

We can also estimate the maximum credit exposure at some level of confidence. This maximum is *not* to be confused with the maximum credit exposure possible. Instead, the maximum credit exposure with which we are concerned is an upper bound on a confidence interval for the estimated replacement cost. If we chose the 95% confidence level, we would therefore have the maximum credit exposure that we could expect on 19 days out of 20. We can regard this estimate as a kind of credit exposure at risk, or credit at risk (CaR) for short, and can formalise it in the same way as the expected exposure. If we again assume that the replacement cost is normally distributed, the credit at risk at the 95% confidence level is:

$$\text{Credit at risk} = 1.65\sigma \qquad (9.5)$$

This figure gives us an estimate of our maximum likely credit exposure by a certain future time. This can be very useful when making purchase and sale decisions, pricing contracts, setting and/or monitoring credit limits, evaluating performance and allocating capital.[14]

   We can also estimate the maximum default loss (as opposed to credit exposure) at the same confidence level. This tells us the maximum loss to expect from default in 95% of cases. It is therefore a measure of the value at risk arising from credit risk, as compared to the earlier VaR that arises from market-price risk. In other words, it is a measure of *default-related value at risk*, or *default VaR* for short. Assuming normality and an exogenous default probability, this default VaR is:

$$\text{Default VaR} = 1.65\sigma \, prob[default] \qquad (9.6)$$

This default VaR is extremely useful, and has all the obvious uses of other VaR figures: it can be used to assist purchase/sale decisions, price contracts, allocate capital, and so forth. Since it gives us the maximum likely loss from counterparty defaults, but ignores market risks, it is a mirror image of, and in fact a natural complement to, traditional VaR, which looks at market risks but ignores default-related risks.

1.4.4. Dynamic Profile of Credit Exposures

These measures, however, give us information about prospective exposures or losses only over a specified future period, and this information is usually not enough for reliable credit analysis. Credit analysis is not like, say, VaR analysis, where we can usually assume that the VaR over one holding period is highly correlated with the VaR over some other holding period. The prospective credit exposures on a given portfolio often change dramatically as we look further into the future, so we cannot assume that our prospective exposure two years from now, say, is a simple 'well-behaved' function (e.g., a straightforward extrapolation) of our credit exposure six months from now. Depending on the

---

Box 9.3: Credit at risk and default VaR vs. 'traditional' VaR

Whilst credit at risk and default VaR are analytically similar to 'traditional' market-price VaR, there are nonetheless a number of important differences between them:

(1) CaR and default VaR are more difficult to estimate than market VaR, since they require estimates of recovery rates, collateral, guarantees and other variables. They therefore require more information and are more dependent on the assumptions that go with using such information. Default VaR also requires estimates of likely default rates, and these too are problematic.

(2) The nature of credit risk compels us to consider the dynamic profiles of credit at risk and default VaR. Unlike traditional market-price VaR, we cannot usually get away with looking over only one horizon period, such as the next day. We need to consider credit exposures over a number of different periods.

(3) CaR and default VaR require that we consider each counterparty separately. We therefore have to consider both counterparty and position type, not just the latter.

(4) The very nature of credit risk means that we are dealing with losses that will not be realised in most instances, but will also be much bigger than expected *ex ante* in those cases where they do occur. The distribution of losses will therefore exhibit potentially very fat tails.

---

position, our credit exposure may rise or fall over time, or move around in all sorts of convoluted ways.

Some examples of typical credit exposures for simple positions are given in Figure 9.1. Figure 9.1(a) shows the mean and maximum exposure curves for a forward contract, while Figure 9.1(b) shows the same curves for an interest-rate swap. As we can see, in both cases the two curves begin at a zero exposure – reflecting the initial zero market value of each contract – and then rise as the horizon increases. These increases in exposure reflect a diffusion effect: exposures rise because the underlying variable on which exposure depends is likely to move more over a longer horizon than over a shorter one. However, the exposures of the two contracts differ at medium and long horizons. With the forward contract, there is no offset to diffusion so the exposure continues to rise as the horizon increases. However, in the case of the swap contract, each set of regular payments reduces the value of outstanding obligations. The contract amortises over time, and this amortisation process serves initially to dampen the diffusion effect and then eventually to overcome it. As the swap approaches maturity, most payments will have been made already and there will be relatively little credit still outstanding. The swap exposure therefore peaks somewhere in the mid-term of the contract and then gradually goes back towards zero as the swap approaches maturity.

However, these are only the credit exposures of uncomplicated positions, and even simple alterations of the contract terms can make a big difference to the exposure profile. Imagine, for example, that we introduce a mutual termination option in the swap contract that gives us the right to close out the contract after two years. Assume too that we expect this right to be exercised and a three-year swap to be initiated at that point to replace what is left of the terminated swap agreement. The credit exposure in Figure 9.1(b)

Box 9.4: A shortcut to credit at risk and default VaR

If we are prepared to make certain simplifying assumptions, we can estimate credit at risk and default VaR easily from existing estimates of market-price VaR. Suppose we wish to estimate our credit exposure over the same period for which we estimate VaR (e.g., over a month). If we start with zero credit exposures, assume that the recovery value of defaulted contracts is zero and ignore non-credit-related profits (e.g., capital gains on equity holdings), then our credit exposure by the end of the next day will equal our accumulated profit. Our credit at risk will therefore be equal to the *upper* fifth percentile of our profit/loss distribution.

If we now assume that the profit and loss distribution is symmetric, with a zero mean profit, the upper fifth percentile profit (i.e., the CaR) will be equal to the lower fifth percentile loss (i.e., the VaR itself), so the CaR is equal to the VaR. We can then estimate a shortcut default VaR by applying a default rate to the CaR just estimated. (For example, if the estimated default rate is 1% and the CaR is $100 million, our default VaR would be $1 million.) We therefore have the following two shortcut formulas:

$$\text{Credit at risk (CaR)} = \text{VaR}$$

$$\text{Default VaR} = \text{prob[default].VaR}$$

We can of course modify the formulas accordingly if we wish to relax the assumptions that the profit and loss distribution is symmetric and has zero mean. We can also relax other assumptions, such as that of zero recovery value. For example, we could assume a certain average recovery value, which would lead to CaR being a known fraction of maximum likely profit. Alternatively – and this might be particularly appropriate if recovery value is low and/or recovery itself particularly uncertain – we could keep the zero recovery assumption and regard the CaR and default-VaR figures as conservative (i.e., upper-bound) estimates.

This approach has the attraction of giving us a short cut to the estimation of credit and default risk without the need for 'real' credit data. However, it is also dependent on a number of obviously dubious assumptions. It is also limited by the requirement for a VaR figure predicated on the horizon period in which we are interested. If we are interested in credit/default risk over the next year, we would want a VaR figure that was also based on an annual holding period, and so on. The only practical solution in these circumstances is to fall back on the assumption that the underlying profit and loss distribution is appropriately well behaved (e.g., normal). Only then can we infer the VaR(s) for the relevant horizon period(s). Hence, this short cut implicitly requires normality or some substitute distributional assumption, and such an assumption will often not be appropriate.

---

would then dip back down to zero after two years, only to rise again and show another hump over the two- to five-year period. This simple adjustment would therefore lead to two peak exposures, one occurring after about one year and the other after about four years, rather than one single peak exposure occurring mid-way over the five-year period.

FIGURE 9.1   Expected Credit Exposure and Credit at Risk

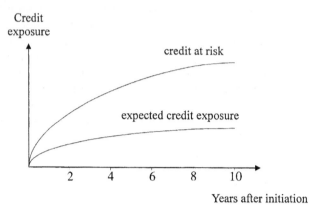

(a) Expected Credit Exposure and Credit at Risk
    for Hypothetical Forward Contract

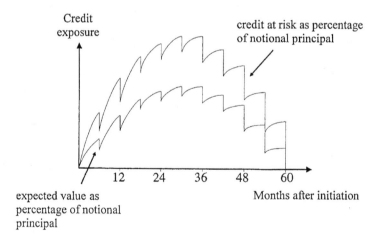

(b) Expected Credit Exposure and Credit at Risk
    for Hypothetical Five-year Interest-rate Swap

Furthermore, the adjusted contract would show relatively little exposure at the very time when the exposure on the unadjusted one was peaking. This example illustrates the importance of looking at the whole profile and not just at the prospective exposure at one particular date. Naturally, the credit exposures of more sophisticated derivatives positions can be even more complicated.[15]

1.4.5. Portfolio Effects

We must also consider how individual credit exposures interact with each other when put together in a portfolio, and we cannot assume that a portfolio's aggregate exposure is simply the sum of individual exposures taken on their own. If we had a portfolio of two similar contracts, a given change in the underlying price would have much the same effect on the values of both contracts. The credit exposures of both contracts would therefore change in the same way, and the change in portfolio exposure would be the sum of the changes in individual contract exposures. However, in general, a change in a risk factor will lead to changes in the credit exposures of individual assets that are less than perfectly correlated with each other. Indeed, where portfolios are hedged, changes in risk factors will have no major effects on the portfolio as a whole, and hence no major effect on overall exposure. Individual positions may be exposed to a given source of risk, but whether and to what extent the portfolio is exposed will depend on how the individual exposures interact. Everything comes down to the interaction of the exposures.[16]

Perhaps the best way forward is to map our exposures onto core risk variables and use a variance-covariance approach to allow for these interactions. The resulting credit-at-risk estimate is analogous to our earlier portfolio VaR estimates: it estimates the relevant maximum likely exposure at a given level of confidence, taking into account interactions among the exposures of the individual positions.

We would also want some idea of prospective losses and not just exposures. We would therefore want a default-VaR system as well. The simplest way to construct such a system is to assume that default probabilities and recovery rates are constant and translate expected exposures into expected default-related losses using (9.6). This default-VaR figure would then give us the maximum amount we are likely to lose from counterparty defaults, at some level of confidence, taking into account the interactions of different underlying risk variables.[17]

2. CREDIT RISK MANAGEMENT

There are thus three elements of credit risk: default probability, recovery rate and risk exposure. Credit risk management can therefore be regarded as a set of techniques for reducing default probability and risk exposure, and increasing the recovery rate.

2.1. Netting Arrangements

There are a number of different ways institutions can achieve these ends. One way is to use netting arrangements. These help to reduce credit exposures and are widely used in derivatives contracts. Netting arrangements stipulate that each party should be liable for the net rather than the gross amount they owe the other party. If there are two contracts between A and B, and the first contract has positive value to A and the second one has positive value to B, a netting arrangement means that A owes B only the difference between the values of the two contracts, if that is positive, or zero otherwise. Without netting, A would still be liable to pay B the whole of what it owes on the second contract, even if B defaults on the first. A netting arrangement protects the non-defaulting party from a situation where its counterparty defaults on one contract and yet simultaneously insists on the payment due on the other.

Without netting, the loss in the event of counterparty default is the sum of the net market values of all contracts (i.e., the market values net of collateral and the expected recovery value of counterparty assets) in the agreement, if the sum is positive, or zero, if the sum is negative:

$$\text{Potential loss} = \sum_{i=1}^{n} Max(V_i, 0) \tag{9.7}$$

where there are n contracts between the two parties and V_i is the net market value of the ith contract. With netting, the potential loss is the sum of all positive-value contracts, viz.:

$$\text{Potential loss} = Max\left(\sum_{i=1}^{n} V_i, 0\right) \tag{9.8}$$

This netted amount will usually be less than the gross amount given in (9.7). The only exception is where all replacement costs are perfectly correlated, in which case the two amounts will be the same – and often very much less.[18] The total potential loss to any party is then the sum of the potential losses over all counterparties – the sum of the gross potential losses (9.7), if there is no netting, or the (usually) smaller sum of net potential losses (9.8), if there is netting. In general, the reduction in credit exposure created by netting will also be greater, the greater the number of deals outstanding with a counter-party and the more nearly aligned the individual contracts are (in terms of maturities, contract size, and so on).[19]

2.2. Periodic Settlement

We can also reduce credit risk by agreeing to the periodic settlement of outstanding obligations at certain points during the lifetime of the contract (e.g., every quarter). Credit exposures are therefore periodically eliminated. An extreme version of periodic settlement is the daily marking to market that takes place on futures exchanges: gains or losses are realised in full at the end of each business day. Periodic settlement arrangements can be useful where counterparties are restricted in their ability to pledge assets or where there is legal uncertainty about the rights of collateral holders in bankruptcy.[20] Alternatively, parties can simply agree to give each other options to terminate the contract early, provided outstanding obligations are settled. Creditor parties can then use such options to realise their profits and cut short the credit extended to the debtor party. Creditors' potential exposures can also be limited by stipulating that positions will be closed out if settlement/margin demands are not met.

However, these periodic settlement arrangements can also create liquidity problems. Firms that suffer adverse market moves will need to settle their losses quickly, and there is the danger that the need to settle quickly will provoke a liquidity crisis. *Ex ante*, a firm is taking on a potential liquidity risk when agreeing to such clauses, and the management ought to take this risk into account and consider how they would meet these liquidity demands if called upon to do so.

2.3. Margin and Collateral Requirements

Institutions can also reduce their exposure by means of margin or collateral requirements (i.e., so the counterparty makes available some particular asset that it would forfeit to a creditor in the event of default). Collateral might be demanded upfront, for example, as with the margin requirements of organised exchanges and many derivatives brokers. This margin is usually set to cover a specified large adverse move in the underlying price over some horizon period (e.g., a day for an organised exchange, but longer for some dealers). The size of the margin requirements can be determined by theoretical considerations (such as extreme value theory, as suggested by Longin (1994)) and/or by reference to past experience. The margins could also be tailored to reflect the size of the position and the credit ratings of counterparties. The contract could then be marked to market, with collateral being returned if the market moves in favour of a particular party, and more collateral being demanded if the market moves against. This marking to market ensures that gains or losses are realised quickly and so prevents the build-up of large credit exposures. If these additional margin demands were not met, the creditor party would have the right to close out the contract and so stop its credit exposure from rising any further. In other cases, there may be no margin upfront, but margin would be required if a contract's value reached a threshold level. For instance, two parties might agree on an interest-rate swap with an initial value of zero, but also agree that the losing party would give the other a stipulated amount of collateral if the contract value reached a certain level. We can think of this as a marking-to-market arrangement by which a losing party agrees to realise its loss on the contract whenever the loss hits a threshold level. Again, credit exposure is limited by providing for positions to be closed out if required margin payments are not made.

2.4. Credit Guarantees

Credit risk can also be reduced by seeking guarantees from third parties. Such guarantees mean that default on the contract can occur only if *both* the counterparty *and* its guarantor default, and can sometimes lead to a major reduction in credit risk. Suppose that our counterparty has an estimated probability of default of 10% over a horizon period. Now suppose that that party gets a guarantee from a company with an estimated default probability of 1% over the horizon. The probability of default on our contract then falls to 1% or less, depending on how the default probabilities are correlated (e.g., the probability of default will be 0.10 times 0.01, or 0.1%, if the probabilities are uncorrelated, and less if they are negatively correlated). Guarantees from third parties can therefore reduce credit risks drastically.[21]

2.5. Credit Triggers

Credit triggers are clauses that allow a contract to be terminated on pre-agreed terms if the credit rating of a counterparty falls to some trigger level. These clauses are similar to the covenants often used in commercial lending that specify that the debtor must

maintain minimum net worth or credit ratings. They are often used in long-term derivatives contracts and typically specify that a party has the right to have the contract
immediately settled if the counterparty's rating falls below investment grade. A credit
trigger protects against the credit exposure that would arise from a deterioration in the
counterparty's rating: should the counterparty's credit rating deteriorate, the contract is
terminated and the creditor can (hopefully) escape with his profit. It therefore ensures that
default can occur only while the counterparty still has a strong credit rating (i.e., default
can occur only when it is least likely to), and simulation evidence suggests that the
reduction in default probabilities can be very substantial.[22]

However, as with periodic resettlement, credit triggers can put considerable liquidity
pressure on the losing party to a derivatives transaction. In fact, credit triggers go even
further in that they hit the losing firm at a vulnerable time (i.e., when its cost of credit has
risen and its access to credit has become more restricted). A credit trigger can therefore
precipitate a liquidity crisis when a firm is downgraded, particularly if the firm has a
number of outstanding contracts each of which includes similar credit triggers. Credit
triggers therefore have a potentially serious downside, and the parties concerned need to
think carefully about this before they agree to them.

2.6. Position Limits

Institutions can also limit credit risks by placing position limits on their counterparties.
Such limits might be based on both notional amounts (i.e., counterparty x might be
allowed up to $\$y$ credit) and credit-at-risk figures. The latter limits would reflect measures
of the total exposure to any given counterparty (e.g., maximum total exposure), given
other relevant factors (e.g., existing exposure to that industry, prospective risks and
returns elsewhere). From what has already been said, it should be clear by now that this
total exposure is not just the sum of the individual exposures associated with each
contract with that counterparty, but an aggregate exposure that takes account of the way
individual position exposures interact.[23]

2.7. Credit Derivatives

Finally, firms can also manage their credit risks using credit derivatives.[24] These are
derivatives contracts with payments conditional on credit events of one sort or another.
The most common credit derivatives are: default swaps, in which one party makes
periodic payments to another party in return for a promise of payment in the event of a
default by some other party; credit spread swaps, in which periodic payments are made
in return for the promise of a spread-contingent payment; and total-return swaps, in
which parties swap bond payments, where at least one of the bonds involved is credit-
risky.[25]

Credit derivatives enable firms to trade credit risks, and such trades can help firms
manage their credit risks in many different ways. Firms that sell their credit risks can
benefit by: freeing up credit lines to good customers, so they can do more business with
them; reducing their exposure to key or weak customers, so reducing their vulnerability
to those customers defaulting; reducing their exposures, in the event that other occurren-

ces (e.g., credit-rating downgrades) make existing exposures too high; and generally separating out credit risks from project risks, so good projects are not unduly hindered by credit-risk considerations. At the same time, other firms might benefit from acquiring particular credit risks: such firms might want to increase particular exposures or gain new exposures (e.g., as part of a credit-risk diversification strategy), or they may benefit from the higher yields obtained by accepting new credit risks. [26] In the words of Mike Parsley:

> The potential of credit derivatives is immense. There are hundreds of possible applications: for commercial banks which want to change the risk profile of their loan books; for investment banks managing huge bond and derivatives portfolios; for manufacturing companies over-exposed to a single customer; for equity investors in project finance deals with unacceptable sovereign risk; for institutional investors that have unusual risk appetites (or just want to speculate); even for employees worried about the safety of their deferred remuneration. The potential uses are so widespread that some market participants argue that credit derivatives could eventually outstrip all other derivative products in size and importance. (Parsley, 1996, p. 28)[27]

Credit derivatives thus have many uses in helping to manage derivatives risks, and risk managers need to give serious attention to how they can best make use of them.

3. INTEGRATING DEFAULT VaR AND MARKET VaR

As we have seen, it is quite possible to set up a system to estimate the maximum we are likely to lose from default (i.e., default VaR), but this default VaR ignores the risk of loss from market price movements. By contrast, traditional VaR allows for this market risk but ignores default risk. In practice, we usually face the prospect of losses from both sources of risk, so we should really take both risk sources into account. But how can we derive an overall VaR figure that takes account of both market and default risk?[28]

One way to do this is simply to carry out the two sets of calculations separately and add the two resulting VaR numbers. This at least gives us a very quick and easy answer, especially if we have already carried out the separate default-VaR and market-VaR calculations. However, if we really want an integrated VaR that covers both market and default risks, we should in theory redo our VaR analysis from first principles, taking both default risk and market risk into account from the beginning. (Some short-cut ways of doing this are explained in Box 9.5.)

We therefore need to go back to basics. As with the earlier VaR analysis, the best approach is to work out the combined default-plus-market VaR of the basic building block positions, and then derive the combined VaRs of more complex positions by reverse-engineering them into their building-block equivalents. However, this time there are only three building-block positions to consider: equity positions, fixed-income positions, and forward positions. The fourth building block – the FX building block – is the same as it was with market risks because there is no credit risk attached to it.

Box 9.5:   Some short cuts to integrated VaR

Estimating integrated VaR does not *necessarily* have to be difficult. One approach is to use the short cut outlined in Box 9.2 to estimate default VaR from an estimate of market VaR. We can then estimate or overall VaR by adding the default VaR thus obtained to the original market VaR. The most basic version of this approach leads to an overall VaR, $VaR^{overall}$, given by:

$$VaR^{overall} = (1 + p)VaR^{mkt}$$

where VaR^{mkt} is the market VaR and p is the probability of default. This approach enables us to estimate overall VaR without any real credit data. However, it is extremely simplistic (e.g., it relies on arbitrary parameter assumptions and normality)[29] and is also open to objection precisely because it does not use real credit data.

   A more sophisticated approach is to estimate the market VaR and default VaR separately, and then combine them into an overall VaR estimate that also makes allowance for the correlation between them. If VaR^{def} is the default VaR, and the correlation coefficient between VaR^{def} and VaR^{mkt} is ρ, then $VaR^{overall}$ is:

$$VaR^{overall} = \sqrt{(VaR^{mkt})^2 + (VaR^{def})^2 + 2\rho VaR^{mkt}VaR^{def}}$$

This second short cut is clearly very easy to use once we have our two VaR estimates and some historical data to estimate their correlation. It is also less simplistic than the first approach and makes use of real credit data. However, this procedure is still a short cut and the basic approach of estimating the two VaRs separately and then adding them is *not* the same as constructing an integrated VaR figure that takes both sources of risk fully into account throughout the analysis. There is no such thing as a free lunch!

3.1. Integrated Equity VaR

The simplest building block is a basic equity position. Imagine we wish to estimate the VaR of a position made up of the equity of a firm that may go bankrupt. Default risk affects our equity holding because a default would lead to the firm's assets being used to pay creditors, and if that happens we can assume that the value of our equity holding would go to zero. One possible way[30] to analyse this problem is by means of a geometric Brownian motion procedure. Assume that the firm will default over any interval of time Δt with probability $\lambda \Delta t$, which we assume for convenience to be constant. If the firm does default, we can presume that our equity holding will be worthless. If the firm does not default, we assume that its return is governed by a discretised geometric Brownian motion process. Our return at the end of a period of length Δt is therefore 0 with probability $\lambda \Delta t$, and approximately

$$S(\mu \Delta t + Z\sigma\sqrt{\Delta t}) \tag{9.9}$$

with probability $1 - \lambda\Delta t$. After a certain amount of manipulation, the variance of the return to the equity position is approximately[31]

$$\sigma_R^2 = S^2(\lambda + \sigma^2)\Delta t \tag{9.10}$$

In this simple model, the return variance is equal to the sum of a credit-risk factor (given by λ) and a market-risk factor (given by σ^2). The greater the probability of default, the greater the return variance. If λ is small enough, the distribution of the return will be roughly normal, and the VaR will be:

$$VaR = -\alpha S\sqrt{(\lambda + \sigma^2)\Delta t} \tag{9.11}$$

Obtaining the VaR of a basic equity holding subject to default risk thus involves a simple modification of the earlier market-VaR approach with no default risk.

3.2. Integrated Fixed-Income VaR

Incorporating credit risk into VaR analyses of fixed-income positions is more difficult, but one reasonable approach[32] is the zero-arbitrage approach suggested by Jarrow and Turnbull (1995, 1996).[33] Suppose we hold a zero-coupon bond issued by a firm with a particular credit rating. We now wish to model the price of our default-risky bond in such a way that there is no room for unexploited arbitrage opportunities. We begin by subdividing the period between now (i.e., 0) and T into a number of sub-periods, each of length Δt. At the start of each sub-period the issuer is either in default already or not. If they are already in default, we assume they remain in default and are unable ever to repay in full. Instead, they wait till T, when they pay a fraction δ of the face value of the bond. If they are not already in default, they either default over the sub-period or they get through the sub-period without defaulting. They then either default or do not default the next sub-period, and so on. In other words, over any given sub-period starting at τ, there is a (risk-neutralised) probability $\mu(\tau)\Delta t$ that the issuer will default, and a probability $(1 - \mu(\tau)\Delta t)$ that they will not default. We assume that the default process is independent of interest rates, so we can take default as an exogenous event.

Our next task is to estimate these probabilities for each sub-period over the period 0 to T, and we can do this by applying a zero-arbitrage argument to the information we already have about the prices of default-free and default-risky bonds. For example, suppose we are dealing with zero-coupon bonds that mature next sub-period and have face value of \$1. The relevant value of τ is then $T - \Delta t$. The expected pay-off on the risky bond is therefore the sum of the expected pay-off if the issuer does not default (i.e., 1 times $[1 - \mu(T - \Delta t)]$) and the expected pay-off if the issuer does default (i.e., δ times $\mu(T - \Delta t)$), that is,

$$\text{expected pay-off} = \{[1 - \mu(T - \Delta t)] + \delta\mu(T - \Delta t)\} \tag{9.12}$$

Under conditions of no arbitrage, this pay-off discounted by the risk-free interest rate (i.e., the pay-off multiplied by the price of the risk-free bond) should equal the price of the risky bond. (9.12) should therefore equal the price of the risk-free bond B^f divided by the price of the risky bond B^r. It follows that $\mu(T - \Delta t)$ must be:

$$\mu(T - \Delta t) = [1 - B^f/B^r]/(1 - \delta) \tag{9.13}$$

The other $\mu(.)$ terms can be found in a similar manner.

Jarrow and Turnbull go on to show, using zero-arbitrage reasoning, that the price of a default-risky bond is equal to the price of the corresponding default-free bond times an adjustment factor $\Phi(T)$:

$$B^r(0, T) = B^f(0, T)\Phi(T) \tag{9.14}$$

and $\Phi(T)$ is the expected present value of the promised pay-off at T taking into account the risk of default.[34] For example, with one sub-period, $\Phi(T)$ would be $\Phi(1) = 1 - \mu(0) + \delta\mu(0)$, with two sub-periods $\Phi(T)$ would be $\Phi(2) = [1 - \mu(0)][1 - \mu(1) + \delta\mu(1)] + \delta\mu(0)$, and so on.

(9.14) is the key to the whole approach: it tells us how to model the bond price in terms of $\Phi(T)$ and the price of the equivalent default-free bond. To price a default-risky bond all we therefore need to do is: (a) apply bond price and recovery ratio (i.e., δ) information to (9.13) and its analogues to derive the various $\mu(\ )$ terms; (b) use this information to calculate $\Phi(T)$; and (c) substitute $\Phi(T)$ and the price of the default-free bond into (9.14) to derive the price of the risky bond.

We are now in a position to model the price of the risky bond, and thence to estimate its VaR. (9.14) tells us that modelling the price of the risky bond boils down to modelling the price of the default-free bond and calculating $\Phi(T)$. If we continue to assume that the default probabilities and recovery rate δ are exogenously given, then $\Phi(T)$ is a known constant, or at least an estimated one, and all we now need is a way to model $B^f(0, T)$, which takes us back to the earlier discussion of modelling default-free fixed-income instruments. We can choose an approach that is as simple or as sophisticated as we like, but suppose for the sake of illustration that we choose the simplest possible, a straightforward duration approximation. The standard deviation of the price of the default-free bond is therefore:

$$\sigma_{Bf} \approx D^m \sigma_r \cdot r \tag{9.15}$$

where D^m is the modified duration of the bond. The standard deviation of the price of the default-risky bond is then:

$$\sigma_{Br} \approx D^m \sigma_r \cdot r \Phi(T) \tag{9.16}$$

Finally, if we assume that the interest rate r is normally distributed, the VaR of the default-risky bond is approximately equal to minus α times σ_{Br} times the present value of the default-risky bond. Alternatively, if we do not assume that r is normally distributed, we can derive the VaR on the basis of whatever other assumption we make about the distribution of r.

The JT approach extends naturally to a large number of other fixed-income securities and fixed-income derivatives. Extending it to coupon-paying bonds is very easy: we simply treat coupon-paying bonds as portfolios of zero-coupon ones. The approach also extends to options on risky bonds and other bond-based derivatives such as interest-rate caps and swaps.[35] It handles not only derivatives where the underlying instrument is subject to credit risk, but also cases – and these are particularly important in OTC markets – where the derivative itself is subject to the risk that the counterparty might default.[36]

3.3. Integrated Forward VaR

It is also straightforward to incorporate credit risk into the VaR analysis of forward positions. Consider a typical forward contract in which one party agrees to make a certain fixed payment at a future date, and the other agrees to make some kind of delivery. This contract therefore consists of two legs, a bond contract and a contract to deliver a particular item or financial asset, or pay an amount contingent on the asset's price. The presence of credit risk means that both of these legs are risky to the respective parties. The first leg is a default-risky zero-coupon bond, which we have just dealt with, and the second is a default-risky delivery contract. As with corporate bonds, we can consider the default-risky contract as equivalent to a portfolio consisting of the corresponding default-free contract and a short option position. In this case, the option position is a call option that allows the deliverer to buy back the item at a strike price equal to the value of his or her liable assets. He or she then exercises the option if the value of the contractual asset exceeds his or her liable wealth, in which case the net result is that he or she hands over his or her liable assets, an outcome we can consider as default. The VaR of the default-risky contract is therefore the same as the VaR of the combined default-free contract and short call position, and we can estimate their VaRs from what we already know from Chapter 3.

4. CONCLUSIONS

The analysis of credit-related risks is one of the most rapidly developing areas in risk management, and the days when credit risk analysis was a quiet backwater compared to the analysis of market risk are well and truly over. Perhaps the key points to emerge are these:

● There are not one, but two credit-related risks to worry about: the risk of credit exposure, and the risk of default loss. Ultimately, it is the risk of default loss that most concerns us, but we need to concern ourselves with risk of credit exposures because managing this latter risk is one of the main ways in which we can keep down our default risks.

● The trend in credit risk analysis is very much towards importing methodologies – most notably, VaR methodologies – that have already made their mark in the analysis of market risks, and it is already clear that credit-related risks are very amenable to such approaches. However, in applying VaR approaches to credit-related risks we must also make allowances for additional factors – default probabilities, and collateral and recovery issues – that are not (directly) present with market risks. Credit-at-risk and default-VaR systems are therefore much more than the mere application of VaR techniques already developed for the analysis of market risks; instead, they represent major developments of VaR methodology in their own right.

In closing this chapter there is also one other point that should not be overlooked. Credit-at-risk and default-VaR systems suffer from many of the same generic problems as other VaR approaches, and need to be used with at least as much caution. In setting up and using such systems, it is therefore critical to supplement them with a regime of stress tests, not to mention plenty of judgement and plain common sense.

ENDNOTES

1. Some useful general discussions of credit risk are to be found, e.g., in Geske (1996), Jorion (1996, Chapter 13), Masters (1997), Oda and Muranaga (1997), Spinner (1996b) or Wakeman (1996a,b).
2. This recovery value would also include any collateral offered as well as whatever assets are recovered through a bankruptcy procedure. We are also concerned here with the present value of the assets recovered, as viewed from the time of default, not with the undiscounted value of the assets at the time they are eventually recovered.
3. To some extent, the return skewness that results from the default-generation process can be mitigated by diversifying our portfolio across different counterparties. However, as Masters (1997, p. 13) observes, 'the limitation of upside opportunity, combined with the remote possibility of severe losses, still causes asymmetry and fat, long tails in typical credit portfolio distributions'. It is also harder to diversify away the idiosyncratic risk with a credit portfolio, because we need considerably more individual positions in a credit portfolio to achieve the same level of diversification as we would get in an equity portfolio (Levin, 1997).
4. See Wakeman (1996a, pp. 314–5).
5. See, e.g., Altman (1984).
6. The object of the exercise is to produce a model that allows us to forecast default probabilities over the relevant horizon, and there are a number of other approaches we can use besides the discriminant analysis discussed in the text. One such possibility is the lognormal default probability model of Oda and Muranaga (1997, pp. 6–7). This model predicts the probability of default based on the assumption that movements in creditworthiness follow a Brownian motion process. Predictions of default can be further improved by adding macroeconomic or ARIMA (autoregressive integrated moving average) factors to the basic model. An alternative is to predict default probabilities on the basis of the spread between comparable default-free and default-risky instruments. Under conditions of no arbitrage, the price of the default-risky contracts, P_t^r, would be

$$P_t^r = (1 - p)P_t^f + p\delta P_t^f$$

where P_t^f is the price of the equivalent default-risk-free contract, p is the (risk-neutralised) probability of default, and δ is the recovery rate in the event of default (see Jarrow and Turnbull (1995), Jorion (1996, p. 258); for more on risk-neutralised versus 'real' probabilities, see Tuckman (1995, pp. 65–74)). If we know the prices of the risky and default-free instruments (which we sometimes do), this equation allows us to infer the probability of default if we have an estimate of the recovery rate. Finally, we can also forecast default probabilities using techniques such as logit/probit analysis or neural networks.
7. Pézier (1996, p. 12)
8. See Wakeman (1996a, p. 320).
9. Estimating recovery rates is not easy and is subject to a number of potentially large sources of error. If we wish to do it properly, we would need to estimate the value of the assets left in the firm at default, the resources used up by the bankruptcy proceedings, the time taken to pay creditors, the discount rate, and other factors. In so doing, we may also need to anticipate the bargaining strategies of different parties and the exercise of judicial discretion (e.g., over the implementation of priority rules).
10. As an aside, there is an interesting analogy between credit exposure and the intrinsic value of a call option: in the one case, the credit exposure is the maximum of the value of the position and zero; in the other, the intrinsic value of the call option is the maximum of the price of the underlying minus the strike price, and zero. This analogy suggests that we can model credit exposures by applying option theory, and Zangari (1997, pp. 16–17) actually does so. This approach to forecasting credit exposures is insightful and elegant, but also appears to be quite demanding of data and does not extend easily to cases with more than one risk factor.
11. See Jorion (1996, pp. 262–3).
12. See Jorion (1996, p. 263). It is of course blindingly obvious that in practice we do not know the true probability of default but would work instead with a forecast over the relevant horizon; hence the need discussed earlier for a default-probability forecasting model.
13. See, e.g., Wakeman (1996b, p. 17).

14. In practice we would usually also want to take account of other relevant factors such as collateral, recovery rates, netting agreements, and so on, in estimating credit exposures. We may therefore want supplementary models to predict collateral and recovery values, and also have to take some view about the enforceability of netting agreements. For more on these sorts of issues, see Oda and Muranaga (1997).

15. The text assumes normality for convenience, but in practice we may wish to make alternative distributional assumptions and/or may prefer to use MCS or other simulation methods (as in Oda and Muranaga (1997) or Zangari (1997)) rather than analytic approaches (such as (9.5)) to estimate credit exposures.

16. We must also take account of any bilateral netting arrangements with counterparties when estimating exposures, and these will generally reduce our exposures. We have more to say on netting arrangements shortly.

17. In practice, we would also have to pay attention not just to the size of particular positions, but also to the size of our exposure to particular counterparties: if we grant too much credit to one counterparty, we become very vulnerable to that counterparty defaulting. In theory, the correct way to handle counterparty identity properly is to distinguish every position by counterparty identity as well as by the type of instrument involved. However, this can quickly lead to a proliferation of specific positions and potential problems with matrix operations. In practice, one would look for various short cuts (e.g., not worrying about the identity of a particular counterparty if our exposure to that counterparty is small). Research on these issues is still only at an early stage.

18. An indication of the scope of credit risk reductions created by netting is given by the results of a 1992 survey of US financial intermediaries active in derivatives markets. The results indicated that these intermediaries had gross positions valued at $64 billion, but net positions of only $27 billion. Netting therefore produced a fall of 58% in credit exposure (Wakeman, 1996a, p. 313).

19. See Wakeman (1996a, p. 313)).

20. Wakeman (1996a, p. 312)

21. See also Wakeman (1996a, p. 317).

22. See, e.g., Wakeman (1996a, p. 317).

23. Such limits could be based on much the same principles as the VaR position limits discussed in Chapter 11 (e.g., they could be graded, ranging from earlier warnings that exposure was getting high to absolute prohibitions against further exposure).

24. For more on credit derivatives, see, e.g., Parsley (1996) or Neal (1996). *The Treasurer* also has a number of good short articles on them (e.g., Baldwin (1996), Reoch (1996) or Eldridge (1997)).

25. The development of credit derivatives has been quite astonishing. The first credit-derivative deals were done in 1993, and since then the London market alone (which, admittedly, is the biggest market) has already grown to over $20 billion in notional-principal open interest. A recent report by the British Bankers' Association suggested that open interest in notional principal terms in London would double that figure in 1998, and reach $100 billion by 2000 (Rivett and Davies, 1996, p. 1).

26. See, e.g., Eldridge (1997, p. 43).

27. Finally, we can also keep our credit risk down by dealing with counterparties that satisfy minimum credit ratings. This leads us into the difficult and controversial issue of derivatives product companies. It used to be argued not so long ago that banks and securities houses would meet the demand for high-quality counterparties by setting up highly capitalised subsidiaries with very high credit ratings – the derivatives products companies (DPCs) – and channelling their derivatives business through them. However, this point of view has come under considerable attack in the last couple of years (see, e.g., Boughey (1996) or Remolona, Bassett and Geoum (1996)). DPCs have failed to win over the lion's share of the market from lesser rated institutions, as the credit quality argument just sketched above would have led us to expect. While the precise reasons for this failure are still not clear, it appears that the reassurance that DPCs provide is too expensive, given the costs of setting up DPCs (and hence the DPCs' need to charge accordingly), the legal uncertainties about their status in the event their parents default, and the other techniques of credit enhancement discussed in the text.

28. While the theoretical case for integrating default risk into VaR is strong, there is a question of whether a combined default-plus-market VaR – a kind of mega-VaR – is worth the effort involved in estimating it. The point is that default VaR will often be very low relative to market VaR, so

integrating the two VaRs into one new VaR will often produce a figure that is only slightly bigger than the original market VaR. (For example, a casual glance at (9.6) shows that default VaR has an order of magnitude equal to that of the market VaR times the probability of default.) The new integrated-VaR figure will therefore differ noticeably from the original market VaR only if there is a significant probability of default. Whether there is any point integrating default risk into VaR in many practical applications is therefore still an open issue.

29. We can, however, also modify this procedure to make it slightly less simplistic (e.g., by making some allowance for non-zero recovery in default).

30. An alternative procedure is a contingent-claims approach that would accommodate this risk by viewing equity as an option on the firm's underlying assets, along the lines of Merton (1974) and Geske (1977). Rather than seeing equity as directly owning the firm's assets, we instead see equity as a call option on those same assets. If the value of the firm's assets exceeds a certain threshold, the equity owner calls the option and 'buys' the firm's assets, in which case the firm carries on in business. If the value of the firm's assets falls short, on the other hand, the equity owner lets the option lapse. In this case, the equity holder gets nothing, the firm goes bankrupt and the firm's assets go to the creditors. However, to implement this approach requires information about the value of the firm's assets, and this information will often not be available. This approach is also more difficult to handle than the approach in the text, since it requires that we model the relevant call option.

31. See also Pézier (1996, p. 28).

32. There are also several alternatives we could use. The first is a contingent-claims approach which would view these positions in terms of their embedded options. It is straightforward to show (see, e.g., Ritchken (1996, pp. 394–5)) that the pay-off to a default-risky bond is the same as the pay-off to a portfolio that is long a comparable risk-free bond and short the put option on the firm's assets. We can therefore infer the VaR of the risky bond from the VaR of the equivalent position consisting of risk-free bond and short put, and we can infer both these VaRs using the procedures discussed in Chapter 3. However, this approach has its drawbacks, relative to the one outlined in the text: (1) It is computationally more difficult, because it forces us to model options. (2) It requires data on the value of firm assets, which may not be readily available. (3) To estimate the VaR of any fixed-income security, we would need to estimate the VaRs of all claims senior to that security (e.g., if we were dealing with junior bonds, we would also have to handle senior bonds at the same time). This can not only create more work, but also introduce further sources of error (e.g., errors in our estimates of the VaRs of senior claims will affect our estimates of the VaRs of junior ones).

Another alternative is the simulation approach suggested by Oda and Muranaga (1997). This approach simulates cash flows in a framework in which cash flows depend on interest rates, collateral prices, the probabilities of future default and the realisations, if any, of actual defaults. Each combination of risk variable paths produces a particular cashflow path, and we simulate enough cashflow paths to be able to infer the VaR from the resulting histogram of portfolio profits and losses. This approach allows us to estimate VaRs whilst taking into account diversification and liquidity factors, effects of collateral and recovery values, the interactions of market and credit risks, and whatever stochastic processes we think govern the probabilities of default. This approach thus takes account of the major 'complications' we would want to consider, and also appears to work reasonably well in practice. How it compares to the Jarrow-Turnbull approach discussed in the text is as yet an open question.

33. Duffie and Huang (1996) also suggest a fairly general procedure to value default-risky derivatives claims. They focus particularly on the valuation of default-risky claims that can alternately be assets or liabilities to each party in the contract. The reader is referred to their article for further details and references to other related literature.

34. See Jarrow and Turnbull (1996, pp. 264–9).

35. Jarrow and Turnbull (1995, pp. 64–5; 1996, 271–7)

36. See, e.g., Jarrow and Turnbull (1995, pp. 65–6). The JT approach can also be extended to relax its dependence on the assumptions that the probabilities of default are independent of interest rates and that recovery ratios are known constants (e.g., Lando (1994) allows default probabilities to depend on spot interest rates). Similarly, the assumption that recovery rates are known constants can easily be replaced with alternatives, provided we stick to simple ones and assume that recovery rates are exogenous.

10

Liquidity, Operational and Legal Risks

H AVING covered credit risks in the last chapter, and market risks in earlier chapters, we turn in this chapter to consider the other main types of risk: liquidity risks, operational risks and legal risks.

I. LIQUIDITY RISK

Liquidity risk is the risk of loss arising from the cost of liquidating a position, and arises where markets are less than perfectly liquid. Typically, market illiquidity manifests itself in the forms of significant transactions or search costs, low market turnover, a relatively small number of traders at any time, and significant bid-ask spreads. These factors mean that traders who wish to liquidate positions may have to pay significant costs to do so: they may have to pay high transactions costs, take time to find a trading partner, or sell at a relatively disadvantageous price, particularly if they need to sell quickly.

It is obvious that most markets most of the time are less than perfectly liquid. Indeed, most markets are imperfectly liquid *all* the time, and there are only a very small number of markets – such as the big capital and money markets – that can be characterised as being close to the ideal of being perfectly liquid. Furthermore, even the liquidity of these markets cannot be taken for granted. These markets are highly liquid almost all the time, but occasionally experience major crises in which their liquidity dries up: the most notable examples are the ERM crisis of 1992 and the stock market crash of 1987. Hence, even in these markets operators cannot necessarily take market liquidity for granted. There are therefore *no* markets that can be regarded as *fully* liquid *all* the time. In short, liquidity risks are always important, or at least potentially so, and we ignore them at our peril.

There are two types of liquidity risk. (1) The first is the normal liquidity risk that arises from dealing with markets that are less than fully liquid in their normal day-to-day operation. We encounter this risk in most markets except the big financial markets. The degree of liquidity, however, varies very greatly from one market to another, from almost no liquidity at one extreme (as with certain types of specialist OTC financial instruments), to very high, but not perfect, liquidity at the other. (2) The other type of liquidity risk is more insidious and in many ways more dangerous. It is the risk of liquidity costs arising because of a market crisis, when we find that the market has lost its normal level of liquidity and we can liquidate positions only by taking much larger losses than under normal circumstances. We can refer to this as crisis liquidity risk to distinguish it from the earlier, normal liquidity risk.

1.1. Normal Liquidity Risk

Recall that our primary concern is with potential loss, and our potential loss depends on the price we might get. So far, we have tended to focus on market price risk: the risk of loss arising because of adverse movements in the market price. However, when dealing with liquidity risk, we should not make the mistake of thinking that we can necessarily obtain 'the' going market price at the time we want to sell. Where liquidity is limited, the very notion of a market price becomes less clear. Bid-ask spreads widen, so the price at which we trade depends in part on whether we are buying or selling. When dealing with everyday market illiquidity, there also tend to be fewer traders and lower turnover. The price also depends on the size of the trade we wish to make and, most importantly, on how long we take to search the market. Other things being equal, if we wish to sell an asset in a hurry, we are likely to get a relatively poor price, but if we are prepared to search (and wait) longer, we can usually get a better price. The price therefore gets better as the relevant search/holding period rises.

We therefore need to modify our VaR to take these liquidity costs into account. The relationship between these everyday liquidity costs and VaR is shown in Figure 10.1. The figure shows a highly liquid position and an illiquid one. We can sell the liquid position at short notice and obtain the market price, whatever that might be, without any significant liquidation costs. However, we can sell the illiquid position only by paying some liquidation cost. Hence, other things being equal, the illiquid asset has a higher VaR, since we must take account of the costs of liquidation. Moreover, the liquidation cost (or, if one prefers, the price we can expect) also depends on how long we are prepared to wait: the longer we wait, the lower the cost. The VaR of the illiquid asset therefore also depends on period involved: the longer the holding period, the lower the VaR.

FIGURE 10.1   VaR, Holding Period and Normal Liquidity Cost

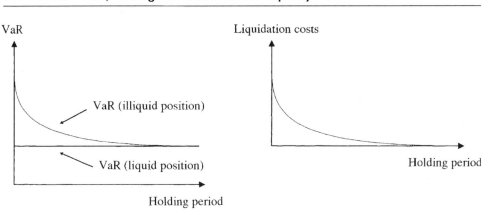

Box 10.1:   Adjusting VaR estimates for liquidity risk

How do we estimate VaR allowing for liquidity risk? Ideally, we should go back to first principles and redo our earlier analyses of market (and, indeed, credit) risks to take liquidity risk into account. However, this is easier said than done.

An alternative is to adopt an 'add-on' approach by which we estimate our market-risk VaR in the usual way and then make some adjustment for liquidity risk. A simple way to do this is as follows:

We begin by estimating market-price VaR in the usual way, presumably taking the market price to be the mean of the bid and ask prices in the relevant market. We then seek a multiplying factor that we apply to this market VaR to adjust for liquidity risk.

To construct this factor, we first need a measure of market illiquidity. A plausible measure of illiquidity, but not necessarily the only one, is the expected normalised bid-ask spread (i.e., the size of bid-ask spread divided by the average of the bid and ask prices, all as expected *ex ante*). The bigger this spread, the less liquid the market.

We would then need to do some background work to simulate prospective losses taking market illiquidity into account. This research would give us VaR estimates inclusive of liquidity risk, and should be carried out for a variety of different types of position. The idea is to take any type of position, categorised by whatever characteristics we think relevant, and estimate its VaR. The multiplier factor we seek is this inclusive VaR estimate divided by the market VaR estimated earlier. This ratio would be 1.5, 1.2 or whatever, telling us that the VaR inclusive of liquidity risk is 50%, 20%, etc. greater than the market VaR exclusive of liquidity risk.

For each type of position, we map the multiplier against the measured illiquidity of that type of position. The result is a table that tells us that any particular amount of measured illiquidity is associated with a particular liquidity multiplier, and we should find that the multiplier increases with the measured amount of illiquidity.

In any given context, all we then need to do is estimate the degree of illiquidity (which is easy to do) and refer to our multiplier tables. Our particular multiplier is the one associated (or most closely associated) with our particular illiquidity estimate, and our VaR estimate is our initial market-price VaR times this factor (e.g., market VaR times 1.5, or whatever).

The importance of liquidity costs will vary across positions, but plausible estimates put forward by Lawrence and Robinson (1995, p. 55) suggest that they can be very significant. Their estimates suggest that 'true' VaRs, inclusive of liquidity costs, can be very much higher for some positions than conventional market-price VaRs that ignore liquidity costs. Indeed, their estimates suggest that liquidation costs can easily dominate the losses that arise from adverse market price movements – in other words, that liquidity risk could easily dominate market-price risk. Conventional estimates of VaR could therefore be very poor and understate the 'true' VaR by a considerable amount.

There is also a need to monitor liquidity on an ongoing basis, both to be able to assess liquidity risk and to spot particular problems coming. In the words of one recent study:

To protect against liquidity risk, it is imperative to constantly monitor the total level of and locational distribution of liquidity readily available within the company. Careful monitoring and execution might be warranted to prevent the settlement dates and trigger/strike prices of option transactions from concentrating within a narrow range. (Mori, Ohsawa and Shimizu, 1996a, p. 9)

In doing this, we should also take account of non-linear issues:

> In order to prepare for non-linear risks of options it is necessary to establish a good reporting system where every single option-related position is uncovered...quite frequently and regularly. There are cases where some non-linear risk is completely ignored because it is hidden in complex financial transactions. Far-out-of-the-money positions also tend to be discounted [i.e., overlooked] in daily risk management. (Mori, Ohsawa and Shimizu, 1996a, p. 10)

Ideally, we should monitor *any* factors that affect our liquidity. We might therefore carry out stress tests to see if we can identify any particular factors that might impinge significantly on our cash flow, or we might apply VaR methodology to look at our cash flow at risk in much the same way as we would look at market risks.[1] We might also examine our derivatives positions for their liquidity implications. Amongst the things we might look at are the prospect of margin calls or collateral requirements that might hit us if currently positive-value positions (such as in-the-money futures positions) become net liabilities, or the prospect of early repayments on collateralised mortgage securities. The more complex the firm and its positions, the more potential liquidity traps there are to look for.

Box 10.2: Hedging liquidity risks

Companies that provide derivatives to end-users can also reduce their liquidity risks by hedging. When they hedge or unwind a position, they typically do so not by writing an offsetting derivatives contract with another derivatives provider (to do so would only destroy their profit margins) but by reverse engineering complex contracts into their component building blocks and hedging or unwinding these instead. These building blocks would be the more basic futures, swaps, options, and so forth. This hedging/unwinding strategy reduces liquidity risks because the company would unwind the position not in highly illiquid OTC markets, but in markets for the building-block components which are much more liquid than the OTC markets.[2]

1.2. Crisis Liquidity Risk

Liquidity risk can also arise in another, more dangerous context. A market can be very liquid most of the time, but lose its liquidity in a major crisis. Typically, the trouble begins with a major fall in price which triggers a huge number of sell orders and makes traders reluctant to buy. The bid-ask spread therefore rises dramatically. The flood of sell orders can also overwhelm the market and drastically slow down the time it takes to get orders executed. Selling orders that would take minutes to execute in normal times instead take hours, and the prices eventually obtained are much lower than sellers had anticipated. Market liquidity therefore dries up, and does so at the very time market operators need it most.

Any strategy that relies on ongoing market liquidity then becomes unhinged. The need to watch for crisis liquidity risk is amply illustrated by the losses inflicted on portfolio insurance and other dynamic hedging strategies in the stock market crash of October 1987. These strategies involved frequent buying and selling to maintain a particular portfolio balance in response to changing prices. They generally work well in normal market conditions, but failed dismally when the stock market crashed:

> Fund managers who thought they were protected found out that their losses were not limited because the insurance programmes could not sell stock or futures fast enough to keep up with the plummeting market. Also as the market plunged, buyers disappeared. The strategy broke down because portfolio insurance...presumes orderly and liquid markets and that there would always be buyers of the constituent stocks...As the market plunged, there were none. Even those who were initially brave enough to stick up their heads above the parapet were swept away by the torrent of sell orders.[3] (Chew, 1996, p. 100)

The only solution to this problem is for institutions

> to address the liquidity risk issue by making worst case assumptions about close-out costs. Before buying such instruments they have to consider what potential bid/ask spreads could be when markets are distressed, and the effect such high close-out costs could have on the financial performance of the instrument. They have also to ask themselves if there was no bid/ask spread whether they will be prepared to hold the instrument to maturity. (Chew, 1996, pp. 102–3)

In other words, they should think through what these risks entail and decide if they can live with them.[4]

2. OPERATIONAL RISK

Operational risks are any and all risks associated with operational issues. They 'relate to all phases of the business process, from origination through to execution and delivery, spanning the front, middle and back office' (Hoffman and Johnson, 1996, p. 60). These risks cover a huge variety of specific risks: risks from unauthorised trading, fraud, and human error, loss of personnel, communication failures and breakdown of control systems, problems with valuation and simulation models, computer breakdowns and other technological problems, failures of suppliers and/or customers, terrorist attacks and natural disasters, and many others. By their nature, operational risks are often less visible than other risks and are often difficult to pin down precisely. Operational risks are everywhere, ranging from the very small (e.g., the risk of losses from minor office mistakes) to the very large (e.g., the risk of institutional bankruptcy because of uncontrolled rogue trading), and encompass every level of the organisation.

Some operational risks are critically important. Most big losses arise from operational risks that have not been properly handled, and most, if not all, the major institutional disasters of recent years – Barings and so on – were the result of failures to control operational risk. The other risks – market, credit and liquidity risks – may make a difference to profits, but will seldom be life-threatening. Operational risk is more danger-ous and much more likely to lead to institutional failure.

2.1. Controlling Operational Risk

The key to handling operational risk is to get the right control systems in place and have good people running them. If the control systems are wrong, or the people responsible are incompetent, then it is only a matter of time before major problems will emerge. It should therefore not come as any surprise that most of the recent high-profile financial disasters occurred in institutions that had both poor control systems and incompetent people operating them. A good, albeit extreme, example is the case of Barings Bank, which failed dramatically in February 1995 due to a combination of poor systems and gross incompe-tence. (This case is discussed in Box 10.3.)

2.1.1. Risk Control Systems

The main points of any good risk control system are fairly obvious.

A clear policy on risk: Senior management should articulate a clear institutional risk policy: the types of risks they want the firm to take, those they want the firm to avoid, and the general amount of risk-taking they want the firm to engage in. (We have more to say on these issues in Chapter 11.)

Proper rules and documentation: Rules, procedures and responsibilities should be clearly set out.

Separation of front and back offices: Separating control of trading activities and docu-mentation cuts down considerably on the ability of rogue traders and other fraudsters to remain unnoticed.

A credible, independent risk management (or middle-office) function: (1) Risk should be managed on a firm-wide basis. This helps to ensure that risks are managed consistently and from a firm-wide perspective. It also provides another cross-check against fraud and human error. (2) The institution's risk management unit should be independent of both front and back offices and report directly to senior management. The independence of the risk management unit then provides another check against fraud and error. (3) The risk management unit should have control over risk measurement and risk-reporting issues below board level. As far as possible, it should also have a consistent (and, where appropriate, integrated) approach to different risks. (4) It should set the position and other limits within which traders and asset managers operate, and monitor compliance with those limits. (5) It should undertake stress testing and contingency planning. (6) It should periodically review and update risk measurement and risk management systems. (7) It should advise senior management on risk management issues and warn them of outstanding or prospective problems.

A credible audit function: Audit trails should be clear, and internal (as well as external) auditing should be independent of front, back and middle offices. Senior management should also take auditors' advice seriously.

Appropriate decision rules: Portfolio decisions should be made using the generalised Sharpe rule discussed in Chapters 7 and 8.

Appropriate incentive structure: Traders and asset managers should be rewarded on a risk-adjusted basis. They should *not* be rewarded on the basis of raw (i.e., unadjusted) profits alone.

Appropriate risk controls and limits: Risk control systems need to be set up to impose limits on decision makers, inform management of breaches (or impending breaches) of those limits and, where appropriate, institute automatic system responses (e.g., blocking additional trades if they would further increase excessive exposures). Limits themselves would often be expressed in terms of incremental VaR rather than just notional values. Stop loss policies also need to be clear and well understood, and properly enforced.

2.1.2. People Issues

The other key point in controlling operational risk is to have good people at all levels. Again, the main points are obvious:

- Senior management must understand the business they are in.
- Senior management should employ good risk measurement/management people and pay them well.
- Senior management should be able to delegate to risk managers beneath them, and should work on the presumption that their risk management specialists know more about risk management than they do.
- At least some senior managers should take some interest in risk management issues: they should talk to their risk management people and make some input in stress-testing exercises.
- Everyone involved should understand that no risk management system is perfect. They should be aware of the weaknesses of whatever risk management systems they work with, and they should clearly understand that the ultimate protection against risk is simply vigilance.

2.2. Other Aspects of Operational Risk

2.2.1. Model Risk

There are also a number of specific types of operational risk that need to be considered. One of the trickiest of these is model risk, the risk of loss arising from the use (or, perhaps more often, misuse) of models, usually for valuation purposes. Model risk is very widespread, and arises any time one has to rely on an estimated value rather than a market one.

Model risk manifests itself in various forms. One obvious form is the risk of loss arising from arbitrage attack by rivals with better models, or more skill at using models:

> Banks that fail to keep up [in the models arms race]...run the risk of...being outmanoeuvred by their more sophisticated competitors. There are well-known, if largely apocryphal, stories of trading strategies which capitalise on model arbitrage: of New York firms arbitraged by their London colleagues, firms systematically exploited by rivals with inside knowledge of their systems and ex-traders turning on their former employers' frailties. (Paul-Choudhury, 1997, p. 23)

Model risk can also manifest itself as the risk of loss from inappropriate hedge positions.

Box 10.3: How *not* to manage operations risk: the case of Barings

The case of Barings Bank is a perfect example of how not to manage operational risk. In the period before its failure in February 1995, Barings broke just about every rule of sound operational risk management:

(1) Barings' senior management did not understand the business they were in (more particularly, they did not understand futures markets) and had no idea what was going on in Barings' Singapore subsidiary.

(2) Management allowed the Singapore manager, Nick Leeson, to control both front and back offices, thus breaking the absolutely basic rule that control of front and back offices be separated.

(3) Management failed to ask elementary questions, the pursuit of any one of which might have led them to discover what was going on before it was too late. Why did Leeson need cash injections from London? (Answer: he needed them to cover his losses.) Who were the mysterious clients that Leeson claimed to be making advances to? (There weren't any.) Why did they need so much money? (Answer: they didn't, but Leeson did.) Where were the repayments from the advances Leeson was making to his mysterious clients? (Answer: What advances?) How could Leeson be making such huge profits from arbitrage activity, which was all he claimed to be doing? (Answer: Leeson wasn't arbitraging; he was speculating with a vengeance.) How could a low-risk activity (i.e., arbitrage) generate high profits? (Answer: it shouldn't.) Why did Leeson need such large cash injections if he was making the large profits he claimed to be making? (No answer.) And where were the profits anyway?

(4) Management failed to monitor Leeson's activities or check the veracity of his reports. Simple checks would have sufficed to discover the fraud, or even phone calls to the Osaka and Singapore exchanges to ask them what Barings' positions were in those markets. Most people out there apparently knew that Barings was taking on huge positions, even if Barings management didn't. Barings also failed to check Leeson's explanations despite their manifest implausibility and very clear evidence he was lying.*

(5) Management failed to heed auditors' warnings that Leeson had too much operational control and ignored their recommendations that management control be tightened up and Leeson be deprived of back-office control. They apparently didn't want to upset Leeson and were satisfied with his claim that he 'didn't mind' the burden of looking after the back office. The fact that Leeson didn't mind the burden of looking after the back office should also have suggested to Barings that there might have been a problem. Leeson was effectively allowed to operate without any control.

It was perhaps hardly surprising that the bank failed.

This arises where we misjudge delta, gamma or other hedge parameters, and as a result take positions that are not as hedged as we think they are. Model risk can also arise where models are applied inappropriately. A model might work very well when applied to the particular financial instrument for which it was designed, but its success might lead practitioners to start using it on other instruments for which it is less suited. A form of model risk can also arise from the sensitivity of model results to particular assumptions, many of which might be fairly arbitrary. If we are not careful, we can get results that we are think are coming from the model, but that are really coming from the particular arbitrary assumptions that we plugged into the model. Our results could then be highly unreliable.

Some other model-related risks are those associated with managing people who use models.[5] The problem here is potentially acute in that managers will not understand the model the way the practitioners do. The practitioners therefore have a major information advantage over their superiors, and there is the danger that they could use this advantage to hide problems or take risks they shouldn't take. There is no magic solution to this problem, but there are several ways that managers can respond to it, beyond the obvious one of making some effort to understand the risks involved:

- They can set up a strong compliance outfit staffed by people who have the knowledge to challenge practitioners, and the only people who can do this are people who could easily be practitioners themselves. The firm therefore needs to pay its compliance people well if it is to induce qualified people away from trading or asset management. Moreover, in order to ensure that the compliance function is independent of trading or asset management, the remuneration of compliance officers should not be linked directly to the profits from trading or asset management.
- Managers and compliance officers should be on their guard for people who 'game' models by keeping to model-specific limits (e.g., Greek limits with derivatives models, or VaR limits with VaR models) whilst deliberately taking additional hidden risks that the models overlook or at least underrate.
- Remuneration packages for traders and asset managers should have some element of conditional deferred payment. If problems subsequently become apparent, the firm can then recover at least part of the remuneration it would otherwise have paid the person who made the decision. Conditional deferred payment helps discourage traders from leaving hidden time bombs and then moving on to other firms before those bombs explode.

2.2.2. Fraud Risk

A more sinister, and often more dangerous, operational risk is that of fraud. There are perhaps two recurrent underlying factors behind most frauds. The first of these is a lack of awareness on the part of senior management of the risks of fraud occurring. Senior management generally get a rarified view of the firm's operations and are often very unaware, until it is too late, of the possibilites of fraud in their own organisations. They are often particularly ignorant of their vulnerability in subsidiary operations, especially overseas ones. In the words of Huntington (1996, p. 34), 'Time and again [even] organisations who are highly experienced in running international operations have found themselves bearing losses from improper practices allowed to flourish in overseas operations they thought were well controlled.' Thinking that everything is under control when it isn't is one of the classic traps into which management routinely fall, and managers should not underrate the ability of fraudsters to conceal things from them. As one investigator recently observed,

When we asked the risk managers [about this issue], the conversation went something like: 'No, they couldn't [hide trades]. But, you know, if the trader did this...but he'd never think of that'. It's quite hard to find a trader who's never broken limits, who's never done a trade he shouldn't have, who's never dumped a [forbidden] position on someone overnight and bought it back again in the morning. (Simon Nelson, quoted in Paul-Choudhury (1997, p. 21))

The second recurrent factor is the desire to conceal losses that have already been made:

Many major financial frauds have had their roots in commercial problems resulting in losses which have been inconvenient to reveal. Management or individuals responsible for the losses have deluded themselves in the first instance that they will conceal them in the hope or expectation that the situation will be resolved or that the losses can somehow be made up.

Many of the fraud losses in trading areas begin with traders going outside their limits, not because of the desire for a bonus but rather to conceal and make up for losses they have incurred on ordinary, authorised trading. Large-scale management frauds have begun with relatively small credit losses being concealed to maintain a financial track record. The common feature among these traders and management fraudsters has been that the problems have got worse...but once on the treadmill they have felt themselves bound to continue with concealing them until, normally, a funding crisis intervenes and the fraud is revealed. (Huntington, 1996, p. 33)

This sort of problem is most likely to occur in situations where a business is fast moving (e.g., because the firm has just gone into a new area, especially an overseas one), where local managers are under pressure to perform and make key decisions quickly, where products are complex and hard to value, and where central control is loose or non-existent. The lessons for senior managers are, I think, fairly self-evident.

2.2.3. Contingency Planning

Another important element in managing operational risk is good contingency planning:

It is critical for all companies, irrespective of the nature of their business, to have sound and thorough contingency plans. In order to achieve this it is essential that all staff understand the importance of detailed contingency planning and the role that they play in the creation of such, irrespective of how trivial or minor they may consider their role. Planning needs to be as intricate as possible, including at an off-site location such items as blank forms and basic office supplies, phone lists of customers, vendors, and employees, special requirements such as facsimile machines, bond calculators, fire proof cabinets, and other speciality needs.

The quality of a contingency plan is directly related to the time and effort that each department...takes in its preparation. It is also necessary that this plan be reviewed and updated on a frequent periodic basis to ensure that the plan will be effective and workable in a time of need. (Anon, 1995a, p. 18)

The benefits of good contingency planning were illustrated by the ability of Fuji Capital Markets Corporation to recover from the loss of its office when the World Trade Center in New York was bombed in 1993. The bombing occurred on a Friday, but the institution was already operating from a back-up site the next Monday. Nonetheless, their experience also indicated that attention to detail is very important (e.g., the firm had difficulty confirming trades because they found that they didn't have address lists readily to hand).[6]

As with stress testing, contingency planning exercises are also useful for highlighting hidden assumptions and other sources of weakness. The process of developing contingency plans can therefore be as useful as the final plan itself.

Box 10.4: Learning from mistakes

One of the keys to handling operational risks is to learn from past mistakes. Serious failings should therefore be investigated. However, everyone involved should also bear in mind the following lessons which Kletz (1993, pp. 107–9, 111) draws from the accident investigation literature:

(1) Reports should avoid the temptation to produce long lists of 'causes' that no one can do much to put right. Such lists give little guidance about how best to avoid problems recurring.

(2) Reports should not produce long lists of recommendations without indicating their relative usefulness. Management will seldom, if ever, put all recommendations into effect. Reports should therefore help them to prioritise if they wish to do so.

(3) Investigators and management should avoid the temptation to overreact. They should also bear in mind that many problems arise because procedures are not followed, not because the procedures as such are inadequate.

(4) Everyone should keep in mind that no accident ever has a single cause. Accidents arise because of conjunctions of different events.

(5) When examining witness and other statements, investigators should be on the lookout for things that are not said. Management should do the same when reading investigators' reports.

(6) Be wary of blaming accidents on human error. In a sense, all accidents are due to human error, but it is difficult to make meaningful recommendations to stop human error occurring again in the future. Also bear in mind that 'human error' is often used to absolve senior management and pass the blame to people lower down the hierarchy. This is unfair to the people who get blamed and also unhelpful to the organisation.

(7) Keep in mind that most accidents occur because people fail on routine tasks. Try to prevent such failures from turning into serious problems by designing systems with built-in redundancy: if problems are not caught at one point, design systems to try to catch them at another.

(8) Design systems with negative feedback, to catch problems before they develop into major headaches. Kletz (1993, p. 111) quotes the example of Brunel's ship, *Great Britain*, which was the first iron-clad ocean-going steamship ever built. On her maiden voyage from Liverpool to the Isle of Man she ran aground in Northern Ireland (!) because no one foresaw that the iron in the ship would affect the compass. (Of course, it didn't help that there was also (not surprisingly) an error in the charts.)

2.3. Quantifying Operational Risks

While many operational risks are clearly impossible to quantify, there are also some operational risks that can be quantified (Wilson, 1995, Hoffman and Johnson, 1996). As with the other risks considered earlier, risk quantification means that we can attach loss estimates to particular risk events and can also say something about the likelihood of such events occurring. Any such quantification exercise must begin by categorising different types of operational risks (people risks, technology risks, and so forth). In order to be able to manage these risks, each type of risk should also fall into a clearly delineated area of functional responsibility (e.g., so some people risks become the responsibility of relevant business line managers, others become the responsibility of the personnel department, the security department, etc.).

The difficult part of this process is to collect and organise the relevant database, covering both the size and frequency of particular types of loss. The approach adopted by Bankers Trust, outlined by Hoffman and Johnson (1996), was to collect data from two main sources: the comparable experiences of other firms to cover fairly common risks (e.g., those relating to certain types of computing risks, compliance risks), and estimates based on scenario analyses supplemented by expert judgements to cover less frequent risks (e.g., the losses and risks associated with computer breakdowns or terrorist attacks). The result of this exercise was a database that covered five main risk categories: (1) people risks (covering human error, fraud, loss of staff, and so on); (2) technology risks (covering technology failures, virus problems, losses due to antiquated systems, etc.); (3) relationship/liability risks (covering legal and/or contractual risks); (4) physical asset risks (covering loss of physical environment, interruption of business, etc.); and (5) external risks (covering changes in regulations, external fraud, and so forth).[7]

This database is then used to quantify the relevant risks. The expected loss would then be the mean of the PDF and the VaR would be the relevant quantile of the PDF. This risk information can be used for a number of purposes:

- It can be used to allocate capital reserves to cover relevant risks. Without such information, there is a clear danger that decision makers will overlook risks and allocate insufficient capital to cover them. This in turn could lead to an imbalance of resource allocation between different units and result in insufficient capital allocation (i.e., excessive risk-taking) at the level of the firm as a whole.
- Risk estimates (or capital reserves) are useful for pricing positions and/or estimating their prospective returns. These risk estimates therefore help to identify relative profitability. For example, a particular line of business might appear to be profitable when operational risks are ignored, but have such high levels of operational risk that it is actually making a loss when one allows for the cost of capital needed to support it. We would therefore be better off terminating that line of business. However, we would find this out only if we had some estimate of operational risk.
- Risk estimates can also indicate where the firm is vulnerable. For example, an operational risk assessment might suggest that the firm is very vulnerable to losses arising from the loss of skilled personnel. This would give the relevant managers a clear signal that they should do something to maintain or improve staff retention.

There is no denying the usefulness of the Wilson and Hoffman-Johnson approaches to operational risk. Nonetheless, it is vital that we appreciate the limitations of these approaches: they can quantify only those operational risks that are actually quantifiable. They are therefore useful for handling a certain subset of operational risks. However, we must never forget that there are many *other* operational risks that *cannot* be quantified. How could Barings quantify the risk of Nick Leeson? How do we quantify the risk of a major war or the risk of a major technological breakthrough that would make most current computers redundant? There are certain risks that it is clearly futile to attempt to quantify.

There are two important lessons here. The first is that the principal defence against operational risks must inevitably be sound systems of control staffed by good people, as outlined in the last section. Many operational risks cannot be handled any other way. We know these risks are there and that they are potentially dangerous, but we can't measure them. Since we can't measure them, we can't capture them in any quantifiable risk measurement system, and so approaches such as those of Wilson and Hoffman and Johnson will miss them. Moreover, the fact that we can't *measure* them also means that we can't *manage* them in the way that we could manage, say, market risks. All we can do therefore is try to keep the lid on them (i.e., to control them).

The other lesson is that we should use quantitative risk measurement/management systems with extreme care. In theory, these systems are fine, but we should also recognise that using them creates new risks, albeit more subtle ones:

- One of these is the risk of trying to measure what cannot be measured. Certain operational risks are very difficult to measure, and others are clearly immeasurable. We should therefore recognise the limits to measurability, and also be careful that the attempt to measure a particular risk does not distort it out of all recognition and in so doing undermine the point of trying to measure it in the first place.
- There is also a second and much more insidious risk, and one that lies in the minds of the risk managers and senior management. This is the risk of falling into the trap of thinking that what is not measured does not exist. We should never think that an operational risk measurement/management system captures all operational risks. The use of such a system can, at best, only pick up the measurable risks, and we should never let it lull us into a false sense of security about the other, more dangerous risks that we cannot measure. If we are not very careful on this point, an operational risk measurement/management system could, paradoxically, leave us much more exposed to operational risks than we would be without it, because it would undermine our ultimate and best line of defence against such risks (i.e., vigilance). Quantitative systems to handle operational risks should therefore be used *only* with extreme caution: they are helpful when used by institutions that already have a good handle on their operational risks, and potentially disastrous to institutions that don't.

3. LEGAL RISK

Legal risk is the risk of loss arising from uncertainty about the enforceability of contracts. It includes risks arising from disputes over insufficient documentation, alleged breach of conditions, uncertain legality (e.g., about the legal authority of counterparties), and uncertainty about the enforceability of contract provisions (e.g., as regards netting, collateral or third-party guarantees) in default or bankruptcy. Legal risks can also arise

---

Box 10.5:   Dealing with organisational complexity

Many organisations are very complex, and management should be aware of the
dangers and problems that complexity creates. Reason (1990, pp. 178–83) suggests a
number of responses to these problems:
(1) Managers can build in additional defences (i.e., incorporate systems redun-
    dancy). The more systems there are, the smaller the chances of things going
    seriously wrong.
(2) Complexity makes organisations opaque, and this opacity makes it difficult for
    managers to know what is happening and for those working within complex
    systems to do their jobs properly. Managers should respond by simplifying
    tasks and procedures, and by ensuring that staff are adequately trained and
    understand their roles.
(3) Very routine or highly automated procedures can be difficult for humans to
    monitor, and even good operators can have difficulty catching occasional
    problems, precisely because they happen so infrequently. Systems therefore need
    to be designed to facilitate the ability of humans to monitor them.
(4) No system is failure-proof, and some contingency will always occur that no one
    had planned for. Systems therefore need to be designed so that skilled human
    operators can take them over if necessary and sort problems out manually.
    Management should ensure that such people are always available and are
    qualified and/or experienced enough to be able to handle such emergencies if
    and when they occur.

---

because of uncertainty over legal jurisdictions and over prospective changes in legal and
regulatory systems.

Legal risk has been a particular issue with derivatives contracts. For example, many
financial institutions entered into swaps contracts with UK local authorities in the late
1980s only to find their contracts voided when the London Borough of Hammersmith
and Fulham defaulted on its obligations and its default was upheld by the House of Lords
in 1991 on the grounds that the Borough did not have the legal authority to enter into
such agreements in the first place. The result was to nullify all such agreements involving
UK local authorities and in so doing inflict considerable losses on their counterparties.
Legal risks can also arise from disputes over the behaviour of counterparties and over
particular contract features (e.g., the legal status of netting agreements). The very novelty
of derivatives contracts also produces considerable legal uncertainty, since many derivatives contracts have not yet been legally tested. All of this of course creates major
headaches, albeit lucrative ones, for corporate lawyers.[8]

Legal risks can be handled in a number of ways. The first and most fundamental
response to legal risk is for firms to ensure that they have access to good legal advice
before key decisions are made. When dealing with foreign counterparties, it is also
particularly important to get expert legal advice about the foreign jurisdictions involved.
Legal advice is very important when getting into new territory, or when dealing with new
or unfamiliar products. Lawyers should also be involved in advising risk managers about
prospective legal developments, alerting them to legal traps, and working with them in
conducting stress tests, contingency planning, and the like.

Institutions can also reduce legal risk by using standardised master agreements. These help to reduce mistakes and misunderstandings, and are in any case designed to reflect current best practice. Even where the legality of certain features is unclear, the use of a master agreement (as opposed to an ad hoc one) at least encourages courts to enforce them, and many legal authorities have indicated a willingness to do so. The use of master agreements also encourages institutions themselves to honour their contracts. Even if an institution thinks it can default on a contract with legal impunity, a default on a master agreement would be badly received by other institutions, since it would increase their own legal risks. An institution that tried to default on a master agreement would therefore come under pressure from other institutions to honour its obligations, and the effectiveness of this pressure should not be underrated.[9]

Institutions can also reduce their legal problems by taking due care to fulfil their legal obligations and thereby try to prevent legal disputes arising. Many legal disputes arise because one party claims that the other has failed to fulfil some obligation. Disputes also often arise because of inadequate documentation or because of failure to follow procedures. These sorts of legal risks can be reduced by tightening up operational controls and making fulfilment of legal obligations – officials getting documentation right, following procedures, acting in good faith, and so on – a priority.

There are also quantitative aspects to legal risk. For some types of legal risk it is possible to put figures to the costs involved (e.g., one can assess lawyers' fees, managerial resources spent dealing with legal cases, the costs of lost business, lost reputation, etc.) as well as to the likelihood of disputes arising (e.g., an insurance company can estimate how many of its customers will sue it). As with other risks, this quantitative information can help a firm to allocate capital, price products and assess profitability. It also helps in certain aspects of decision making (e.g., a company might realise that it is better off getting its act together to provide better service, in order to reduce its legal costs). In other words, certain legal risks can be handled in much the same quantitative way as some of the other risks we have considered.

There is also another quantitative aspect to legal risk. Even where one is unsure of prospective losses and the likelihood of such losses occurring, it can still be useful to measure (and manage) certain types of legal exposure. The obvious exposures are those to particular legal jurisdictions or particular product lines. The same goes for exposures to new or unfamiliar product lines, particularly some of the newer financial derivatives. These exposures can be managed by informing senior management of current and prospective exposures so that they can make appropriate decisions, and also by setting limits on overall exposures to particular types of legal risk.

ENDNOTES

1. We shall have more to say on cash flow at risk (CFaR) in Chapter 12.
2. Other companies are less able to reduce liquidity risks than derivatives providers, for several reasons. (1) They would be end-users of derivatives, who had agreed to particular derivatives contracts because they wanted the particular risk exposures those contracts gave them. They would not therefore normally want to hedge their derivatives positions because doing so would undermine the reasons for taking them on in the first place. (2) Whilst end-users can theoretically reduce their liquidity risks by making themselves aware of how they can be reverse-engineered and unwound in

more liquid building-block markets, they frequently lack the specialist expertise to do this successfully. After all, derivatives companies presumably don't pay their rocket scientists huge salaries for nothing.

3. The massive widening of bid-ask spreads in these crises also creates serious valuation issues, since the usual procedures (e.g., taking market value to be the mean of bid and ask prices) become unreliable indicators of value. In other words, mark to market becomes less reliable. This problem is particularly acute in cases where buyers cannot be found (as when the market for collateralised mortgage obligations collapsed in March 1994). Strictly speaking, mark to market would lead to the conclusion that such positions had zero value. In such circumstances, one has little option but to resort to alternative valuation procedures (e.g., mark to model, or just 'judgement', so-called) and face up to all the problems they entail (i.e., openness to abuse/fraud, difficulty of verifying values, etc.).

4. It may help, too, if institutions had some sort of early warning system to indicate whether 'a stressful situation was approaching. This is not to say that market participants could easily predict market stress well in advance, but rather that it is important to monitor regularly and on a continuous basis any kind of factors likely to indicate stress consequences such as changes in market liquidity and [in] credit risk of counterparties' (Mori, Ohsawa and Shimizu, 1996a, p. 10).

5. For more on these issues, see Paul-Choudhury (1997).

6. Anon. (1995a, p. 18)

7. Hoffman and Johnson (1996) have more details on the Bankers Trust approach. An alternative approach is that used by Touche Ross, which is discussed by Wilson (1995).

8. There is also considerable legal risk attached to the use of VaR itself. VaR figures are inevitably inaccurate – sometimes they will be too high, and sometimes too low – and, as Brown (1997, p. 70) points out, a good corporate lawyer can make any of the assumptions or adjustments on which VaR figures are based look like management manipulation. Moreover, Brown continues

> Board and management responsibility for derivatives risk is still an unsettled area of law. VaR was originally designed outside the framework of existing legal theory, and then was suddenly thrust in the middle of it by regulatory agencies. Is management responsible for maintaining a stable VaR? Keep VaR low? Fully disclosing VaR? Acting on VaR information? Understanding VaR? Ensuring VaR is accurate? Ensuring VaR is conservative? Nobody knows, but it will be expensive to find out. (Brown, 1997, p. 70)

9. This pressure can be very effective. Traditionally, merchants' courts had no legal authority, and yet were able to enforce compliance with their judgements by the threat of ostracism, the carrying out of which would put offending merchants out of business (see, e.g., Benson (1990)). This pressure can be more effective than the pressure exercised by law courts. The strength of this pressure in the derivatives area was illustrated by the aftermath of the failure of Drexel Burnham Lambert in 1990. Most of DBL's swap agreements contained a walk-away clause that enabled counterparties to cease payment even if they owed DBL money. However, DBL counterparties that were tempted to exploit this loophole were dissuaded from doing so, in part by the fear that other counterparties would be less likely to do future business with them if they took advantage of the clause (Jorion, 1996, p. 250).

11

Allocating Capital

WE now turn to capital allocation. There are two aspects to this issue. Within the institution, capital allocation is the process of allocating investment resources between different units. These units might be individual traders or asset managers, the particular business units to which these individuals belong, or broader business units within the institution.

The other aspect is capital allocation at the level of the institution as a whole. The central issue here is to determine the amount of capital (i.e., equity, retained earnings, and so forth) needed to ensure that the institution is strong enough to withstand prospective losses and still command the confidence of its various stakeholders.

1. ALLOCATING CAPITAL WITHIN THE INSTITUTION

1.1. 'Ideal' Allocations to Business Units

Any institution can be broken up into business units on a variety of levels. At the lowest level, the unit might be the individual trader or asset manager. At the next level, the unit might be the group or section to which those individuals belong (e.g., UK fixed-income traders). And at the next highest level, it might be a group of similar such units (e.g., all fixed-income traders). If we carry on aggregating these units, we then eventually reach the level of the institution as a whole.

In examining investment, it therefore makes sense to start with the investments of individual traders or asset managers. We then aggregate their investments to determine the investments of their respective business units, aggregate these in turn to determine the investments of broader business units, and carry on in this way until we arrive at the amount invested by the institution as a whole (see Figure 11.1).

It helps if we begin by assuming away any 'frictions' – such as moral hazard between the individual trader and the institution, asymmetric information problems between individuals and their line managers, asymmetric information across business units, and so on – within the organisation. If we make this assumption, each individual unit should decide whether or not to make any prospective investment on the basis of the (*ex ante*) generalised Sharpe rule introduced in Chapter 7. This rule tells the trader to make the investment if and only if its prospective return, R_A, is greater than or equal to a particular required return, given by the right-hand side of (7.10) or its analogues. If we are using (7.10), we therefore make the investment if R_A exceeds $[1 + \eta_A(VaR, a)]R_p^{old}$.

The optimal amount of investment is then determined by diminishing returns. Our unit

FIGURE 11.1   Investment Levels throughout the Business

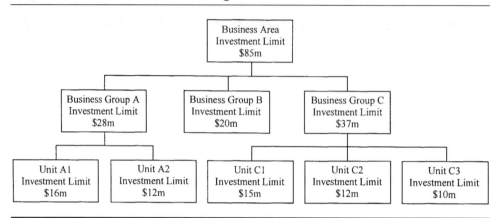

has a certain pool of potential investments. In choosing between those assets, it will naturally prefer more promising ones over less promising ones, taking account of both expected return and risk. As the level of investment increases, it therefore finds itself investing in assets whose expected risk-adjusted returns are lower than those it has already invested in. As investment continues to rise, the marginal expected return, net of financing costs, will eventually fall to a level where it is no longer worthwhile to expand any further, i.e. where:

$$R_A \approx [1 + \eta_A(VaR, a)]R_p^{old} \qquad (11.1)$$

This condition determines the optimal investment level for the business unit concerned. If the unit invests less than this amount, it is forgoing chances to increase its risk-adjusted portfolio return. If it invests more, it is taking on marginal investments that bring down the risk-adjusted portfolio return. The optimal level of investment is therefore the level at which marginal and portfolio returns are equal, after adjusting for risk.

This condition (or its various analogues) applies to any and all business units, at any level of the organisation. The expected marginal return for any one unit must therefore be equal to the expected marginal return for any other unit, after making appropriate allowances for risk. If this condition does not hold, it is possible to increase expected risk-adjusted profitability by changing the allocation of investments between units. If unit 1 can expect a higher risk-adjusted net return than unit 2, efficient use of investment capital requires that capital be shifted away from unit 2 towards unit 1, to enable unit 1 to obtain a better return. This shift will lead to a fall in unit 1's risk-adjusted return and a rise in unit 2's risk-adjusted return, and resources should continue to be shifted until the two risk-adjusted returns are equalised at the margin. Only then is there the right balance of investments between different units.[1] Condition (11.1) thus implicitly tells us what investment levels should be, in all business units at all levels of the firm.[2]

1.2. Position Limits

Unfortunately, there are also the various 'frictions' to contend with: trader/manager moral hazard, asymmetric information across the institution and so forth. The existence of these frictions makes it essential that management impose some system of position limits to control unit risk-taking and provide a basis on which to manage overall institutional risk. Management must therefore impose some system of *position limits* on risk-takers throughout the organisation.

1.2.1. Choosing Units in Which to Express Position Limits

The first issue with position limits is to choose units in which to express them. Traditionally, position limits have been expressed in nominal (i.e., monetary) amounts: trader 1 has a position limit of \$30 million, trader 2 has a position limit of \$10 million, and so on. Nominal limits have the advantages that they are easy to understand and compliance with them can easily be monitored. However, they have the drawback that they can be very poor at controlling risks. The overall risk of any portfolio depends on its leverage as well as its nominal size. If traders wish to increase their risk-taking, they can often do so by increasing the leverage of their position even without expanding the portfolio's size. Fixed-income traders can opt for longer-maturity instruments, for example, or traders can opt for derivatives positions with greater (and often hidden) leverage. Nominal limits alone are therefore not enough to give effective control over position risks, particularly where derivatives are concerned. In addition, nominal limits make it difficult to make comparisons across different positions, and this makes it difficult to manage risk properly and ensure that resources are sensibly allocated between different units.[3]

Position limits in VaR terms avoid some of these problems, and have a number of specific attractions:

- They tell us how much risk we are taking on the position as a whole, and incorporate both portfolio size effects and leverage effects. In the latter respect, they are clearly superior to nominal position limits.
- VaR enables heterogeneous positions to be compared on a common basis, which is not otherwise possible. In other words, VaR gives us a common risk metric, across all units and types of position.
- The process of setting limits can be simplified, and the complex manuals currently used in conjunction with nominal position limits can be scrapped.
- A VaR position limit gives management a reasonably clear idea of what they stand to lose on a position, and thereby facilitates good risk management.
- A VaR position limit is dynamic, and adjusts in response to relevant exogenous changes. If a key volatility rises, for instance, then the VaR of a position will often rise and the business unit concerned will be under pressure to scale the position back. A VaR position limit therefore responds automatically to external events, encouraging decision makers to scale back positions that have become more risky, and encouraging them to expand positions that have become less risky.
- A VaR position limit incorporates diversification effects that nominal limits cannot handle. We can then allocate resources to different units whilst taking into account the extent to which these risks diversify. This leads to hierarchical limit structures in which the risks at higher levels can be lower than the sum of the risks reporting to them, as illustrated in Figure 11.2.

En passant, one should also note that for the business units within the organisation, as

FIGURE 11.2   VaR Position Limits

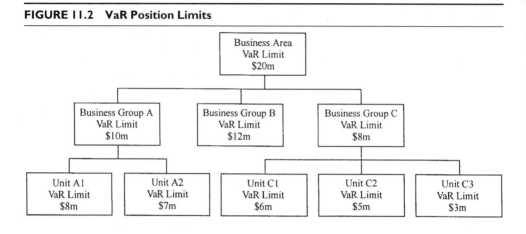

Source: Guldimann (1995, p. 38)

opposed to the institution taken as a whole, the VaRs in which position limits are expressed are incremental VaRs – the extent to which that unit adds to overall institutional VaR. Incremental VaRs take into account the extent to which the individual decision makers' risk-taking interacts with risks taken on elsewhere in the institution. Expressing limits in terms of incremental VaRs therefore allows each unit to add a certain amount to total institution risk, but does not limit any unit's ability to take profitable risks that offset risks taken elsewhere in the institution.

A drawback of VaR limits is that they are more difficult for traders or asset managers to understand. Moreover, VaR limits also have the property that they may force positions to be revised in response to exogenous changes. For example, a position might initially satisfy a VaR limit but then expected volatility might rise and push that position over its limit. The trader or asset manager would then have to scale the position back to reduce its VaR.[4] This need to respond to exogenous changes implies that it will often make sense to express VaR limits in graded terms, ranging from limits that trigger warnings that the position may need looking at, up to limits that force immediate response by the decision makers concerned. These graded limits would then give decision makers some leeway to accommodate exogenous shocks without necessarily being forced to change their positions too drastically. We can also mitigate the disruptions caused by exogenous changes affecting position limits by having limits based not just on currently expected VaR, but also on VaRs over longer periods (e.g., a decision maker could have a VaR target expressed in terms of average daily VaR over some period). The decision maker could then absorb an increase in volatility by adjusting his/her VaR over that longer period.[5]

1.2.2. Setting and Revising Position Limits

Once we have chosen a unit in which to express position limits, we then have to choose levels at which to set them, for each business unit. Ideally, we would like to set position limits so that they produce the optimal investment levels implied by (11.1). If position limits are much higher than these levels, there is a danger of excessive investment (i.e.,

---

Box 11.1:   Profit-related pay and notional position limits: a dangerous combination

Securities houses and investment banks traditionally pay their traders and asset managers according to the profits they generate, whilst subjecting them to position limits stated in nominal terms. This combination is potentially very damaging.

Profit-related pay encourages traders to maximise profits. However, given that higher profits imply higher risks, encouraging them to maximise profits is tantamount to encouraging them to take large risks. Furthermore, since traders' downside risks are cushioned (if risks don't turn out, they can only lose their jobs), traders also have an incentive to take more risks than are in the interests of the institutions they work for.

Notional position limits are particularly ill-suited to control this risk-taking. A trader can often increase risk-taking whilst respecting a nominal position limit by increasing leverage: replacing equities with options, short-dated bonds with long-dated ones, and so on. Controlling the nominal size of a position does not control its risk, and this is particularly the case where derivatives are concerned.

In short, profit-related pay encourages excessive risk-taking and notional position limits do little to control that risk-taking. Particularly where management control is poor, there is a danger that a trader might make losses and be tempted to gamble his/her way out of them. Moreover, this is not a theoretical danger, but something that has happened repeatedly in recent years, as anyone who reads the papers knows. The combination of profit-related pay and notional position limits can therefore leave institutions far more exposed than they should be.

---

letting traders take on marginal investments that are really not worth bothering with from the institution's point of view); but if position limits are too tight, profitable investment opportunities will be passed over. We therefore want position limits that are large enough to allow for all worthwhile investments to be made, but are not so large that they allow units to invest too much.

The usual approach to position limits is to start off with some initial allocation of limits and alter them periodically.[6] We would want to increase the position limits of those units that perform better than average, and decrease the position limits of units that perform worse than average. At the same time, we would also want our position limits to change in response to changes in the level of institution-wide risk-taking, as reflected in the institution-wide VaR. A simple rule that combines these two factors would specify that the percentage change in position limit ($\Delta PL_t/PL_{t-1}$) be set according to something like:

$$\Delta PL_t/PL_{t-1} = \gamma(SR_{t-1}^+ - SR_{t-1}^-) + (VaR_t - VaR_{t-1})/VaR_{t-1} \qquad (11.2)$$

where $\gamma > 0$ is a feedback parameter, SR_{t-1}^+ is the previous-period Sharpe ratio of the institution including the unit in question, SR_{t-1}^- is the Sharpe ratio of the institution excluding that unit, and VaR_t and VaR_{t-1} are the institution-wide VaR targets for periods t and $t-1$.

If the unit performs better than the rest of the institution, SR_{t-1}^+ will exceed SR_{t-1}^- and the rule will cause the unit's position limit to increase. If the unit performs less well than the average, SR_{t-1}^+ will be less than SR_{t-1}^- and the unit's position limit will decrease. The beauty of this type of rule is that it directs our capital towards the better-performing units and away from the worse-performing ones. As units become better or the opportunities available to them improve, their superior performance will gradually lead to their position limits being increased and more capital being directed their way. By contrast, as units deteriorate or as their opportunities diminish, this rule will gradually lead to their position limits and capital allocations being reduced. Were we to use such a rule, we would also want a value for γ high enough to make the position limits genuinely responsive to performance, but not so high as to destabilise position limits (and more importantly, investment levels) from one period to another.

(11.2) also stipulates that the position limit should change in response to the firm-level position limit (i.e., the aggregate VaR). Other things being equal, if the institution increases aggregate VaR next period, we would expect all position limits down the line to increase by the same proportion. If the VaR decreases, we would expect position limits down the line to decrease by the same proportion.

However, it is doubtful that management in practice would ever use a rule such as (11.2) as anything more than a rough guide in making essentially discretionary adjustments to position limits. The reason is that the process of revising position limits is complicated by other factors that require proactive management rather than the application of mechanical rules. One of these factors is the need to take a view on the permanence (or otherwise) of particular changes in portfolio volatility. Suppose the estimated volatility of our portfolio increases by a certain amount. If positions remain the same, the estimated VaR will increase, and a mechanical application of a VaR trading limit would require an immediate cutback in the size of our position (e.g., under normality, VaR would increase proportionately with the increase in portfolio standard deviation, and a strict VaR limit would require that the position be cut back by the same proportion by which volatility rises). However, such a response may not (and, in general, will not) be appropriate. If the increase in expected volatility is temporary, it may not make much sense to cut positions right back, only to increase them again shortly afterwards when volatility has increased again. Hence, in such circumstances it may make sense to make only minimal cutbacks in VaR limits. Even if the increase in volatility is perceived as permanent, the appropriate response will often be a gradual reduction in the VaR back towards its longer-term target rather than an immediate drastic cut in the VaR limit.[7] In short, it is seldom, if ever, optimal to force VaR immediately back to a target level in response to an exogenous volatility change. Moreover, the appropriate response to such a change will also depend on management's perception of how long the change will last. The need for managers to form a view on the permanence or otherwise of volatility changes is thus one reason why managing VaR limits requires discretion, and cannot be left to some automatic rule.[8]

Another reason for management to make discretionary decisions about position limits is that circumstances will sometimes arise in which different types of limit give conflicting signals about the way in which positions should be adjusted in response to exogenous changes. Suppose that an institution has both VaR limits and limits or targets expressed in terms of, say, delta. This latter might reflect a policy of delta hedging. If volatility rises, a VaR limit would suggest that our position be cut back, but a delta limit might suggest the opposite. However, we can't both cut back and expand the position at the same time, so one limit must give way to the other: either we cut back, in which case our delta hedge position becomes unhedged, or we maintain the delta hedge and violate our VaR limit.[9] The appropriate response in any given context presumably depends on other factors, and can therefore be determined by management only on the basis of those other factors.[10] Once again, there is no avoiding the need for management to make discretionary decisions.

2. INTERNAL CAPITAL REQUIREMENTS

2.1. Measuring Capital Strength

We now turn to capital issues at the level of the institution as a whole, and our first task is to measure an institution's overall capital strength. The main purpose of institutional capital is to absorb losses whilst still protecting the institution's solvency. The greater its capital, the greater the losses it can absorb whilst still remaining solvent, and, other things being equal, the lower the probability that the institution will get into distress over any given period.[11] We can therefore assess an institution's strength from the probability of distress implied by its current capital level, given other relevant factors.

Given these factors, let us suppose that an institution has a particular probability of distress, p^d. The institution gets distressed when its return is so negative that it more than wipes out the value of its allocated capital. p^d is therefore the probability of R taking a value less than $-K/W$, and this probability is given by the shaded area in the left-hand tail of Figure 11.3. Assuming for illustrative purposes that the institution's return is normal, p^d can be written as a function – in fact, the normal PDF – of a parameter α^d, where $-\alpha^d$ is the distance of the left-hand tail of the distribution from the mean of the distribution in standard-deviation units, i.e.,

$$p^d = \Phi(\alpha^d) \tag{11.3}$$

It follows that

$$-\alpha^d \sigma_p = K/W \tag{11.4}$$

and, hence, that $-\alpha^d$ is a natural measure of institution strength:

$$\text{Strength} = -\alpha^d = K/(W\sigma_p) \tag{11.5}$$

The bigger the strength measure, the smaller the tail in Figure 11.3, and the lower the

---

FIGURE 11.3   The Probability of Distress and the Level of Capital

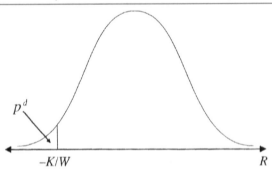

probability of distress, and vice versa. The measure itself is simply the capital/asset ratio K/W divided by the portfolio standard deviation σ_p. The institution therefore gets stronger (and its probability of distress gets smaller) as the capital/asset ratio rises, other things remaining equal. However, unlike traditional measures of soundness, this measure of strength also takes account of the riskiness of the institution's portfolio. In particular, it tells us that the institution becomes stronger as the portfolio standard deviation falls and the portfolio itself becomes less risky.

Some indicative strength values and their associated distress probabilities are given in Table 11.1. Very low strength measures indicate that the institution is highly unsound and in serious danger of distress. However, the probability of distress declines as strength increases, and any strength value beyond, say, 4.5, implies a probability of distress so small that we can barely measure it.

A slight drawback with the measure in the form given in (11.5) is that it requires us to have a measure of the portfolio standard deviation, and we may not have such information to hand. However, this problem is easily remedied by resorting to VaR theory. Under normality we know that the VaR of our portfolio is given by:

$$VaR = -\alpha\sigma_p W \qquad (11.6)$$

where α is the usual confidence level parameter on which the VaR is predicated. If we have a VaR estimate, we can infer the portfolio standard deviation by rearranging (11.5) to obtain:

$$\sigma_p = -VaR/(\alpha W) \qquad (11.7)$$

Substituting (11.7) into (11.5) then gives us an alternative measure of strength:

$$\text{Strength} = -K\alpha/VaR \qquad (11.8)$$

Strength is therefore equal to minus bank capital times the confidence level parameter on which the VaR is predicated, divided by the VaR itself.[12]

This measure requires minimal, easily available information and has a number of potential uses:[13]

- It allows us to derive an implied probability of distress for any given institution over some specified time period.
- It allows us to assess the changing strength of an institution over time, by looking at how the measure (and/or the implied distress probability) changes.
- We can use it to compare the relative strengths of different institutions.[14]

Table 11.1 Strength Values and Distress Probabilities

Strength measure	Distress probability
0	0.5
1	0.16
1.5	0.067
2	0.023
2.5	0.0062
3	0.0014
4	0.00003

However, one should recognise that the strength measure and any implied probability of failure are inevitably fairly crude, so one would be unwise to attach any significance to minor differences, and this is particularly true when we are dealing with very high strength values and very low probabilities of distress.[15]

Box 11.2: The new strength measure vs. traditional measures

The traditional rule-of-thumb measure of institutional financial strength is the raw capital ratio, K/W.[16] In the case of banks, the raw ratio is sometimes replaced by the (so-called) risk-weighted capital ratio set out in the Basle Accord (1988) and its later amendments. This ratio is given by K/W^w, where W^w is a risk-weighted (sic) measure of the bank's assets. Each asset is classified into one of a number of categories, and each category carries a fixed weight (e.g., 100%, 50%, 10% or 0%). If w_1 is the weight attached to assets in category 1, and we have W_1 category 1 assets, and so on, then W^w is $w_1 W_1 + w_2 W_2 + \ldots$This 'risk-weighted' ratio is then used by the bank supervisory authorities to determine minimum capital requirements.

The new strength measure proposed here – $K/(W\sigma_p)$, or its normal equivalent, $-K\alpha/VaR$ – is superior to both these older measures of capital strength.

The problem with the raw capital ratio K/W is that it fails to take account of the portfolio standard deviation. The raw capital ratio will therefore give a misleading indication of the change in an institution's capital strength if the portfolio standard deviation changes. Similarly, when comparing two different institutions, the raw capital ratio will also give a misleading indication of their relative strength if portfolios have different standard deviations.

The problem with the 'risk-weighted' capital ratio is that the very principle of such a ratio is fundamentally unsound.[17] We *cannot* generally assess the risk of a portfolio by any procedure that aggregates individual risks without considering the extent to which these risks interact within the portfolio. The 'risk-weighted' approach attempts to do exactly this, and is therefore tantamount to denying the most basic lesson of portfolio theory (i.e., that risks usually interact).

The new capital strength measure is free of these problems and takes account of risk factors in the theoretically correct way (i.e., via the portfolio standard deviation).

2.2. Determining the Internal Capital Requirement

We now turn to the actual capital requirements, and there are two such requirements to consider. The first of these is the internal capital requirement: the level of capital required by the firm for its own risk management purposes, irrespective of any regulatory pressures to maintain any particular minimum level of capital. This internal capital requirement is therefore the level of capital the institution would choose to maintain, provided regulators don't force it to maintain a higher level.

2.2.1. A VaR Approach

One approach to internal capital is to substitute (11.7) into (11.4) and rearrange to get:

$$K = -\alpha^d \sigma_p W = \alpha^d VaR/\alpha \qquad (11.9)$$

The required capital, K, can be written as the product of α^d and VaR divided by α. We can then think of the internal capital requirement as determined by the choice of VaR/α (and therefore, in effect, by the choice of VaR), and by the choice of α^d, which itself reflects an implicitly chosen probability of distress. We now consider each of these in turn.

Aggregate VaR   We can think of the VaR at the aggregate level as determined by the same process that determines the appropriate VaRs of different units within the organisation. As the institution increases its level of aggregate investment, the investment opportunities still remaining will become less attractive, and the institution will face a diminishing marginal, risk-adjusted return. The appropriate level of investment is therefore that which makes the expected return on the marginal asset (R_A) equal to its required return as given by (7.10) or (7.15). This level of investment tells us our portfolio standard deviation, and the combination of investment level (or portfolio size) and portfolio standard deviation gives us our VaR.[18]

Nonetheless, achieving the appropriate VaR is seldom as clear-cut in practice as it might look on paper. The senior management will seldom, if ever, have the information to make use of this rule directly, and will in practice tend to arrive at their VaR target by a looser judgemental process. The management will usually start from the existing VaR and review whether it needs to be altered in response to changing circumstances. They will then want to reduce VaR if they feel overly exposed (e.g., because volatility seems to be rising, or because prospective profits seem to be low), and will want to increase VaR if expected returns look promising. The target VaR would be altered accordingly, and the new target made effective by appropriate alterations in position limits down through the organisation.

Determining α^d   Determining α^d is more problematic, because it is difficult in practice to determine exactly what α^d should be, based only on a chosen probability of distress. The difficulty here is one of practice rather than theory. On paper, we can always work out α^d exactly, given a precise target probability of failure, by using (11.4). However, in practice we cannot do so, for two reasons. (1) Our reasons for choosing any particular target probability of distress are never so precise that we can nail down the target probability with any genuine (as opposed to merely spurious) precision, and our inability to nail down this probability implies a corresponding lack of precision for α^d as well. (2) Even if we did have a very precise target probability of failure, which would then give us our exact value of $-\alpha^d$, we still lack the means to deliver exactly this target probability.

The Actual Capital Requirement   All we can reasonably say is that our capital requirement then becomes a multiple (i.e., α^d/α) of the VaR, with some arbitrariness coming from our inability to pin down α^d. Instead of working with a spuriously precise point target for $-\alpha^d$, it is therefore better to work with a minimum target for $-\alpha^d$, say $-\alpha_L^d$. However, we would also presumably want $-\alpha^d$ not to be vastly in excess of this minimum target, so we would also want to ensure that $-\alpha^d$ remained within a certain range, from $-\alpha_L^d$ up to $-\alpha_H^d$. We then aim for a level of capital in the range:

$$\alpha_L^d VaR/\alpha \leqslant K \leqslant \alpha_H^d VaR/\alpha \qquad (11.10)$$

Since it is mainly the relative size of K and VaR that matters for capital adequacy purposes, it makes more sense to focus on the ratio of K/VaR. Managing our capital adequacy therefore requires that we monitor K/VaR to see if it is in the appropriate range, viz.

$$\alpha_L^d/\alpha \leqslant K/VaR \leqslant \alpha_H^d/\alpha \qquad (11.11)$$

and then take whatever remedial action might be called for. If K/VaR is well within this range, no specific action is called for, but if K/VaR starts getting close to either end, we should start thinking about action to push it back. If K/VaR is getting too big, we should be thinking about policies to reduce K (e.g., increasing dividends) and/or increase VaR (e.g., investing more or taking more risks). If K/VaR is getting too small, we should be thinking about policies to increase K (e.g., by increasing retained earnings, issuing more equity, etc.) and/or reduce VaR (i.e., invest less or reduce risk-taking). If K/VaR is already over our range, we are clearly overly conservative and should expand our investments and/or take more risks; and if K/VaR is below the bottom end of the range, we are in danger and should take remedial action immediately.

Box 11.3: The hysteria factor

Equation (11.9) sheds some light on the hysteria factor built into the BIS internal models approach to regulatory bank capital, as proposed by the BIS in April 1995. This approach allows a bank to calculate its regulatory capital requirement as the daily VaR at the 99% confidence level, multiplied by a figure of three (or sometimes a little more), which is simply pulled out of thin air.[19] Industry legend has it that it arose as a compromise between the US regulatory authorities who wanted a multiplier of one (i.e., in effect, no multiplier at all) and the German authorities who wanted a multiplier of five.

If we measure our VaR using the same confidence level as that which reflects our preferred probability of distress – which, implicitly, is what the BIS internal model approach seeks to do – then α^d should equal α and the capital requirement collapses to the VaR (see (11.9)). The US regulatory authorities were therefore right, and the multiplier should be one.

2.2.2. A Stress Test Approach

Another approach to internal capital is to use stress tests to determine the losses we might face under extreme but plausible scenarios. To use stress tests we need to make judgements about the types and magnitudes of possible shocks, and about the impact they would have on the institution. In using stress tests for capital purposes, we also have to draw a line somewhere between those shocks that we want to live with (e.g., significant but not necessarily huge rises in interest rates) and therefore want to make provision for, and those shocks (e.g., a combination of stock market crash, bond market crash, exchange rate crisis and major war) that might be so bad that there is no point even trying to provide for them.[20] Our capital requirement is then the level of capital needed to absorb the former losses and carry on in business.[21]

2.2.3. A Combined Approach

These approaches to capital each have their advantages and disadvantages. The VaR approach is excellent for handling 'everyday' (i.e., frequent, but not too extreme) risk factors. It is also relatively objective, notwithstanding the difficulties of estimating VaR and pinning down the confidence parameter α^d, and provides a decent operational rule to guide capital decisions. Its major drawback is that it provides no protection against unusual extreme events that could plausibly occur and would inflict large losses if they did. Reliance on a VaR approach alone can therefore expose us to the danger of being wiped out by the first major 'shock' that comes along.

By contrast, the stress test approach is excellent for handing these unusual shocks; indeed, handling these shocks is exactly what stress tests are designed for. However, stress testing is no use for handling everyday risks. It is also very subjective and the results depend critically on a range of judgemental decisions that are inevitably difficult to assess: the scenarios to be considered, the effects of these scenarios on the institution, and perhaps most difficult of all, deciding which scenarios we should provide for and which we should not. In the final analysis, the usefulness of stress tests depends very heavily on the skill or otherwise of the stress tester.

Not surprisingly, there is considerable controversy between those who believe that capital should focus on ordinary market risks and those who believe that it should focus on extraordinary shocks. My view is that both views have some merit and it would be a mistake to see the issue in either/or terms. At the end of the day, the purpose of capital is to absorb plausible losses, and we cannot say a priori whether those losses will be due to ordinary market risks or unusual shocks. We therefore need to consider both market risks and the shocks that we would want to be able to live with. If the capital needed to absorb everyday market losses is higher than the capital needed to absorb unusual shocks, then we can reasonably say, if we want to, that capital is determined by ordinary market risks. If the capital needed to absorb the shocks is greater than the capital needed to absorb everyday market risks, we can equally reasonably say that capital is determined by the extraordinary shocks. It all comes down to empirics and judgement. In my view, the market risk and extraordinary shock approaches are natural complements – each is strong where the other is weak – and prudence would suggest that we should really make use of both. We should therefore estimate the capital needed to absorb both market and extraordinary shocks, and take the required level of capital to be the larger of the two.

3. DEALING WITH REGULATORY CAPITAL REQUIREMENTS

The other capital requirements are regulatory ones. These apply to some institutions (e.g., securities firms and banks) but not to many others (e.g., most industrial corporates). Where they apply, institutions have to decide how to live with them. In doing this, they presumably have no choice about *whether* to obey the regulations, but they do have some choice about *how* to respond to them. If regulations are imposed that force an institution to maintain higher levels of capital than its management would prefer, the management must consider how to minimise the burden that the regulation places on them. The analogy here is that of a tax: we have little choice but to pay tax where it is due (i.e., we should not *evade* the tax), but we should arrange our affairs to reduce the amount of tax we have to pay (i.e., we should try to *avoid* the tax). In trying to minimise the burden of capital regulation, the management needs to consider how to switch out of activities that attract high regulatory capital requirements (i.e., are relatively heavily taxed) and into activities that attract relatively low regulatory requirements (i.e., are relatively lightly taxed).

Assume we already know our internal capital requirement. If we face a regulatory capital requirement, our first task is to determine what the regulatory capital requirement actually is. If the regulatory capital requirement is less than (or equal to) the capital we would hold anyway, then we have no problem because our preferred level of capital already satisfies the regulatory requirement. Our regulatory tax burden would therefore be zero. But if the regulatory requirement exceeds our internal requirement, the regulatory constraint forces us to maintain a higher level of capital than we would prefer (i.e., we have to pay some regulatory tax). Our capital requirement is then the amount specified by the capital regulation. In short, our actual capital requirement is the maximum of the internal capital requirement and the regulatory capital requirement:

$$\text{Capital requirement} =$$
$$\text{Max [internal capital required, regulatory capital required]} \quad (11.12)$$

Where our capital is determined by the regulation, we then seek to minimise the regulatory burden (i.e., to avoid the regulatory tax). We do so by using our earlier investment decision rule – the (*ex ante*) generalised Sharpe ratio (GSR) introduced in Chapter 7, equation (7.15) – but with finance costs that allow for the capital regulation. This rule tells us to make the additional investment if and only if:

$$R_A \geqslant R_p^{old} + [(\sigma_d^{new}/\sigma_d^{old} - 1)(R_p^{old} - R_b^{old})/a] + \Delta R_b/a \quad (7.12)$$

We therefore make the investment if and only if the expected return on the investment exceeds the required return given by the right-hand side of (7.15). In order to implement this rule, we need to pin down the last term in (7.15), the change in the cost of finance associated with the investment. However, we also know that this term is:

$$\Delta R_b = (K^{new}/W^{new} - K^{old}/W^{old})(c^k - c^d) \quad (7.17)$$

where the notation is again the same as it was in Chapter 7. It therefore merely remains to determine the two capital ratios, and we can infer these from the regulations themselves.

The procedure therefore involves three steps: (a) We infer the before and after regulatory capital ratios from the regulations. (b) We combine these capital ratios with estimates of c^k and c^d to estimate ΔR_b. And, (c) we plug our estimate of ΔR_b into the right-hand side of (7.15), estimate the other terms, and see if (7.15) actually holds.

We then use this modified GSR to re-evaluate our portfolio and minimise our regulatory tax burden. To do this, we start with our existing portfolio and apply this criterion to any one of our assets. This exercise tells us whether to keep or sell the asset. If the decision is to sell the asset, we adjust our portfolio accordingly. We then proceed to a second asset, apply the same procedure to that, and move on to a third asset. We go through each asset in turn, and by the end we will know which of our current assets we should continue to hold. We then repeat the process all over again for any additional assets that we don't currently hold, but think we might want to hold in our rearranged portfolio. The net effect is to get rid of more heavily taxed assets and replace them with more lightly taxed ones. This process eventually leads to our final, tax-efficient portfolio.

ENDNOTES

1. This condition not only gives us a theoretical optimum, but also gives us a practically implementable decision rule, as discussed in Chapter 8. All we need to do in this context is take each business unit and identify its marginal (i.e., least worthwhile) investment. Condition (11.1) then tells us that the risk-adjusted returns on these investments should be much the same, if capital is allocated optimally. If we find that this condition is not met, then we should reallocate capital away from those units with low marginal risk-adjusted returns, towards units with higher risk-adjusted returns. As we reallocate, we should check to see whether the risk-adjusted marginal returns have been equalised, and we stop reallocating when they have been.

2. The discussion in the text does, however, sweep one awkward issue under the rug. The VaR in (11.1) does not refer just to market VaR, but to *any* VaR. It therefore includes default VaR and any VaRs we may impute to operational, liquidity or other risks. If we are to use this type of rule for these types of risk, we therefore need estimates of these other VaRs as well, and not just estimates of market VaRs. As is clear from previous chapters, this is sometimes easier said than done.

3. An alternative often used for derivatives positions is to express position limits (or in this case, strictly speaking, targets) in terms of the Greek parameters – the delta, gamma, vega and so forth. We would do so primarily to hedge positions. For example, if we wanted to hedge a particular stock position using call options, we might use the delta parameter to tell us the size of the option position needed to delta-hedge us against the underlying stock price risk. Of course, such positions depend on our estimates of the relevant Greek parameters and (as with VaR limits) need to be revised continuously in response to exogenous changes.

4. This dynamic readjustment of positions in response to exogenous changes is disruptive, naturally, but should not be regarded as a disadvantage of VaR-based position limits. As discussed already in the text, if a position has become more risky then, other things being equal, there *should* be pressure to cut it back, and this pressure is exactly what the VaR limit provides. The only issue is whether the VaR limit provides the right amount of pressure to adjust positions, and this is one reason why we might want a system of soft as well as hard VaR limits.

5. However, it is important that VaR-based position limits be introduced gradually and, in the first instance at least, as a complement to existing position limits rather than a substitute for them. Since one never really knows in advance how new systems would work in practice, it would be very unwise for any management to abandon established systems of position limits until experience has demonstrated how any new system of position limits would actually work. The big question then is whether to introduce VaR limits with the ultimate aim of having them replace or instead merely supplement existing limits. For what it is worth, my own feeling is that relatively few firms would want to rely on VaR limits alone, for three reasons: (1) No system of limits is ever going to be perfect, and non-VaR limits would help protect the firm against the 'blind spots' in VaR-based limits. For example, if limits are expressed only in VaR terms, there is always a danger that traders or asset managers will find ways to keep their VaRs down whilst taking other risks that are not adequately reflected in their VaRs. Having additional limits at least provides an additional layer of protection for the firm against such behaviour. (2) Nominal position limits still seem to have their niche for certain types of position (e.g., in cases where hidden leverage is not a major problem). (3) There will often be cases where we want to hedge certain types of risk, particularly with derivatives positions, and in these cases it is entirely appropriate to use targets expressed in terms of the relevant Greek parameters. No VaR target, however good, will beat a delta target if we want to delta hedge, for example. There is therefore no reason to suppose that VaR-based position limits dominate other types of position limit for all possible types of position.

6. An alternative and more imaginative approach to position limits is to try to set them to mimic the optimal investment levels implied by (11.1), and this should now be technically feasible. Essentially, we identify each unit's marginal investments and reallocate position limits away from

those units whose marginal returns are low towards those whose marginal returns are high. We can identify the marginal investments from the trades made by each unit. If we are concerned about position limits being dependent on a very small number of trades we can take the marginal required return to be an average of the marginal x investments over the day, or we could take the marginal required return to be a weighted average of marginal required returns over a number of past days. I would expect to see this sort of approach starting to be used over the next few years, as a supplement at least to the more reactive approach outlined in the text.

7. There will also be times when the appropriate response to an exogenous rise in volatility is to allow VaR to rise temporarily, before bringing it down towards its new lower target level. As Aaron Brown puts it, 'getting from a $10,000,000 to a $5,000,000 VaR may require a temporary stopover at $15,000,000 VaR' (Brown, 1997, p. 69).

8. There are also other reasons to caution against allowing VaR limits to produce excessive changes in positions in response to changes in exogenous factors. (1) A policy of making major position changes in response to such changes will often increase the volatility of returns, and thus be potentially self-defeating if the ultimate objective is to trade off risk and expected return (Brown, 1997, p. 69). (2) Relevant exogenous factors are usually forecasts (e.g., of portfolio volatility), and these forecasts usually have errors. If we make major changes to our position every time volatility forecasts change, we will end up making a lot of changes in response to statistical shadows.

9. Brown gives a nice analogy to this problem. He compares it to a traffic emergency:

> The VaR philosophy, since it is computed on an unmanaged position, assumes you cannot steer. Therefore, it always recommends hitting the brakes. Yet in some situations, accelerating gives you more control over the car. The only solution, in finance and driving, is to have a strategy for dealing with emergencies. Either try to steer your way out or shut your eyes, hit the brakes and hope for the best. But don't try both at once. (Brown, 1997, p. 68)

10. . Managing both Greek and VaR targets can also be particularly difficult in a crisis, and Brown (1997, pp. 69–70) points out that in such circumstances proprietary and hedge positions can interact in very damaging ways. In a crisis volatility will rise and the VaR of hedged positions (which have low VaR under normal conditions) will often shoot up. A tight VaR limit will therefore force a major reduction in proprietary positions not only to meet their share of the VaR target, which is presumably bad enough, but also to accommodate the ballooning VaR of (supposedly) hedged positions. The institution would therefore have to liquidate a large number of profitable proprietary positions to meet its VaR target.

11. Distress is where an institution gets into financial difficulties somehow defined, and we can best think of it as the firm making a loss above a specified maximum target. The notion of distress encompasses default or outright failure, but also includes other situations where the firm is in financial straits or merely misses its financial targets. In managing its capital, we can think of the firm first setting out an operational definition of distress over the relevant horizon period and then managing its capital to maintain a particular probability of distress so defined. Distress is therefore not to be confused with failure or default, particularly if the firm is using VaR-based targets. After all, it makes no sense at all to have the firm operate a VaR risk management policy where the firm is expected to go bust every hundred days or so. The probability of failure or default must be very rare (e.g., once every hundred years), and yet the bad event on which VaR is predicated must be one that happens every so often. Hence, in using VaR for capital purposes, we must operate with a notion of bad events that is less severe than outright failure.

12. When using this measure, we need to make sure that σ_p and VaR are based on the same holding period. Since σ_p is usually quoted in annualised terms (i.e., σ_p is the standard deviation of annualised portfolio returns), we may need to de-annualise σ_p and translate it into the standard deviation relevant to the holding period on which the VaR is based.

13. The measure also has the attraction that it is not limited to normal return distributions, but also applies to other 'well-behaved' distributions such as the t-distribution. However, any implied probabilities of failure that we derive from such measures are obviously dependent on the assumed PDF. Moreover, and self-evidently, we can only compare one strength value with another if they are based on the same PDFs or if we make appropriate allowance for any differences in PDFs.

Hence, we cannot compare the raw strength value of one institution with that of another without making some, at least implicit, assumptions about their PDFs.

14. Consider the two cases of JP Morgan and Barings, for instance. Over 1994, Morgan's capital was about \$9.6 billion, and we need to divide this by the confidence parameter -1.65 and the annualised VaR, \$237 million. (This latter figure can be obtained by taking the daily average VaR, the DeaR in Morgan terminology, and scaling it up by the square root of 250.) The result is an average strength measure over 1994 of 66.8 and a negligible (to put it mildly) implied annual probability of distress. (Morgan is clearly a very strong bank, but no one in their right mind would ever believe that any financial institution, however sound, was *that* strong.) Now consider the case of Barings on the eve of its failure. Barings had a capital of about £615 million, and an annualised VaR of about £2 billion (!). (This figure comes from an estimated daily VaR of £126 million, scaled up to its annualised equivalent.) Dividing 615 by the product of 2,000 and 1.65 then gives us a strength value of 0.51, and an implied annualised probability of distress of about 0.3. (Again, one should not take this figure too seriously. The true probability of distress was probably much higher.) The most elementary calculations would therefore have shown that Morgan was very sound and that Barings was in mortal danger, provided of course that one used half-decent data. While one should never trust the strength measure to give precise probabilities of distress, these examples at least demonstrate its ability to separate the sheep from the goats.

15. By minor, I mean all differences other than those that would make a major impact on the implied probability of distress, and one has to keep in mind that there comes a point where the probability of distress becomes so low that further increases in strength values become meaningless. Thus Morgan had a measured strength of over 66 during 1994, but it would not make the slightest difference if that value were to fall to only 10, say, because the probability of distress is still negligible: a negligible rise in a negligible probability of distress still leaves a negligible probability of distress.

16. Of course, sensible analysts have always used the raw capital ratio not as an absolute measure as such, but as a kind of rough indicator in conjunction with various judgemental factors. Nonetheless, however much it is tempered by judgement, the use of the raw capital ratio is still open to the objection set out in the text, namely, that it does not allow for portfolio risk as reflected in σ_p.

17. There are many problems with the 'risk-weighted' measure (e.g., the weights and classifications are arbitrary, the weights bear no relationship to market risks, the risk-weighted capital requirements are only loosely related to real portfolio risks, and so on). The 'risk-weighted' scheme is covered in more detail in the Appendix to this chapter. For other references, see, e.g., Benston (1989) or Dowd (1997).

18. Assuming, of course, that we make some appropriate assumption for the distribution of the portfolio return. For example, under normality, $VaR = -\alpha\sigma_p W$, where W is the level of investment. Hence, given the confidence parameter α, the choice of W and σ_p determines VaR.

19. Strictly speaking, the new BIS regulations allow an institution that meets certain conditions to have the market risk component of its regulatory capital requirement on any given day be the maximum of its previous daily VaR and three times the average of the daily VaR for the previous 60 days. The VaR is based on a one-day holding period, but VaR measures are calibrated on a ten-day movement in prices or rates (i.e., we start with a ten-day holding period, calculate the VaR for the ten-day holding period and then infer the corresponding VaR for a one-day holding period). The multiplier of three can also be raised if the institution's regulatory supervisor feels that the results of model validation tests (i.e., backtests, to use the regulatory jargon) are sufficiently poor. The actual regulatory capital requirement will also include a specific risk component as well as the market risk component just estimated. The reader who wants more details really needs to look at the regulatory documents (e.g., US Treasury, Federal Reserve System and Federal Deposit Insurance Corporation (1996)).

20. If we are excessively demanding in our stress testing, we will come up with capital requirements that are too high to be feasible. As Greenspan observed, we should resist the 'temptation…to embrace the notion that bank capital must be capable of withstanding every conceivable set of adverse circumstances…it is important…to recognise that bank shareholders must earn a competitive rate of return on the capital they place at risk…' (quoted in Chew (1994, p. 63)).

21. In using stress tests for capital purposes, it is also good practice to break the process down into two stages. In the first stage, we go through our various scenario analyses and come up with a

putative capital requirement. This capital requirement will be the amount of capital needed to absorb the worst-case scenario and still be able to carry on. Since the capital requirement hinges on this particular scenario, it is therefore wise for the stress tester and/or more senior management to re-examine this scenario in more detail, to satisfy themselves that the scenario is plausible, that loss estimates seem reasonable and that they do wish the institution to be able to absorb these losses without getting distressed. If management are satisfied on these points, the capital level is the level suggested by the stress test. If not, the stress tests need to be repeated.

APPENDIX TO CHAPTER 11: REGULATORY CAPITAL REQUIREMENTS

Most financial institutions are subject to regulatory capital requirements of one form or another. These capital adequacy regulations are intended to make financial institutions stronger than they would otherwise be, and are usually defended as means of protecting small depositors and/or investors, reducing the chances of bank failure, protecting the safety and soundness of the financial system, or mitigating the effects of information asymmetries between managers and outsider investors.

1. MAIN TYPES OF CAPITAL ADEQUACY REGULATION

1.1. The Comprehensive Approach

The simplest type of capital adequacy regulation is the 'comprehensive' approach. This approach sets capital requirements as a proportion of the sum of the firm's total long position plus a qualified amount of its total short position. Typically, the capital requirement would be:

$$\text{Capital requirement} = \tau[L + Max(S - \beta L, 0)] \tag{11A.1}$$

where $0 < \tau < 1, 0 \leqslant \beta < 1$, L is the total long position, S is the total short position, τ is the capital requirement parameter and β is an offset parameter that determines how much of the short position qualifies for the capital requirement.

The comprehensive approach has been used for decades by the US Securities and Exchange Commission and by securities regulators in many other countries. The parameter τ varies from 10% to 40% across different jurisdictions, and some regulatory systems allow positive offsets (i.e., $\beta > 0$) while others do not.[A1] In the latter case, the capital requirement boils down to a certain proportion of the gross book value.

1.2. The Building Block Approach

The building block approach takes capital requirements as determined by the sum of specified weighted position values. In the case of securities firms, these positions are net or gross book positions. In the case of banks, positions are divided into a number of categories (e.g., fixed income, equity, etc.; they are also distinguished by the status of the issuer) and each category carries a fixed weight (100%, 50%, etc.). If w_1 is the weight attached to assets in category 1, and we have W_1 category 1 assets, and so forth, the weighted overall position is $w_1 W_1 + w_2 W_2 + ...$, and the relevant capital requirement would be a certain proportion of this weighted total position.

Building block approaches were used in the UK for decades to determine the capital requirements of both banks and securities firms. A building block approach was then adopted by the Basle Accord (1988) and subsequently applied to banks in the G-10 countries. While the original Basle Accord focused heavily on the risks associated with the issuer (i.e., credit risks, of a sort), the recently agreed Amendment to the Basle Accord (which is due to come into effect in January 1998) has sought to extend the categories to give more coverage to market-related risks.[A2] A similar building block approach has also been adopted by the EU's Capital Adequacy Directive (CAD), which came into effect in most EU countries in January 1996.

1.3. The SFA's Simplified Portfolio Approach

Another approach is the simplified portfolio approach used by the UK Securities and Futures Authority since 1992 to determine the regulatory capital requirements of UK securities firms. This approach takes the capital requirement to be a multiple of the portfolio standard deviation calculated under the simplistic but convenient assumptions that all assets have a market beta of one and have equal standard deviations.[A3]

1.4. The VaR Approach

Capital requirements can also be based on VaR. However, since the regulators/supervisors do not necessarily observe an institution's 'true' VaR estimate, the regulators who use VaR models to set capital requirements also need to provide the institution with some inducement to report its VaR truthfully. If not, the institution might be tempted to under-report its VaR to lower its capital requirement.

The use of VaRs for regulatory purposes was set out by the Basle Committee on Banking Supervision in its 1996 Amendment to the Basle Accord. The new BIS rules suggested that qualified banks be allowed to have their capital requirements determined according to a standardised VaR (or 'internal model') approach. A daily VaR was to be based on a 99% confidence level and an observation period of at least a year. Correlations could be recognised both within and (to a limited extent) between major categories (e.g., fixed income, equities). The capital requirement for market risk would then be equal to the maximum of the previous day's VaR, or the average VaR over the last 60 days times a multiplier (i.e., the hysteria factor) of at least three. (This multiplier would be set by the local bank supervisor in accordance with the results of validation or backtesting exercises. The multiplier would be raised if backtesting exercises revealed that a bank had been overly optimistic in its VaR forecasts. The purpose of this provision was to discourage banks from under-reporting their true VaR forecasts to lower their capital requirements.) As with the building block approach, the total capital requirement was also to include an additional 'specific risk' charge for issuer-specific risks (e.g., credit risks).[A4,A5]

2. PROBLEMS WITH CAPITAL ADEQUACY REGULATION

2.1. The Different Approaches Compared

2.1.1. The Comprehensive Approach

The worst approach is easily the comprehensive one, which can only be described as 'grossly inadequate' (Dimson and Marsh, 1995, p. 830). Its most glaring drawback is that it makes no allowance for portfolio factors, but it also makes little or no allowances for balanced books, which means that it particularly penalises hedged positions. Empirical evidence also suggests that it generates capital requirements that have no correlation at all with market risks.[A6] The comprehensive approach is therefore useless as a means of strengthening institutions against market risks.

2.1.2. The Building Block Approach

The building block approach is marginally better than the comprehensive approach. It gives greater recognition to the lower risk of hedged positions, and it is arguable that allowing for differential weights to be applied to different positions (as is the case with the capital adequacy regulations applied to banks under the Basle and CAD rules) is an improvement on allowing for no weight differentiation at all.[A7] The empirical evidence of Dimson and Marsh also suggests that this approach produces capital requirements that are correlated, albeit only modestly, with market risk.[A8] However, the building block approach still ignores portfolio factors and therefore fails to meet the most minimal criterion for intellectual respectability (i.e., that it be consistent with portfolio theory).[A9]

2.1.3. The Simplified Portfolio Approach

The simplified portfolio approach at least attempts to meet this criterion, and the empirical evidence of Dimson and Marsh (1995) confirms that the capital requirements it produces are more closely tied to portfolio risks than the capital requirements produced by either of the other two approaches. However, this approach has the drawback of relying on excessively simplified assumptions (different equities do not all have betas equal to one or returns with equal standard deviations) that will virtually never hold for any real-world portfolio. Moreover, these assumptions are so restrictive that this approach actually gives very little room for portfolio factors.[A10]

2.1.4. The VaR Approach

In theory, a VaR approach is superior to the SFA approach because it does not depend on the simplistic assumptions on which the latter is based and can therefore do justice to portfolio factors. It also has the major attraction, at least to the regulators, that it enables regulatory capital requirements to be tied to institutions' own assessments of their risks, as proxied by their VaRs. Instead of the regulators second-guessing what the institutions need, when they lack the information to do so, a VaR approach allows them to impose requirements based on institutions' own (and, presumably, better informed) assessments of their risks.

However, VaR approaches also have their own problems. (1) There are obvious problems relating to the arbitrariness and/or size of parameters – the choice of confidence level, holding period, the multiplying (i.e., hysteria) factor, and so forth. (2) There are also potentially serious model validation problems because of the poor statistical power of validation tests (Kupiec, 1995). These are a particular problem in the present context not only because they affect model validation for internal purposes, but also because they affect the ability of regulatory supervisors to verify that institutions are not producing excessively low VaR forecasts to get lower capital requirements (i.e., they affect the ability of supervisors to conduct backtesting exercises). (3) The VaR approaches set out in the Basle and CAD frameworks lead to capital requirements that are high relative to the capital requirements that emerge from the building block approaches. This clearly discourages institutions from opting for their capital requirements to be assessed via the VaR approach, and may also discourage institutions from adopting their own VaR systems in the first place. (4) Finally, it makes sense to use a VaR or any other portfolio approach to assess capital requirements only if we believe that capital should be set at a level to cover ordinary market risks (as opposed to occasional extraordinary shocks), and most regulators do not accept that capital requirements should focus on market risks. If capital is meant to cover the odd shock, as regulators themselves seem to accept, then capital requirements should be determined by stress tests, and everyday portfolio risk factors should be irrelevant.

2.2. Generic Problems with Capital Adequacy Regulation

There are also some generic problems that affect all types of capital adequacy regulation.

2.2.1. The Weakness of the Rule-making Process

One problem is that there is no reason to trust – indeed, every reason to distrust – the process by which capital adequacy regulations are formed. This process is one of negotiation in and around committees, which in itself often leads to compromise decisions that are frequently unsatisfactory and sometimes downright irrational. The pressure to satisfy interested parties also produces excessively long and detailed rulebooks that often reflect the concerns of participating parties rather than real issues on the ground, and these rules are frequently drawn up in almost total disregard of the costs they inflict on regulated institutions. There is also a tendency to produce 'one size fits all' rules that may be quite inappropriate when applied to real-world situations. Furthermore, the difficulty of getting agreement makes it difficult to change the regulations once they have been agreed upon. Regulations therefore tend to be ossified and very difficult to change – an obvious drawback in a fast-moving area like modern risk management.

There is good reason, too, to distrust the inputs into the regulation-making process as well as the process itself. The inputs consist of: the private interests of regulators and, sometimes, of their government masters; the influences of powerful lobbying groups, which can lead to regulatory capture (i.e., regulations that reflect the interests of the regulated firms); the prejudices and personalities of the main players involved; and chance events, such as a particular crisis that produces a knee-jerk reaction that pushes the outcome in one direction rather than another.

It is therefore naive, to put it mildly, to believe that the combination of this process and these inputs can produce a logically defensible outcome.[A11]

2.2.2. Distortion of Risk Management

Another problem with capital adequacy regulation is that it can undermine internal risk management, which not only imposes costs on the regulated institutions, but also undermines the supposed objective of making institutions stronger. The problem is that the regulation pressures institutions to assess and manage their risks in the particular ways favoured by the regulatory agencies. However, as we have seen, there is no reason to suppose that the regulatory procedures are actually the most appropriate ones to use. The regulations also impose an unnecessary and restrictive uniformity across institutions, which can hamper the spontaneous development of best risk management practice. The regulations therefore impose a straitjacket on regulated institutions which is not only costly, but can also undermine their own attempts to manage their risks.

2.2.3. Effects of Capital Adequacy Regulation Unclear

A further problem is that the regulators themselves have very little idea what effects their regulations actually have. This problem goes deeper than the Dimson-Marsh evidence that the most widely used types of regulation (i.e., the comprehensive and building block approaches) produce capital requirements that are either not correlated or at best only modestly correlated with market risks. The point is that any set of regulations creates incentives on the part of regulated institutions to try to avoid the regulations. Regulators may force institutions to comply with capital adequacy regulation, but institutions will respond by rearranging their portfolios to make the regulations less onerous (i.e., they will legitimately seek to avoid the regulatory tax). A regulator can therefore assess the effects of the regulations only by *anticipating* how institutions will react to them, and by taking those reactions into account when framing the regulations in the first place. Needless to say, this is a task well beyond the regulators' capability. So regulators impose regulations, but do not know what effects those regulations have because they have no idea how institutions respond to them. This makes it difficult, to put it mildly, for the regulators to know how to set or justify the regulations they impose.

2.2.4. Questionable Rationale for Capital Adequacy Regulation

Finally, it is highly questionable whether capital should be regulated at all. Most regulators and academics believe that the case for regulating capital is so obvious as to require little further investigation. To the extent that they pursue the issue any further, they tend to fall back on arguments – sometimes very nebulous ones – about capital adequacy regulation being needed to protect small depositors/investors, protect the stability of the financial system, protect the economy against bank failures, or counter market failures arising from asymmetric information between managers and outside investors.[A12] However, any plausibility these arguments have is superficial, and none of them in my view withstands close scrutiny.[A13] The only other argument sometimes made is that we need capital adequacy to counter the moral hazard (i.e., the incentive for institutions to take excessive risks) created by deposit insurance systems and/or the existence of a lender of last resort.[A14] This latter argument is also questionable, but even if we accept it, it merely establishes that one particular policy (i.e., capital adequacy regulation) may be needed to offset the effects of other governmental or regulatory policies (i.e., deposit insurance and the lender of last resort). Either way, the economically best solution is simply to abolish capital adequacy regulation *and* the other regulatory interventions that go with it. Capital standards would then be determined by market forces, and depositors and investors would get the levels of capital protection they demand (and, by implication, are willing to pay for).

3. CONCLUSIONS

Nonetheless, at the end of the day, arguments about the faults of capital adequacy regulation are of academic interest as far as the regulated firms are concerned. What really matters to them is that they have to live with the regulations and must therefore choose how to respond to them. Consequently, their main concerns should be to ensure that the regulations are complied with, as much as is appropriate, whilst also rearranging their positions to minimise the burden that regulations place on them.

Box 11A.1: Confessions of a regulator

Vicki Fitt, the deputy director of the UK Securities and Futures Authority, recently provided an interesting perspective on capital regulation in an article in the July 1996 issue of *Risk*. She wrote:[A15]

'For many years now, I have been contributing to and defending the European Union's Capital Adequacy Directive, and observing the evolution of the Basle Committee on Banking Supervision's proposals on market risk capital requirements...But I find it increasingly difficult to support them. In fact, I feel that between them they have the potential to deliver the greatest disservice to the financial services industry of any regulatory initiative I have witnessed. Why?

Directives have proved to be wholly unsuitable vehicles for technical detail. They are political documents which contain, almost by necessity, uneasy, arbitrary and irrational compromises, born of differences in the experience, understanding, culture and personality of those empowered to vote on them. Moreover, to crystallise regulations to such a degree of detail – when the process to amend them is so lengthy and tortuous – is hard to justify. Rules which are unworkable in practice are already fossilised in the CAD. As products and practice develop, the supervisory regime will get further and further behind the reality of industrial practice...

The driving force behind both the CAD and the Basle proposals is regulators' desire to set capital requirements. But in so doing, they dangerously confuse risk management and regulatory capital, as though they were interchangeable. The discipline of having capital to back risk is clearly necessary. Risk management is, however, entirely different and, indeed, more valuable. At the end of the day, it is robust risk management, not capital, that protects a firm.

Risk management is not an exact science; the mechanical process of calculating capital requirements, of course, is...

An over-prescriptive recipe for calculating capital charges with value-at-risk models can create the dangerous illusion that "the right answer" will result; both the naive senior manager and the inexperienced regulator might be unable to resist relying on the output. There is no right answer. Moreover, the language of "precision" has no place in a discussion of risk management...

There is an extreme danger in the value-at-risk framework that regulators will impose their views of risk management on the industry. No regulator is justified in doing this. Firms should implement the models they consider best enable them to monitor and control the businesses; this places the responsibility for risk management where it should properly lie. Furthermore, it is in no-one's interest to standardise practices in this area – disagreement is healthy as it allows the industry to trend continually towards better solutions while accepting that there is no best.

Where does this leave us? Preoccupied with rules when we should be preoccupied with risk, knee-deep in numbers emanating from spurious calculations performed ostensibly for the regulators' benefit, caught up in the micro-detail of market risk which, for most firms, is unlikely to be the type of exposure which causes their downfall. But, despite the irritation that we may all feel about this, the industry is highly adaptable and will find ways through and around inappropriate or rigid regulation.'

Endnotes

A1. Dimson and Marsh (1995, p. 829)
A2. Basle Committee on Banking Supervision (1996); see also Dale (1996, pp. 289–317) and Jorion (1996, pp. 48–9).
A3. Dimson and Marsh (1995, pp. 826–7)
A4. The use of VaR models for regulatory purposes was also endorsed in the CAD. There are a number of smaller differences between the Basle Committee and CAD approaches (e.g., over implementation dates, coverage of countries and institutions, and treatment of issues such as counterparty risk, large exposures, capital, consolidation, and so forth; see Vipond (1996)). However, perhaps the most important difference between the two is the astonishing stipulation in the CAD that the capital requirement be the higher of a standard building block requirement and a

VaR-based capital requirements modelled on, although not identical to, the Basle VaR capital requirement (see Dale (1996, pp. 214–5)). The CAD therefore allows institutions to derive their capital requirements using a VaR approach, but only if the VaR-based capital requirement is equal to or exceeds the building block requirement. The CAD therefore provides no incentive for institutions to adopt VaR systems and those institutions that do have VaR systems are positively discouraged from asking to have their capital requirements based on them.

A5.   In 1995, the Federal Reserve Board endorsed another approach to capital adequacy regulation, the pre-commitment approach of Kupiec and O'Brien (see, e.g., Kupiec and O'Brien (1995a, b, 1996)). Under this approach, institutions would be allowed to set their own prospective maximum loss limits (on which their capital requirements would be based), subject to a penalty schedule for losses in excess of these levels. The regulators could then induce the capital requirements they want by setting the penalties at suitable levels. This approach has the advantage, relative to the BIS/CAD VaR approach, of allowing the banks more freedom to decide on their own VaR parameters. It also has the advantage of making verification much easier: either the bank breaches its loss limit, in which case it should be penalised, or it does not, in which case it shouldn't be. However, the pre-commitment approach has its own problems (e.g., regulators need to know what penalties to set to achieve their desired outcomes, the penalties may not be feasible, and so on; see, e.g., Gumerlock (1996) or Prescott (1997)) and will not be adopted for regulatory purposes for some time yet, if ever.

A6.   See, e.g., Dimson and Marsh (1995, p. 838). The poor performance of the comprehensive approach is also confirmed by the later empirical evidence of Dimson and Marsh (1996).

A7.   However, everything depends on the weights chosen, and one must never forget that the very principle of assigning fixed weights to positions to reflect their risks contradicts the very basis of portfolio theory, and is therefore fundamentally unsound.

A8.   See Dimson and Marsh (1995, p. 848). Similar results were also found by Dimson and Marsh (1996).

A9.   It also has other serious drawbacks. (1) It covers market price risks poorly. Even if there is only one asset in a portfolio (i.e., so there are no portfolio effects to worry about), the market risk of that position will depend on market factors such as correlations, durations, and so on, and we cannot capture these risk factors by a single fixed 'risk' parameter, as the BIS/CAD rules attempt to do. (2) The building block approach is reliant on notional values, which makes it ill-suited to handling derivatives positions. (3) It does not account for netting agreements. For more on the weaknesses of the building block approach, see Jorion (1996, pp. 47–8) or Dowd (1997).

A10.   However, the later work of Dimson and Marsh (1996) sounds a warning about the use of simplified portfolio approaches. Dimson and Marsh evaluate the performance of two other simplified portfolio-based approaches, and one of these – their net capital-at-risk approach – performs dreadfully. There is an important lesson to draw here: while portfolio-based or VaR approaches are theoretically superior to the approaches traditionally used by regulators, we cannot assume that any particular simplified approach will necessarily work well, or even that it will necessarily beat its Stone Age competitors.

A11.   A good real-world example that illustrates these problems is the process of attempting to reach international agreement on harmonising the capital requirements of securities firms in the early 1990s. It was widely recognised that a portfolio approach was theoretically superior to the comprehensive and building block approaches, and yet a portfolio approach was eliminated as an option during the negotiations. The debate was also highly political, with the SEC holding out for a comprehensive approach in the (irrational) belief that a building block approach per se would produce more prudence (Dimson and Marsh, 1995, pp. 831–2). The theoretically correct view is that it is not the type of system that determines whether capital requirements are prudent or otherwise, but the actual size of the capital requirements.

A12.   See, e.g., Miles (1995).

A13.   This is not the place to pursue these arguments in detail, but one can at least sketch the problems with them. (a) The investor protection argument boils down to pure paternalism (i.e., the premise that government should protect people against losses) and is not necessarily persuasive even if one accepts a paternalistic stance (e.g., why should 'small' taxpayers have to pay to protect 'small' investors?). (b) The systemic fragility argument gets its plausibility from our collective memory (and a distorted one at that) of the US banking collapses of the 1930s. In fact, there is no reason to believe that individual bank failures would threaten the financial system as a whole (e.g.

the evidence indicates that bank failure contagion is limited, at most). Moreover, banks failures seem to have much the same effects on economic activity as the failures of comparably sized firms. (c) The asymmetric information argument ignores the point that management have an incentive to maintain the confidence of depositors and investors, and will therefore have an incentive to do whatever is required to maintain that confidence (e.g., provide relevant information, offer credible assurances, and so on). For more on these issues, see Dowd (1996, 1997).

A14.   See, e.g., Benston and Kaufman (1996).

A15.   Fitt (1996, p. 17).

12

Firm-wide Risk Management

T HE final chapter of the book examines risk management at the firm-wide level. There are three main topics to consider: (1) strategic risk management; (2) enterprise-wide risk management (ERM); and (3) the usefulness of VaR approaches to corporates, particularly non-financial ones.

1. STRATEGIC RISK MANAGEMENT

1.1. Strategic Risk Management Policy

The most basic requirement of strategic risk management is a clear policy on the firm's approach to risk: senior management must take a view of the sorts of risks they want the firm to manage. To some extent the answer depends on the firm's line of business, and the management would normally want the firm to bear those risks peculiar to its own particular business. The answer will also depend on the size of the firm's exposures to different risks and on its capability to handle them, although its risk management capability will itself depend on decisions management have made about building up and/or maintaining particular risk management capabilities. The alternatives to the firm managing particular risks itself are to avoid them (e.g., by prohibiting employees from taking on certain risk exposures or by taking out appropriate insurance or hedging cover) or to pay others to manage them on its behalf (e.g., by hiring outsiders who are specialists in managing such risks).

Such a policy goes a long way towards determining the general environment and specific parameters within which everyone works, and is important for a number of reasons. One reason is to protect the ability of the firm to attend to its core business. More particularly, it is to protect stakeholders and thereby ensure that the firm gets the best out of them. Managers and workers are vulnerable to the risk of losing their jobs if the firm gets into difficulties, long-term customers are vulnerable to losses if their supplier goes out of business, and the firm's suppliers are vulnerable to loss if their customer gets into difficulties. A good risk management policy is therefore valuable to all these stakeholders: it can protect the jobs of managers and workers, protect the sources of supply of customers, and protect the suppliers' market. Part of the reason for risk management is therefore to protect the interests of these stakeholders.

However, risk management is also in the interests of the firm itself, even if shareholders and/or management do not care about the welfare of other stakeholders as such. The point is that the firm needs these other stakeholders to make investments and other commitments to it, and they will be more inclined to do so if they feel secure about the firm and its prospects. The firm needs managers and workers to invest their human capital in the firm, it needs suppliers to make appropriate longer-term investments and it needs customers to stay loyal. By making stakeholders more secure, a good risk management policy helps to encourage managers and workers to stay with the firm and invest their human capital in it, encourages suppliers to make risky investment decisions, and encourages customers to continue buying its products. If the firm fails to manage its risks well, its staff will start looking for jobs elsewhere, suppliers will avoid longer-term commitments, and customers will look for alternative sources of supply, all of which are obviously detrimental to the firm. The firm therefore needs a good risk management policy to protect its core business.[1]

Risk management can also directly or indirectly benefit stakeholders in other ways:[2]

- It can enable the firm to improve its performance by specialising appropriately in its handling of risks. As a general (albeit crude) rule, it makes sense for the firm to have a risk management policy that enables senior management to concentrate most of their energies on those risks they have a comparative advantage in handling.

- Risk management can benefit all stakeholders by facilitating optimal investment decisions.[3] It can do this in one of two ways. (1) It can protect a firm's cash flows, so that it has the cash to invest in positive-net-value projects whenever they appear. (2) It can ameliorate conflicts of interest among stakeholders that might otherwise lead to good investment opportunities being passed over. The classic example is the conflict of interest between bondholders and shareholders which can discourage shareholders from approving of otherwise good investments if too many of the gains would go to bondholders in the form of lower expected default losses; risk management can resolve this type of problem by ensuring that more of the gains from additional investments go to shareholders; management are then more likely to approve such projects, and everyone gains.[4]

- Risk management helps to reduce the deadweight costs of financial distress, such as the extra legal and administrative costs of filing for bankruptcy, the loss of tax write-offs, and so on. The reduction in these costs potentially benefits everyone concerned.

- By making earnings less volatile, risk management also makes financial statements, dividend announcements, and so forth, more informative. This helps those concerned to make more informed (and therefore, presumably, better) decisions.

Greater earnings stability also tends to reduce average tax liabilities when those liabilities are convex functions of earnings, as they usually are.[5]

1.2. Managing Strategic Risk

Having set out a policy framework, senior management must then manage strategic risk within the context of that framework. There are three major aspects to this task:

- Management should think ahead strategically: they should anticipate major new developments so the firm can take advantage of them, or at least ensure that they are not caught unprepared.

- They should make certain risk management decisions that can be made only at the most senior level: to determine corporate capital structure, to decide how to handle major exposures, major investments, major joint ventures, and so on.
- They should set out the policies governing position limits and targets for the institution as a whole, and for business units lower down the line.

In making these decisions, senior management should take account of a large variety of factors: overall business objectives, past performance of the units and individuals concerned, market liquidity and volatility, what competitors are doing, and other factors. They should also bear in mind the following.

Medium- to long-term view: They should take a medium- to long-term view to complement the shorter-term view usually taken by more junior managers or traders (e.g., traders will usually look over the next day). In any case, only they have the responsibility and firm-wide perspective to make major longer-term decisions.

Narrowness of profit and loss figures: Senior management should be aware that market measures of profit and loss are often unduly narrow, even for financial institutions.[6] Thus, a bank will often make a considerable profit from fees and commissions, but these profits do not derive directly from trading and cannot therefore be measured on a mark-to-market basis. At the same time, such profits are often related to positions in traded instruments and we must take account of such income when assessing the overall risks and returns associated with particular tradable positions. A fortiori, these sorts of issues – the narrowness of conventional profit and loss figures, and the hidden relationships between different positions, which might themselves be accounted for under different business units – arise with non-financial firms at least as much as with financial ones. If senior management do not pick up on these issues, it is very unlikely that anyone else will.

Interaction with expenses: Senior management need to take account of how profits and incomes interact with expenses, particularly because expenses are often ignored or dealt with by arbitrary rules of thumb at the level of the business unit. They might discover that business units that appear to be highly profitable are not in fact so when one takes account of how much they cost to operate, or vice versa. It is particularly important to be aware of the impact of overheads regimes and other intra-institutional cost accounting conventions on reported incomes and profits, and also to be aware of the incentives they create and the conflicts they can produce between different business units.

2. ENTERPRISE-WIDE RISK MANAGEMENT

2.1. Why Enterprise-wide Risk Management?

2.1.1. What is ERM?

The philosophy of risk management outlined in this book leads naturally to and, indeed, depends upon, a system of enterprise-wide risk management (ERM). The essence of ERM is the management of overall institutional risk across all risk categories and business units.[7] An ERM system deals with broad risk categories (e.g., market risk or credit risk), the different risks attached to differing instruments and portfolios (e.g., equity risks,

---

Box 12.1: Making risks transparent

Firms need to decide how much they wish to communicate the risks they are taking to actual or potential stakeholders. Annual reports and other financial statements are still, as a rule, relatively uninformative about the risks the firm is taking on.[8] However, in the last couple of years many firms have started providing more public information to investors, partly by providing more information about their derivatives positions and their general policy towards derivatives, and partly by providing VaR information.[9]

There are several reasons why firms should think seriously about increased risk disclosure:

- There is a strong argument that they have a duty to provide interested parties with adequate information on which to make informed investment and other decisions.
- Various factors over the last two decades – the increasing use of derivatives, the increased complexity of many firms and of their business relationships, and increased (or at least high) volatility in the environments in which they operate – have combined to make the older standards of disclosure less informative to interested parties. Increased VaR disclosure helps to restore the balance.
- Increased disclosure may be in a firm's own interest. (1) It reassures investors who might otherwise assume the firm is taking more risks than it really is (i.e., disclosure tries to indicate that the firm has nothing to hide). (2) It sends a signal to investors and other interested parties that management have a confident and progressive approach to risk. (3) It puts pressure on rivals who might not be so keen to reveal themselves.

---

commodity risks, swap risks), the risks associated with different business units up to the level of the institution as a whole, and the risks associated with having offices in different locations operating under differing legal and regulatory systems. An ERM system needs to be able to measure and aggregate all these risks on a consistent basis, taking all correlations and interrelationships into account, and give the firm or business unit exposure to any given risk factor at any given time.

The ERM approach to risk management is very recent, and the development of ERM is led, as one might have expected, by the bigger banks and securities houses. Despite its relative novelty, most informed observers already believe that it is only a matter of time before ERM systems become standard among larger corporations. Information technology and finance theory have now developed to the point where the biggest obstacles to setting up systems of integrated risk management are no longer technical or analytical, but organisational and, to some extent, economic. Business units need to be pulled together, procedures standardised, and new systems set up to facilitate both centralised control and centralised risk management. Setting up ERM systems can therefore involve major upheaval and considerable expense. Nonetheless, firms that establish them can also reap very significant benefits.

2.1.2. Benefits of ERM

One benefit of ERM is a major improvement in the quality of risk-return analysis. We clearly need to measure the risk taken by the institution, and we can measure this risk only if we have an enterprise-wide risk management system. ERM enables decision makers – both junior decision makers such as asset managers or traders, and senior management – to make decisions taking the broader risk picture into account. In so doing ERM also helps to resolve co-ordination issues between decentralised agents in different business units (e.g., when making credit decisions and in taking advantage of netting) and should, in theory, lead to better quality risk management decisions at all levels of the firm. It should also of course lead to greater economic efficiency in other ways as well (e.g., in allocating capital).

An ERM system also imposes a discipline on the firm that makes for greater consistency in data collection, measurement and processing, highlights gaps or other inadequacies in the data, facilitates auditing and monitoring, makes it more difficult for human error or fraud to slip by unnoticed, and improves overall management control, particularly as regards subsidiary units. There is no doubt that sound ERM systems would have prevented most of the high-profile financial disasters of recent years had the institutions concerned had them.

The benefits of ERM also increase – and the case for ERM becomes more pressing – as the firm becomes more complex and growing complexity makes risks more difficult to manage. Senior management has a tremendous task managing risks if the firm is large, has many different lines of business, and operates all over the world across different legal systems, cultures and languages. As global conglomerates become ever more complex, the older systems of management control and risk management become increasingly unreliable, and the chances of major problems such as uncontrolled rogue trading increase. There comes a point where a large conglomerate has to adopt ERM if it wishes to re-establish strong management control and get a proper handle on risk management.

In addition, ERM also helps a firm to provide stakeholders and potential investors with better risk information. The firm can report its risk positions more fully and more accurately and thereby enable these parties to make more informed decisions. This is not just a matter of reporting VaR figures, but also a matter of giving some idea of the firm's risk exposures and hedging policy, so that interested parties know what risks they are taking when they invest in the firm or get involved with it.[10]

2.2. Main Features of an ERM System[11]

Any ERM system has the following basic features.

2.2.1. Centralised Data Warehouse

The first is a centralised data warehouse in which to store all position, credit and transaction data. Needless to say, establishing a centralised warehouse implies a major restructuring of the firm's organisation and it is important that firms do not underrate the task involved:

Box 12.2:   Problems of risk management before ERM

It is only relatively recently that sophisticated ERM systems have become practically feasible for large complex organisations. The absence of such systems in the past led to a variety of problems that firms with ERM systems can now, hopefully, avoid:

- Rarely, if ever, did an individual decision maker have a clear idea of the risks taken on by the firm as a whole. This applied to decision-makers at the firm-wide level as well as those at the micro level. The former had an imperfect idea of firm-wide risks because data were often inconsistent and risk measurement systems did not allow for intra-firm risk correlations; and the latter seldom, if ever, had a clear idea of what was happening in other units or at the firm-wide level.
- The absence of ERM made it easier for problems caused by fraud or human oversight to go undetected. In practice it often led to problems being overlooked, particularly when they involved subsidiaries. These overlooked problems have sometimes led to major losses (as in the cases of Daiwa, Sumitomo and MG) and even fatal ones (as in the case of Barings).
- The lack of information led to co-ordination problems that were both costly to live with and costly to avoid. Offices in different locations might independently extend credit to the same counterparty, thereby leading to an excessive overall credit exposure. Yet it was also difficult to co-ordinate decisions taken by people in different offices, and systems to limit each business unit's freedom to make decisions often prevented them from exploiting profitable opportunities.
- These problems – flawed risk information, weak management control, lack of knowledge about what is going on, and poor co-ordination – tend to increase as the firm and its activities become more complex. Furthermore, firms often respond to these problems by becoming more bureaucratic and more hierarchic, and this response undermines flexibility and discourages initiative and innovation.

Underestimating the complexity and difficulty of assembling a centralized data warehouse can have such dire consequences in time and cost that firms have thrown in the towel way before the goal was achieved. Others have rushed the job or not fully completed the integration. As a result, they run the risk of making key business decisions based on incomplete reports. (Spinner, 1996a, p. 40)

Establishing a centralised data warehouse requires that an institution get to grips with an enormous mass of information, unify a potentially large number of inherited data systems and ensure that output is standardised and made comparable across the institution. This is a huge task in any large firm – definitions, conventions and procedures need to be standardised across the whole enterprise – and is easily the most demanding aspect of establishing an ERM system.[12] We need to establish positions by product, office, country and client. This means collecting and cleaning data from each office, each of which will have its own particular data system. Some offices will use mainframes, some will use PCs,

Macs or other computers, and there will be all sorts of differences in the software used, the quality of the data they deal with, the conventions and procedures used in different offices, and so forth. A very considerable amount of effort will therefore have to go into cleaning up the data. In addition, when dealing with credit information, we also need to break positions down by client identity and take account of netting agreements, guarantees, collateral terms, legal issues, and other relevant factors. Decisions also have to be made about how frequently data are to be revised, how data systems are to be made secure against fraud, and the like.[13]

2.2.2. Analytics

We also need analytics systems to process our data. These systems would depend on the risks the institution faces and the level of sophistication required by management. The main issues here were largely covered in earlier chapters. Where market risks are concerned, the analytics would be one or more VaR systems – variance-covariance, historical simulation, or Monte Carlo simulation – as appropriate, combined with some system for stress testing. The institution would also want appropriate systems to analyse credit risk, ranging from a traditional, fairly simplistic credit analysis system to a more sophisticated credit at risk system. There are also issues of how far the analysis of credit risk should be integrated with the analysis of market risk and the extent to which credit risk analyses should be supported by credit stress testing. Finally, senior management need to make decisions on how to handle liquidity, operational and legal risks.

2.2.3. Monitoring and Evaluation

The analytics of an ERM system would feed into centralised systems of monitoring and evaluation. These would include:

- Systems to verify data and flag up data problems.
- One or more systems to monitor and enforce compliance with position limits and other constraints on decision makers.
- Systems to collect and process data for purposes of risk adjustment and performance evaluation.
- Systems to validate the pricing, VaR and other models used for analytical purposes.

2.2.4. Decision Making

The output produced by these systems then feeds into the risk measurement and risk management processes. Reports on data verification problems and compliance issues would be fed to the people responsible for ensuring that data are sound and that limits are complied with; some output would be inputted directly into the computer systems that enable decision makers to choose between alternative positions; some output would also go into performance evaluation to determine remuneration; and reports on validation issues would be sent to the people concerned.

Box 12.3: Principles of successful ERM

ERM implies major changes in corporate structure and considerable commitments of management time and other resources. Oldfield and Santomero (1995, p. 20) suggest that there needs to be a 'focus on the central businesses of the organization' and a full-scale review of the risk management implications of all major lines of business. This review process should observe the following guidelines:

- Risk management must be integral to an institution's business plan, and appropriate policies must be developed for each business unit. Oldfield and Santomero also suggest, with good reason, in my view, that activities that are not part of the institution's focus should be dropped to reduce the danger that management might overlook the risks involved.
- The specific risks of each business activity should be identified and measured, where possible. Obviously, databases need to be developed and risks should be treated consistently across the organisation.
- Procedures should ensure that 'risk management begins at the point nearest to the assumption of the risk' in order to 'maintain management control, generate data in a consistent fashion, and eliminate needless exposure to risk'.[14]
- Senior management must have a clear and effective overall risk management system. This system must look at the performance of all business units down to the level of the individual decision maker and be closely integrated into the firm's business planning and management control processes.

2.3. Approaches to Enterprise-wide Risk Management

Institutions will want to adopt ERM in different ways suited to their own particular business needs. ERM systems can therefore differ enormously from each other.

2.3.1. Type and Sophistication of ERM Systems

At the most simple level, ERM might merely involve the sharing of information across the organisation. A decision-making unit can then make decisions knowing more about what is going on elsewhere in the organisation. Local management and senior management could share more information with each other, and local managements could share information with their counterparts in different locations. It can also be helpful if the central office disseminates information about rate forecasts, firm-wide projections and the like, so that people have a better idea of the assumptions colleagues are working to.

ERM systems can also be more sophisticated. They can involve centralised controls on particular risk exposures, such as the total exposures to given counterparties or currencies. Individual decision makers would then have a better idea of the effects of their decisions on the firm as a whole, and systems could be set up to encourage them to promote the objectives set out by senior management (e.g., through appropriate performance evaluation schemes). Credit decisions, say, could be made knowing the firm's current aggregate exposure. By providing such information, ERM systems also make for better allocation of credit exposures (e.g., instead of giving different offices their own fixed credit limits, individual offices could make credit decisions against a firm-wide credit limit, taking other factors into account). Such systems can also tell decision makers when they are approaching (or have breached) credit or other limits and, if desired, can be set up to block trades if they would break such limits.

2.3.2. Timeliness

ERM systems also differ in the degree of timeliness of the information they provide. Since this information is used for making decisions in real time, we would, other things being equal, obviously prefer information to be up to date when decision makers use it. However, obtaining up-to-date information is not easy. Each transaction

> changes the bank's risk profile. The calculations that must be performed to determine the impact of each transaction, multiplied by the volume of transactions, makes it nearly impossible to update the risk calculations continuously with each transaction, for every product, in every bank location. (Williams, 1996, p. 34).

The ideal of real-time processing – up-to-the-second data, continuously provided – is therefore almost impossible to achieve across the institution as a whole, at least with the present cost of information technology. At the moment, real-time information systems are more or less confined to trading rooms, where dealers need them to make their decisions in a rapidly changing environment. Real-time systems are also expensive, even when used restrictively, as when used only in dealing rooms.

In practice, the best that can be done for the rest of the enterprise is to provide information on a batch basis: to provide updated information periodically, either every so often and/or when so many changes have been made that the old information can no longer be regarded as sufficiently up to date to be useful. We are therefore dealing with systems that operate in realistic rather than real time.[15] The frequency with which information is updated would also depend on the type of position involved, the rapidity with which positions and/or values change, and the cost and difficulty of updating information.

2.3.3. Degree of Integration of Risk Analysis

Different institutions can also opt for different degrees of risk analysis integration. Traditionally, different types of risk analysis have been carried out by different people in different departments using different methodologies, with very little co-ordination between them.[16] However, this type of separation is increasingly anachronistic:

- One reason is that the analysis of different risks is now converging – much credit risk analysis now uses the same VaR methodology as the analysis of market risk – and this convergence makes it increasingly pointless to carry out different risk analyses separately.
- Integration helps ensure that results are mutually consistent and, as far as possible, comparable with each other to facilitate decision making (e.g., in allocating capital between different activities).[17]
- It makes sense to avoid unnecessary duplication: there is no point in a market risk unit going through a complex valuation procedure to estimate market risks whilst the credit

risk unit is going through much the same procedure to estimate credit risks. Integration therefore helps to ensure that avoidable duplication is eliminated.

- It is important to ensure, where possible, that the assumptions, data and valuation models used in analysing different types of risk are the same, or are at least consistent with each other.
- Co-ordinating analyses helps us to pick up their interactions. Market risk analysis can have implications for the analysis of credit risk, and vice versa.[18] A large gain on a position will often imply a corresponding large increase in credit exposure, until the debt is settled and the profit is realised, and a large loss will often imply a reduction in credit exposure. Market and credit risks will therefore often counteract each other – we will gain on one where we lose on the other – and where they do, we should not add the separate risks together as if they were independent. However, it is very difficult to avoid adding risks together unless we have an integrated approach that takes their correlations into account.[19]
- We need an integrated approach to be able to handle new hybrid instruments that involve a combination of different types of risk and cannot sensibly be handled if we examine these risks separately.[20] Traders who are used to dealing with market risks must increasingly take account of credit risks as they venture into new instruments in less liquid markets; similarly, lenders, who used to be concerned only with credit risks, are now forced to pay more attention to market risks as their loans become more liquid.[21] There is thus an increasingly important middle ground of financial instruments that are sensitive to both market and credit risks, and we need an integrated approach to handle them.[22]

3. VaR FOR CORPORATES

3.1. Limitations of VaR for Corporates

We now turn to our last substantive issue, the usefulness of VaR approaches to corporates. It should be clear by now that the VaR approach outlined in this book is best suited to financial institutions, and particularly to those such as investment banks and securities houses that have large portfolios of traded financial instruments. One reason for this is that most of the instruments they handle are traded on fairly liquid markets and marked to market, so their positions are straightforward to value and profits and losses are relatively easy to ascertain. In addition, the daily marking to market of these positions usually ensures that there are enough profit/loss observations to make VaR approaches feasible, bearing in mind the large numbers of observations these approaches require.

By contrast, other financial institutions and almost all corporates have at least some assets or liabilities that are less amenable to VaR methodologies. Part of the explanation is that their positions are often more difficult to value.[23] Most corporates have substantial asset holdings that are not traded in organised markets and therefore cannot be valued by marking to market. Typical examples are fixed plant, equipment, real estate, labour contracts and brand names. Such assets make up the bulk of the asset portfolios of almost all non-financial corporations. There are also many financial institutions that

Box 12.4:   Integrating risk analysis

One approach to integrating the analysis of different types of risk is suggested by Drzik (1996, p. 15). He suggests that different risks be positioned along a liquidity continuum that recognises both the common elements among different risks as well as their differences from each other. Their position on this continuum then determines how those risks should be handled. Drzik sets out four key points on this continuum:

(1) *Smooth markets*: These are textbook liquid markets with large numbers of participants and high turnovers. Standard examples are currency markets or markets for US Treasuries. Positions are easily valued by marking to market and risk is assessed on the basis of VaR supplemented by stress tests.

(2) *Choppy markets*: These markets are less deep and less liquid, and have fewer participants and lower turnover. Examples are OTC markets in equities. Participants tend to use similar methods to those of participants in smooth markets, but these methods are less reliable in choppy markets because of liquidity and valuation problems.

(3) *Icy markets*: These markets are even thinner and less liquid, and secondary markets exist, but are very limited. Trades tend to be negotiated rather than screen-based, and prices are often not transferable across deals. Pricing is usually mark to model supplemented by some marking to market with adjustments for liquidity and other concerns. Risk calculations are mainly carried out by loss modelling, with some VaR analysis adjusted for liquidity risks.

(4) *Frozen markets*: These markets are extremely thin and there are few, if any, secondary markets. Assets are usually bought to hold to maturity and products are highly tailored. Pricing is highly judgemental, and often based on reserve-adjusted book values supplemented by marking to model and relatively arbitrary allowances for illiquidity. Risk evaluation is highly problematic.

Each point on this continuum is characterised by certain features:

Valuation: Market prices are good valuation guides in smooth markets, of somewhat less use in choppy markets, even less use in icy markets, and no use in frozen ones. We therefore rely almost entirely on mark-to-market valuation for smooth markets. When markets become choppy we make more use of mark-to-model valuation and to some extent judgemental methods. With icy markets the balance shifts further towards judgemental methods, and with frozen markets we rely on little else.

Risk control: Risk control in smooth markets is straightforward, since profits and losses are easy to ascertain, and relies mainly on limits backed up by *ex post* monitoring and performance evaluation. Risk control in choppy markets is similar except for the need to pay more attention to issues of liquidity and unrealised gains/losses. In icy and frozen markets we have to devote even more attention to these issues, and also to systems to mitigate or stop losses from accumulating.

Remuneration: As markets become less liquid, we should place increasing emphasis on deferred compensation. Deferment enables us to reduce the compensation of individuals whose decisions produce losses that become apparent only later. The prospect of such penalties then gives them more incentive to act responsibly.

have substantial holdings of relatively illiquid assets (e.g., commercial banks) and others whose liabilities are substantially illiquid (e.g., insurance and pension companies). The illiquidity of these positions makes it difficult to value them by their market prices and alternative means of valuation have other problems: ascertaining replacement costs can be difficult, historical costs may have little bearing on current value, and marking to model might not be appropriate because models may be inadequate or non-existent.

A second reason why corporates (and other financial institutions) cannot use VaR-type systems with the same (relative) ease as securities houses is because corporates usually attempt to manage risks over considerably longer horizons than a day or a month, and typically want horizons varying from months to years. This longer-term perspective then means that it is almost impossible to get enough observations on which to carry out VaR and related calculations. It also means that it becomes harder to justify convenient modelling assumptions (e.g., the assumption of normality).

3.2. Potential Corporate Uses of VaR Approaches

3.2.1. Managing Market and Credit Risks

Nonetheless, corporates can still benefit from applying VaR approaches to particular risks, and three potential applications come readily come to mind:

- A firm can use a VaR approach to manage the market risks of particular positions, even if the non-marketability of other positions prevents such approaches being applied across the firm as a whole. A VaR system could help a large firm manage its fixed income positions, say, or help an international corporation manage its FX positions. VaR approaches can also be used by corporates to help manage the market risks of their derivatives positions.
- A VaR risk management system could enable a firm to manage exposures resulting from other decisions. For example, a firm might have particular FX or other exposures from a foreign investment, and use a VaR system to assess and manage the risks resulting from this investment.
- Systems based on VaR principles can also be useful to corporates when handling non-market-price risks. The most obvious such risks are credit risks (as discussed in Chapter 9), but VaR methodologies might also be useful in managing liquidity and possibly other risks as well (as discussed in Chapter 10).

3.2.2. Cash Flow at Risk (CFaR)

Many corporates can also benefit from VaR approaches applied to their prospective cash flows. Such cash flow at risk (CFaR) systems enable them to quantify cash flow risks and aggregate them in ways that take account of the correlations between them (i.e., they do to cash flows what VaR systems proper do to position values). The key feature of such systems is the definition of risk 'in terms of earnings, or some other measure of operating performance, rather than asset value' (Turner, 1996, p. 38). We can then think of the actual cash flow at risk as the lowest likely cash flow over some period at some chosen confidence level. Since we are dealing with operating cash flows, we can also think of CFaR in terms of the risks of missing targets in our business plans (loc. cit.).[24]

A CFaR system would be set up to reflect the horizons and planning cycles used in budget planning (e.g., if a firm measures earnings quarterly, it would set up a CFaR system with a quarterly holding period). Typically, a CFaR system would also be set up to encompass the firm as a whole, or at least its major operating units, and would use the same definitions, conventions and operating units used by the firm's budgetary process.

The system itself consists of a method of simulating cash flows based on certain assumptions about underlying risk factors and the sensitivities of cash flows to those factors. A CFaR analysis will usually begin with the firm's key financial variables – sales revenue, interest expense, cost of goods, and the like. These are then linked to risk variables by positing appropriate relationships between them. These relationships might be the equations suggested by theoretical models, where such models exist (e.g., in relating interest costs to spot interest rates). Alternatively, and more normally, these relationships would be presumed behavioural equations based loosely on economic theory. Thus foreign sales might be related to an exchange rate, the prices of competitors' goods, and so on. The sensitivies of relevant cash flow variables – foreign sales, or whatever – to the risk factors that influence them can come from empirical estimates based on past data or from expert assessments of what those sensitivities are likely to be.[25] These relationships should as far as possible incorporate whatever relevant information we have to hand. For example, if our policy is to swap from making floating to fixed interest rate payments when interest rates reach a certain threshold, we should incorporate this information when modelling interest costs. These relationships should also avoid violating known zero-arbitrage conditions. Ideally, too, the simulated output from any CFaR system should match the volatilities, correlations and other general features of the real-world variables being simulated. The cash flow at risk would then be inferred from the histograms or other output produced by this CFaR system.

CFaR systems have a number of attractions: (1) They are a useful complement to VaR systems. A firm can use a CFaR system to look at risks over a longer horizon than is usual with a VaR system. A firm can therefore benefit from a CFaR system even if it has a good VaR system already in place. (2) A CFaR system is useful to firms that are unable to make much use of VaR because of the valuation and data problems that limit the applicability of proper VaR systems. (3) A CFaR system can be applied to the firm as a whole and take account of correlations among individual cash flows. (4) By highlighting the underlying risk factors, a CFaR system helps managers think more clearly about their longer-term risks. (5) The results of CFaR exercises are readily interpretable in terms of budgetary and other planning exercises. (6) Data collection and processing costs are (hopefully) fairly low because CFaR uses much of the same data and data conventions as the ordinary budgetary process. (7) The costs of CFaR systems can also be kept down by making the system fairly crude: there is no point having a system give more precise forecasts than the budgetary system on which it depends.[26] (8) The results of CFaR systems help improve budgetary and longer-term planning, and the process of carrying out CFaR exercises can highlight hidden assumptions, weaknesses and interactions that might otherwise be overlooked.[27]

4. CONCLUSIONS

Looking further afield, the VaR approach to risk management is still very young and no one can yet say with any certainty where it will all lead. Nonetheless, certain points are already very clear. First, VaR is not another one of those management fads that periodically shake everyone up and then disappear without trace. There is little doubt that VaR is here to stay and those involved in risk management – risk managers themselves, senior managers, regulators, and so on – need to brace themselves for yet another risk management revolution, and perhaps the most drastic one yet. Second, the VaR revolution is still in its early stages. Even the bigger investment banks and securities houses – the institutions in the vanguard of the VaR movement – are still very much learning about it, and other institutions lag well behind them. Nonetheless, it is already clear that VaR approaches to risk management will become universal among financial institutions within a relatively short period of time. Thirdly, the VaR revolution will go well beyond financial institutions. With corporates, the emphasis will be less on VaR as such – although VaR systems will still have a useful role to play – as on credit-risk, CFaR and ERM systems, and work on these has really only just begun. ERM systems in particular will drastically alter the way that large corporates go about their business, and I would venture to predict that it will be in the adoption of ERM systems, rather than in the adoption of VaR systems in a narrow sense, that the VaR revolution in risk management will have its greatest impact.

ENDNOTES

1. See also, e.g., Campbell and Kracaw (1993, pp. 11–12).
2. Shareholders also benefit from risk management, although there is some controversy on this issue. Shareholders differ from (some) other stakeholders in that they (usually) have more opportunities to diversify their risk. This makes them less vulnerable to firm-specific risk and leads some writers to conclude that they get no benefit from firm risk management. However, I believe this argument goes too far and ignores a number of relevant points. (1) The argument itself is valid only in a restrictive – usually CAPM – world, and it is now widely accepted that the CAPM framework is unduly restrictive for many of the questions in which we are interested. (2) Risk management benefits shareholders if it induces other stakeholders to make commitments to the firm which they might not otherwise make, and which it is in shareholders' interests that they do make. (3) Risk management benefits shareholders for similar reasons as it (directly or otherwise) benefits other stakeholders, as explained in the text: it facilitates risk specialisation, encourages worthwhile investments, makes earnings more informative, and reduces average tax liabilities.
3. See, e.g., Smithson (1996b).
4. See, e.g., Smith and Stulz (1985).
5. The point is that the proportion of income paid as tax usually increases with the level of pre-tax income. A firm that has a very stable income from year to year would therefore usually have a lower average tax liability than a firm that has the same average income, but more income volatility from year to year. In other words, average tax liabilities tend to rise as income becomes more volatile, for any given level of average income. Hence, measures to stabilise income (i.e., risk management) help to reduce firms' average tax liabilities. Further convexity of the tax schedule can also arise in tax systems where firms are not allowed to carry forward losses against future income. Even if the tax rate is flat, a firm with a stable income would then pay lower tax than one with a very volatile income.
6. For more on this and related issues, see Baliman (1996, pp. 11–12).

7. See, e.g., Paul-Choudhury (1996) or Williams (1996).

8. See, e.g., Chew (1996, 190–5).

9. Providing information about VaR also goes some way towards revealing risks that might otherwise be hidden in derivatives positions. As we already know, VaR is very informative about market risks, including derivatives risks, when the instruments themselves are fairly straightforward (i.e., when pay-offs are linear functions of well-behaved risk factors). VaR is less informative when positions are non-linear in risk factors or otherwise more involved (as with options positions). Nonetheless, the combination of VaR information and further details of non-linear and other awkward derivatives positions goes a long way towards disclosing risks. Firms should also consider revealing something of their approach to stress testing (e.g., the kinds of scenarios they look at, and their impact on the firm), although in doing so they will obviously want to get the right balance between providing sufficient information to reassure stakeholders and giving away commercially sensitive information to competitors.

10. See also Paul-Choudhury (1996). Setting up ERM systems can be expensive, but it is important that firms do not try to cut corners by paying low salaries to back- or middle-office staff or leaving them with antiquated equipment to work with. As Jorion observes,

> Back [and middle] offices suffer from the perception that they do not directly contribute to the bottom line. This perception is seriously mistaken, as many institutions have suffered losses that could have been avoided by decent back-office support. The $1.1 billion loss incurred by Daiwa, for instance, has been partly blamed on an inadequate back-office system. (Jorion, 1996, p. 291)

The losses suffered by Barings are also strong testimony to the value of proper office support.

11. The principles of what is now referred to as ERM evolved in the early and mid-1990s. Some of these were set out in detail by the G30 Report of July 1993 and elaborated upon in subsequent industry and regulatory documents. Others have been developed in the trade literature, an example being the excellent Supplement on ERM in the July 1996 issue of *Risk*. For further discussions, see, e.g., Chew (1996, pp. 231–9) and Jorion (1996, pp. 299–305).

12. Williams (1996)

13. Spinner (1996a) offers some useful advice on how to (and how not to) establish a centralised data warehouse. To do the task right, she suggests four main guidelines: (1) Ensure that top management is seriously committed, if only to ensure that the project is resourced properly. (2) Establish firm-wide standards about nomenclature to avoid ambiguities and misunderstandings. This is inconvenient, but cannot be avoided. (3) Try to avoid local turf battles and aim to minimise opposition to the project by involving departmental and regional managers in the process. (4) Lastly, but not least, make sure that everything is documented, so information can be easily recovered.

The main traps to avoid are fairly obvious: disorganised IT departments, excessive staff turnover, particularly of IT staff, excessive multiplicity of systems, outdated legacy systems, lack of common standards, inter-departmental feuding, and incompatibility of systems.

14. Oldfield and Santomero (1995, p. 27)

15. Williams (1996, p. 34)

16. Drzik points out how

> risk management in most financial institutions has been practised as a collection of relatively insular specialties: credit experts evaluate default risk; mortgage specialists evaluate and manage prepayment risk; traders and derivatives specialists evaluate, price and manage market risks; and actuaries evaluate and price mortality, liability and other insurance risks.
>
> Each group has evolved its own approach supported by its own language, measurement standards and policy norms. This inhibits potentially productive communication across groups and limits the degree to which senior management can develop policies which transcend individual risk-taking activities. (Drzik, 1996, p. 14)

17. See R. Allen (1996, p. 21).

18. See, e.g., Spinner (1996b) or R. Allen (1996).

19. An integrated treatment will also be necessary if we are to pick up interactions of a different sort. In making a choice between two investments, we might also want to take into account the

implications of existing credit exposures. Imagine that we were a net creditor to one party and a net debtor to another. If we invest in the former, we would extend that party more credit and hence increase our credit exposure. We would then have to set aside capital against this higher exposure and cost the increase in exposure into our profit calculations. If we lend to the other party, on the other hand, there would be no increase in our credit exposure and therefore no increase in credit-exposure costs. We might therefore prefer the latter investment to the former, even if its expected return were a little lower (R. Allen, 1996, p. 24).

20. See, e.g., R. Allen (1996, p. 25).

21. See Drzik (1996, p. 14).

22. Organisationally, the integration of risk analysis also requires that there be a single, common risk management authority for the whole organisation (R. Allen, 1996, pp. 28–9). This risk management function can be subdivided into units that specialise in market risks, credit risks, and the like, but it is important that these units report to the same person so that he/she can make final decisions taking all relevant risks into account.

23. See, e.g., McNew (1996, p. 54).

24. For more on these systems, see Linsmeier and Pearson (1996, pp. 23–4), McNew (1996), Shimko (1996) or Turner (1996).

25. See, e.g., Turner (1996, p. 38).

26. Linsmeier and Pearson (1996, p. 24).

27. Of course, CFaR systems have their problems, many of which they share with VaR systems (i.e., they suffer from model risk, etc.). However, they also have other problems. (1) The construction of CFaR systems can involve a lot of judgement and, in some cases, a lot of work. (2) CFaR systems tend to involve a wider set of risk factors than VaR systems (e.g., we might use the outcome of R&D exercises as a risk factor in a CFaR system, but not in a VaR system). (3) Some of these risk factors are difficult to put PDFs to and/or get adequate historical data for. See also Linsmeier and Pearson (1996, p. 24).

APPENDIX TO CHAPTER 12: RISK MANAGEMENT ADVICE FOR SENIOR MANAGERS

Much of what senior management need to know about modern risk management can be summarised by the following guidelines. These fall under four general headings: general risk management, the use of derivatives, value at risk and related issues, and dealing with taxation and regulation.

1. On General Risk Management

1.1. Make sure you know your own business and the risks it entails.

1.2. Remember that you are the senior risk manager. You should have a clear corporate policy on risk that is understood by everyone concerned. You should know the main risks your firm is taking and why.

1.3. The objective of risk management is not to eliminate or even minimise risks, but to manage them appropriately, taking into account the potential benefits from risk-taking.

1.4. Remember that risk management is a form of engineering: it *uses* science, but ultimately *depends* on judgement.

1.5. The ultimate protection against risk is good judgement and alertness – your own and that of your employees.

1.6. Observe what goes on elsewhere and learn from the mistakes of others. If you are sufficiently concerned about similar problems occurring in your firm, do something to prevent them.

1.7. It is particularly important to learn from others when they lose huge amounts of money or go bankrupt. When you see that happen, ask yourself if your firm is *really* covered.

1.8. When firms get into major difficulties, the problems involved are usually ones that senior management thought they had taken care of.

1.9. It is the operational risks – rogue traders and the like – that usually bring institutions down. Remember Barings.

1.10. The best defences against operational risks are sound systems of management control and vigilant managers.

1.11. Be on the lookout for the obvious: business units that are apparently earning very large profits for no clear reason, figures in reports that are clearly suspicious, sudden deteriorations in performance, junior managers under severe stress, very high turnover of staff, and that sort of thing.

1.12. If you are tempted to regard risk management as expensive, think of the alternative. Don't regard risk management as a drain on profits.

1.13. Get good people you can trust, pay them well and back their judgement. Good people are far more valuable than good systems. As one participant once said, 'I would prefer a C-rated model with weaknesses and have people with experience and intuition to run our risk management than an A-rated model with a C-rated team of people who don't understand the model and are therefore unable to question the numbers that the system churns out.'[A1]

1.14. Talk to your risk management people and be aware of their concerns.

1.15. Take some interest in stress testing and contingency planning exercises.

1.16. Never think that a fancy risk management system takes care of your risks for you and thereby relieves you of the need to stay alert.

1.17. Understand the limitations of your risk management systems. Be clear about the risks your systems do not cover well, especially operational ones. Ask what could go wrong, ask yourself if the results seem right, and so forth. Always ask your risk management people where you are vulnerable.

1.18. Have your risk management systems checked over occasionally by outside experts, and listen to their advice. Listen to your auditors as well.

1.19. Remember that risk management is not an exact science, so don't be fooled by spuriously precise answers or be impressed by people who talk in such terms. Remember the words of the physicist Richard Feynman, when commenting on the Challenger disaster: 'If a guy tells me the probability of failure is 1 in 10^5, I know he's full of crap.'[A2]

1.20 Policy statements should give substantial objectives and policy guidelines, as opposed to the meaningless platitudes that abound in modern corporate life. When drawing them up, you should ask yourself: Do they come across as just so much more management nonsense that no one ever pays any attention to? Do they give the impression that they are merely written to protect the management against criticism or lawsuits? Are they condescending to workers, shareholders and other stakeholders? Do they exaggerate the priority really given to risk management issues?

2. Dealing with Derivatives

2.1. Don't be put off the use of derivatives by recent well-publicised problems. Derivatives are very useful tools, when used properly.

2.2. Remember that derivatives have one or more of three uses: to take a position (i.e., to speculate), to hedge, or to reduce funding costs. If you are thinking about using derivatives, be clear why.

2.3. Derivatives can therefore increase or decrease your overall risks, depending on how you use them.

2.4. Be aware of the leverage (i.e., the potential for gains or losses) in your derivatives positions, particularly leverage that might be hidden in complex derivatives positions.

2.5. If you are using derivatives to reduce funding costs, make sure you understand why/how the contract gives you lower funding costs. In particular, make sure that you have not agreed to hidden options or other contingent pay-off clauses that could lead to large losses later on.

2.6. When dealing with derivatives providers, recognise that they always know more than you do.

2.7. When considering contracts with derivatives providers, satisfy yourself that *you* broadly understand the risks you are thinking of taking on.

2.8. When considering any derivatives contract, satisfy yourself that you *want* to take on the risks involved.

2.9. Don't forget that people sometimes make very silly mistakes, especially when dealing with derivatives. Remember the words of one experienced derivatives salesman: 'I've seen things in the market where I scratch my head and can't imagine why people did it…when P&G lost all that money, I couldn't fathom what anyone at the company was thinking when they looked at that formula of that swap and said, "Yes, that's exactly what I want to put [my money] on".'[A3]

2.10. In assessing a derivatives contract, particularly a complex one, have the contract reverse-engineered into its basic building block components (this helps in understanding the risks involved) and consider whether you would be better off taking on the building blocks instead.

2.11. Shop around for quotes from different derivatives providers before agreeing to a particular contract.

2.12. Protect yourself against unscrupulous providers by seeking qualified second opinions.

2.13. You can also protect yourself by asking questions and insisting on full written answers. Questions should focus on prospective losses for different realisations of the underlying risk variable(s).

2.14. If the answers you get are incomplete, unclear or otherwise unsatisfactory, don't get involved in long-drawn-out negotiations. Just assume the worst and take your business elsewhere.

2.15. If you are not sure what questions to ask, seek guidance from your own risk managers or outside consultants. Always check with them anyway before signing anything.

2.16. Know your exit costs. When negotiating with providers, try to nail down your likely liquidation costs in advance by asking for written quotes that specify the terms on which they would unwind your derivatives positions later.

2.17. Before finally agreeing to any contract, decide on your stop loss position, so you know *in advance* the maximum loss you will tolerate before bailing out. Ensure that everyone else involved also knows the stop loss position.

2.18. Having established your stop loss strategy, keep to it.

2.19. When dealing with outside consultants, deal with people you can trust. As a general rule, employ consultants who have no axe to grind because they are not trying to sell you their own systems.

3. Dealing with VaR and Associated Systems

3.1. Do not regard the VaR movement as just another management fad that will go away if you ignore it. VaR is not like business process re-engineering. It is here to stay and you may as well get used to it.

3.2. There are some very good reasons to take the VaR movement seriously. It has a lot to offer.

3.3. Understand clearly what the terms VaR, ERM, CFaR and the like actually mean. More important still, understand what they *don't* mean (i.e., understand that VaR does not give the maximum possible loss, and so on).

3.4. Try to get some feel for what these VaR, ERM and other systems involve – their strengths, their potential uses, their limitations and weaknesses, and the like. This does *not* mean that you have to become an expert on them.

3.5. You should investigate what benefits these various systems – VaR systems, ERM systems, CFaR systems, etc. – could bring to your particular firm. However, also recognise that the benefits can vary a lot from one firm to another, depending on each firm's particular business and circumstances.

3.6. If you decide to adopt any of these systems, be clear why. There is only one good reason: you should adopt them if and because they fit your business needs, as you have identified them.

3.7. *Don't* adopt VaR and associated systems just because your competitors are doing so. Resist the temptation to behave like a lemming.

3.8. *Don't* adopt them just because you have some vague idea that they will help you steal a march on the competition. You are unlikely to steal a march on the competition if you don't know what you are doing.

3.9. *Don't* adopt them in response to pressure from shareholders or systems providers. Shareholders pay you to make these decisions for them and systems providers are looking for business.

3.10. Pay attention to what other firms are doing, and learn from them.

3.11. Don't be hurried, and remember that there is always the option of wait and see. Waiting allows you to see what mistakes other firms make so you can avoid them. Waiting till later will also be cheaper, because costs will fall over time.

3.12. Think carefully (and seek advice) about the level of technology that is adequate for you.

3.13. Establish the level of technology that is adequate for your needs: historical simulation, variance-covariance, or Monte Carlo simulation.

3.14. The systems with the lowest level of technology are historical simulation ones, the highest-tech ones are Monte Carlo systems, and variance-covariance systems are somewhere in between.

3.15. As a general rule, you are best off adopting the system with the lowest adequate level of technology. The higher the level of technology, the greater the expense, the more difficult the system is to use, and the greater the chances of something going badly wrong.

3.16. Don't ever buy a complex system without satisfying yourself that you really need it; don't buy an expensive Monte Carlo system, say, when a simple historical simulation system would do.

3.17. Be discriminating: systems must suit your particular business needs. Remember that there is even more variety (and potential variety) among CFaR and ERM systems than among VaR systems proper.

3.18. As a general rule, large firms need systems fitted for them, as opposed to systems just bought off the shelf and imported without much thought. This is particularly so when it comes to ERM and CFaR systems.

3.19. Be wary of buying expensive systems off the shelf, and be very wary of providers who would sell you very complex systems that only rocket scientists can understand.

3.20. Shop around for systems and service providers, and don't confuse expense with quality. It is very easy to spend a lot of money on a poor or inappropriate system.

3.21. Never, ever, buy complex systems that no one in your firm is comfortable with. Either the systems are unnecessarily complex or else you need to hire people who can work with them.

3.22. Make sure you have access to advice from people who understand the area. Work closely with your risk management and treasury people, and don't go against their advice unless you have good reason to.

3.23. When setting up VaR and related systems, ensure that you also develop good stress testing capability. Make sure that you use these systems in conjunction with regular and detailed stress tests.

3.24. Take some interest in stress testing exercises, if only to inform the broader planning process.

3.25. You should insist that your VaR, CFaR, stress test and other reports be informative, but not unnecessarily so. They should be short and to the point, and written in plain language. Besides reporting key numbers, they should also warn you of important problems or qualifications that you should be aware of.

3.26. Insist on periodic longer reports that go into more detail and keep you warned of medium- to longer-term problems and other issues that would not make it into your more regular VaR reports.

3.27. Keep in mind that no systems ever give guaranteed results. Remember the more general risk management rules set out earlier. Never think that you have some foolproof system that allows you to go to sleep. Never be complacent.

4. Dealing with Taxation and Regulation

4.1. Dealing with Taxation

4.1. Be clear about the difference between avoidance (which is legal) and evasion (which is not). Remember: evasion is what you must avoid.

4.2. The interests of your stakeholders *require* you to avoid (as opposed to evade) taxation as best you can. To do anything else is to give their money away.

4.3. Remember that your primary and, indeed, overriding, responsibilities are to your stakeholders, not to the regulators, the tax authorities or their political masters. It is your *duty* to avoid taxation. In the words of the Scottish jurist Lord Clyde, 'no man...is under the slightest obligation, moral or other, so to arrange ... his business or his property as to enable the Inland Revenue [or the IRS or anyone else] to put the largest possible shovel into his stores.'[A4]

4.4. You should insist that your firm puts some serious effort into avoidance.

4.5. Avoidance is often best done discreetly.

4.6. The more complex the tax system, the more loopholes it has, and the more opportunities there are for avoidance. Remember also that there are all sorts of differences in tax systems across different countries and sectors. Exploit these to the full.

4.7. In avoiding tax, you need people who understand the rules, and the people who usually understand them best are tax officials themselves. You should therefore consider hiring some of the gamekeepers to poach for you.

4.8. Tax specialists can save you a lot of money. You should therefore be willing to pay them well. This also helps give you the edge over the tax authorities, since they can seldom match private-sector salaries.

4.2. Dealing with Financial Regulation

4.9. Work from the premise that regulation as such is a nuisance. You either follow a particular regulatory rule because it embodies good practice for your firm, which you would therefore want follow anyway, or else you want to avoid it.

4.10. You therefore need to distinguish between 'good' rules that you want to follow and 'bad' ones that you don't.

4.11. A good rule is one that is compatible with or promotes your firm's interest, broadly defined. The firm's interest is not just the maximisation of profits, but also encompasses the firm's (and your) various statutory, ethical and other obligations to the people you are dealing with.

4.12. Examples of good rules would be rules of good business practice, useful disclosure rules in financial statements, certain rules specifying your obligations to employees and customers, and the like.

4.13. You have to make the distinction between good and bad rules. You do so by deciding which rules are good. The rest can then be regarded as bad.

4.14. You should regard the bad rules as a form of taxation. They are therefore to be avoided.

4.15. Avoidance of bad regulatory rules is similar in many respects to tax avoidance. The same points therefore apply: you have a duty to avoid them, you should hire specialists, exploit loopholes, be discreet, and so forth.

4.16. Keep in mind that regulation by and large does not work. If a regulation stops you doing what you want to do, you can usually find some way to get round it or at least to mitigate its impact.

Endnotes

A1.   Daniel Mudge, quoted in Chew (1994, p. 70).

A2. Quoted in Adams (1995, p. 213).
A3. Anonymous (1995b, p. 28)
A4. Quoted in Mount (1997, p. 4.).

GLOSSARY OF MAIN TERMS

Basic risk: The risk of loss associated with an imperfectly hedged position.

Binomial procedure: A procedure to price derivatives based on the assumption that there are no arbitrage profits and that the underlying price follows a discretised binomial process.

Capital asset pricing model (CAPM): A security-pricing model based on the idea that the key factor influencing an investment decision is the relationship of the investment's return with the return to a hypothetical market portfolio.

Capital requirements: The capital required to meet certain standards of safety and soundness. Capital requirements can be internal (i.e., implied by the firm's own risk management policy) and/or regulatory (i.e., required by regulators).

Cashflow at risk (CFaR): The lowest or most negative likely cash flow over some holding period at a given level of confidence.

Convexity: A measure of the rate of change of duration with respect to yield.

Correlation: The extent to which movements in two variables are related.

Credit at risk (CaR): The largest likely credit exposure over a given period and confidence level.

Credit derivatives: Derivatives contracts with pay-offs contingent on credit events.

Credit exposure: The total amount of credit granted to a counterparty.

Credit risk: The risk of loss arising from the failure of a counterparty to make a promised payment.

Credit Metrics: The credit-at-risk framework launched by JP Morgan and a number of other leading banks in April 1997.

Curvature: The rate at which the price sensitivity of a position changes in response to changes in the underlying price.

Daily earnings at risk (DEaR): The term use in RiskMetrics literature to refer to VaR based on a daily holding period.

Default risk: See credit risk.

Default value at risk (Default VaR): The largest likely loss from counterparty default over some period and confidence level.

Delta: The change in the value of a derivatives contract associated with a small change in the price of the underlying.

Delta-gamma approaches to VaR: Variance-covariance approaches to the estimation of VaR that handle departures from normal linearity by means of second-order (i.e., delta-gamma) approximations.

Delta-normal approaches to VaR: Variance-covariance approaches to the estimation of VaR that handle departures from normal linearity by means of first order (i.e., delta approximations.

Derivatives: Contracts whose values depend on the prices of one or more other variables, known as underlying variables.

Duration: The average time over which the cash payments of a fixed-income security are due to be received.

Enterprise-wide risk management (ERM): The management of overall institutional risk across all risk categories and business units.

Exponentially weighted moving average (EWMA): A procedure for the estimation of volatilities and/or correlations that assumes that expected volatility (or correlation) next period is an exponentially weighted average of past volatilities (or correlations).

Extreme value approach (EVA): An approach to the estimation of VaR based on the use of statistical extreme value theory.

Factor analysis: A procedure to derive the main sources of variation in a group of time series (such as the returns to assets in a portfolio). It differs from principal components analysis in that it seeks to minimise the off-diagonal elements of the unexplained residual matrix.

Factor push analysis: A form of stress testing in which risk factors are pushed in the most disadvantageous directions and we assess the combined effect of all such changes on our portfolio. It differs from maximum loss optimisation in only examining losses at the extreme values taken by risk factors.

Fat tails: Tails of probability distributions that are larger than those of a normal distribution.

Financial engineering: The process of constructing complex positions (or contracts) from more primitive 'building block' positions (or contracts).

Fixed-income security: A security that promises fixed contractual future payments.

Forward contract: An agreement to buy or sell a particular commodity or asset at a particular future time for a price agreed now but paid on the arranged future date.

Futures contract: A standardised, exchange-traded forward contract. Futures contracts are also subject to margin requirements and marked to market daily.

Gamma: The localised curvature of an options position.

Gamma risk: The risk of loss from a change in delta.

Gap analysis: Analysis of the changes in net interest income resulting from changes in interest rates.

Generalised autoregressive conditional heteroskedastic (GARCH) estimators: A model for forecasting volatilities (or correlations) that assumes that volatility next period depends on lagged volatilities (or correlations) and lagged squared returns.

Generalised Sharpe approach: A decision procedure that applies the Sharpe ratio to an investment plus the existing portfolio, rather than to the investment on its own.

Hedge position: A position that hedges another.

Hedging: The process of decreasing risks.

Historical simulation approach to VaR: An approach that estimates VaR from a profit and loss distribution simulated using historical returns data.

Implied correlation: The correlation implied by the price of a derivative with more than one underlying.

Implied volatility: The volatility implied by the price of a derivative.

Incremental VaR: The change in VaR resulting from a risk management decision.

Legal risk: The risk of loss arising from uncertainty about the enforceability of contracts.

Leverage: The gain or loss on a position relative to the gain or loss on the underlying risk factor.

Liquidity: The ability to unwind a position at little or no cost.

Liquidity risk: The risks arising from the potential cost or inconvenience of unwinding a position.

Margin requirements: Deposits required against the taking of risky positions.

Market (price) risks: The risks of loss arising from adverse movements in market prices.

Marking to market: The process of valuing and periodically revaluing positions in marketable securities by means of their current market prices.

Maximum loss optimisation: A form of stress testing in which risk factors are pushed in the most disadvantageous directions and we assess the combined effect of all such changes on our portfolio. It differs from factor push analysis in that it searches over losses that occur when risk factors take intermediate as well as extreme values.

Mean-variance approach: An approach to portfolio analysis based on the premise that one can determine the optimal portfolio using information about the means, variances and covariances of the relevant returns. It implies that one does not need information about higher moments of return distributions, such as skewness and kurtosis.

Monte Carlo simulation approaches to VaR: Aproaches that estimate VaR from a distribution of future portfolio values that is simulated using pseudo-random number techniques.

Netting arrangements: Arrangements by which the parties in multiple bilateral contracts agree to owe each other the net rather than gross amounts involved.

Normal approach to VaR: Approach that estimates VaR on the assumption that the portfolio is a linear function of normally distributed risk variables.

Normal distribution: The Gaussian or bell-curve probability distribution.

Operational risks: Risks arising from the failure of internal systems or the people who operate in them.

Option: A contract that gives the holder the right, but not the obligation, depending on the type of option, to buy or sell a particular commodity or asset on pre-agreed terms. European options give the holder the right to exercise the option at a particular future date, while American options give the holder the right to exercise at any time over a particular period. Options can be traded on organised exchanges ('exchange-traded') or traded over the counter (OTC).

Performance evaluation: *Ex post* risk adjustment (i.e., risk adjustment after the risks have been taken).

Periodic settlement: The process by which the obligations outstanding between counterparties are periodically paid off.

Portfolio insurance: An equity and bond trading strategy that attempts to mimic the pay-off to an equity call option.

Portfolio theory: A normative theory of portfolio selection making use of mean, variance and covariance information on return distributions.

Position limits: Management-imposed limits on the sizes of the positions that traders or asset managers are allowed to take.

Principal components analysis: A procedure to derive the main sources of variation – the principal components – in a group of time series. It differs from factor analysis in that it seeks to minimise the diagonal terms of the unexplained residual matrix.

Quasi-Monte Carlo approach to VaR: An approach that estimates VaR from a distribution of future portfolio values that is simulated using quasi-random number techniques.

Recovery rate: The proportion of money owing recovered from a debtor in the event of bankruptcy.

Reverse engineering: The process of decomposng complex positions (or contracts) into portfolios of simpler positions (or contracts).

Risk: The prospect of gain or loss. Risk is usually regarded as quantifiable.

Risk-adjusted return on capital (RAROC): The ratio of return to VaR.

Risk adjustment: In general, the process of adjusting returns for the risks involved. However, the term is usually used to refer more specifically to *ex ante* risk adjustment (i.e., to adjustments before the risk are actually taken).

RiskMetrics: The analytical framework developed by JP Morgan to estimate VaR.

Scenario analysis: A form of stress testing that focuses on the impact of one or more specified scenarios or particular states of the world.

Scenario simulation: A procedure that uses the distribution of principal factors to simulate the distribution of the future portfolio value.

Sharpe ratio: The difference between the return to an investment and a benchmark return, divided by the standard deviation of that difference.

Speculation: The process of increasing risks.

Speculative position: A position that increases risks.

Stochastic process: A statistical model describing the random process governing the movement of one or more variables over time.

Stress testing: The process of assessing the vulnerability of a position or portfolio to hypothetical events.

Swaps: Agreements to swap future cash flows.

Tail events: Low-probability events in the extreme tail of a probability distribution.

Underlying: The variable on which the pay-off to a derivatives contract depends.

Value at risk (VaR): The maximum likely loss over some particular holding period at a particular level of confidence. We can distinguish between absolute VaR (i.e., the absolute amount at risk) and relative VaR (i.e., the absolute amount at risk plus expected earnings). We can also talk of a VaR estimation procedure, a VaR methodology, and a VaR approach to risk management.

Variance-covariance approaches to VaR: Approaches to the estimation of VaR that make use of the variance-covariance matrix of the asset returns.

Volatility: The variability of a price, usually interpreted as its standard deviation.

Worst-case scenario analysis: A form of stress testing that estimates the worst of a number of events expected to occur over some particular horizon.

Zero-coupon bonds: Bonds with only one scheduled payment.

BIBLIOGRAPHY

Adams, J. 1995. *Risk*. London: UCL Press.

Alexander, C. 1996. Volatility and correlation forecasting. In *The handbook of risk management and analysis*, ed. C. Alexander: 233–260. Chichester: John Wiley and Sons.

Allen, M. 1994. Building a role model. *Risk* 7 (September): 73–80.

Allen, R. 1996. Together they stand. *Firmwide Risk Management: A Risk Special Supplement*, July: 21–29.

Allen, S. 1996. *Value-at-risk for exotic options*. Paper presented at the *Risk* publications conference on value-at-risk. New York, October.

Altman, E. 1984. A further empirical investigation of the bankruptcy cost question. *Journal of Finance* 39: 1067–1089.

Anonymous 1995a. Controlling the tentacles of operational risk. *Risk Special Supplement*, June: 16–18.

Anonymous 1995b. Confessions of a structured note salesman. *Derivatives Strategy* 1 (November): 24–29.

Artzner; P.; F. Delbaen; J.-M. Eber; and D. Heath. 1996. *A characterization of measures of risk*. Mimeo. Ithaca, NY: Cornell University.

Baldwin, P. 1996. Using derivatives to manage credit risk. *The Treasurer*, May: 18–20.

Baliman, M. 1996. Take it from the top. *Firmwide Risk Management: A Risk Special Supplement*, July: 11–13.

Basle Committee on Banking Supervision. 1995. *An internal model-based approach to market risk capital requirements*. Basle: Bank for International Settlements.

Basle Committee on Banking Supervision. 1996. *Amendment to the capital accord to incorporate market risks*. Basle: Bank for International Settlements.

Basle Committee on Banking Supervision and Technical Committee of IOSCO. 1995. *Joint report, framework for supervisory information about derivatives activities*. Basle: Bank for International Settlements.

Basle Committee on Banking Supervision and Technical Committee of IOSCO. 1996. *Survey of disclosures about trading and derivatives activities of banks and securities firms*. Basle: Bank for International Settlements.

Bassi, F.; P. Embrechts; and M. Kafetzaki. undated. *A survival kit on quantile estimation*. Mimeo. Zürich: Department of Mathematics, ETHZ.

Beckers, S. 1996. A survey of risk measurement theory and practice. In *The handbook of risk management and analysis*, ed. C. Alexander: 171–192. Chichester: John Wiley and Sons.

Beckström, R. A. 1995. VaR, the next generation. *Derivatives Strategy* 4 (October): 11–12.

Beckström, R. A.; and A. Campbell. eds. 1995. *An introduction to VaR*. Palo Alto, CA:

CATS Software, Inc.

Beckström, R. A.; D. Lewis; and C. Roberts. 1994. VaR: pushing risk management to the statistical limit. *Capital Market Strategies* 3 (November): 9–15.

Beder, T. 1995. VaR: seductive but dangerous. *Financial Analysts Journal* 51 (September/October): 12–24.

Benson, B. L. 1990. *The enterprise of law: justice without the state.* San Francisco: Pacific Research Institute.

Benston, G. J. 1989. *International bank capital standards.* Paper presented to the Australian National University–University of Melbourne Conference *Regulating commercial banks: Australian experience in perspective.* August.

Benston, G. J.; and G. G. Kaufman 1996. The appropriate role of banking regulation. *Economic Journal* 106: 688–697.

Bera, A. K.; and C. M. Jarque. 1980. An efficient large-sample test for normality of observations and regression residuals. Australian National University *Working Papers in Econometrics* No. 40.

Best, P. 1998. *Value at risk: a practical guide.* Chichester: John Wiley and Sons.

Black, F. 1976. The pricing of commodity contracts. *Journal of Financial Economics* 2: 167–179.

Black, F.; and M. Scholes. 1973. The pricing of options and corporate liabilities. *Journal of Political Economy* 81: 637–654.

Black, F.; E. Derman; and W. Toy. 1990. A one-factor model of interest rates and its application to Treasury bond options. *Financial Analysts Journal* 46: 33–39.

Boudoukh, J.; M. Richardson; and R. Whitelaw. 1995. Expect the worst. *Risk* 8 (September): 100–101.

Boughey, S. 1996. Why you don't need a triple-A subsidiary. *Derivatives Strategy* 7 (June): 28–32.

Boyle, P. 1977. Options: a Monte Carlo approach. *Journal of Financial Economics* 4: 323–338.

Boyle, P.; M. Broadie; and P. Glasserman. 1997. Monte Carlo methods for security pricing. *Journal of Economic Dynamics and Control* 21: 1267–1321.

Brier, G. W. 1950. Verification of forecasts expressed in terms of probability. *Monthly Weather Review* 75: 1–3.

Broadie, M.; and P. Glasserman. 1996. Estimating security price derivatives using simulation. *Management Science* 42: 269–285.

Brock, W. A.; W. D. Dechert; and J. Scheinkman. 1987. A test for independence based on the correlation dimension. University of Wisconsin–Madison *SSRI Workshop Paper 8702.*

Brotherton-Ratcliffe, R. 1994. Monte Carlo motoring. *Risk* 7 (December): 53–57.

Brown, A. 1997. The next 10 VaR disasters. *Derivatives Strategy* 2 (March): 68–70.

Butler, J. S.; and B. Schachter. 1996. *Improving value-at-risk estimates by combining kernel estimation with historical simulation.* Mimeo. Vanderbilt University and Comptroller of the Currency.

Campbell, T. S.; and W. A. Kracaw. 1993. *Financial risk management: fixed income and foreign exchange.* New York: HarperCollins College Publishers.

Chance, D. M. 1993. Leap into the unknown. *Risk* 6 (May): 60–66.

Chance, D. M. 1994. The ABCs of geometric Brownian motion. *Derivatives Quarterly* 1 (Winter): 41–47.

Chance, D. M. 1995a. Its all greek to me. *Derivatives 'R Us*, 1(10).

Chance, D. M. 1995b. *An introduction to derivatives*, 3rd ed. Fort Worth: Dryden.

Chance, D. M. 1995c. The value of risk management. *Derivatives 'R Us*, 1(32).

Chance, D. M. 1996. Limitations of duration and the concept of convexity. *Derivatives Research Unincorporated* 2(19).

Chappell, D. 1997. *BDS statistics*. Mimeo. Department of Economics, University of Sheffield.

Chappell, D.; and K. Dowd. 1997. VaR: an issue of confidence. Forthcoming in *Risk*.

Chew, L. 1994. Shock treatment. *Risk* 9 (September): 63–70.

Chew, L. 1996. *Managing derivative risks: The use and abuse of leverage*. Chichester: John Wiley and Sons.

Chorafas, D. N. 1995. *Managing derivatives risk: establishing internal systems and controls*. Chicago: Irwin.

Christoffersen, P. F. 1996. *Evaluating interval forecasts*. Mimeo. Research Department, International Monetary Fund. Forthcoming in the *International Economic Review*.

Clewlow, L.; and A. Carverhill. 1994. Quicker on the curves. *Risk* 7 (May): 63–65.

Corrado, C.; and T. Miller. 1996. Volatility without tears. *Risk* 9 (July): 49–51.

Cox, J. C.; J. E. Ingersoll; and S. A. Ross. 1985a. An intertemporal general equilibrium model of asset prices. *Econometrica* 53: 363–384.

Cox, J. C., J. E. Ingersoll; and S. A. Ross. 1985b. A theory of the term structure of interest rates. *Econometrica* 53: 385–407.

Crnkovic, C.; and J. Drachman. 1995. *A universal tool to discriminate among risk measurement techniques*. Mimeo. Corporate Risk Management Group, JP Morgan.

Daigler, R. T. 1994. *Financial futures and options markets: concepts and strategies*. New York: HarperCollins College Publishers.

Dale, R. 1996. *Risk and regulation in global securities markets*. Chichester: John Wiley and Sons.

Daníelsson, J. 1996. *Multivariate stochastic volatility models: estimation and a comparison with VGARCH models*. Mimeo. Department of Economics, University of Iceland.

Daníelsson, J.; and C. G. de Vries. 1996. *Tail index and quantile estimation with very high frequency data*. Mimeo. University of Iceland and Tinbergen Institute, Erasmus University.

Daníelsson, J.; and C. G. de Vries. 1997. *Extreme returns, tail estimation, and value-at-risk*. Mimeo. University of Iceland and Tinbergen Institute, Erasmus University.

Davidson, C. 1996. Risk where credit's due. *Risk* 9 (June): 54–57.

Derivatives Policy Group. 1995. *A framework for voluntary oversight*. New York: Derivatives Policy Group.

Dimson, E.; and P. Marsh. 1995. Capital requirements for securities firms. *Journal of Finance* 50: 821–851.

Dimson, E., and P. Marsh. 1996. Stress tests of capital requirements. Wharton School Financial Institutions Center *Working Paper 96–50*.

Dowd, K. 1996. *Competition and finance: a reinterpretation of financial and monetary economics*. Basingstoke: Macmillan, and New York: St Martin's Press.

Dowd, K. 1997. The regulation of bank capital adequacy. *Advances in Austrian Economics* 4: 95–110.

Drzik, J. 1996. Putting risk in its place. *Firmwide Risk Management: A Risk Special Supplement*, July: 14–16.

Duffie, D.; and M. Huang. 1996. Swap rates and credit quality. *Journal of Finance* 51: 921–949.

EC Council. 1993. *Directive on the capital adequacy of investment firms and credit institutions*. Brussels: EC Commission.

Efron, B. 1979. Bootstrap methods: another look at the jacknife. *Annals of Statistics* 7: 1–26.

Eldridge, A. 1997. Credit derivatives: set to become the most significant derivative product? *The Treasurer*, March: 42–43.

Embrechts, P.; C. Klüppelberg; and T. Mikosch. 1997. *Modelling extreme events for insurance and finance*. Berlin: Springer Verlag.

Engle, R.; and J. Mezrich. 1996. GARCH for groups. *Risk* 9 (August): 36–40.

Estrella, A. 1996. Taylor, Black and Scholes: series approximations and risk management pitfalls. In *Risk measurement and systemic risk. Proceedings of a joint central bank research conference*. Washington, DC: Board of Governors of the Federal Reserve System. 359–379.

Estrella, A.; D. Hendricks; J. Kambhu; S. Shin; and S. Walter. 1994. The price risk of options positions: measurement and capital requirements. Federal Reserve Bank of New York *Quarterly Review* (Fall): 27–43.

Fabozzi, F. J. 1993. *Fixed income mathematics: analytical and statistical techniques*, revised ed. Chicago: Irwin.

Fallon, W. 1996. Calculating value-at-risk. Wharton School Financial Institutions Center *Working Paper 96–49*.

Falloon, W. 1995. 2020 visions. *Risk* 8 (October): 43–45.

Fama, E. F. 1965. The behavior of stock prices. *Journal of Business* 38: 34–105.

Fama, E. F. 1968. Risk, return, and equilibrium: some clarifying comments. *Journal of Finance* 23: 29–40.

Fama, E. F.; and K. R. French. 1988. Permanent and temporary components of stock prices. *Journal of Political Economy* 96: 246–273.

Field, P. 1995. The art, not science, of risk management. *Risk* Special Supplement, June: 2–4.

Figlewski, S. 1994. Forecasting volatility using historical data. New York University *Working Paper S-94-13*.

Finger, C. C. 1996. Accounting for 'pull to par' and 'roll down' for RiskMetrics™ cashflows. *RiskMetrics™ Monitor*, Third Quarter: 4–11.

Fitt, V. 1996. Confessions of a regulator. *Risk* 9 (July): 17.

Frain, J.; and C. Meegan. 1996. *Market risk: an introduction to the concept and analytics of value-at-risk*. Mimeo. Economic Analysis Research and Publications Department, Central Bank of Ireland.

Frankfurter, G. M. 1995. The rise and fall of the CAPM empire: a review on emerging capital markets. *Financial Markets, Institutions and Instruments* 5(4). *Recent developments in financial economics: selected surveys of the literature*: 104–127.

Freund, J. E. 1972. *Mathematical statistics*. 2nd ed. Englewood Cliffs, NJ: Prentice-Hall International.

Frye, J. 1996. *Principals of risk: finding value-at-risk through factor-based interest rate scenarios*. Mimeo. NationsBank-CRT, Chicago.

Garman, M. B. 1996a. *Making VaR proactive*. Berkeley, CA: Financial Engineering Associates.

Garman, M. B. 1996b. Making VaR more flexible. *Derivatives Strategy* (April): 52–53.

Garman, M. B. 1996c. Improving on VaR. *Risk* 9 (May): 61–63.

Garman, M. B. 1996d. *VaRdelta: understanding and using VaRdelta for risk management.* Paper presented at the *Risk* Publications conference on value-at-risk. New York, October.

Garman, M. B.; and S. Kohlhagen. 1983. Foreign currency option values. *Journal of International Money and Finance* 2: 231–237.

General Accounting Office. 1994. *Financial derivatives: actions needed to protect the financial system.* Washington, DC: US GAO.

Geske, R. 1977. The valuation of corporate liabilities as compound options. *Journal of Financial and Quantitative Analysis* 12: 541–552.

Geske, R. 1996. Credit risk from the foundation up. *Derivatives Tactics*, April 1. Palo Alto: CATS Software.

Geske, R., and R. Roll. 1984. On valuing American call options with the Black-Scholes formula. *Journal of Finance* 39: 443–455.

Glaeser, B. 1996. Save a place for VaR. *Risk* 9 (December): 17–18.

Glasserman, P. 1991. *Gradient estimation via perturbation analysis.* Norwell, MA: Kluwer Academic Publishers.

González Miranda, F.; and N. Burgess. 1997. Modelling market volatilities: the neural network perspective. *European Journal of Finance* 3: 137–157.

Group of Thirty. 1993. *Derivatives: practices and principles.* New York: Group of Thirty.

Guldimann, T. 1995. A risk measurement framework. In *RiskMetrics™ – technical document*, 3rd ed., ed. T. Guldimann *et al.*: 6–45. New York: Morgan Guaranty Trust Company Global Research.

Guldimann, T. 1996. Beyond the year 2000. *Risk* 9 (June): 17–19.

Guldimann, T.; P. Zangari; J. Longerstaey; J. Matero; and J. Howard. 1995. *Risk Metrics™ – technical document.* 3rd ed. New York: Morgan Guaranty Trust Company Global Research.

Gumerlock, R. 1996. Lacking commitment. *Risk* 8 (June): 36–39.

Hamilton, C. 1996. Enterprise-wide risk management (ERM): redefining traditional thinking. *Firmwide Risk Management: A Risk Special Supplement*, July: 8–9.

Heath, D.; R. A. Jarrow; and A. Morton. 1990a. Bond pricing and the term structure of interest rates: a discrete time approximation. *Journal of Financial and Quantitative Analysis* 25: 419–440.

Heath, D.; R. A. Jarrow; and A. Morton. 1990b. Contingent claim valuation with a random evolution of interest rates. *Review of Futures Markets* 9: 54–76.

Heath, D.; R. A. Jarrow; and A. Morton. 1992. Bond pricing and the term structure of interest rates: a new methodology for contingent claims valuation. *Econometrica* 60: 77–105.

Hendricks, D. 1996. Evaluation of value-at-risk models using historical data. Federal Reserve Bank of New York *Economic Policy Review* 2 (April): 39–70.

Hentschel, L.; and C. W. Smith, Jr. 1996. Risk in derivatives markets. Wharton School Financial Institutions Center *Working Paper 96–24.*

Ho, T.; 1992. Key rate durations: measures of interest rate risks. *Journal of Fixed Income* 2: 29–44.

Ho, T.; and S.-B. Lee. 1986. Term structure movements and pricing interest rate contingent claims. *Journal of Finance* 41: 1011–1029.

Hoffman, D.; and M. Johnson. 1996. Operating procedures. *Risk* 9 (October): 60–63.

Holton, G. A. 1996a. *Closed form value at risk*. Boston: Contingency Analysis. Available at http://www.contingencyanalysis.com.

Holton, G. A. 1996b. *Enterprise risk management*. Boston: Contingency Analysis.

Hopper, G. P. 1996. Value at risk: a new methodology for measuring portfolio risk. Federal Reserve Bank of Boston *Business Review* July/August, 19–31.

Hsieh, D. A. 1988. The statistical properties of daily exchange rates: 1974–1983. *Journal of International Economics* 13: 171–186.

Huntington, I. 1996. Fraud: the unmanaged risk. *Capital Market Strategies* 9 (March): 30–36.

Jackson, P. 1996. Risk measurement and capital requirements for banks. *Bank of England Quarterly Bulletin* (May): 177–184.

Jackson, P.; D. J. Maude; and W. Perraudin, 1997. Bank capital and value-at-risk. *Journal of Derivatives* 4 (Spring): 73–90.

Jakobsen, S. 1996. Measuring value-at-risk for mortgage-backed securities. In *Risk management in volatile financial markets*. eds. F. Bruni; D. E. Fair; and R. O'Brien: 185–208. Dordrecht: Kluwer Academic Publishers.

Jamshidian, F.; and Y. Zhu 1996. Scenario simulation model for risk management. *Capital Market Strategies* 12 (December): 26–30.

Jamshidian, F.; and Y. Zhu 1997. Scenario simulation: theory and methodology. *Finance and Stochastics* 1: 43–67.

Jarrow, R. A. 1996. *Modelling fixed income securities and interest rate options*. New York: McGraw-Hill.

Jarrow, R. A.; and S. M. Turnbull. 1995. Pricing options on derivative securities subject to credit risk. *Journal of Finance* 50: 53–85.

Jarrow, R. A.; and S. M. Turnbull. 1996. Credit risk. In *The handbook of risk management and analysis*, ed. C. Alexander: 261–278. Chichester: John Wiley and Sons.

Jorion, P. 1995. Predicting volatility in the foreign exchange market. *Journal of Finance* 50: 507–528.

Jorion, P. 1996. *Value at risk: the new benchmark for controlling market risk*. Chicago: Irwin.

Jorion, P. 1997. In defense of VaR. *Derivatives Strategy* 2 (April): 22–23.

Joy, C.; P. P. Boyle; and K. S. Tan. 1995. *Quasi-Monte Carlo methods in numerical finance*. Mimeo. University of Waterloo.

J. P. Morgan and Company. 1997. *CreditMetrics*™ – *technical document. The benchmark for understanding credit risk*. New York: J. P. Morgan and Company.

Kendall, M. G.; and A. Stuart. 1973. *The advanced theory of statistics. Volume 2: inference and relationship*. 3rd ed. London: Griffin.

Kletz, T. 1993. *Lessons from disaster: how organisations have no memory and accidents recur*. Rugby: Institution of Chemical Engineers.

Koutsoyiannis, A. 1977. *Theory of econometrics: an introductory exposition of econometric methods*, 2nd ed. London and Basingstoke: Macmillan.

Kupiec, P. 1995. Techniques for verifying the accuracy of risk management models. *Journal of Derivatives* 3: 73–84.

Kupiec, P.; and J. O'Brien. 1995a. Internal affairs. *Risk* 8 (May): 43–47.

Kupiec, P.; and J. O'Brien. 1995b. Model alternative. *Risk* 8 (June): 37–40.

Kupiec, P; and J. O'Brien. 1995c. *Recent developments in bank capital regulation of market risks*. Mimeo. Board of Governors of the Federal Reserve System. November.

Kupiec, P.; and J. O'Brien. 1996. Commitment is the key. *Risk* 9 (September): 60–64.

Lando, D. 1994. *Three essays on contingent claims pricing*. PhD thesis, Cornell University.

Laubsch, A. 1996. Estimating index tracking error for equity portfolios. *RiskMetrics*™ *Monitor*, Second Quarter: 34–41.

Lawrence, C.; and G. Robinson. 1995a. How safe is RiskMetrics? *Risk* 8 (January): 26–29.

Lawrence, C.; and G. Robinson. 1995b. Liquid measures. *Risk* 8 (July): 52–55.

Lawrence, D. 1996. *Measuring and managing derivative market risk*. London: International Thomson Business Press.

Levin, R. 1997. *Challenges of managing credit portfolios*. Mimeo. New York: JP Morgan Securities, Inc.

Linsmeier, T. J.; and N. D. Pearson. 1996. *Risk measurement: an introduction to value at risk*. Mimeo. University of Illinois at Urbana-Champaign.

Lintner, J. 1965. The valuation of risk assets and the selection of risky investments in stock portfolios and capital budgets. *Review of Economics and Statistics* 47: 13–37.

Litterman, R. 1996. Hot spots™ and hedges. *Journal of Portfolio Management Special Issue*: 52–75.

Løftingsmo, A. 1996. *Risk goes metric: developing a common yardstick for measuring risk in financial markets*. Diploma thesis. Trondheim: Norwegian Institute of Technology.

Longerstaey, J. 1995a. Mapping to describe positions. In *RiskMetrics*™ – *technical document*. 3rd ed. T. Guldimann; P. Zangari; J. Longerstaey; J. Matero; and J. Howard. 107–156. New York: Morgan Guaranty Trust Company Global Research.

Longerstaey, J. 1995b. Adjusting correlations for non-synchronous data. *RiskMetrics*™ *Monitor*, Third Quarter: 4–13.

Longerstaey, J.; C. C. Finger; S. Howard; and P. Zangari. 1996. *RiskMetrics*™ – *technical document*, 4th ed. New York: Morgan Guaranty Trust Company.

Longerstaey, J.; and P. Zangari. 1995a. A transparent tool. *Risk* 8 (January): 30–32.

Longerstaey, J.; and P. Zangari. 1995b. *Five questions about RiskMetrics*™. New York: Morgan Guaranty Trust Company.

Longin, F. 1994. Optimal margin levels in futures markets: a parametric extreme-based method. London Business School Institute of Finance and Accounting *Working Paper* 192–194.

Longstaff, F. A.; and E. S. Schwartz. 1992a. Interest rate volatility and the term structure: a two-factor general equilibrium model. *Journal of Finance* 47: 1259–1282.

Longstaff, F. A.; and E. S. Schwartz. 1992b. A two-factor interest rate model and contingent claim valuation. *Journal of Fixed Income* 3: 393–430.

Lopez, J. A. 1996. *Regulatory evaluation of value-at-risk models*. Mimeo. Research and Market Analysis Group, Federal Reserve Bank of New York.

Louis, J. C. 1997. Worrying about correlation. *Derivatives Strategy* 2 (March): 53–55.

Mahoney, J. M. 1996. *Forecast biases in value-at-risk estimations: evidence from foreign exchange and global equity portfolios*. Mimeo, Federal Reserve Bank of New York.

Mandelbrot, B. 1963. The variation of certain speculative prices. *Journal of Business* 36: 394–419.

Markowitz, H. M. 1952. Portfolio selection. *Journal of Finance* 7: 77–91.

Markowitz, H. M. 1959. *Portfolio selection: efficient diversification of investments*. New York: John Wiley and Sons.

Markowitz, H. M. 1992. Mean-variance analysis. In *The New Palgrave Dictionary of*

Money and Finance. Vol. 2. ed. P. Newman; M. Milgate; and J. Eatwell: 683–685. New York: Stockton Press.

Marshall, C., and M. Siegel 1997. Value at risk: implementing a risk measurement standard. *Journal of Derivatives* 4: 91–110.

Masters, B. 1997. *Introduction to CreditMetrics™.* New York: JP Morgan Securities, Inc.

McNew, L. 1996. So near, so VaR. *Risk* 9 (October): 54–56.

Meegan, C. 1995. Market risk management: the concept of value-at-risk. *Technical Paper* 3/*RT*/95. Central Bank of Ireland.

Merton, R. C. 1974. On the pricing of corporate debt: the risk structure of interest rates. *Journal of Finance* 29: 449–470.

Merton, R. C. 1996. Foreword. In *Managing derivative risks: the use and abuse of leverage,* L. Chew: xiii–xv. Chichester: John Wiley and Sons.

Miles, D. 1995. Optimal regulation of deposit taking financial intermediaries. *European Economic Review* 39: 1365–1384.

Modigliani, F.; and L. Modigliani. 1997. Risk-adjusted performance. *Journal of Portfolio Management* 23 (Winter): 45–54.

Morgan Guaranty Trust Company. 1995. *Annual report.* New York: Morgan Guaranty Trust Company.

Mori, A.; M. Ohsawa; and T. Shimizu. 1996a. A framework for more effective stress testing. Bank of Japan Institute for Monetary and Economic Studies *Discussion Paper 96-E-2.*

Mori, A.; M. Ohsawa; and T. Shimizu. 1996b. Calculation of value at risk and risk/return simulation. Bank of Japan Institute for Monetary and Economic Studies *Discussion Paper 96-E-8.*

Moro, B. 1995. The full Monte. *Risk* 8 (February): 57–58.

Moskowitz, B.; and R. E. Caflisch. 1995. *Smoothness and dimension reduction in quasi-Monte Carlo methods.* UCLA Department of Mathematics Working Paper.

Mossin, J. 1966. Equilibrium in a capital asset market. *Econometrica* 34: 768–783.

Mount, F. 1997. Bishop Brown, oh he of little faith. *Sunday Times,* Section 5, 6 July, 4.

Neal, R. S. 1996. Credit derivatives: new financial instruments for controlling credit risk. Federal Reserve Bank of Kansas City *Economic Review,* Second Quarter: 15–27.

Niederreiter, H. 1992. *Random number generation and quasi-Monte Carlo methods.* Philadelphia: SIAM.

Niederreiter, H.; and C. Xing. 1995. *Low-discrepancy sequences and global function fields with many rational places.* Mimeo. Austrian Academy of Sciences. Vienna.

Oda, N.; and J. Muranaga. 1997. *A new framework for measuring the credit risk of a portfolio: 'ExVaR model'.* Bank of Japan Institute for Monetary and Economic Studies *Discussion Paper 97-E-1.*

Oldfield, G. S.; and A. M. Santomero. 1995. The place of risk management in financial institutions. Wharton School *Working Paper* 95–05.

Olsen and Associates. 1996a. *Views from the frontier: the new science.* Zürich: Olsen and Associates.

Olsen and Associates. 1996b. *Views from the frontier: the risk challenge.* Zürich: Olsen and Associates.

Owen, A. B. 1995. Randomly permuted (t,m,s)-nets and (t,s)-sequences. In *Monte Carlo and quasi-Monte Carlo methods in scientific computing.* eds. H. Niederreiter; and P. J-S. Shiue: 299–317. New York: Springer Verlag.

Owen, A. B.; and D. A. Tavella. 1996. *Scrambled nets for value at risk calculations.* Mimeo. Stanford University.

Page, M.; and D. Costa. 1996. *The value-at-risk of a portfolio of currency derivatives under worst-case distributional assumptions.* Mimeo. Susquehanna Investment Group and Department of Mathematics, University of Virginia.

Papageorgiou, A.; and J. Traub. 1996. Beating Monte Carlo. *Risk* 9 (June): 63–65.

Parsley, M. 1996. Credit derivatives get cracking. *Euromoney*, March: 28–34.

Paskov, S.; and J. Traub. 1995. Faster valuation of financial derivatives. *Journal of Portfolio Management* 22: 113–120.

Paul-Choudhury, S. 1996. Crossing the divide. *Firmwide Risk Management: A Risk Special Supplement*, July: 2–4.

Paul-Choudhury, S. 1997. This year's model. *Risk* 10 (May): 18–23.

Pézier, J. 1996. *Aggregating credit and market risks in a VaR analysis.* Paper presented at the *Risk* Publications conference on Value-at-Risk. New York, October.

Prescott, E. S. 1997. The pre-commitment approach in a model of regulatory banking capital. Federal Reserve Bank of Richmond *Economic Quarterly* 83 (Winter): 23–50.

Pritsker, M. 1996. *Evaluating value at risk methodologies: accuracy versus computational time.* Mimeo. Board of Governors of the Federal Reserve System.

Reason, J. 1990. *Human error.* Cambridge: Cambridge University Press.

Rebonato, R. 1996. Interest-rate option models: a critical survey. In *The handbook of risk management and analysis*, ed. C. Alexander: 31–81. Chichester: John Wiley and Sons.

Reed, N. 1996. Variations on a theme. *Risk* 9 (June): 2–4.

Remolona, E. M.; W. Bassett; and I. S. Geoum 1996. Risk management by structured derivative product companies. Federal Reserve Bank of New York *Economic Policy Review*, April: 17–37.

Reoch, R. 1996. Credit derivatives for corporate treasurers. *The Treasurer*, October: 44–47.

Ritchken, P. 1996. *Derivative markets: theory, strategy, and applications.* New York: HarperCollins College Publishers.

Rivett, P.; and J. Davies. 1996. Credit derivatives. Coopers and Lybrand *Bankers' Digest* (Winter): 19–21.

Robinson, G. 1996. More haste, less precision. *Risk* 9 (September): 117–121.

Roll, R. 1977. A critique of the asset pricing theory's tests. *Journal of Financial Economics* 4: 129–176.

Ross, S. A. 1976. The arbitrage theory of asset pricing. *Journal of Economic Theory* 13: 341–360.

Rouvinez, C. 1997. Going Greek with VaR. *Risk* 10 (February): 57–65.

Schachter, B. 1995. *Comments on 'Taylor, Black and Scholes: series approximations and risk management pitfalls' by Arturo Estrella.* Mimeo. Office of the Comptroller of the Currency.

Sharpe, W. F. 1964. Capital asset prices: a theory of market equilibrium under conditions of risk. *Journal of Finance* 19: 425–442.

Sharpe, W. F. 1966. 'Mutual Fund Performance,' *Journal of Business,* 39 (January) *Supplement on Security Prices*: 119–138.

Sharpe, W. F. 1994. The Sharpe ratio. *Journal of Portfolio Management*: 49–58.

Shimko, D. 1996. VaR for corporates. *Risk* 9 (June): 28–29.

Shimko, D. 1997. Accentuate the positive. *'Risk' VaR for End-users Supplement* (March): 10–14.

Simister, G. 1996. *Market pressures and advanced technology bring in better risk management systems.* Press statement. Cambridge: Brady Plc.

Simons, K. 1996. Value at risk – new approaches to risk management. Federal Reserve Bank of Boston New England *Economic Review* (Sept/Oct), 3–13.

Sinkey, J. F., Jr. 1992. *Commercial bank financial management in the financial-services industry,* 4th ed. New York: Macmillan Publishing Company.

Smith, C. W., Jr.; C. W. Smithson; and D. S. Wilford. 1992 Managing financial risk. In *The financial derivatives reader.* ed. Robert W. Kolb: 3–24. Miami: Kolb Publishing Company.

Smith, C. W., Jr.; and R. Stulz. 1985. The determinants of firms' hedging policies. *Journal of Financial and Quantitative Analysis* 20: 391–405.

Smithson, C. 1996a. Value at risk (2). *Risk* 9 (February): 38–39.

Smithson, C. 1996b. Theory vs. practice. *Risk* 9 (September): 128–131.

Spinner, K. 1996a. Managing the data integration nightmare. *Derivatives Strategy* 1 (December/January): 40–44.

Spinner, K. 1996b. Integrating credit and market risk. *Derivatives Tactics,* 1 April. Palo Alto: CATS Software.

Studer, G. 1995. *Value at risk and maximum loss optimization.* Zürich: Institute for Operations Research, Swiss Federal Institute of Technology.

Studer, G.; and H.-J. Lüthi. 1996. *Quadratic maximum loss for risk measurement of portfolios.* Zürich: Institute for Operations Research, Swiss Federal Institute of Technology.

Taleb, N. 1997a. The world according to Nassim Taleb. *Derivatives Strategy* 2 (December/January): 37–40.

Taleb, N. 1997b. Against VaR. *Derivatives Strategy* 2 (April): 21, 24–26.

Tezuka, S. 1994. A generalization of Faure sequences and its efficient implementation. IBM Research, Tokyo Research Laboratory, *Research Report RTO105.*

Tompkins, R. 1995. Answers in the cards. *Risk* 8 (June): 55–57.

Tuckman, B. 1995. *Fixed income securities: tools for today's markets.* New York: John Wiley and Sons.

Turner, C. 1996. VaR as an industrial tool. *Risk* 9 (March): 38–40.

US Treasury, Federal Reserve System, and Federal Deposit Insurance Corporation. 1996. *Risk-based capital standards: market risk.* Interagency Notice, 29 August.

Venkataraman, S. 1997. Value at risk for a mixture of normal distributions: the use of quasi-Bayesian estimation techniques. Federal Reserve Bank of Chicago *Economic Perspectives* (March/April), 2–13.

Vipond, P. 1996. *An industry view of internal risk models.* Paper presented to the LSE Financial Markets Group conference on internal risk models and financial regulation, 15 October.

Wakeman, L. 1996a. Credit enhancement. In *The handbook of risk management and analysis,* ed. C. Alexander: 307–327. Chichester: John Wiley and Sons.

Wakeman, L. 1996b. *Using value at risk in credit risk management.* Paper presented at the *Risk* Publications conference on value-at-risk. New York, October.

Whaley, R. 1982. Valuation of American call options on dividend-paying stocks: empirical evidence. *Journal of Financial Economics* 10: 29–58.

Williams, D. 1996. Not-so-simple solutions. *Firmwide Risk Management: A Risk Special Supplement,* July: 32–37.

Wilson, D. 1995. VaR in operation. *Risk* 8 (December): 24–25.

Wilson, T. C. 1992. RAROC remodelled. *Risk* 5 (September): 112–119.

Wilson, T. C. 1993. Infinite wisdom. *Risk* 6 (June): 37–45.

Wilson, T. C. 1994a. Debunking the myths. *Risk* 7 (April): 67–72.

Wilson, T. C. 1994b. Plugging the gap. *Risk* 7 (October): 74–80.

Wilson, T. C. 1996. Calculating risk capital. In *The handbook of risk management and analysis*, ed. C. Alexander: 193–232. Chichester: John Wiley and Sons.

Zangari, P. 1995. Statistics of market moves. In *RiskMetrics*™ – *technical document*, 3rd ed. T. Guldimann *et al.*: 46–106. New York: Morgan Guaranty Trust Company Global Research.

Zangari, P. 1996a. A VaR methodology for portfolios that include options. *RiskMetrics*™ *Monitor*, First Quarter: 4–12.

Zangari, P. 1996b. An improved methodology for measuring VaR. *RiskMetrics*™ *Monitor*, Second Quarter: 7–25.

Zangari, P. 1996c. A value-at-risk analysis of currency exposures. *RiskMetrics*™ *Monitor*, Second Quarter: 26–33.

Zangari, P. 1996d. How accurate is the delta-gamma methodology? *RiskMetrics*™ *Monitor*, Third Quarter: 12–29.

Zangari, P. 1996e. When is non-normality a problem? The case of 15 times series from emerging markets. *RiskMetrics*™ *Monitor*, Fourth Quarter: 20–32.

Zangari, P. 1996f. Market risk methodology. In *RiskMetrics*™ – *technical document*, 4th ed., ed. J. Longerstaey; and M. Spencer: 107–148. New York: Morgan Guaranty Trust Company and London: Reuters Ltd.

Zangari, P. 1996g. Appendix E: routines to simulate correlated normal random variables. In *RiskMetrics*™ – *technical document*, 4th ed., ed. J. Longerstaey *et al.* 253–256. 4th ed., New York: Morgan Guaranty Trust Company and London: Reuters Ltd.

Zangari, P. 1997. On measuring credit exposure. *RiskMetrics*™ *Monitor*, First Quarter: 3–22.

AUTHOR INDEX

SUBJECT INDEX